Shojo Beat

Beauty is the Beast ™

5

Story & Art by Tomo Matsumoto

Table of Contents

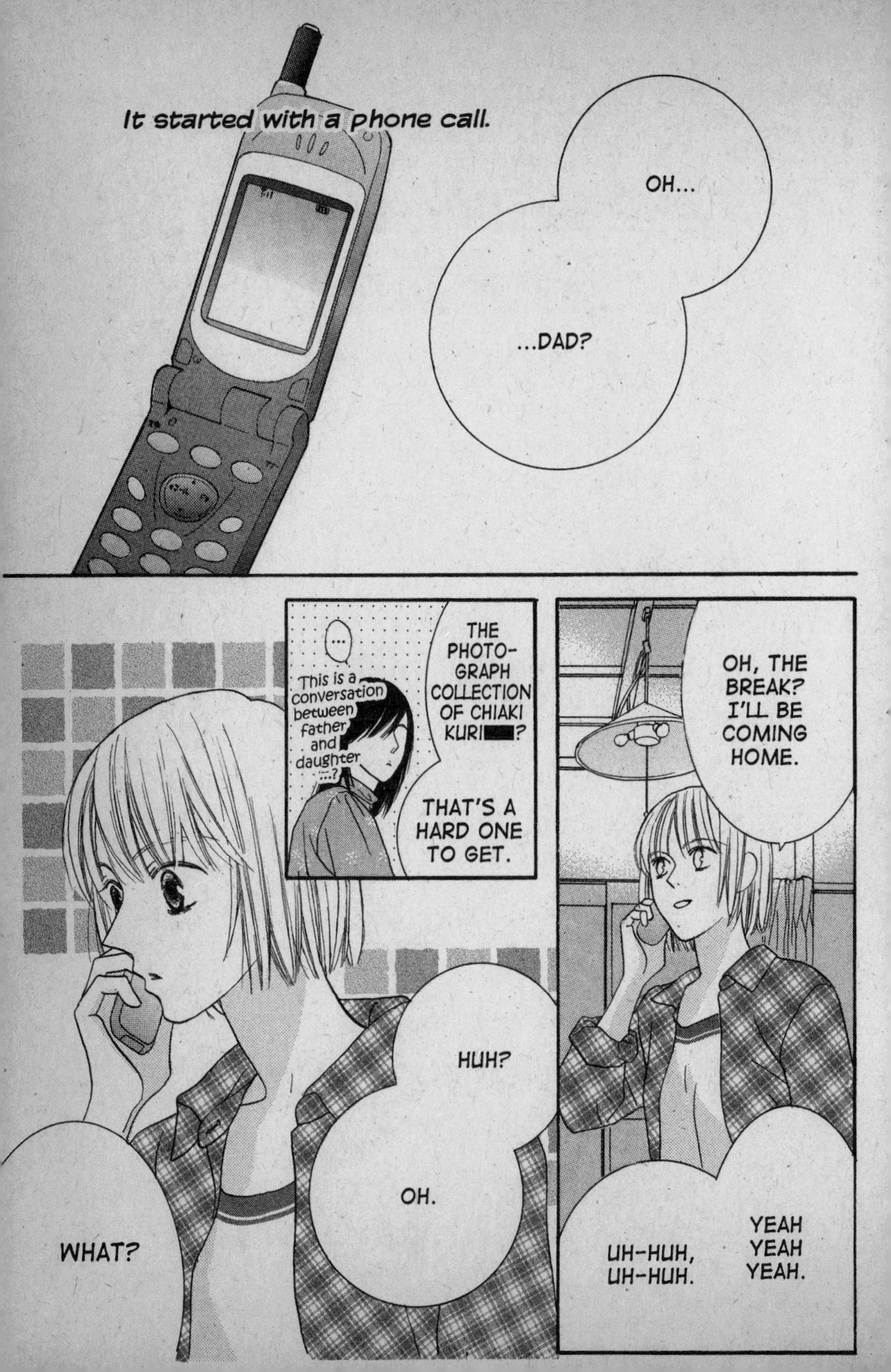
It started with a phone call.
OH...
...DAD?
OH, THE BREAK? I'LL BE COMING HOME.
YEAH YEAH YEAH.
UH-HUH, UH-HUH.
THE PHOTO-GRAPH COLLECTION OF CHIAKI KURI[redacted]?
THAT'S A HARD ONE TO GET.
...
This is a conversation between father and daughter ...?
HUH?
OH.
WHAT?

Beauty is the Beast

Chapter 24

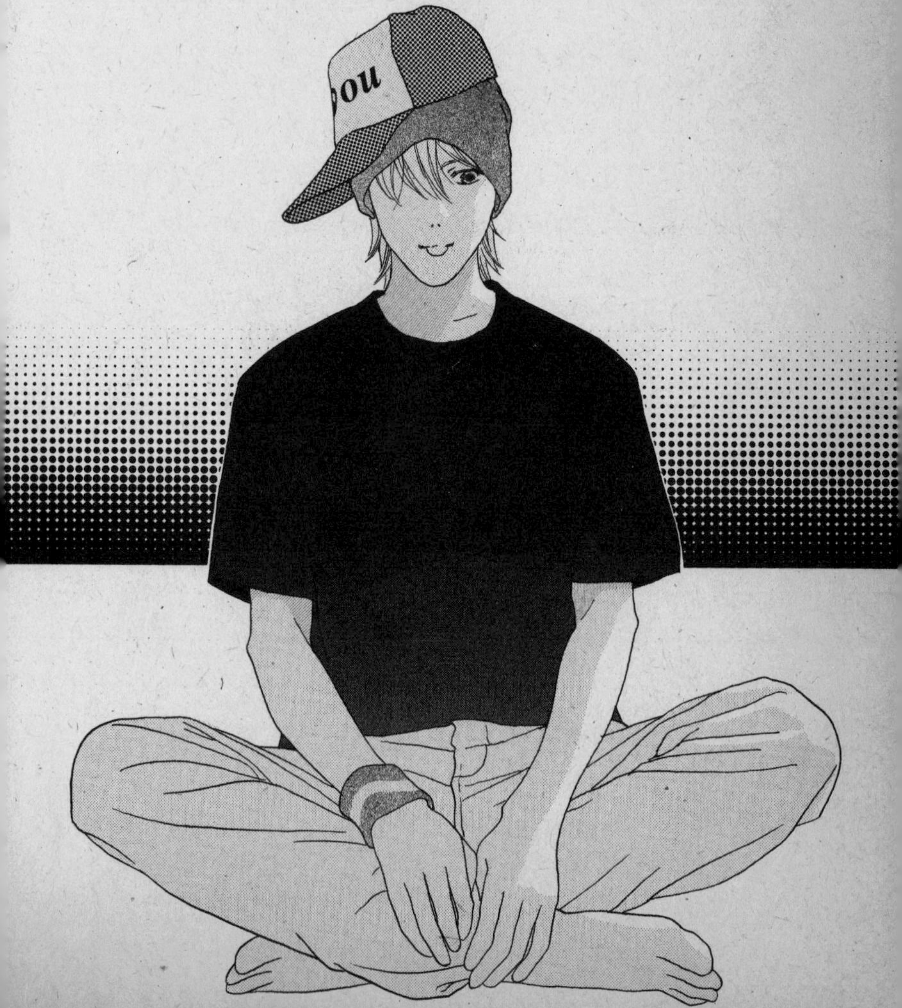

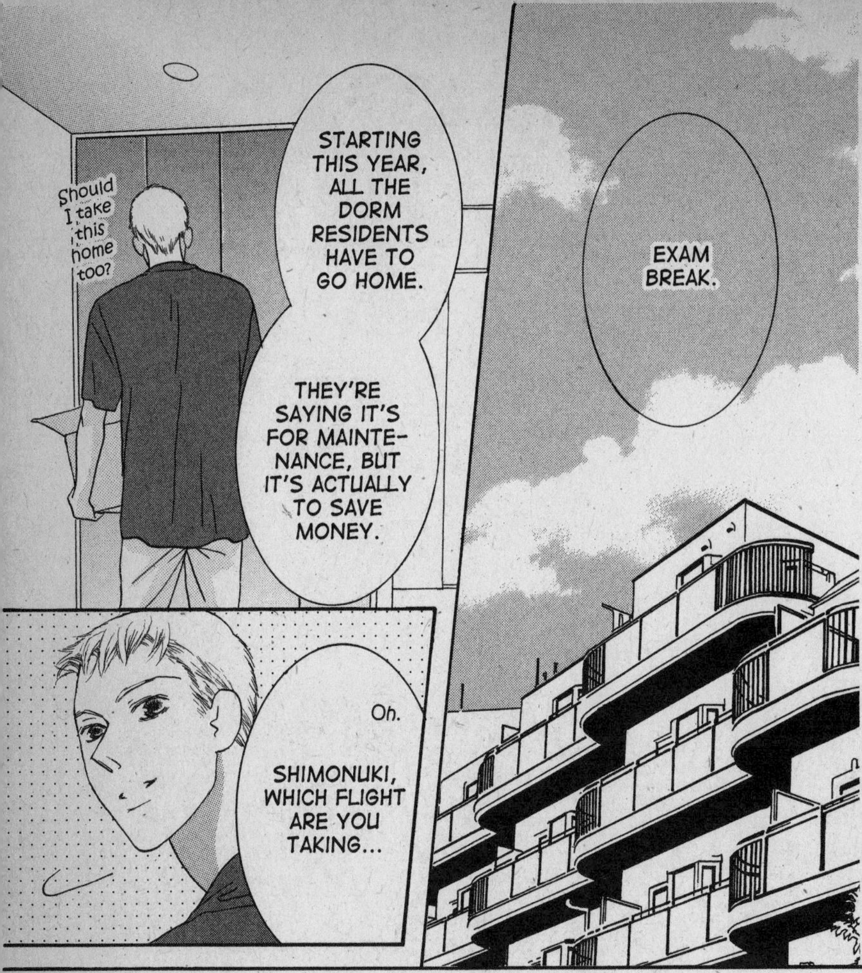
EXAM BREAK.
STARTING THIS YEAR, ALL THE DORM RESIDENTS HAVE TO GO HOME.
Should I take this home too?
THEY'RE SAYING IT'S FOR MAINTE-NANCE, BUT IT'S ACTUALLY TO SAVE MONEY.
Oh.
SHIMONUKI, WHICH FLIGHT ARE YOU TAKING...

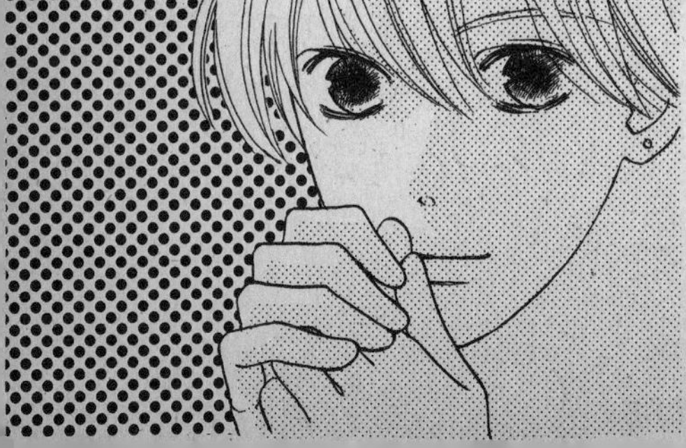

Suzu

After graduating from a national university with a degree in architecture, she started working for an architectural firm. Perhaps due to her experience living in the dorm, she has her own ideas about building insulation and draft prevention. Her clients trust her.

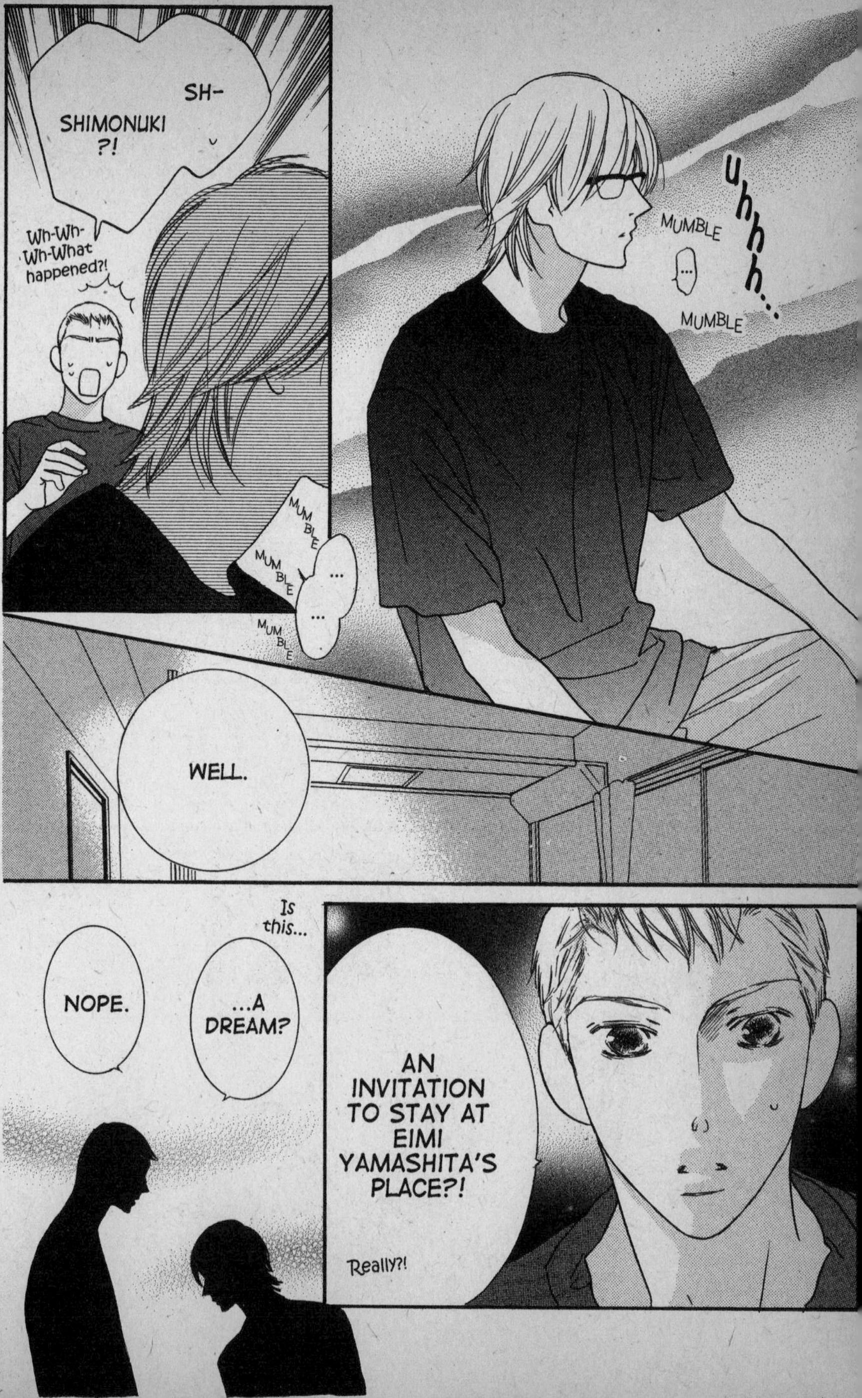
Uhhh...
MUMBLE
...
MUMBLE
SH-
SHIMONUKI ?!
Wh-Wh-Wh-What happened?!
MUMBLE
...
MUMBLE
...
MUMBLE
WELL.
AN INVITATION TO STAY AT EIMI YAMASHITA'S PLACE?!
Really?!
Is this...
...A DREAM?
NOPE.

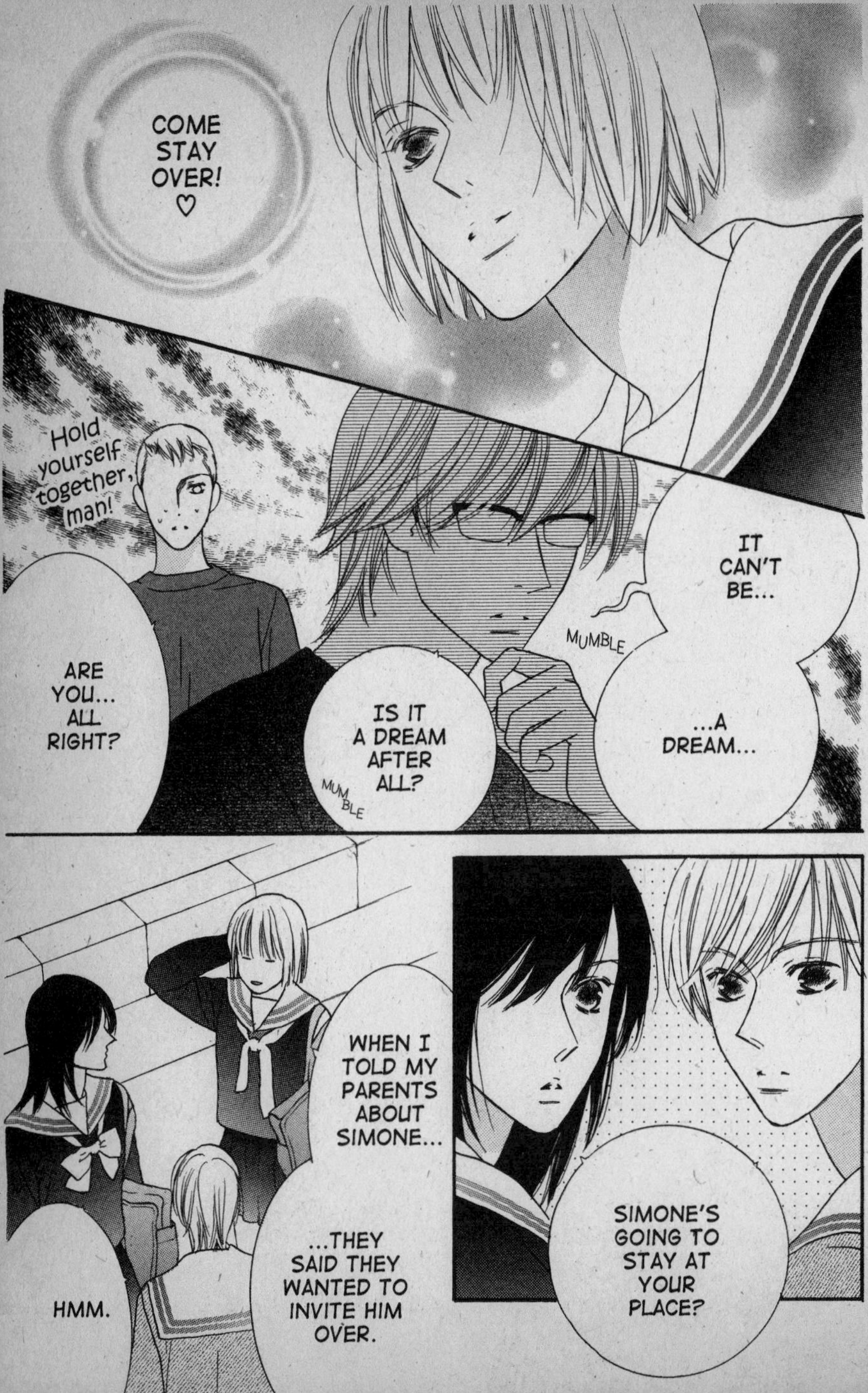
COME STAY OVER! ♡
IT CAN'T BE...
MUMBLE
...A DREAM...
IS IT A DREAM AFTER ALL?
MUMBLE
Hold yourself together, man!
ARE YOU... ALL RIGHT?
SIMONE'S GOING TO STAY AT YOUR PLACE?
WHEN I TOLD MY PARENTS ABOUT SIMONE...
...THEY SAID THEY WANTED TO INVITE HIM OVER.
HMM.

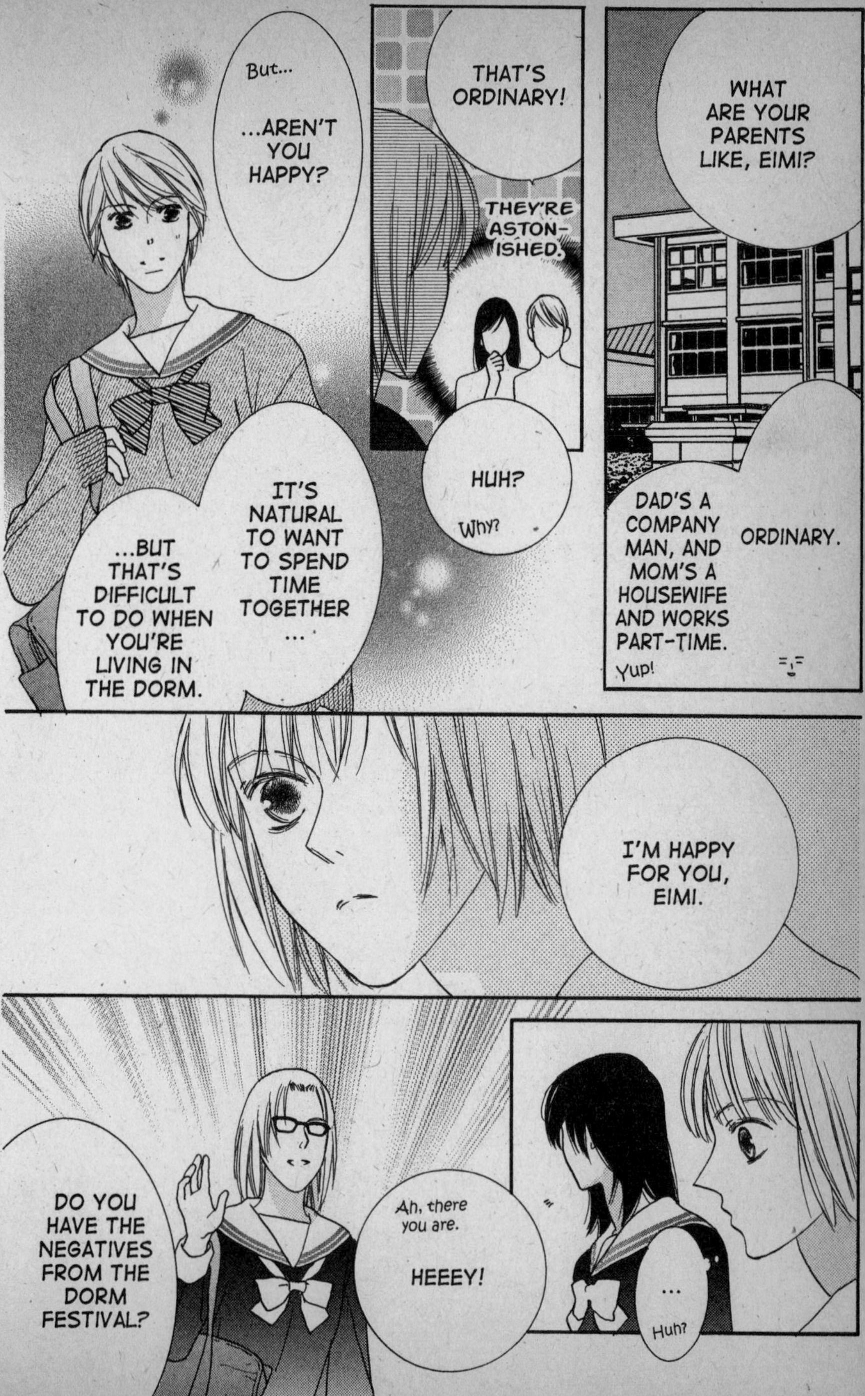
WHAT ARE YOUR PARENTS LIKE, EIMI?
DAD'S A COMPANY MAN, AND MOM'S A HOUSEWIFE AND WORKS PART-TIME.
ORDINARY.
Yup!
THAT'S ORDINARY!
THEY'RE ASTON-ISHED.
HUH?
Why?
But...
...AREN'T YOU HAPPY?
IT'S NATURAL TO WANT TO SPEND TIME TOGETHER ...
...BUT THAT'S DIFFICULT TO DO WHEN YOU'RE LIVING IN THE DORM.
I'M HAPPY FOR YOU, EIMI.
...
Huh?
Ah, there you are.
HEEEY!
DO YOU HAVE THE NEGATIVES FROM THE DORM FESTIVAL?

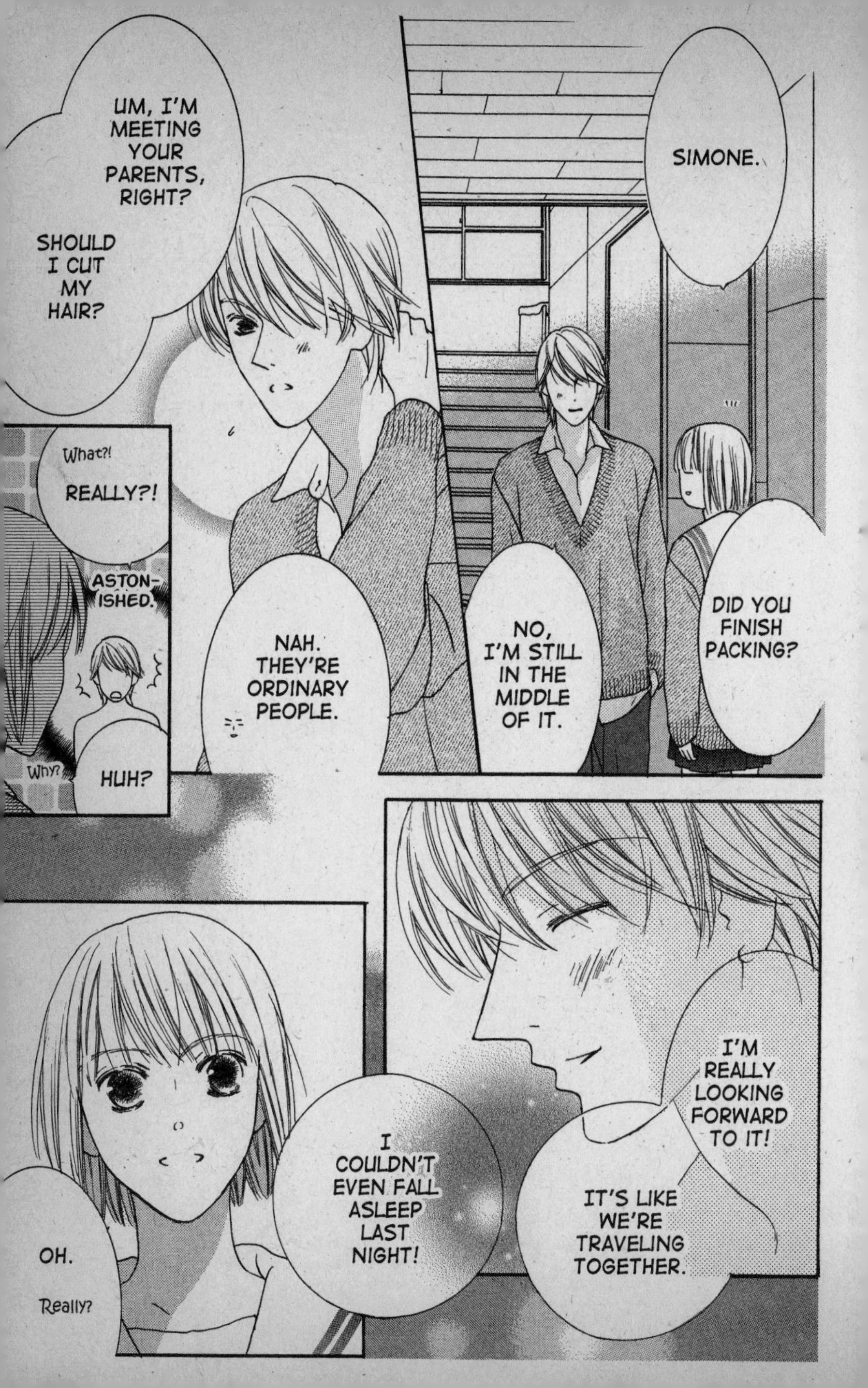
SIMONE.
DID YOU FINISH PACKING?
NO, I'M STILL IN THE MIDDLE OF IT.
UM, I'M MEETING YOUR PARENTS, RIGHT?
SHOULD I CUT MY HAIR?
NAH. THEY'RE ORDINARY PEOPLE.
What?!
REALLY?!
ASTON-ISHED.
HUH?
Why?
I'M REALLY LOOKING FORWARD TO IT!
IT'S LIKE WE'RE TRAVELING TOGETHER.
I COULDN'T EVEN FALL ASLEEP LAST NIGHT!
OH.
Really?

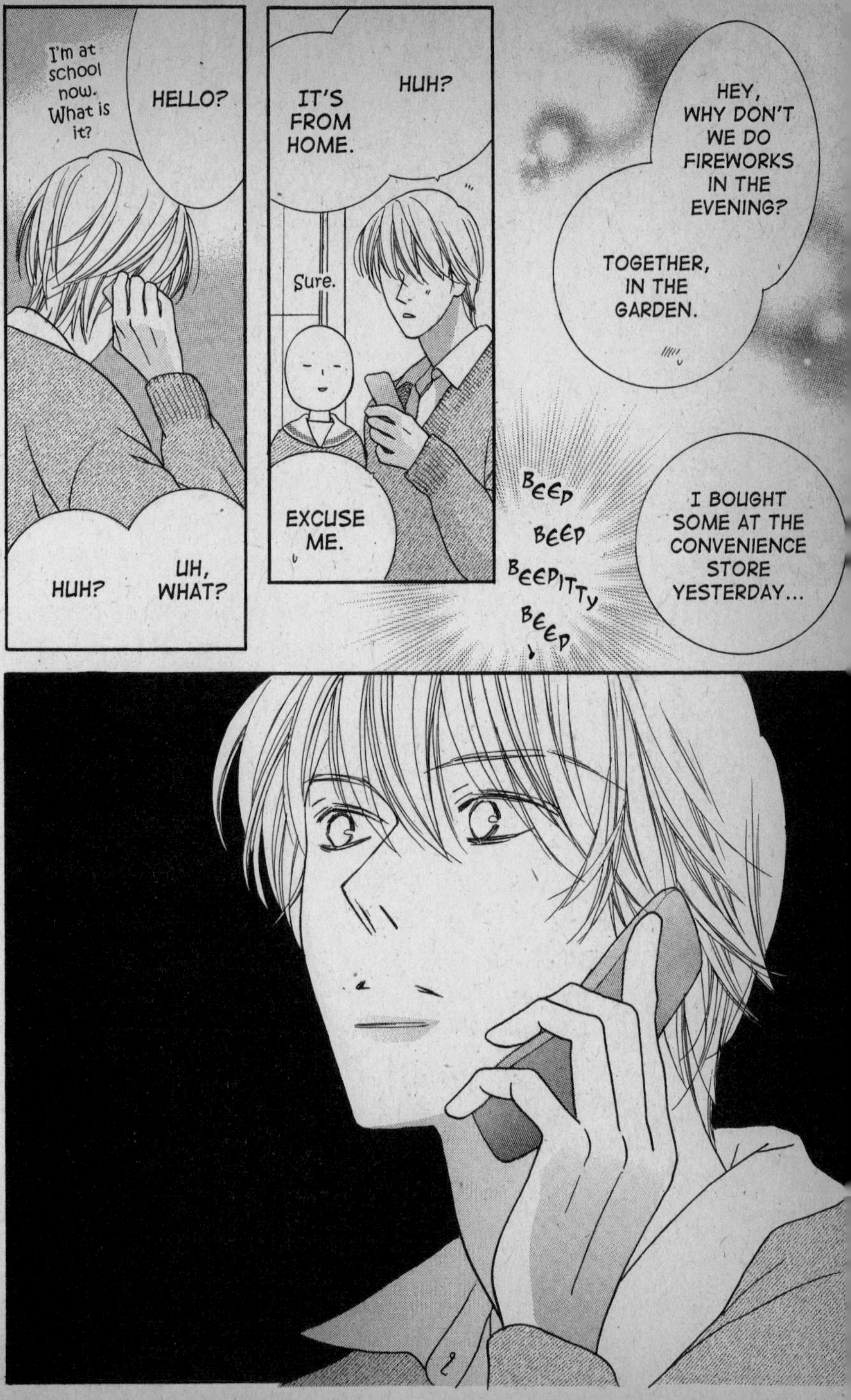
HUH?
IT'S FROM HOME.
Sure.
EXCUSE ME.
HELLO?
I'm at school now. What is it?
UH, WHAT?
HUH?
HEY, WHY DON'T WE DO FIREWORKS IN THE EVENING?
TOGETHER, IN THE GARDEN.
I BOUGHT SOME AT THE CONVENIENCE STORE YESTERDAY...
BEEP BEEP BEEPITTY BEEP

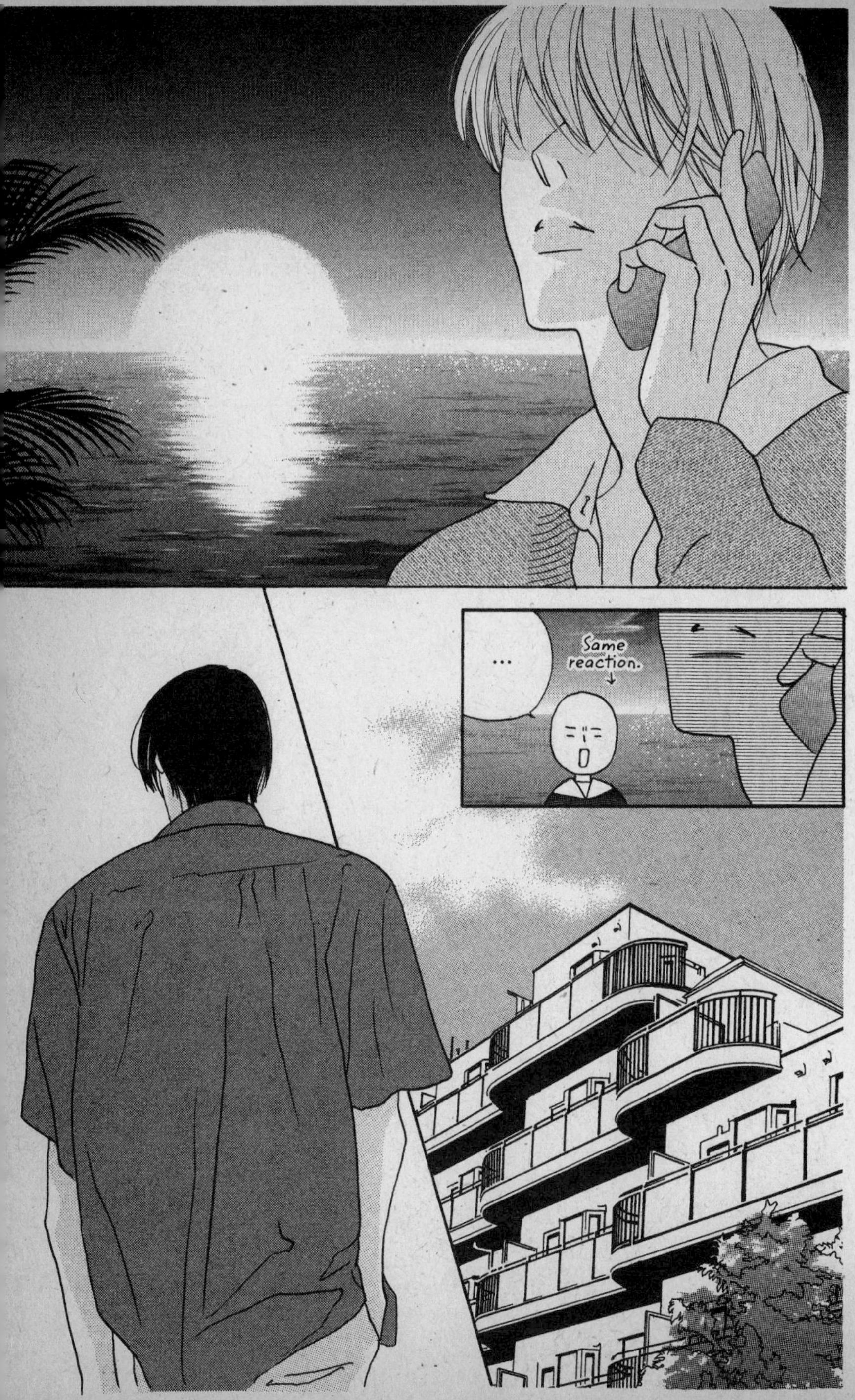
...
Same reaction.

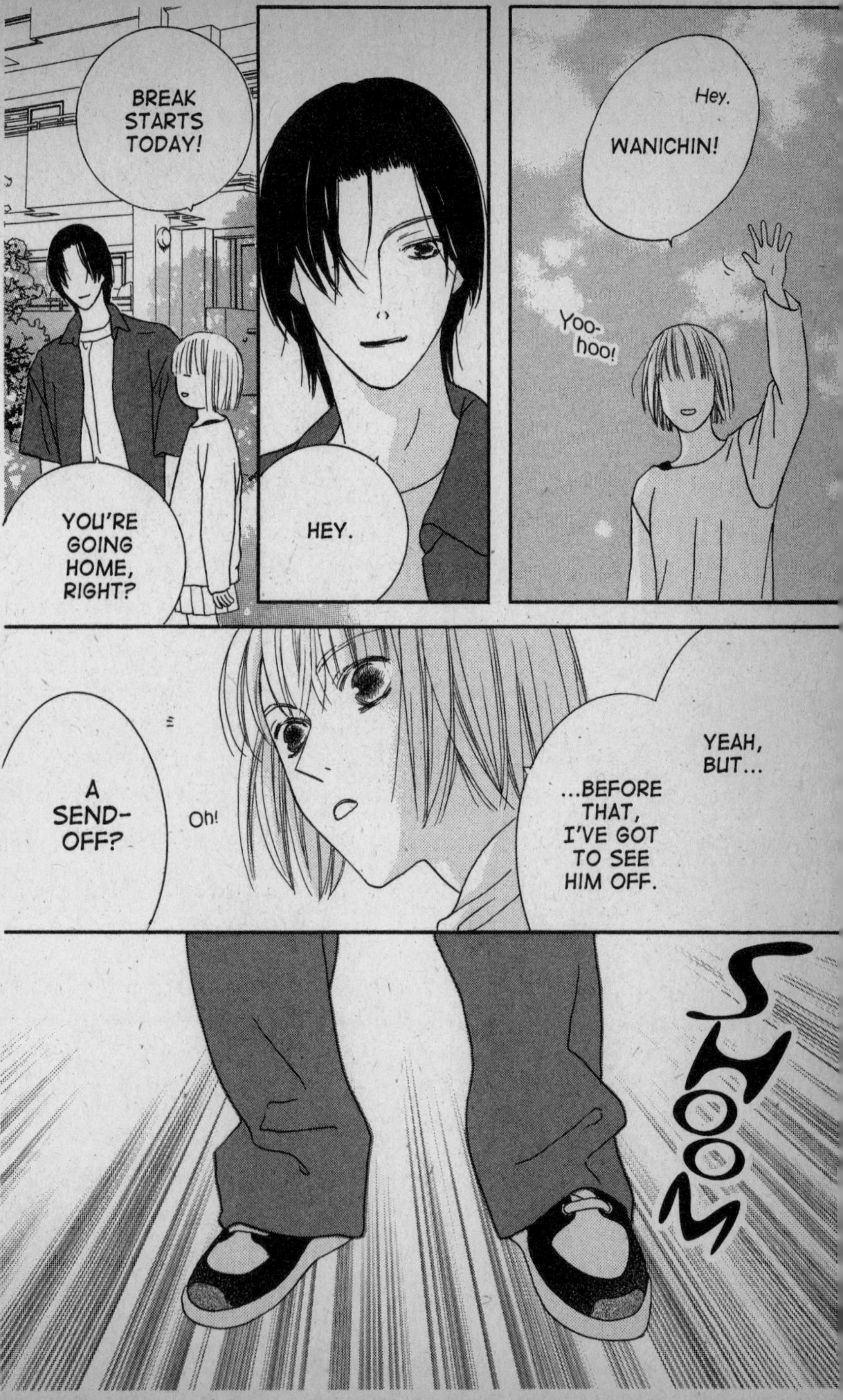

Hey. WANICHIN!
Yoo-hoo!
HEY.
BREAK STARTS TODAY!
YOU'RE GOING HOME, RIGHT?
YEAH, BUT...
...BEFORE THAT, I'VE GOT TO SEE HIM OFF.
Oh!
A SEND-OFF?
SHOOM

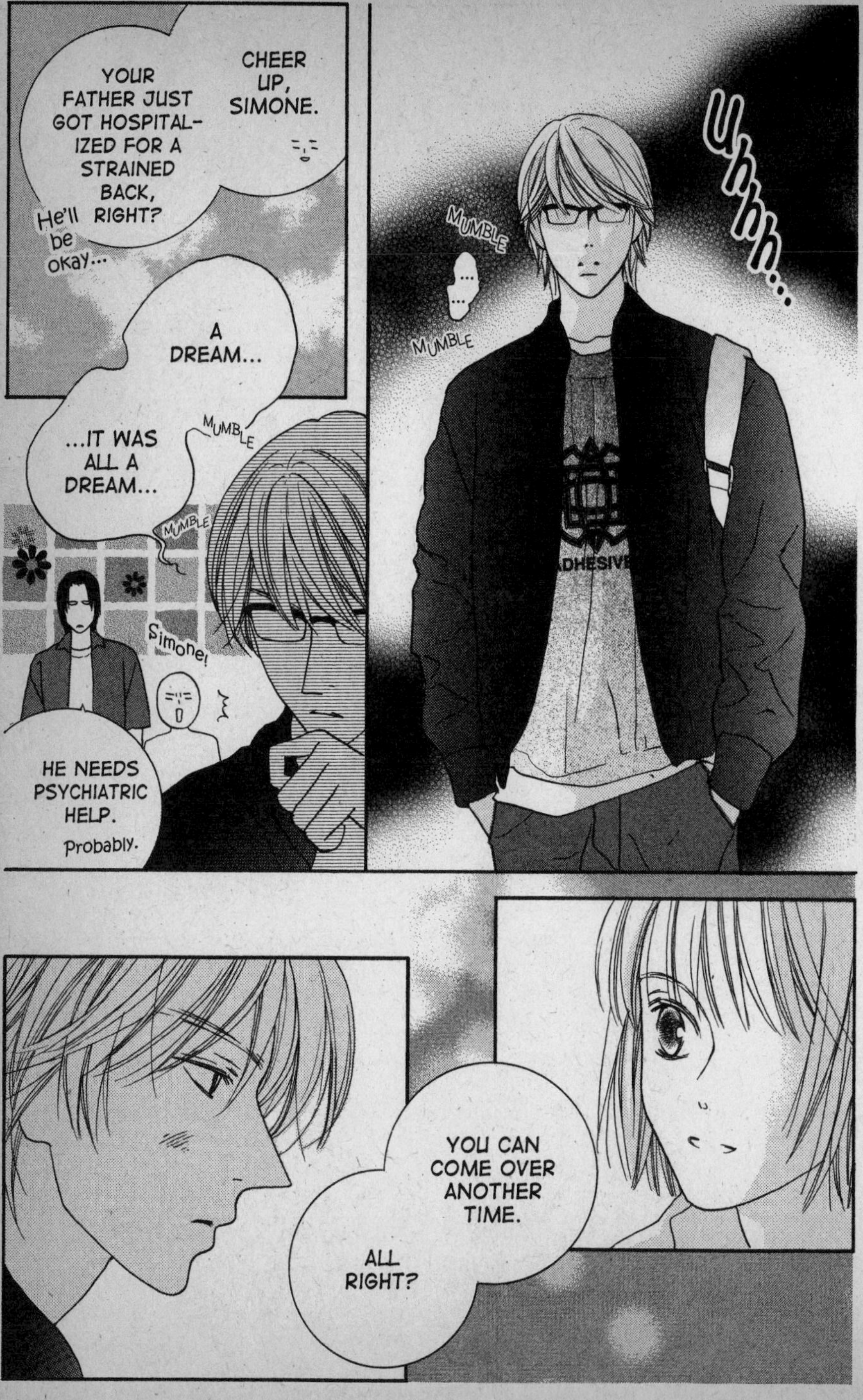
Uhhh...
MUMBLE
... ...
MUMBLE
CHEER UP, SIMONE.
YOUR FATHER JUST GOT HOSPITAL-IZED FOR A STRAINED BACK, RIGHT?
He'll be okay...
A DREAM...
...IT WAS ALL A DREAM...
MUMBLE
MUMBLE
Simone!
HE NEEDS PSYCHIATRIC HELP.
Probably.
ADHESIVE
YOU CAN COME OVER ANOTHER TIME.
ALL RIGHT?

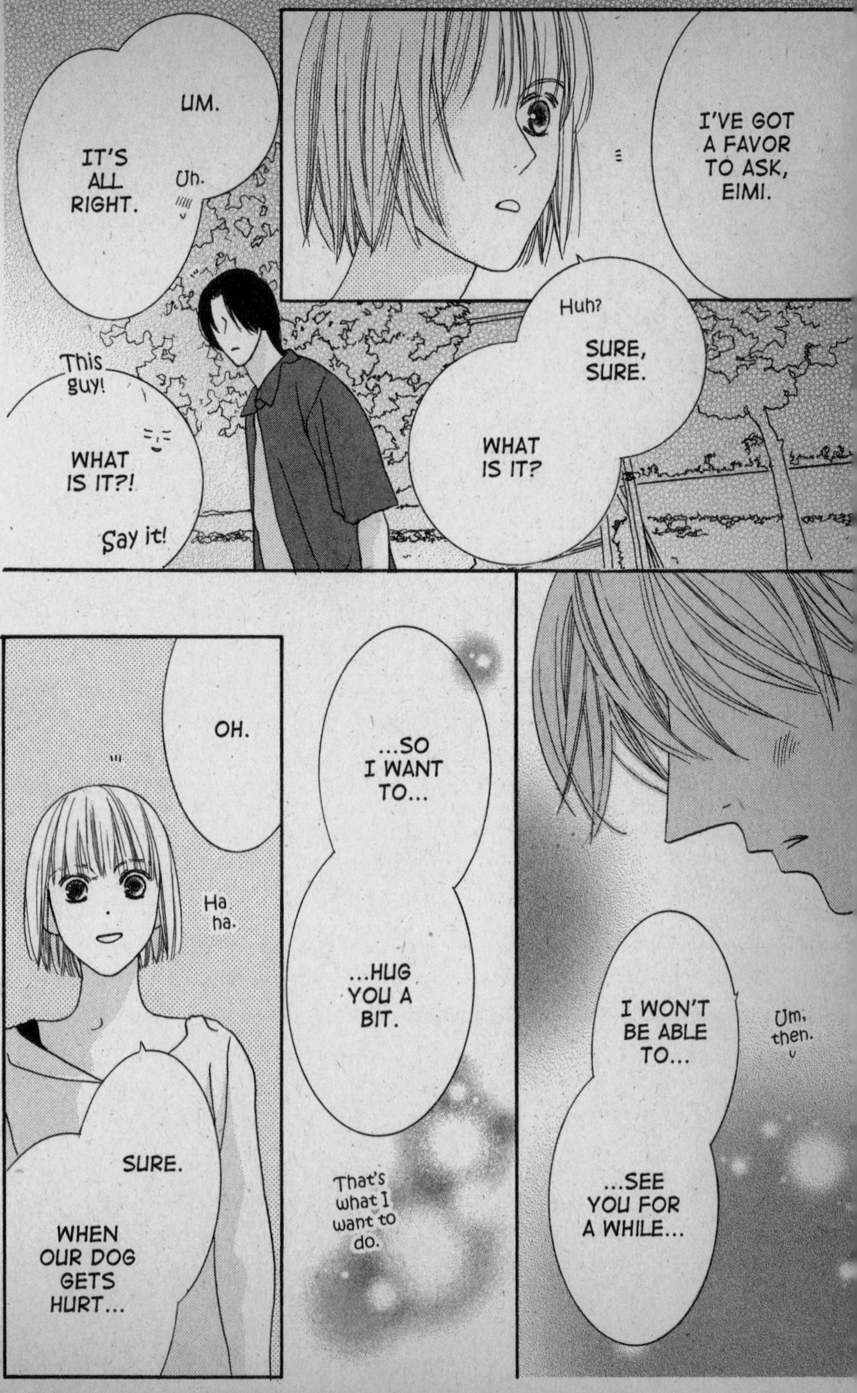
I'VE GOT A FAVOR TO ASK, EIMI.
Huh?
SURE, SURE.
WHAT IS IT?
UM.
Uh.
IT'S ALL RIGHT.
This guy!
WHAT IS IT?!
Say it!
Um, then.
I WON'T BE ABLE TO...
...SEE YOU FOR A WHILE...
...SO I WANT TO...
...HUG YOU A BIT.
That's what I want to do.
OH.
Ha ha.
SURE.
WHEN OUR DOG GETS HURT...

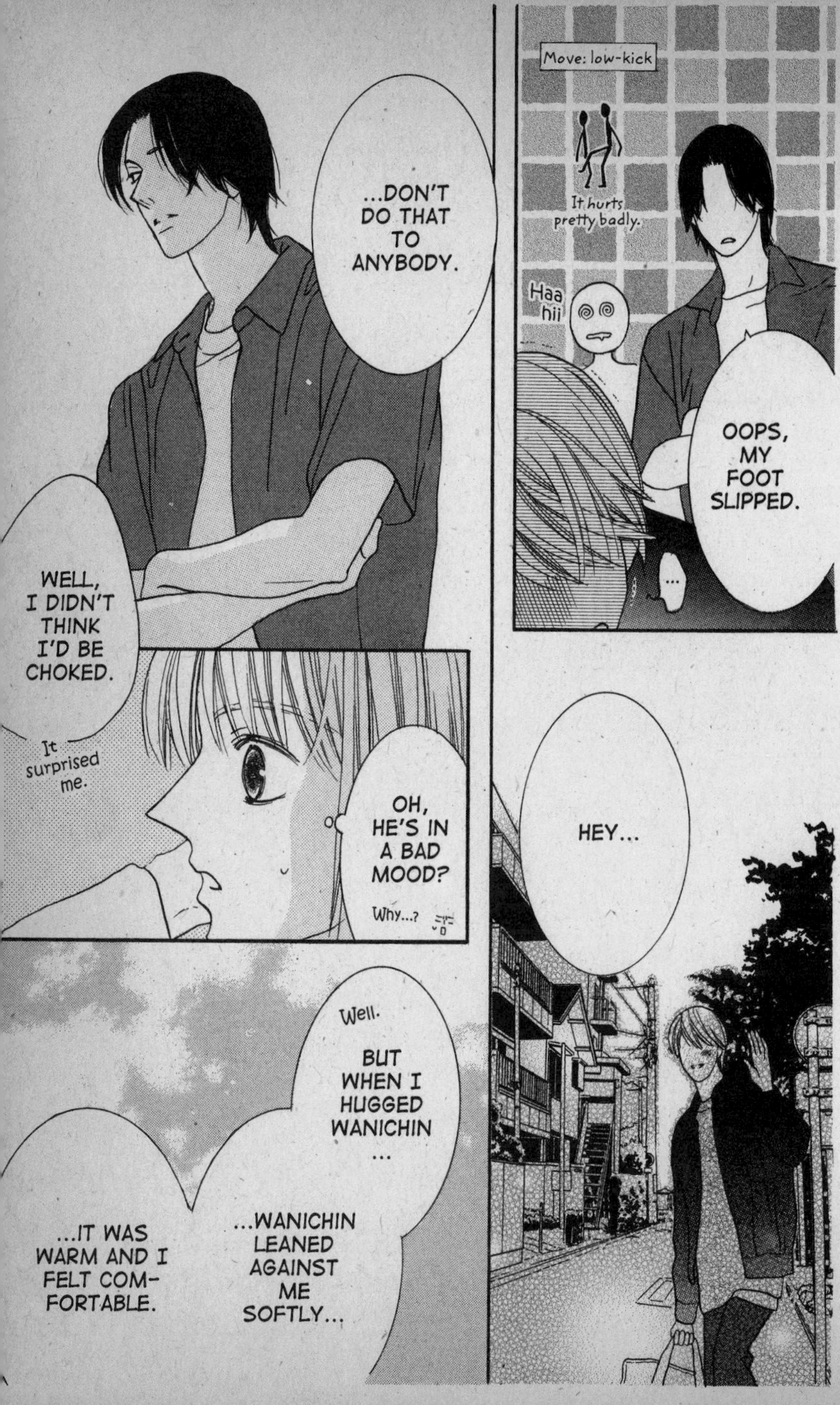
Move: low-kick
It hurts pretty badly.
Haa hii
OOPS, MY FOOT SLIPPED.
...
...DON'T DO THAT TO ANYBODY.
WELL, I DIDN'T THINK I'D BE CHOKED.
It surprised me.
HEY...
OH, HE'S IN A BAD MOOD?
Why...?
Well.
BUT WHEN I HUGGED WANICHIN ...
...WANICHIN LEANED AGAINST ME SOFTLY...
...IT WAS WARM AND I FELT COM-FORTABLE.

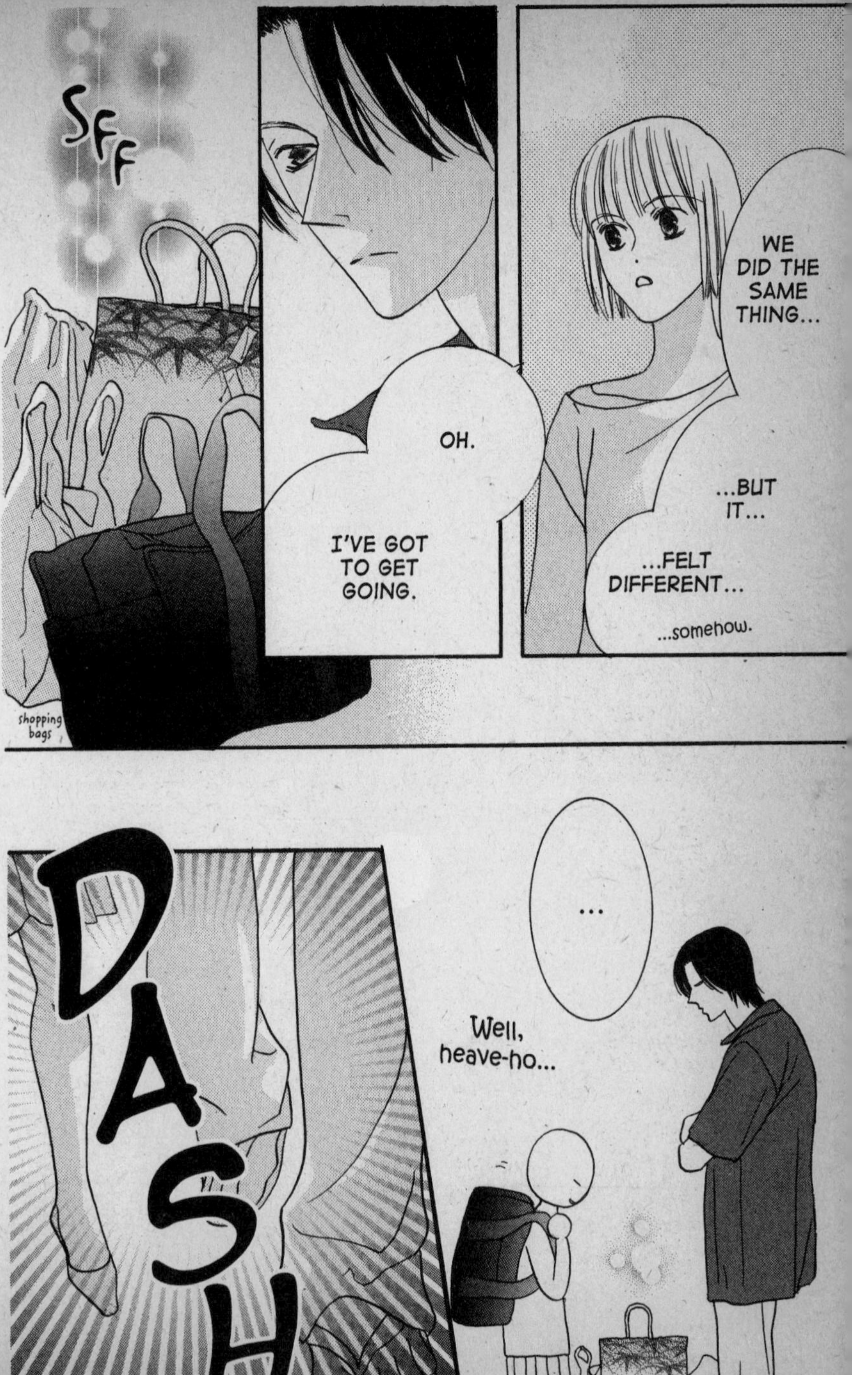
WE DID THE SAME THING...
...BUT IT...
...FELT DIFFERENT...
...somehow.
OH.
I'VE GOT TO GET GOING.
SFF
shopping bags
...
Well, heave-ho...
DASH

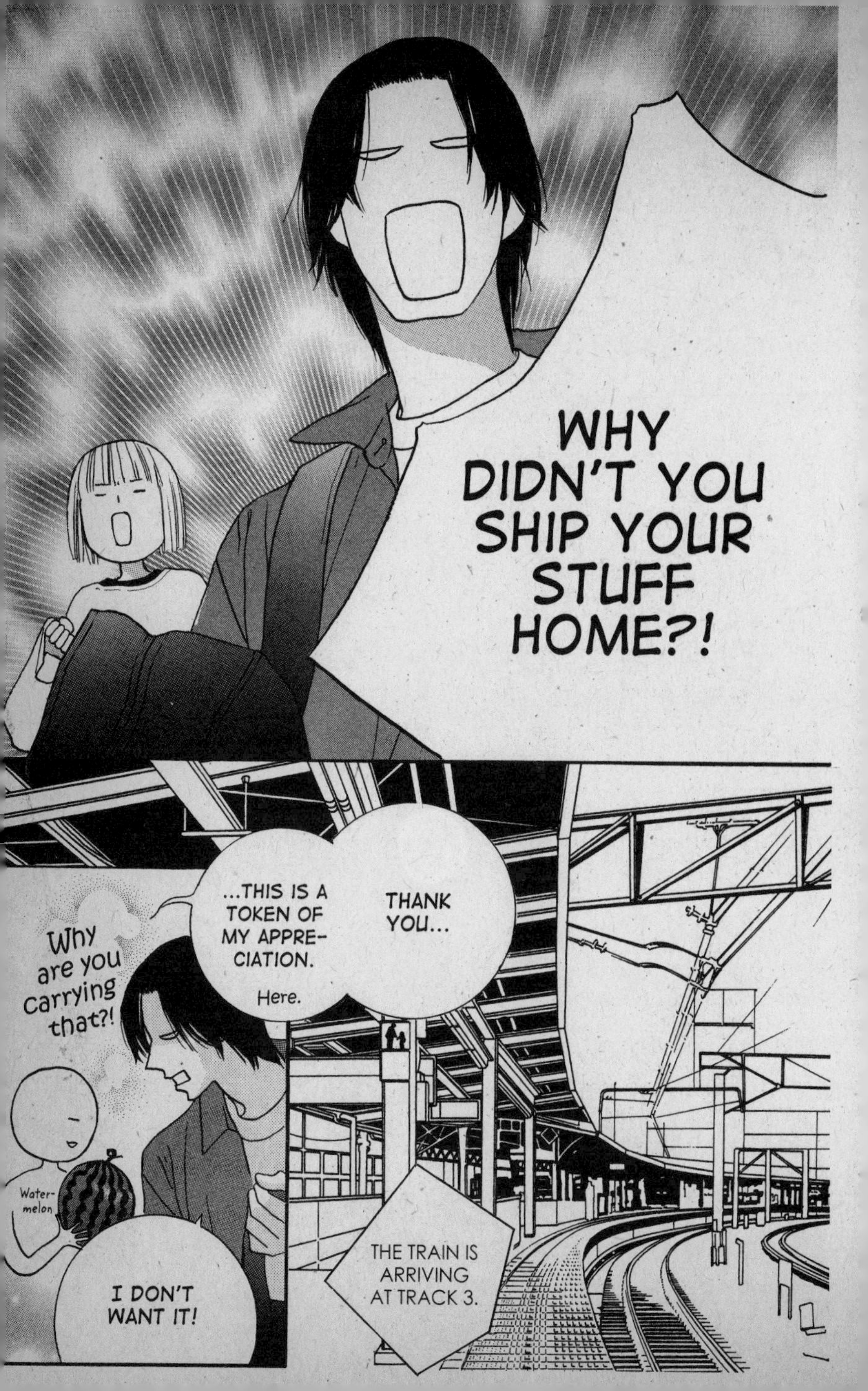
WHY DIDN'T YOU SHIP YOUR STUFF HOME?!
THE TRAIN IS ARRIVING AT TRACK 3.
THANK YOU...
...THIS IS A TOKEN OF MY APPRE-CIATION.
Here.
Why are you carrying that?!
Water-melon
I DON'T WANT IT!

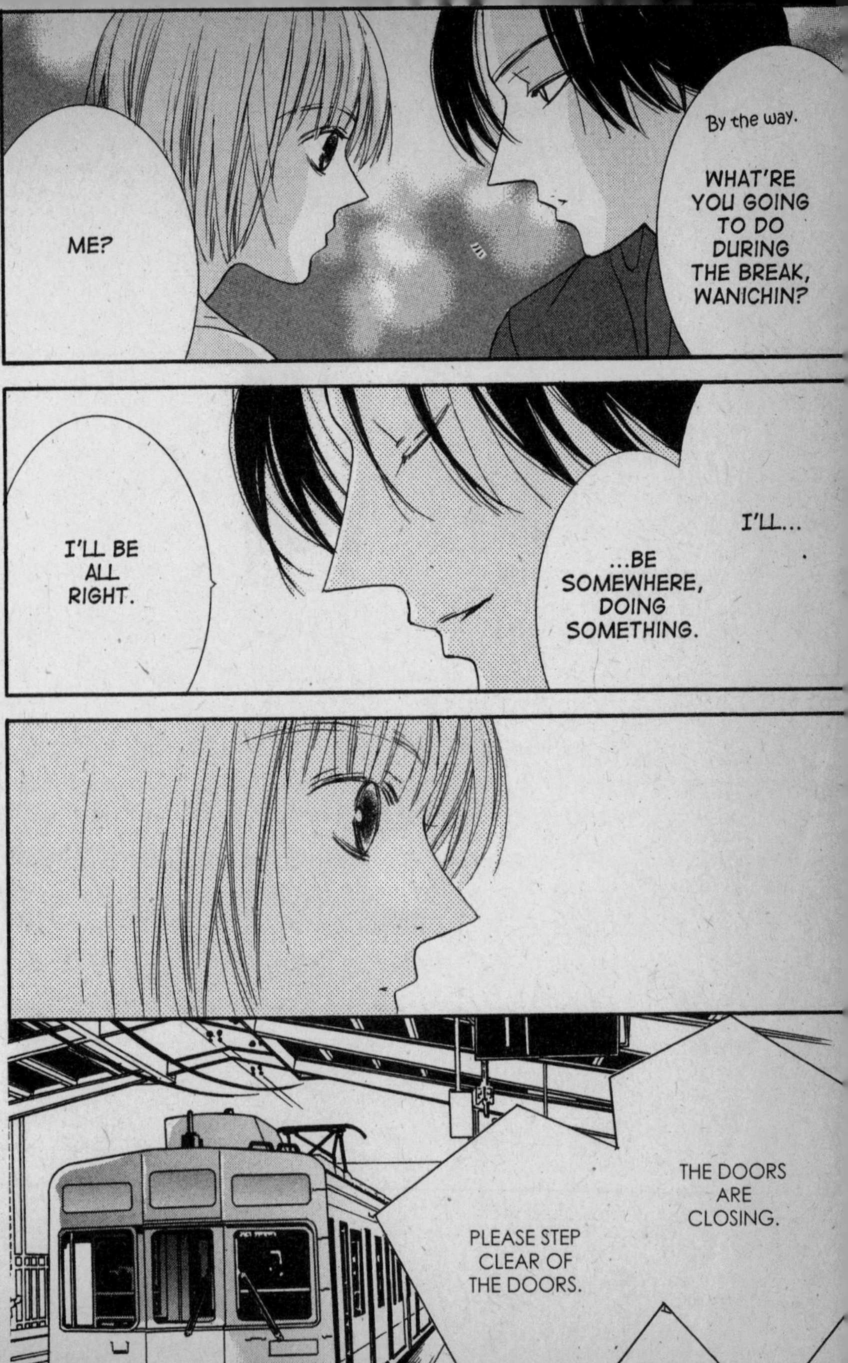
By the way.
WHAT'RE YOU GOING TO DO DURING THE BREAK, WANICHIN?
ME?
I'LL...
...BE SOMEWHERE, DOING SOMETHING.
I'LL BE ALL RIGHT.
THE DOORS ARE CLOSING.
PLEASE STEP CLEAR OF THE DOORS.

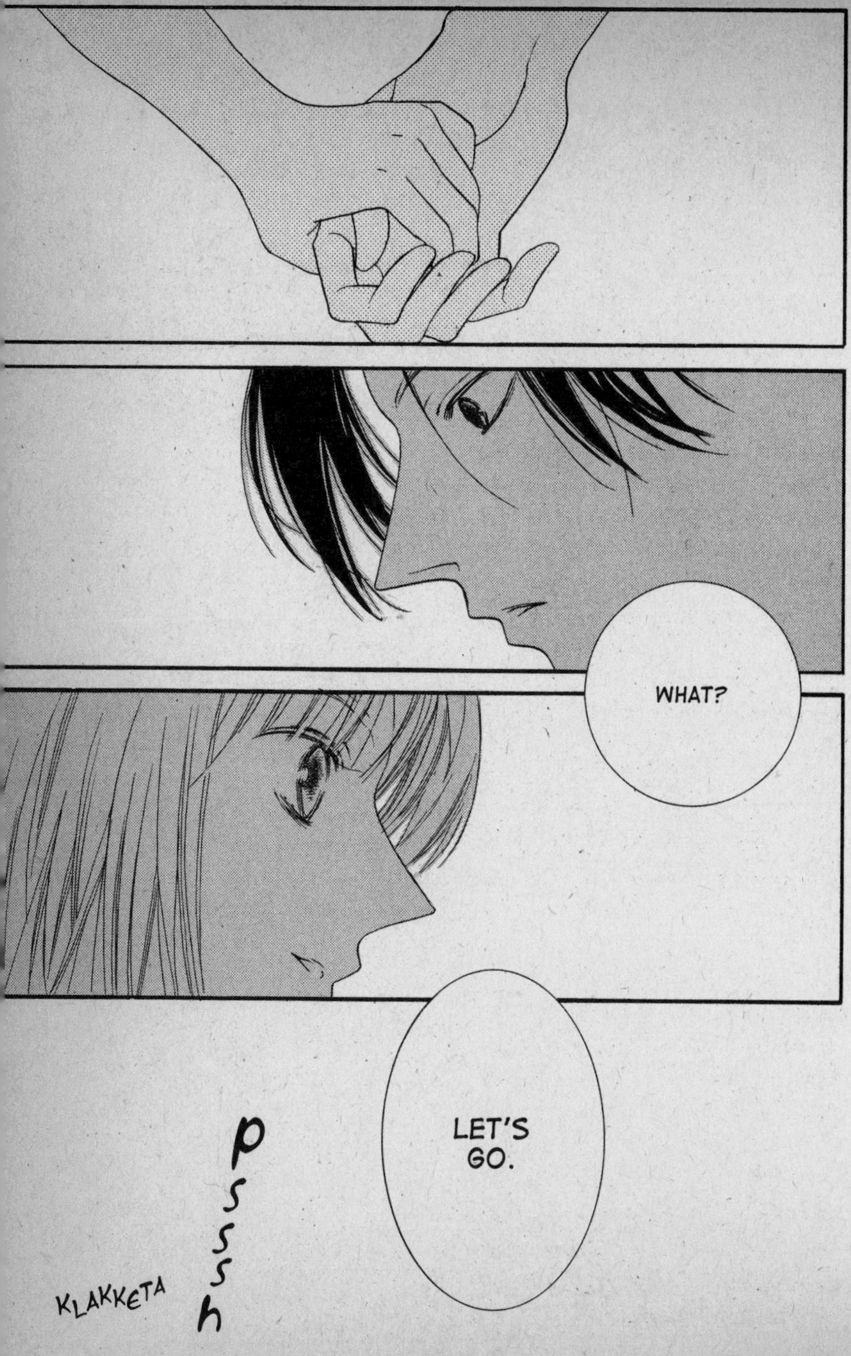
WHAT?
LET'S GO.
PSSSH
KLAKKETA

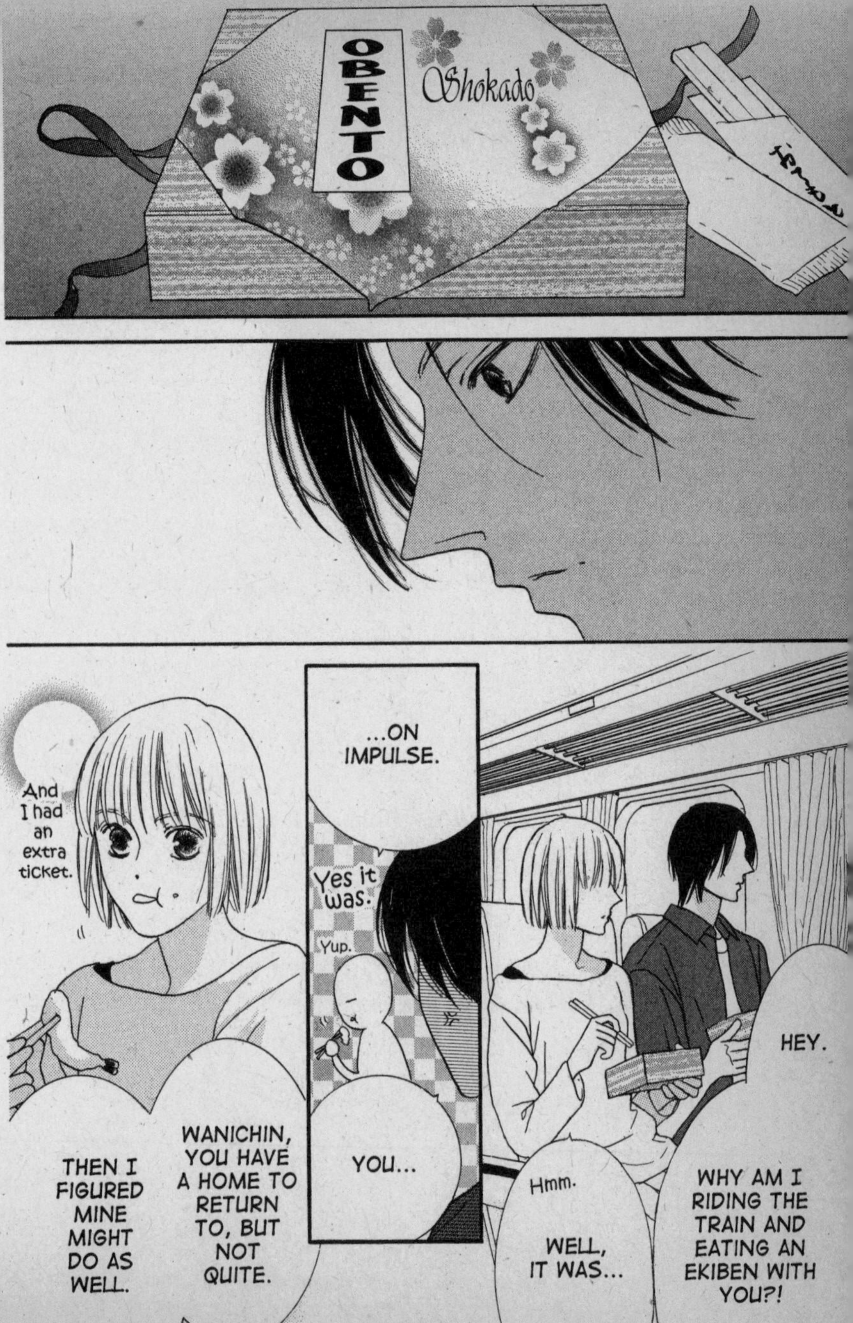
OBENTO
Shokado
HEY.
WHY AM I RIDING THE TRAIN AND EATING AN EKIBEN WITH YOU?!
Hmm.
WELL, IT WAS...
...ON IMPULSE.
Yes it was.
Yup.
YOU...
WANICHIN, YOU HAVE A HOME TO RETURN TO, BUT NOT QUITE.
THEN I FIGURED MINE MIGHT DO AS WELL.
And I had an extra ticket.

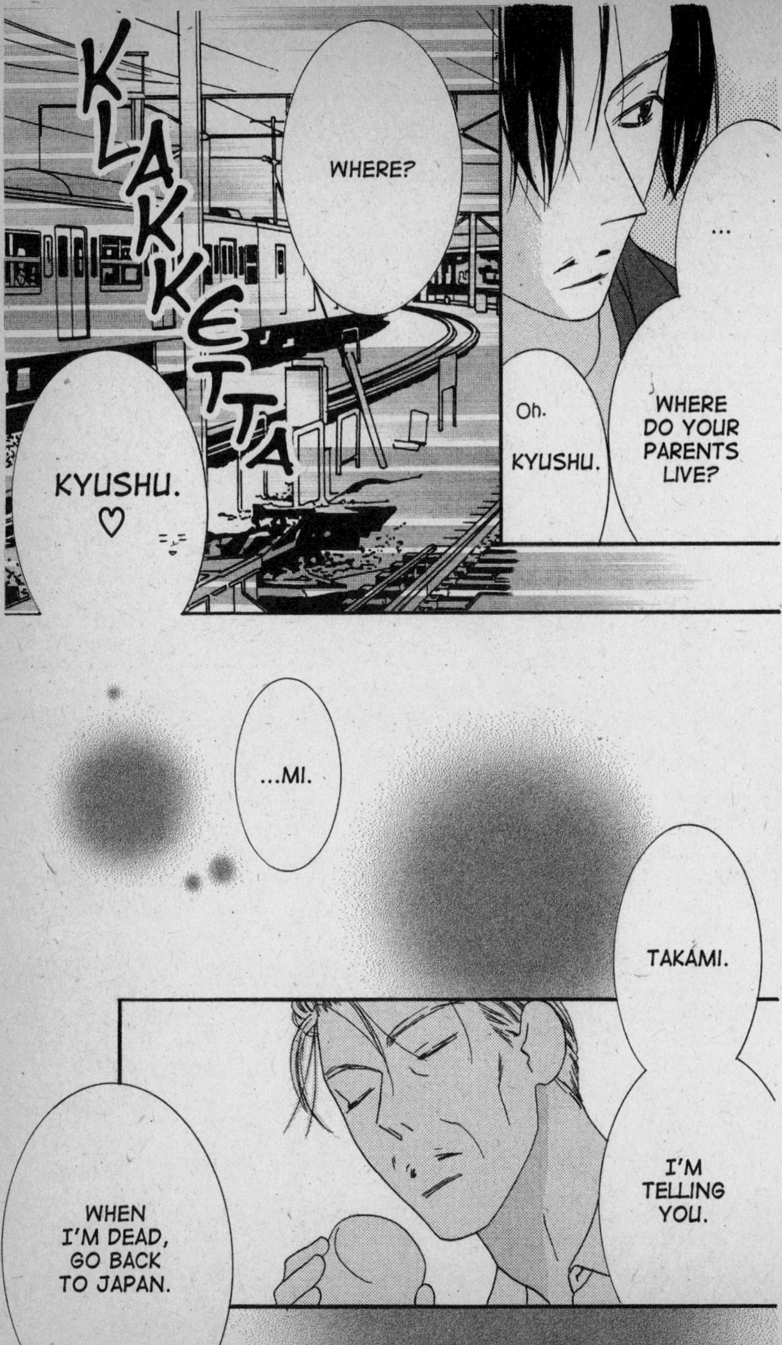
...
WHERE DO YOUR PARENTS LIVE?
Oh. KYUSHU.
WHERE?
KLAKKETTA
KYUSHU. ♡
...MI.
TAKAMI.
I'M TELLING YOU.
WHEN I'M DEAD, GO BACK TO JAPAN.

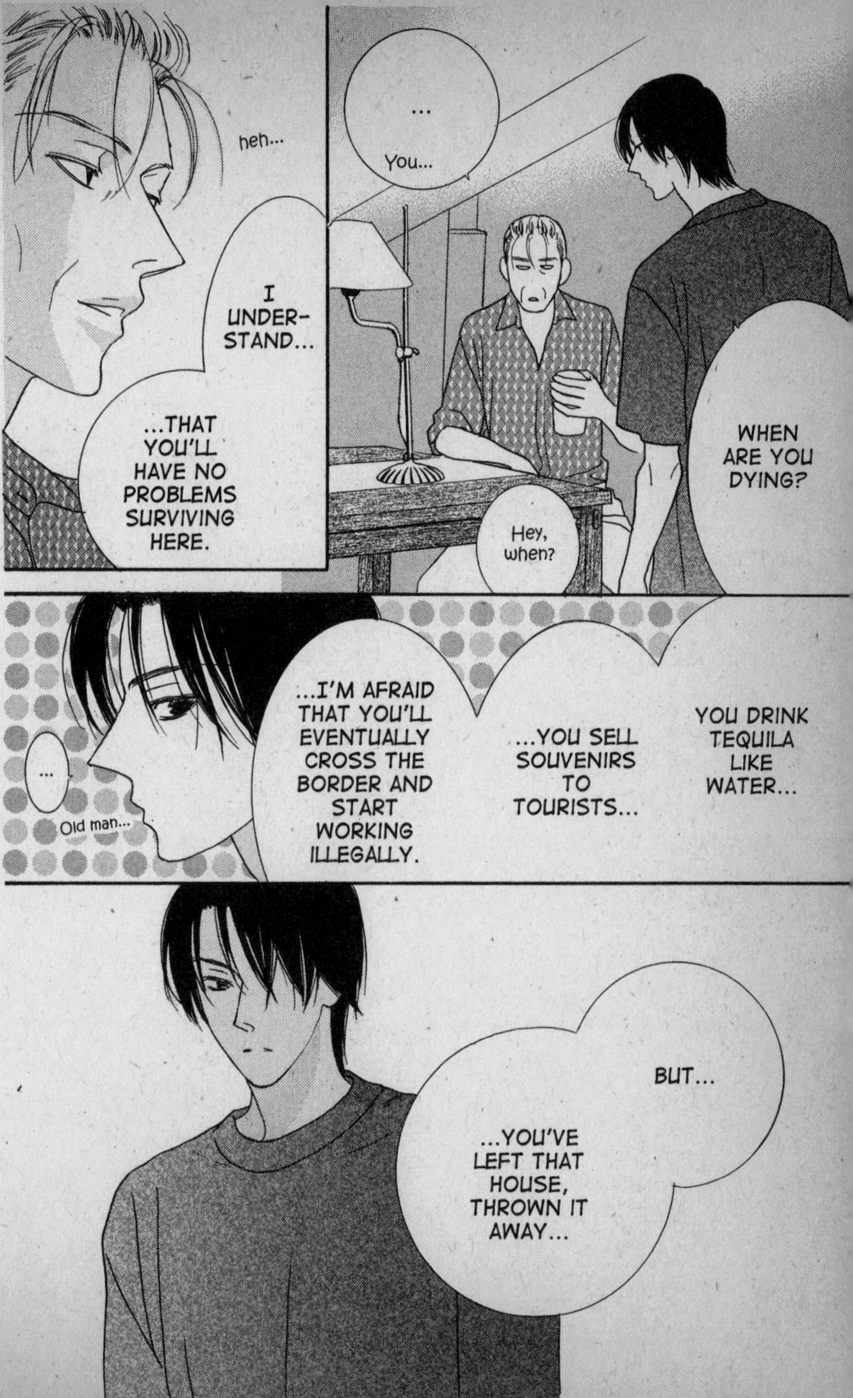
... You...
WHEN ARE YOU DYING?
Hey, when?
heh...
I UNDER-STAND...
...THAT YOU'LL HAVE NO PROBLEMS SURVIVING HERE.
YOU DRINK TEQUILA LIKE WATER...
...YOU SELL SOUVENIRS TO TOURISTS...
...I'M AFRAID THAT YOU'LL EVENTUALLY CROSS THE BORDER AND START WORKING ILLEGALLY.
...
Old man...
BUT...
...YOU'VE LEFT THAT HOUSE, THROWN IT AWAY...

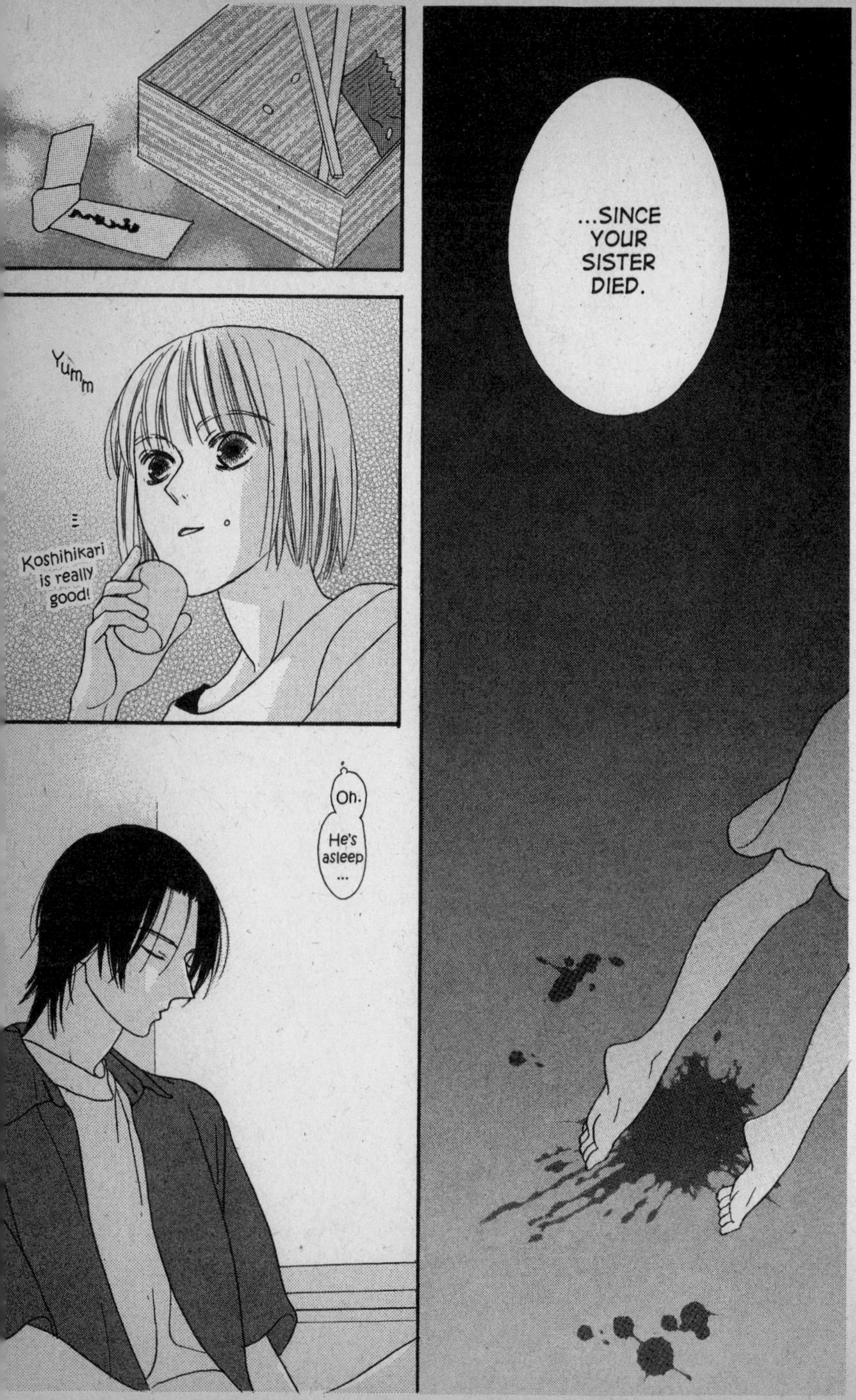
...SINCE YOUR SISTER DIED.
Yumm
Koshihikari is really good!
Oh.
He's asleep ...

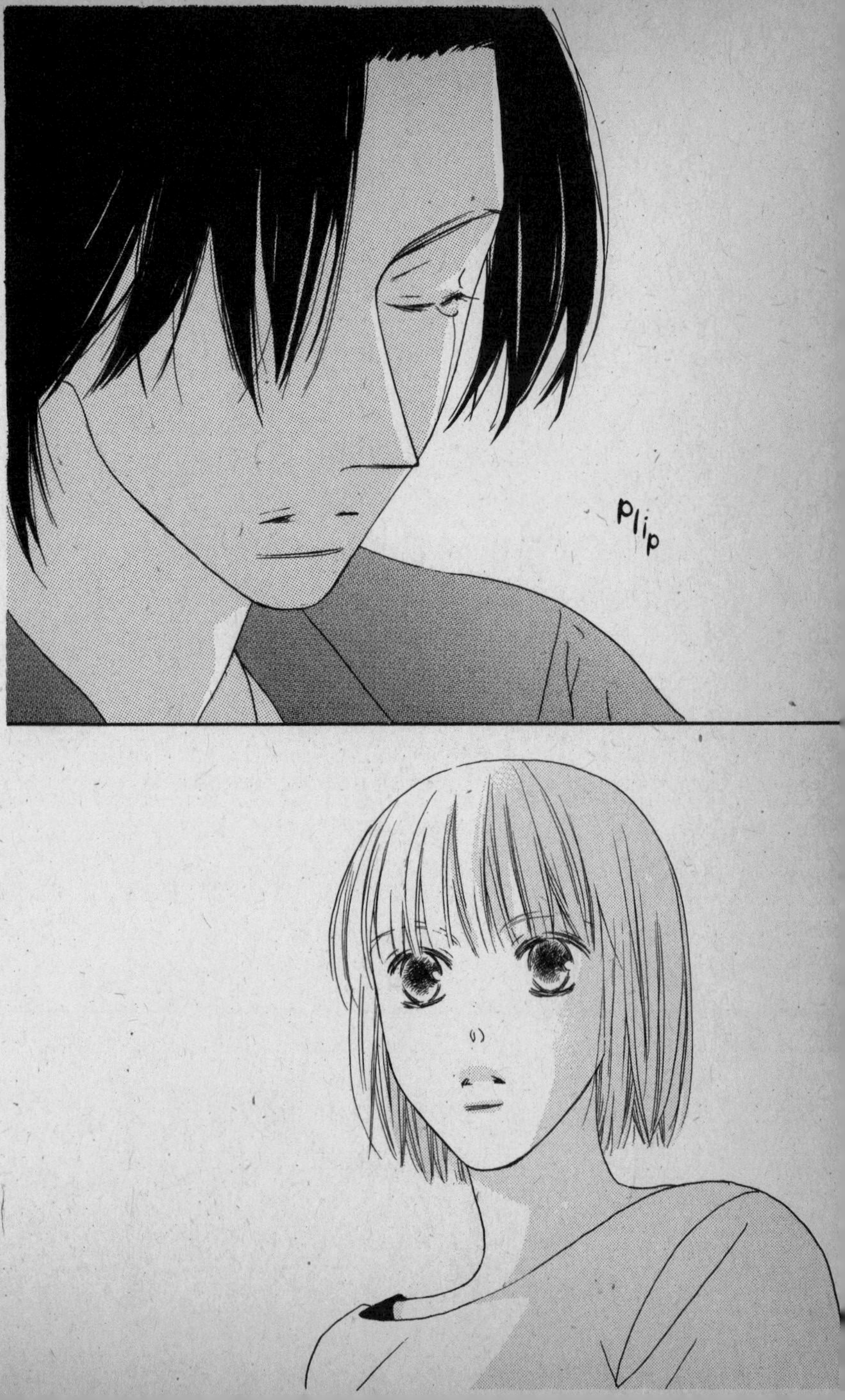
plip

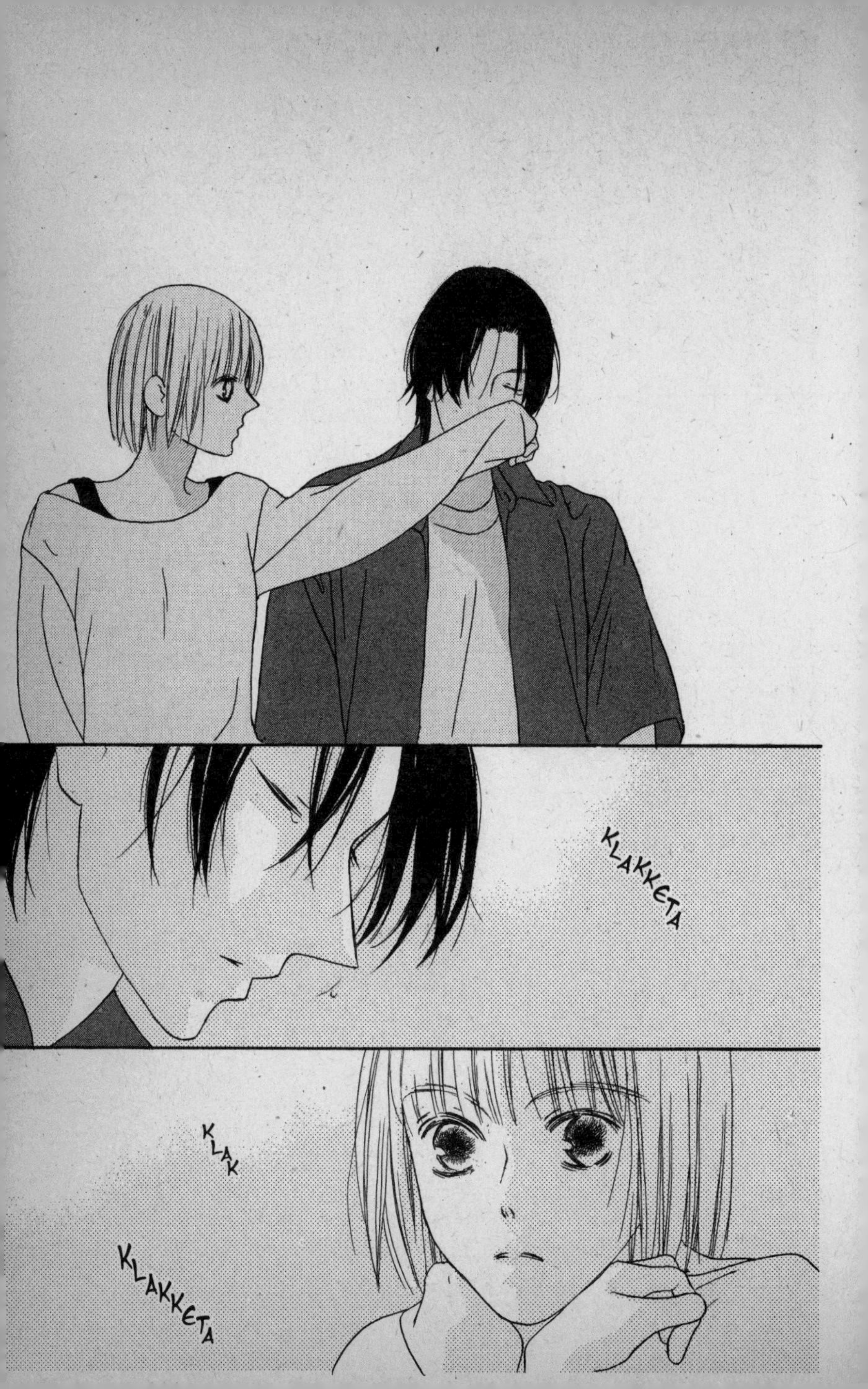
KLAKKETA
KLAK
KLAKKETA

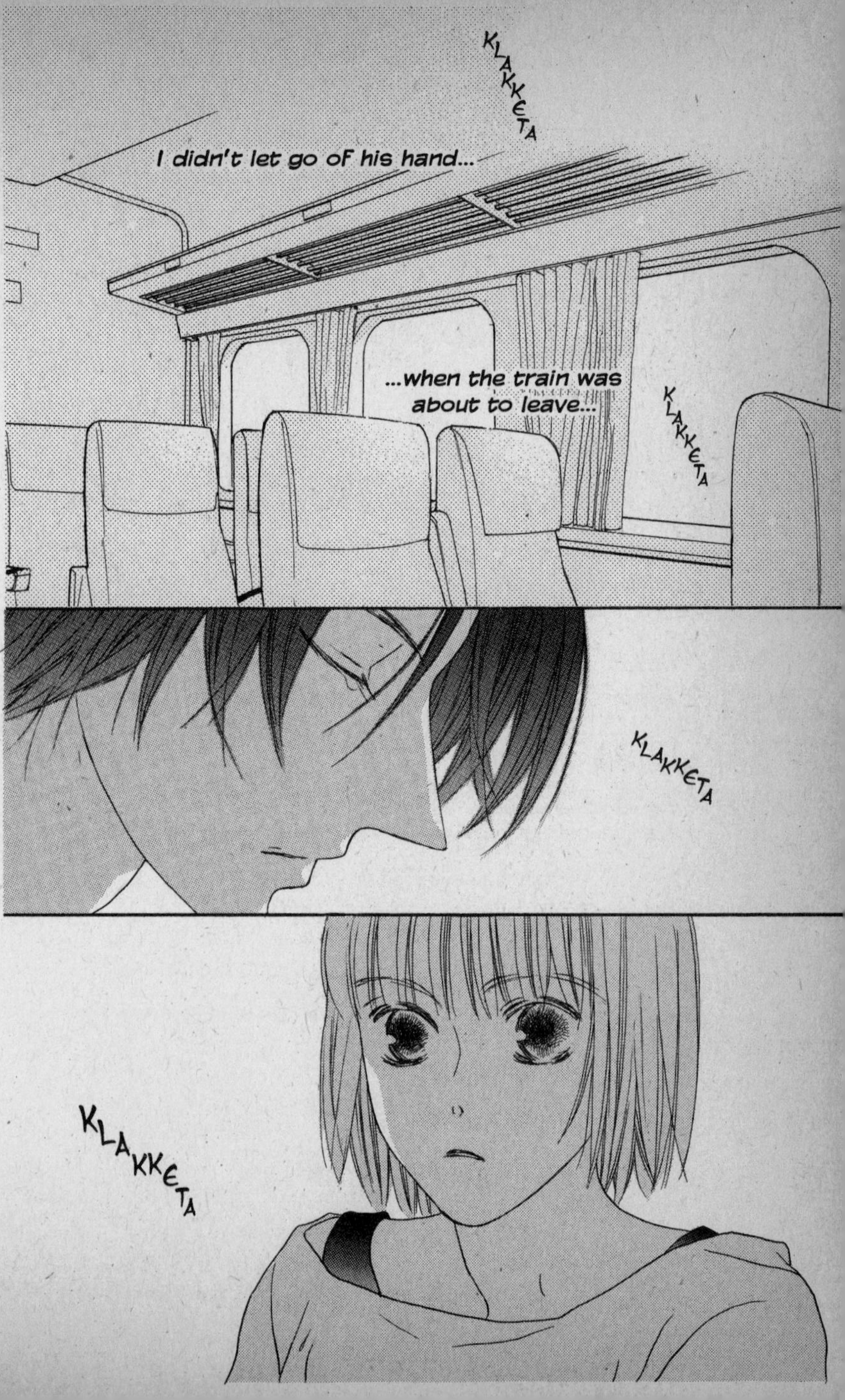
KLAKKETA
I didn't let go of his hand...
...when the train was about to leave...
KLAKKETA
KLAKKETA
KLAKKETA

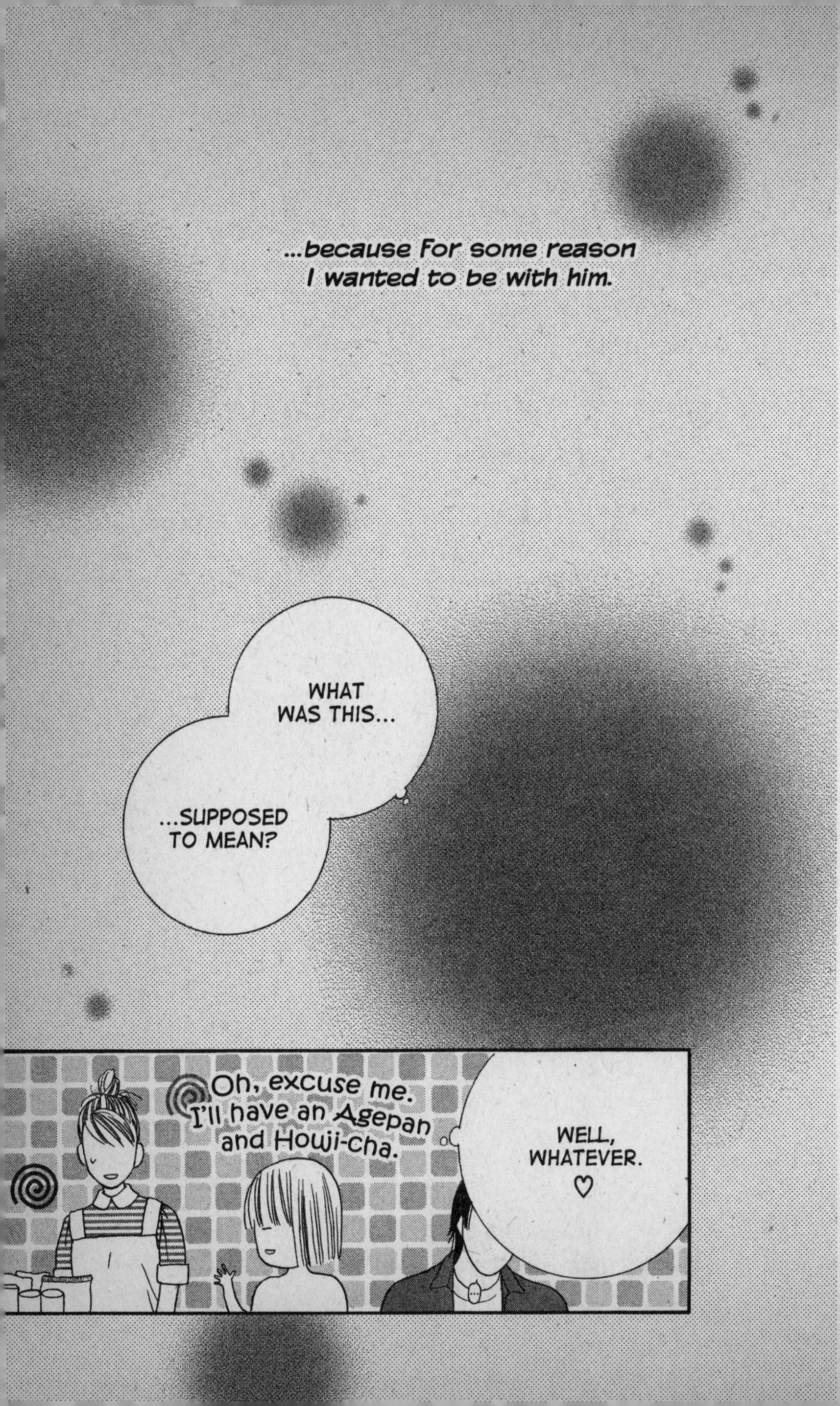
...because for some reason
I wanted to be with him.
WHAT WAS THIS...
...SUPPOSED TO MEAN?
WELL, WHATEVER. ♡
Oh, excuse me. I'll have an Agepan and Houji-cha.

BEAUTY IS THE BEAST

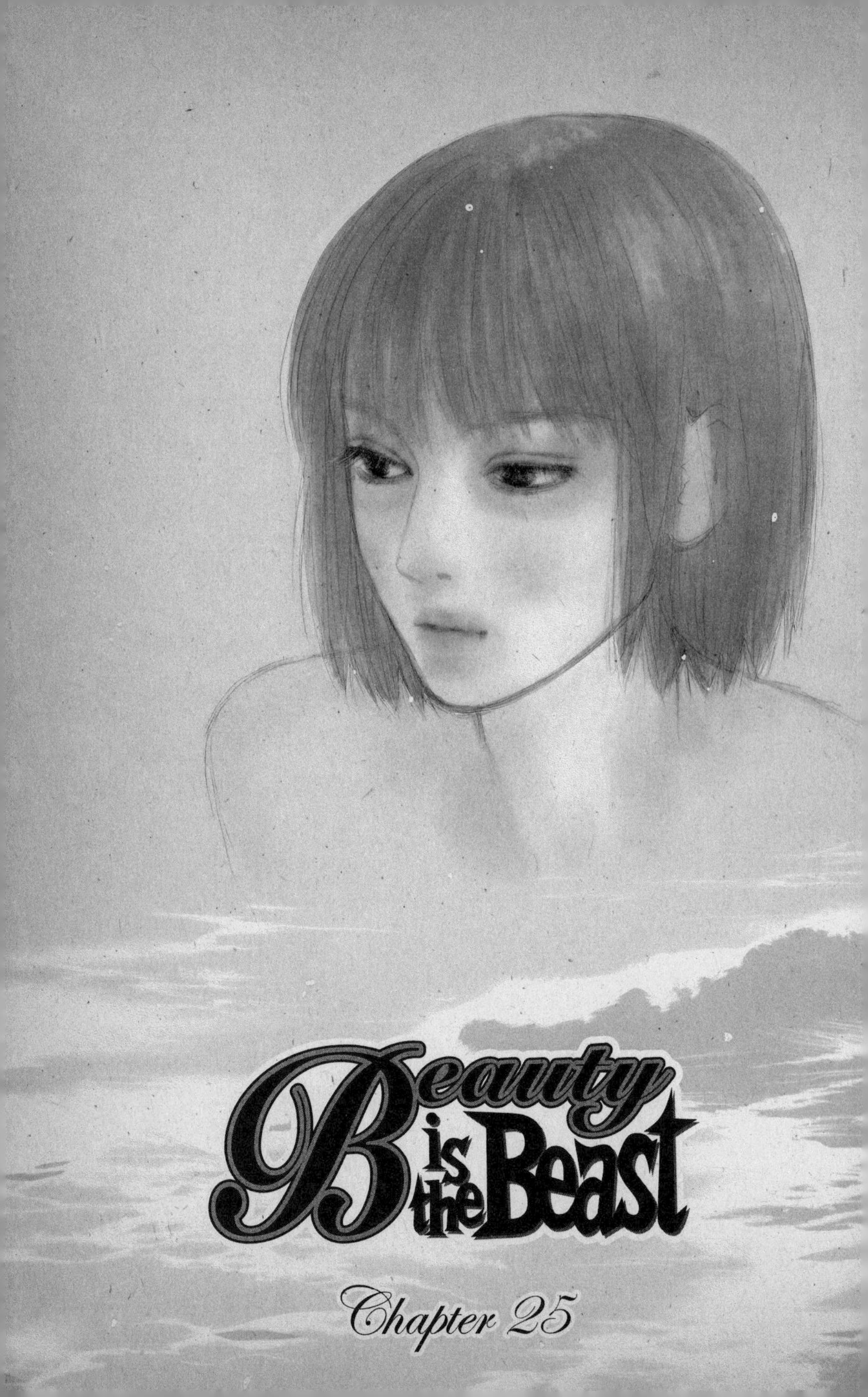
Beauty is the Beast
Chapter 25

BEAUTY IS THE BEAST

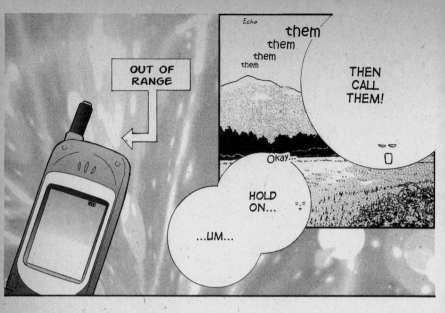

OUT OF RANGE

Echo

them
them
them
them

THEN CALL THEM!

Okay...

HOLD ON...

...UM...

Rahhh!

LOOK ME IN THE EYE AND SAY THAT!

I THINK WE'LL GET THERE IF WE KEEP ON WALKING...

Yup.

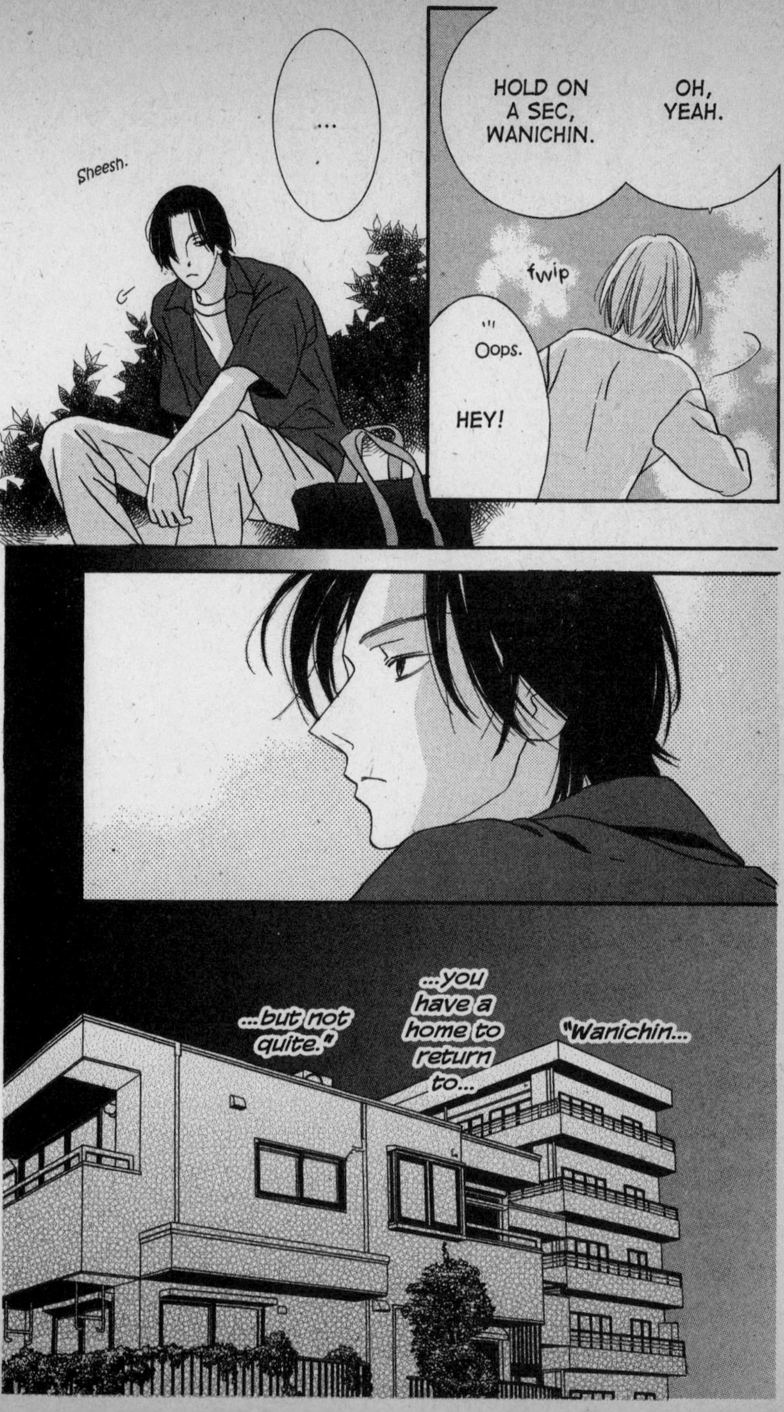
OH, YEAH.
HOLD ON A SEC, WANICHIN.
fwip
Oops.
HEY!
...
Sheesh.
"Wanichin...
...you have a home to return to...
...but not quite."

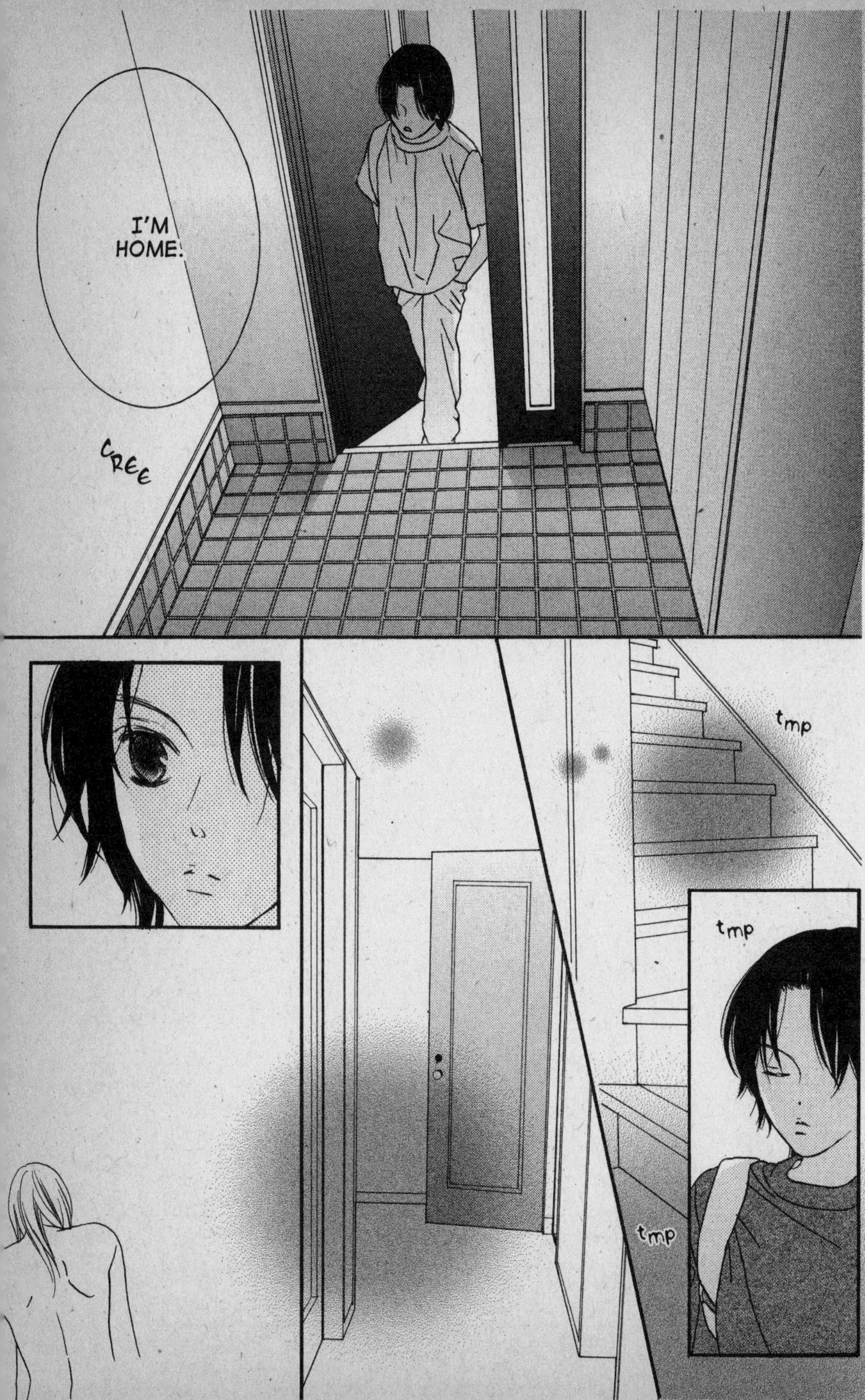
I'M HOME!
CREE
tmp
tmp
tmp

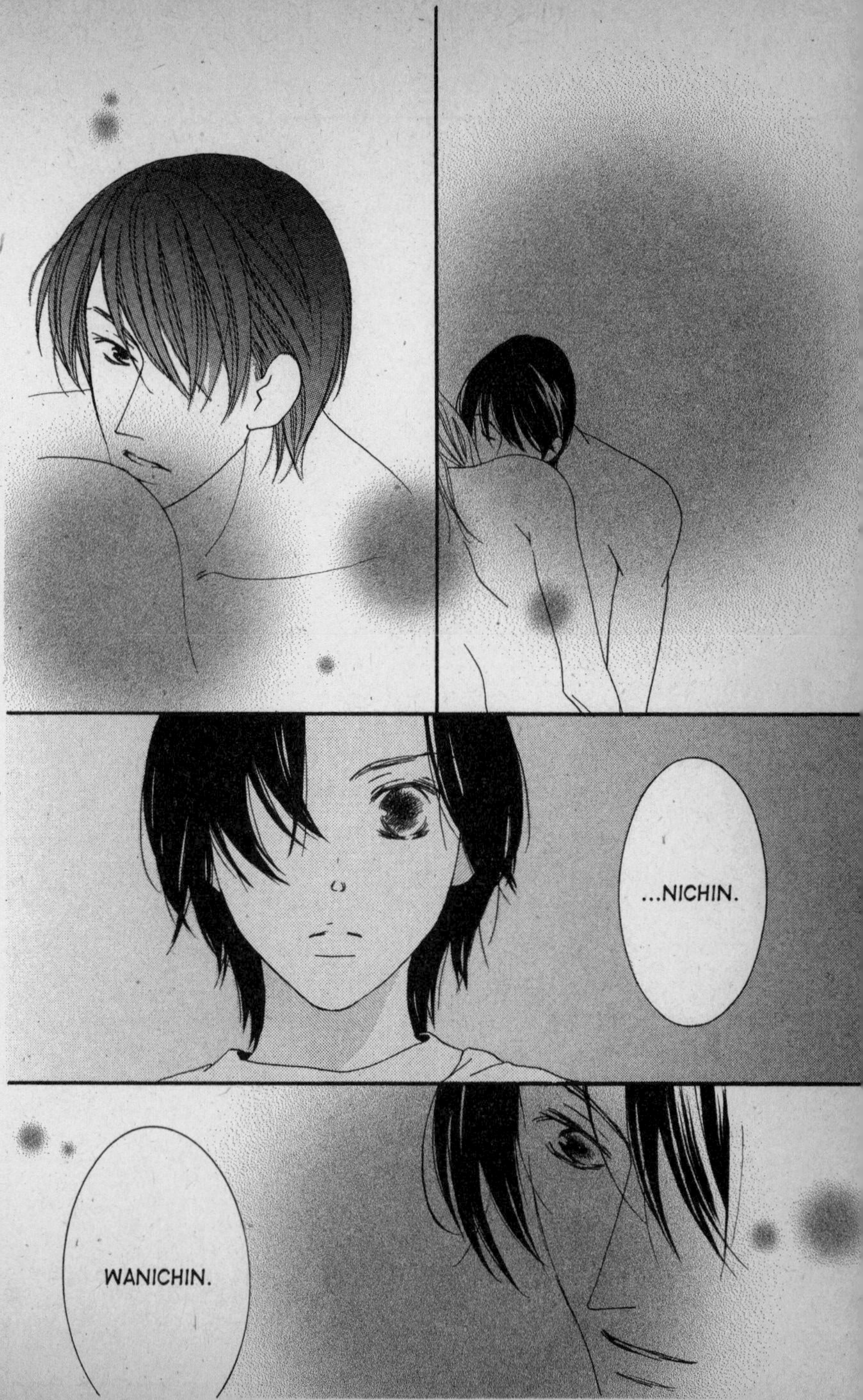
...NICHIN.
WANICHIN.

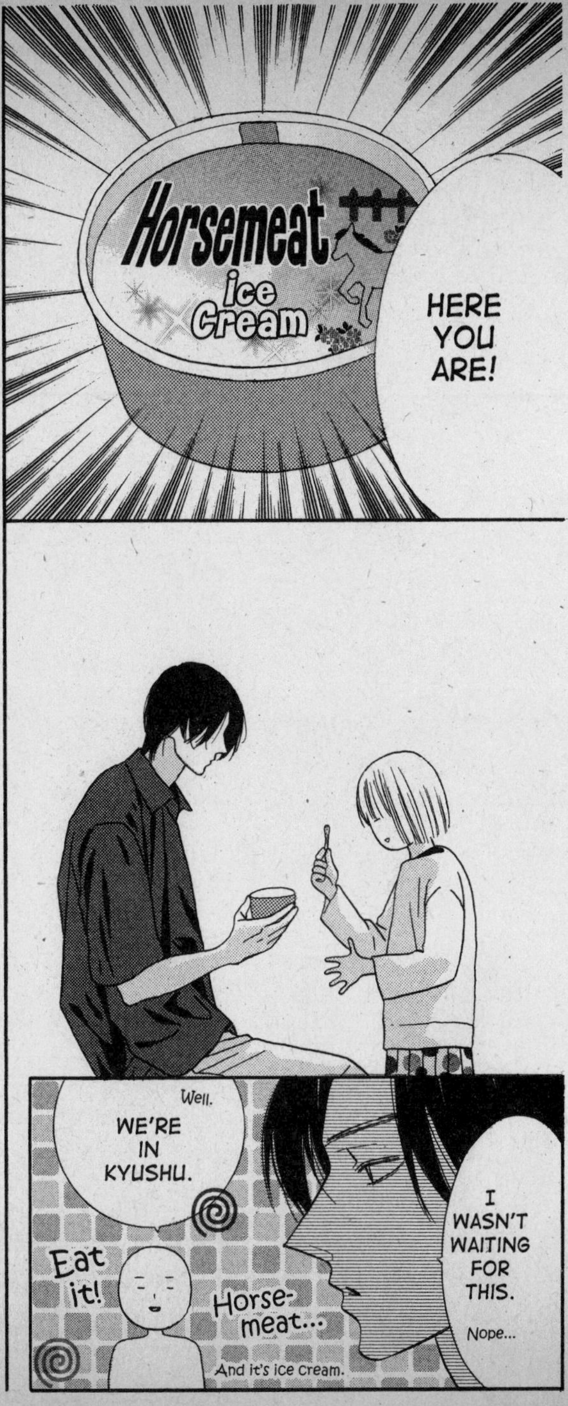
Horsemeat ice Cream
HERE YOU ARE!
I WASN'T WAITING FOR THIS.
Nope...
Well.
WE'RE IN KYUSHU.
Horse-meat...
Eat it!
And it's ice cream.

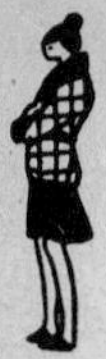

②

Wanichin's dad doesn't like getting hurt.
He's unfit as a parent, but men who have some weaknesses in them wring women's hearts, so that's why women love him (man, that's bad).

Wanichin's relationships, which are like a penance, might be all right if there wasn't any emptiness in them. I thought that as I watched the movie "Monster's Ball" recently.
There is a stormy sex scene in it, so it is the number one movie you should not watch in your living room. (☺)
But it's a delicate story, and I like it.

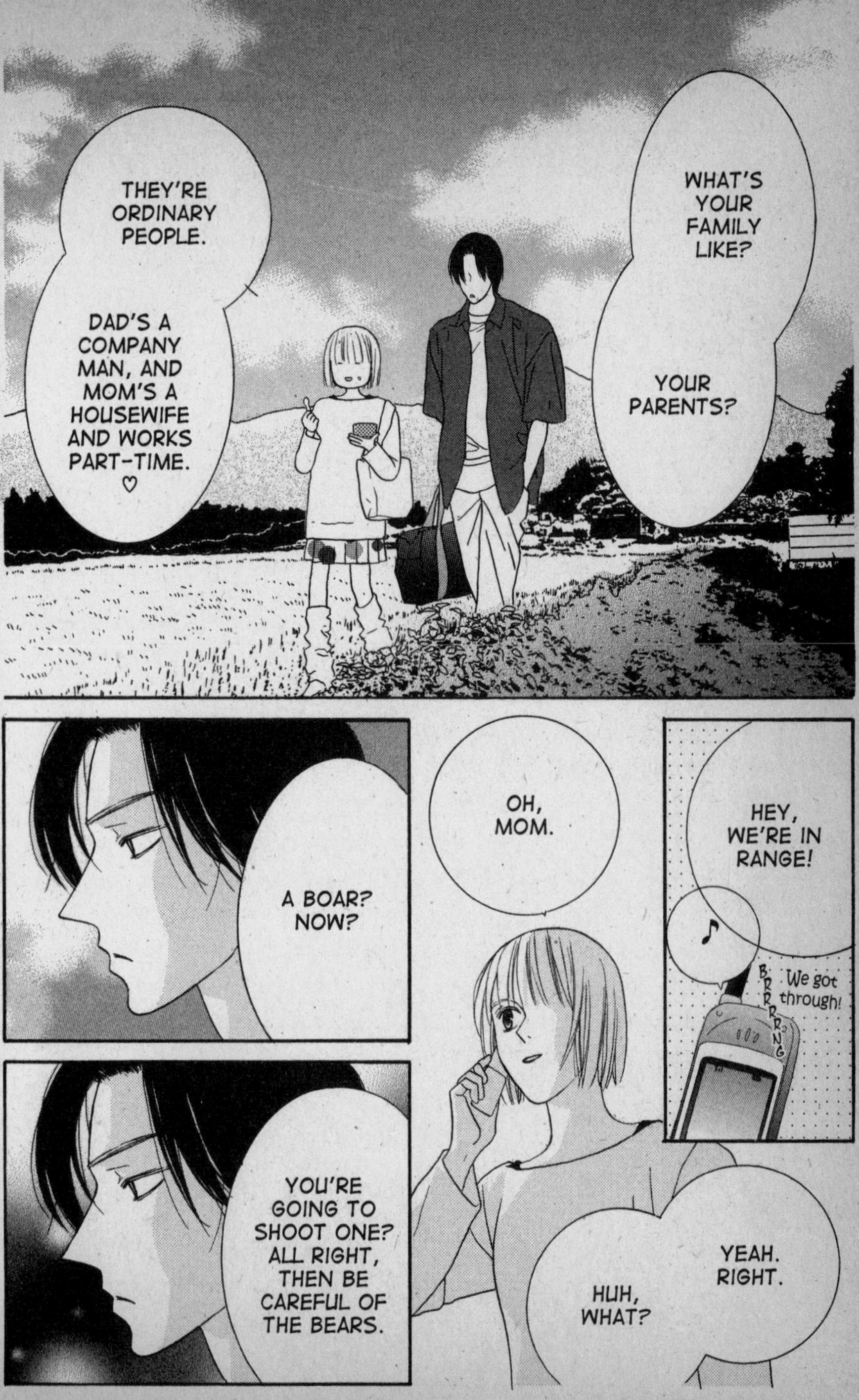
WHAT'S YOUR FAMILY LIKE?
YOUR PARENTS?
THEY'RE ORDINARY PEOPLE.
DAD'S A COMPANY MAN, AND MOM'S A HOUSEWIFE AND WORKS PART-TIME. ♡
HEY, WE'RE IN RANGE!
♪
We got through!
BRRRRRNG
OH, MOM.
A BOAR? NOW?
YEAH. RIGHT.
HUH, WHAT?
YOU'RE GOING TO SHOOT ONE? ALL RIGHT, THEN BE CAREFUL OF THE BEARS.

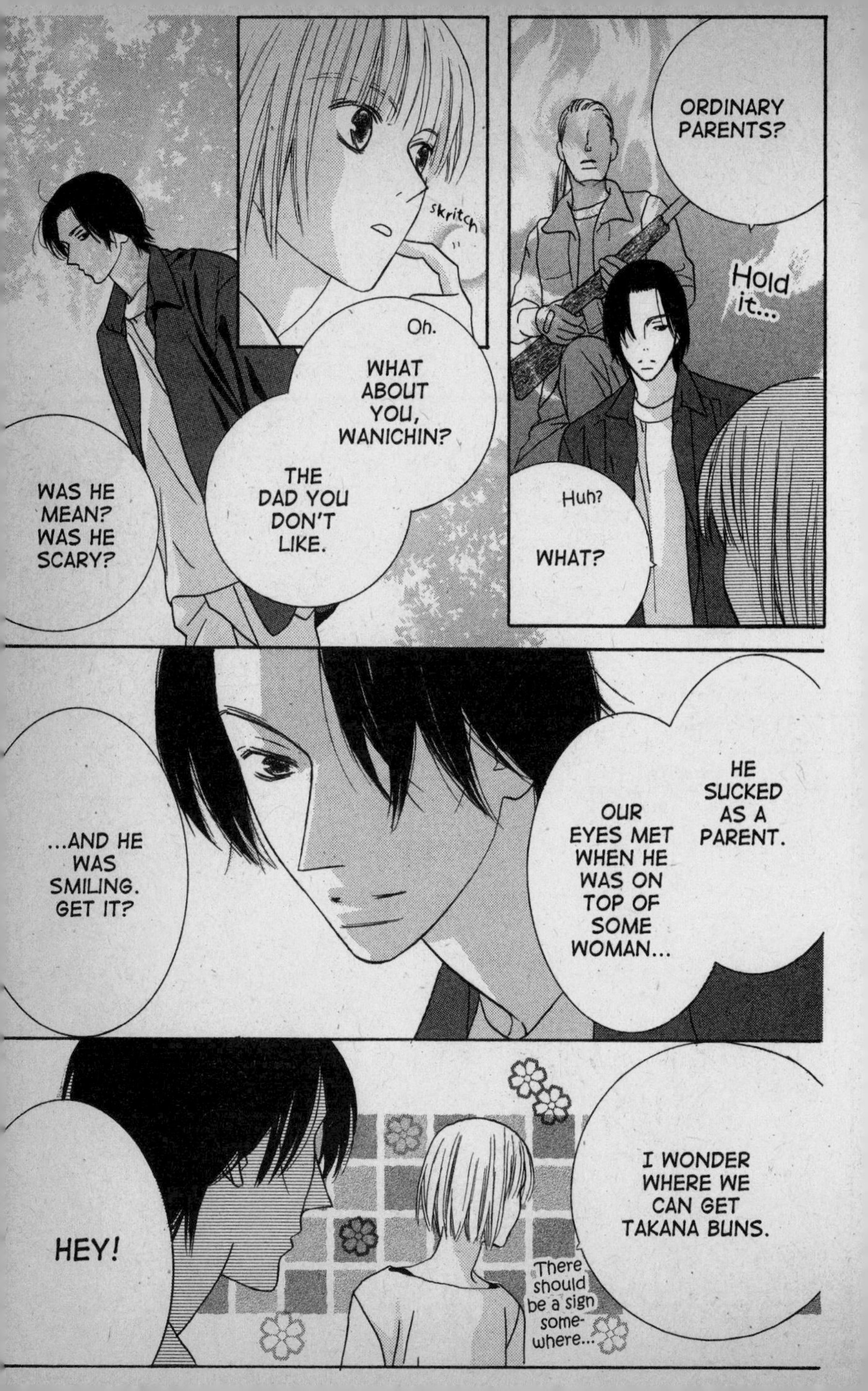
ORDINARY PARENTS?
Hold it...
Huh?
WHAT?
skritch
Oh.
WHAT ABOUT YOU, WANICHIN?
THE DAD YOU DON'T LIKE.
WAS HE MEAN? WAS HE SCARY?
HE SUCKED AS A PARENT.
OUR EYES MET WHEN HE WAS ON TOP OF SOME WOMAN...
...AND HE WAS SMILING. GET IT?
I WONDER WHERE WE CAN GET TAKANA BUNS.
There should be a sign some-where...
HEY!

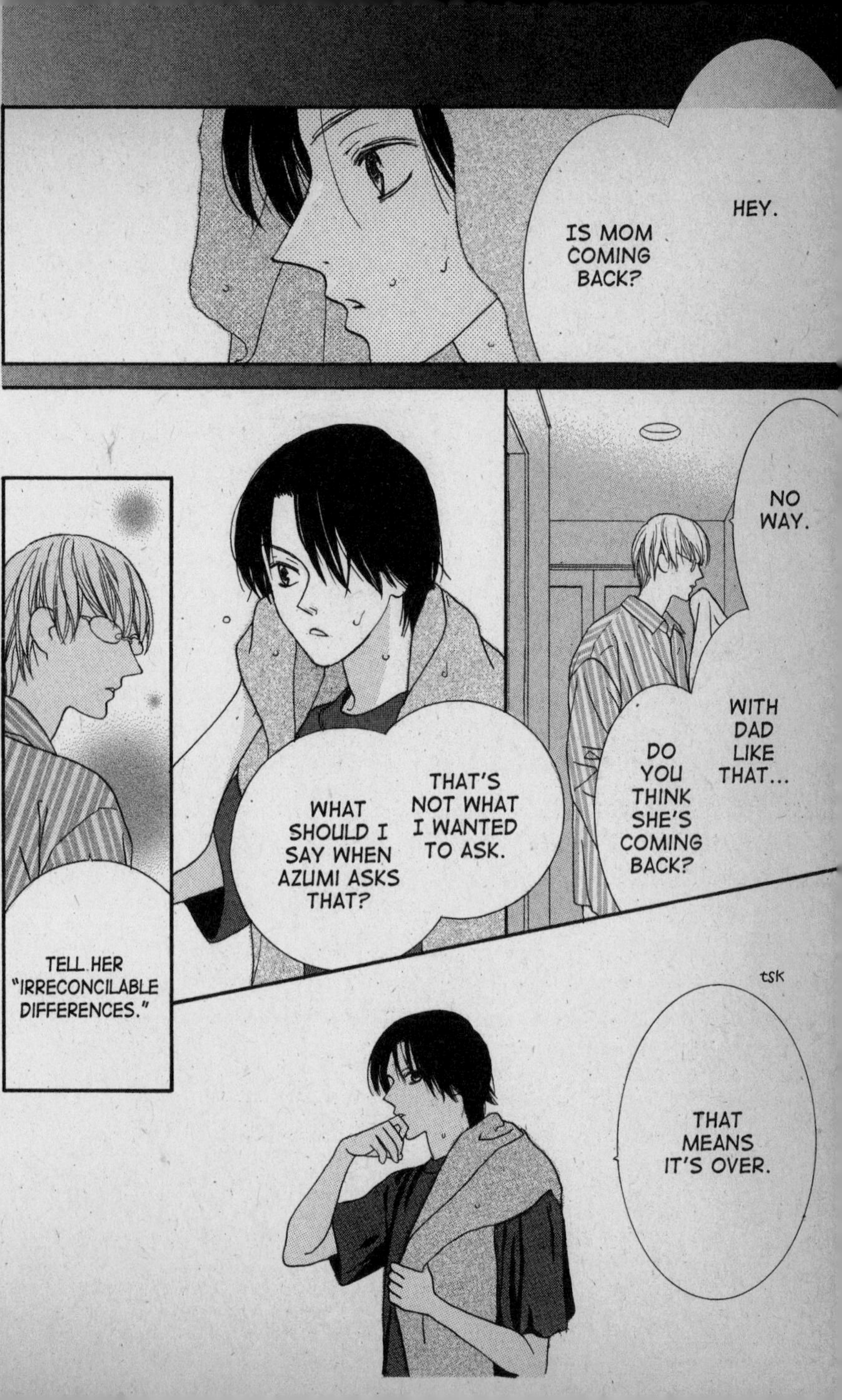
HEY.
IS MOM COMING BACK?
NO WAY.
WITH DAD LIKE THAT...
DO YOU THINK SHE'S COMING BACK?
THAT'S NOT WHAT I WANTED TO ASK.
WHAT SHOULD I SAY WHEN AZUMI ASKS THAT?
TELL HER "IRRECONCILABLE DIFFERENCES."
tsk
THAT MEANS IT'S OVER.

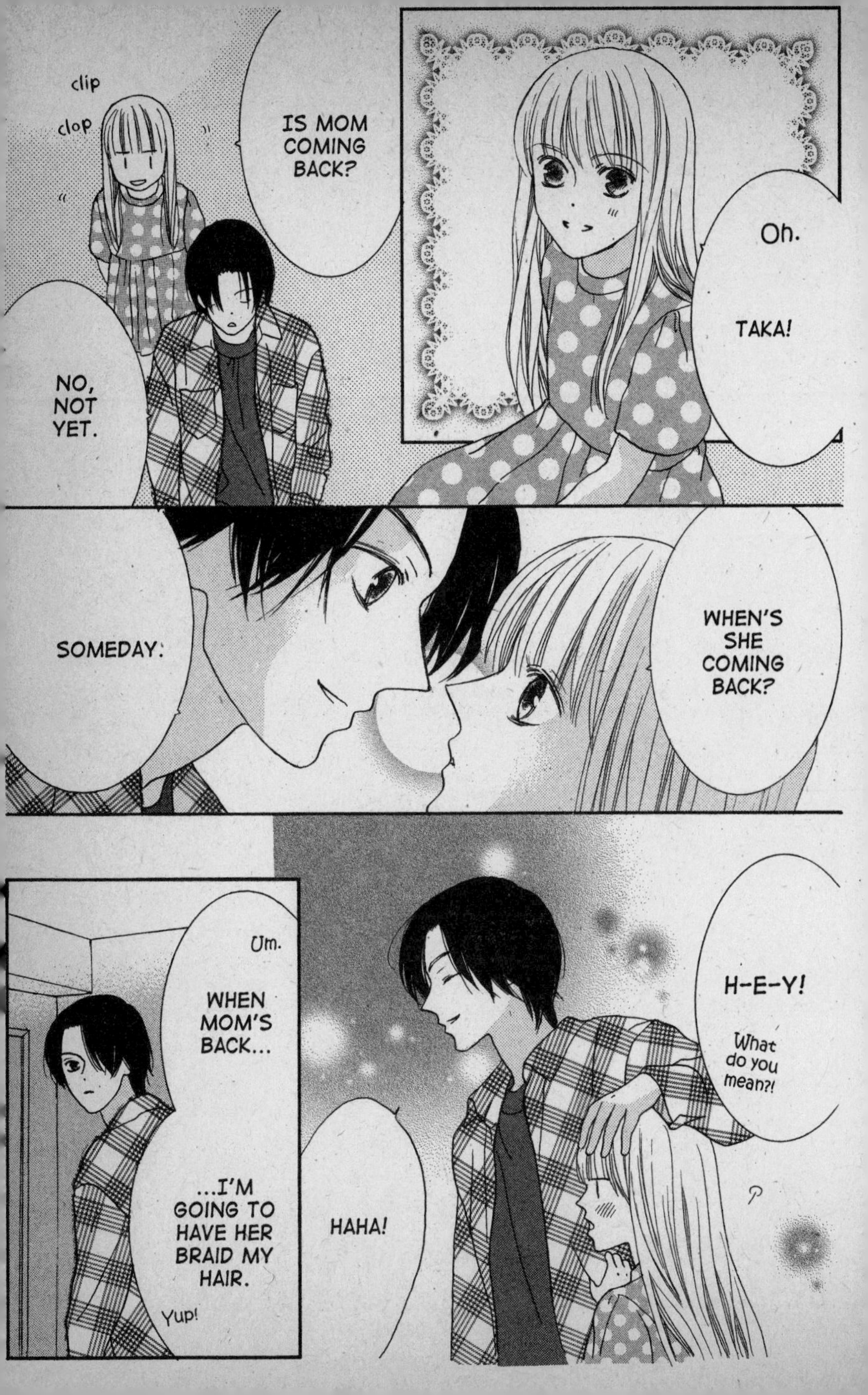
Oh.
TAKA!
clip
clop
IS MOM COMING BACK?
NO, NOT YET.
WHEN'S SHE COMING BACK?
SOMEDAY.
H-E-Y!
What do you mean?!
HAHA!
Um.
WHEN MOM'S BACK...
...I'M GOING TO HAVE HER BRAID MY HAIR.
Yup!

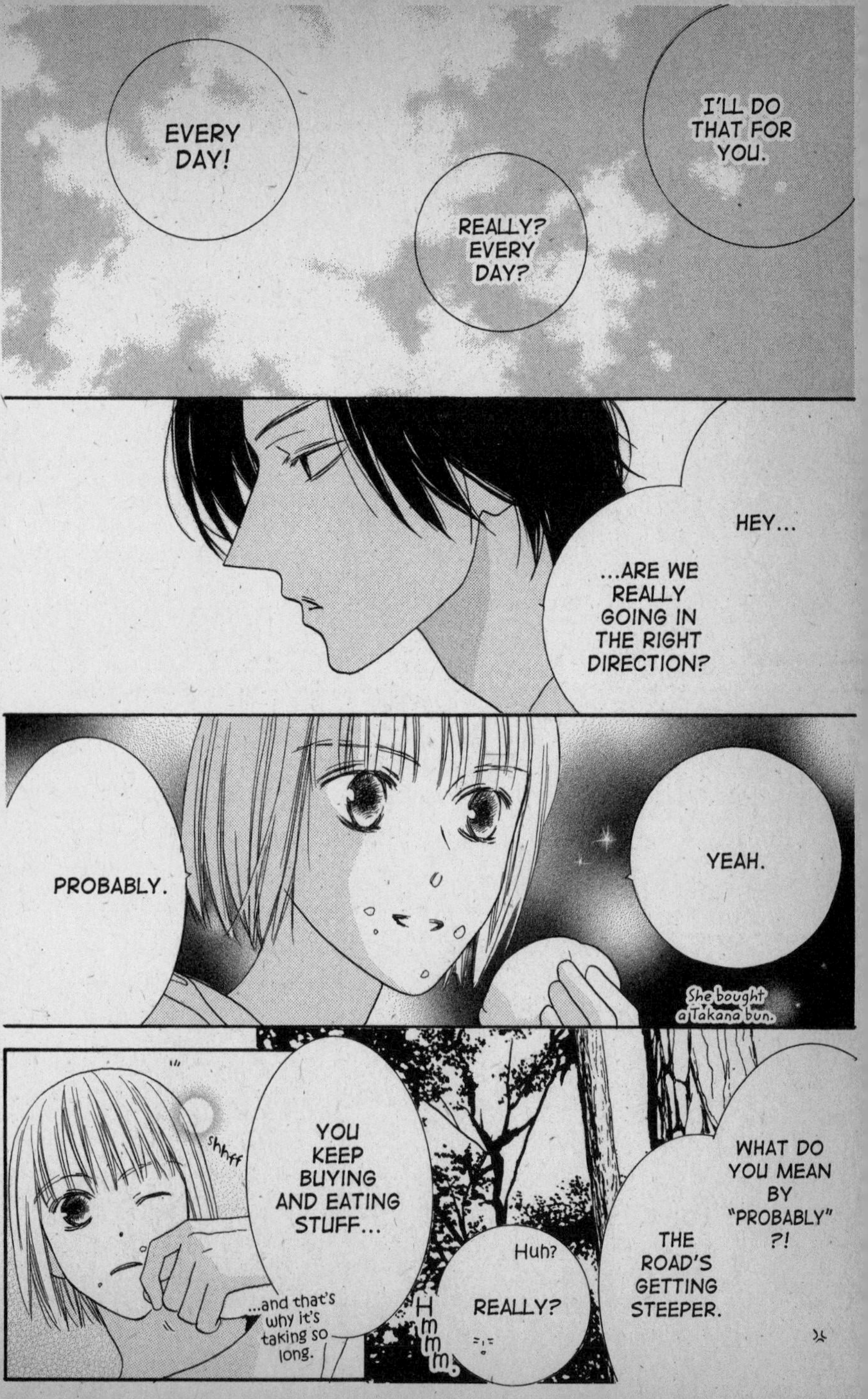
I'LL DO THAT FOR YOU.
REALLY? EVERY DAY?
EVERY DAY!
HEY...
...ARE WE REALLY GOING IN THE RIGHT DIRECTION?
YEAH.
She bought a Takana bun.
PROBABLY.
WHAT DO YOU MEAN BY "PROBABLY" ?!
THE ROAD'S GETTING STEEPER.
Huh?
REALLY?
Hmmm.
YOU KEEP BUYING AND EATING STUFF...
...and that's why it's taking so long.
shhff

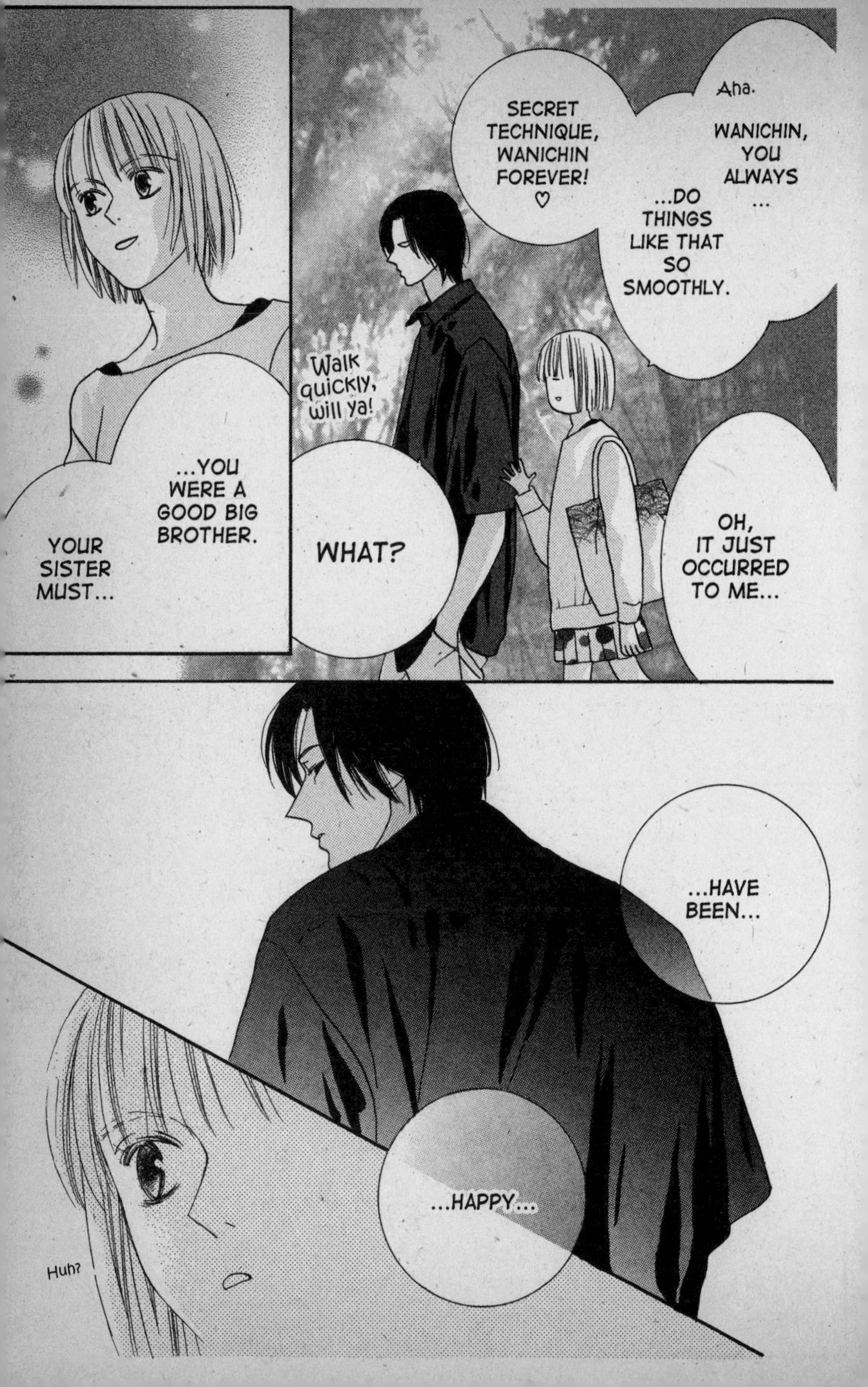
Aha.
WANICHIN, YOU ALWAYS ...
...DO THINGS LIKE THAT SO SMOOTHLY.
SECRET TECHNIQUE, WANICHIN FOREVER! ♡
OH, IT JUST OCCURRED TO ME...
Walk quickly, will ya!
WHAT?
...YOU WERE A GOOD BIG BROTHER.
YOUR SISTER MUST...
...HAVE BEEN...
...HAPPY...
Huh?

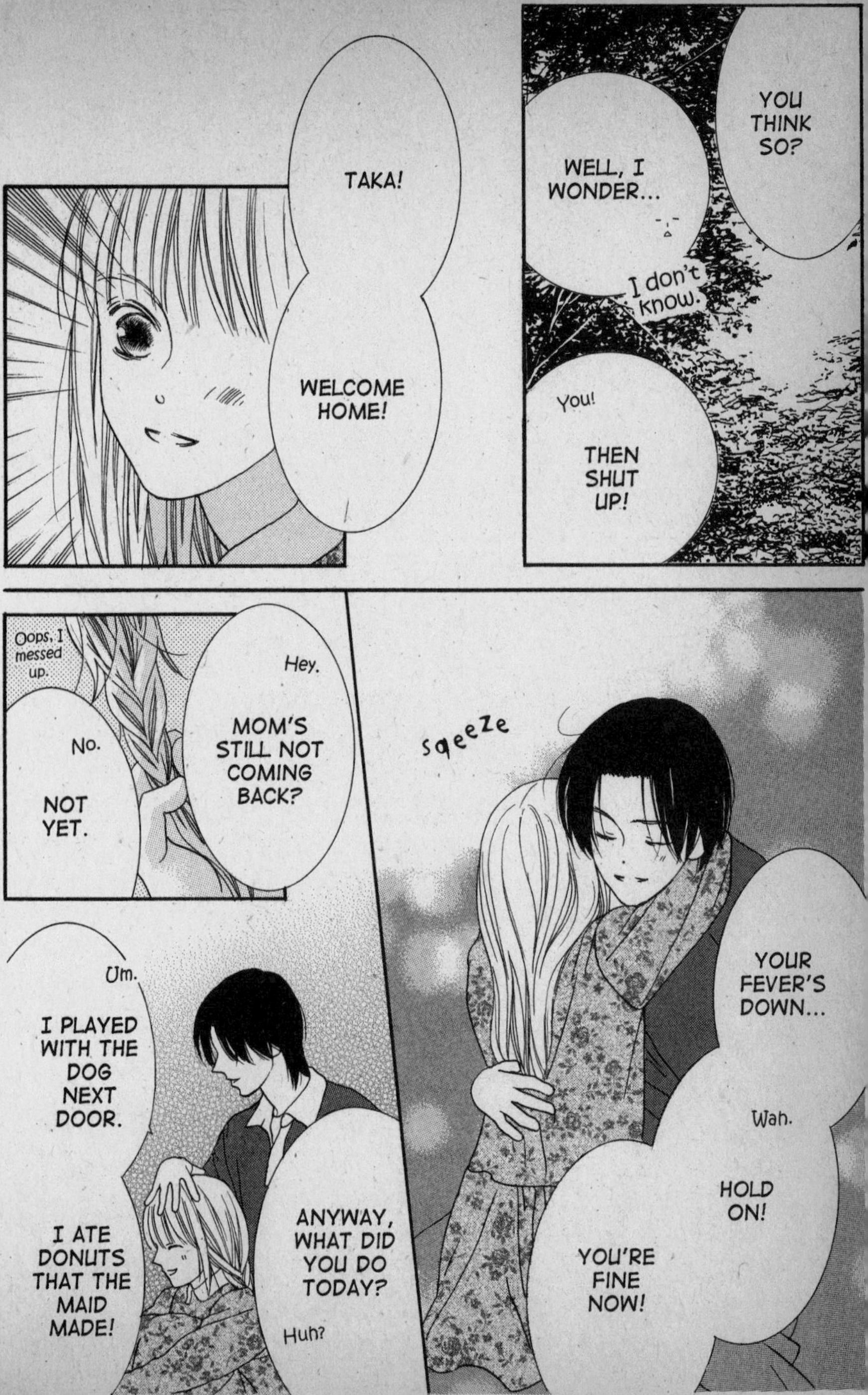
YOU THINK SO?
WELL, I WONDER...
I don't know.
You!
THEN SHUT UP!
TAKA!
WELCOME HOME!
sqeeze
YOUR FEVER'S DOWN...
Wah.
HOLD ON!
YOU'RE FINE NOW!
Hey.
MOM'S STILL NOT COMING BACK?
Oops, I messed up.
No.
NOT YET.
ANYWAY, WHAT DID YOU DO TODAY?
Huh?
Um.
I PLAYED WITH THE DOG NEXT DOOR.
I ATE DONUTS THAT THE MAID MADE!

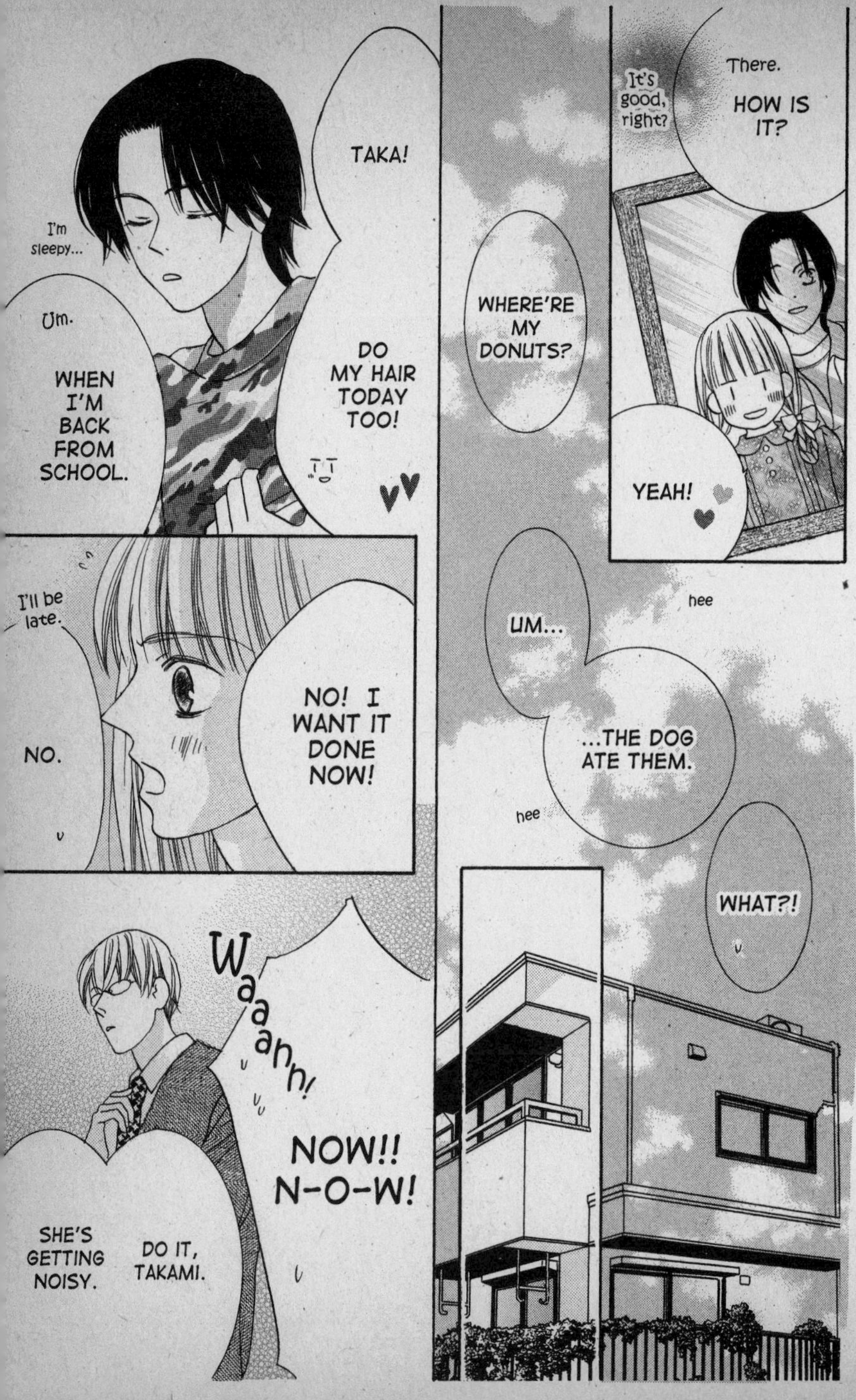
There.
HOW IS IT?
It's good, right?
YEAH!
WHERE'RE MY DONUTS?
UM...
...THE DOG ATE THEM.
hee
hee
WHAT?!
TAKA!
DO MY HAIR TODAY TOO!
I'm sleepy...
Um.
WHEN I'M BACK FROM SCHOOL.
NO! I WANT IT DONE NOW!
I'll be late.
NO.
Waaaann!
NOW!! N-O-W!
DO IT, TAKAMI.
SHE'S GETTING NOISY.

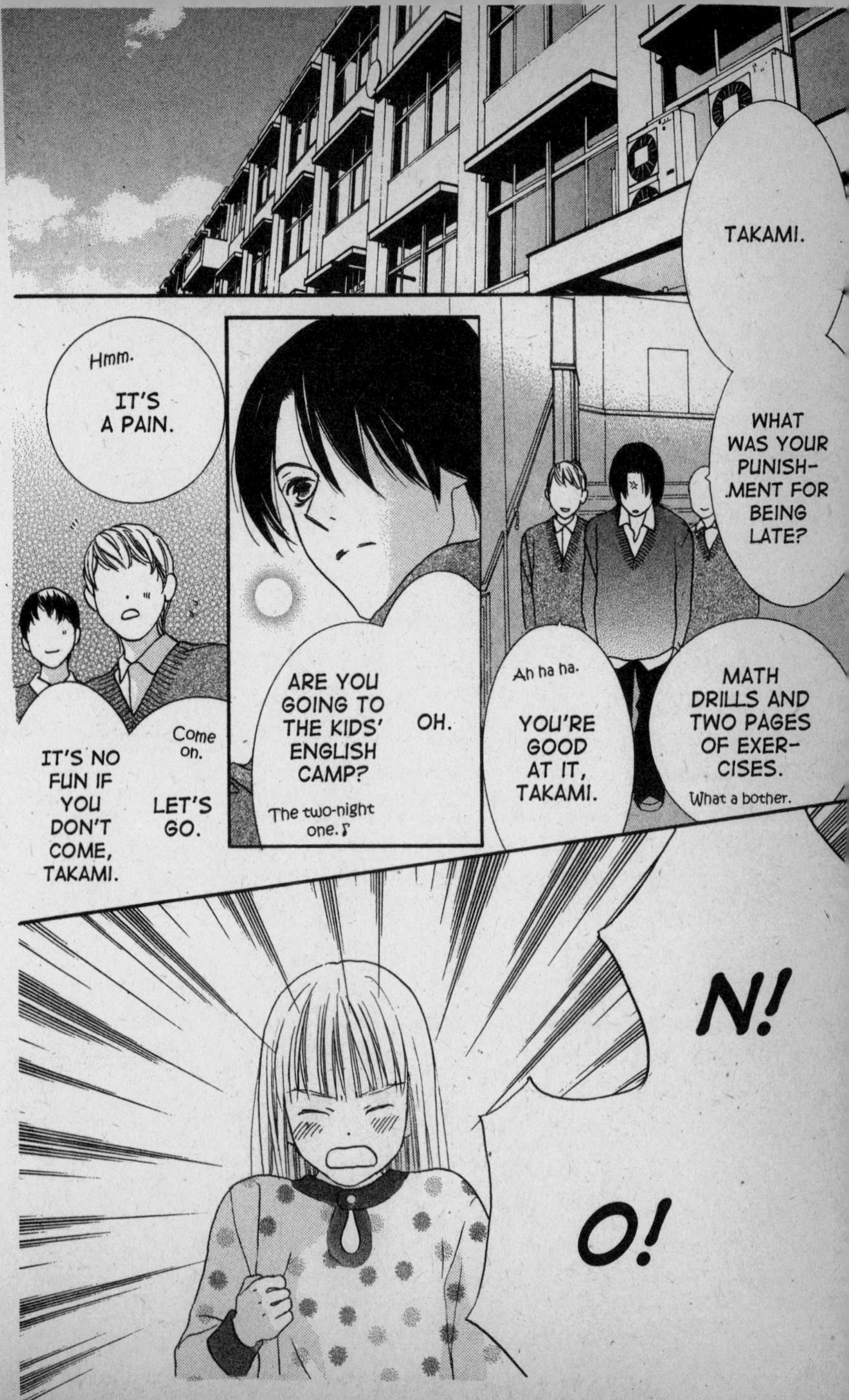
TAKAMI.
WHAT WAS YOUR PUNISHMENT FOR BEING LATE?
MATH DRILLS AND TWO PAGES OF EXERCISES.
What a bother.
Ah ha ha.
YOU'RE GOOD AT IT, TAKAMI.
OH.
ARE YOU GOING TO THE KIDS' ENGLISH CAMP?
The two-night one.♪
Hmm.
IT'S A PAIN.
Come on.
LET'S GO.
IT'S NO FUN IF YOU DON'T COME, TAKAMI.
N!
O!

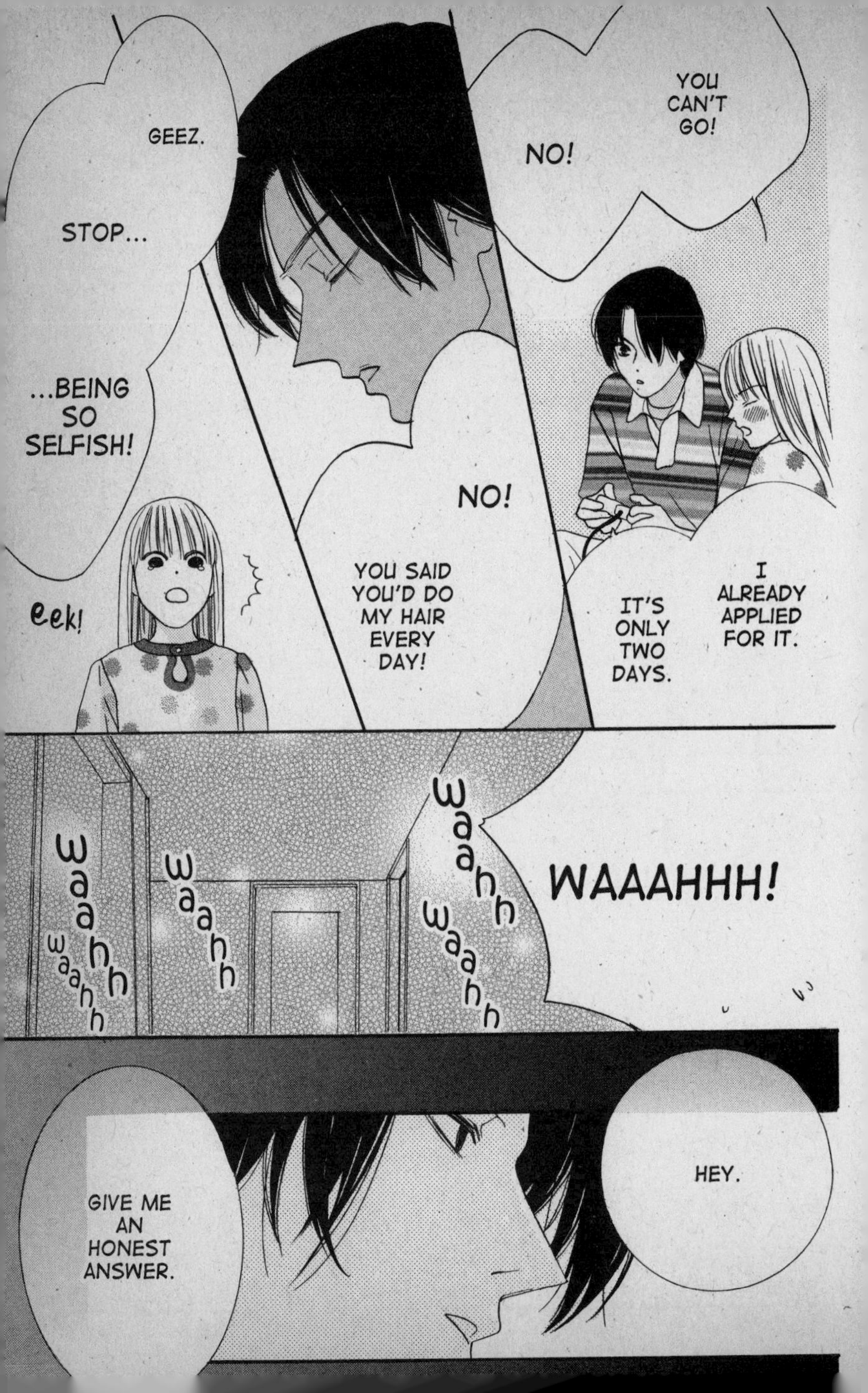
YOU CAN'T GO!
NO!
I ALREADY APPLIED FOR IT.
IT'S ONLY TWO DAYS.
NO!
YOU SAID YOU'D DO MY HAIR EVERY DAY!
GEEZ.
STOP...
...BEING SO SELFISH!
eek!
WAAAHHH!
waahh
waahh
waahh
waahh
waahh
HEY.
GIVE ME AN HONEST ANSWER.

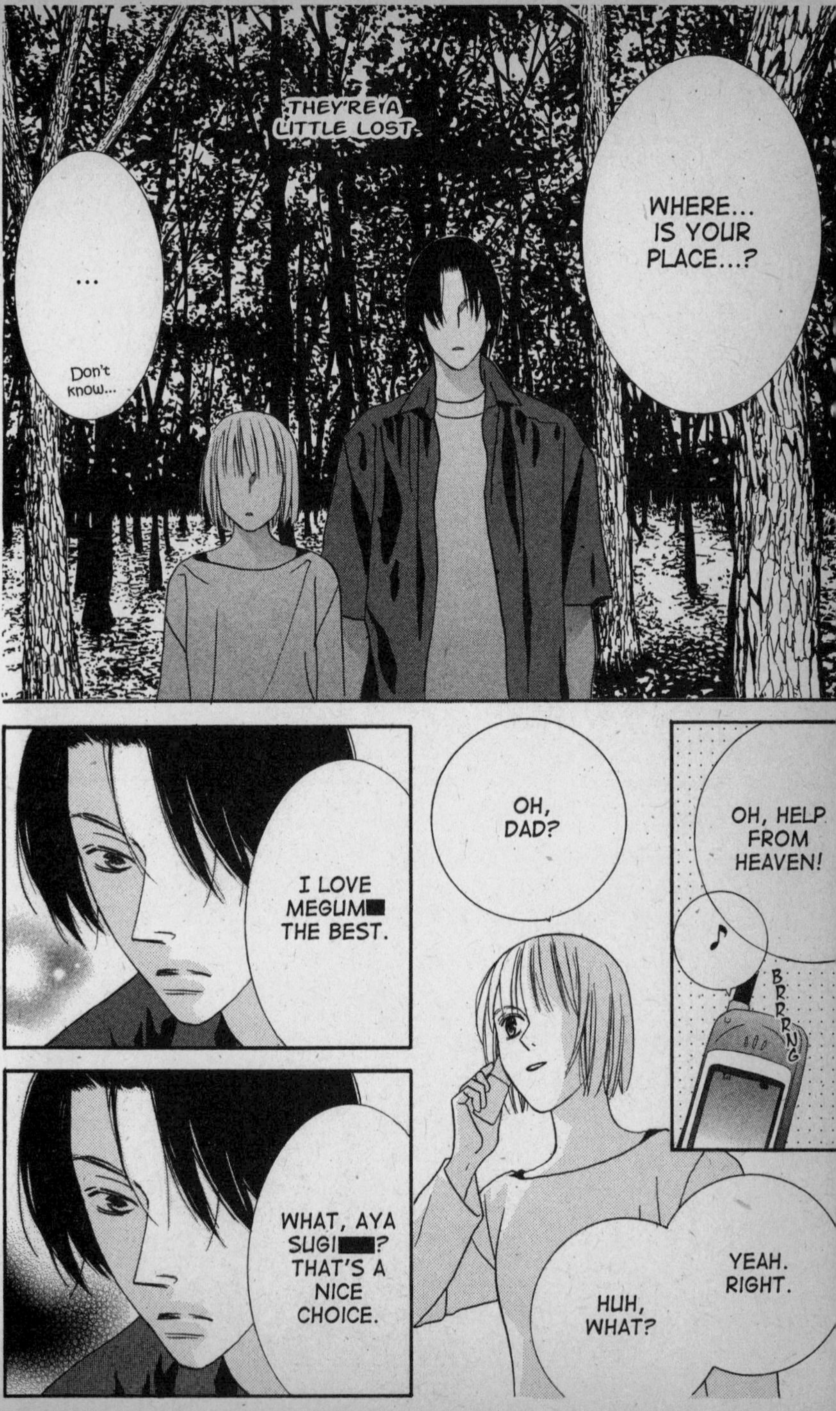
WHERE... IS YOUR PLACE...?
THEY'RE A LITTLE LOST
...
Don't know...
OH, HELP FROM HEAVEN!
♪
BRRRNG
OH, DAD?
I LOVE MEGUM[redacted] THE BEST.
WHAT, AYA SUGI[redacted]? THAT'S A NICE CHOICE.
YEAH. RIGHT.
HUH, WHAT?

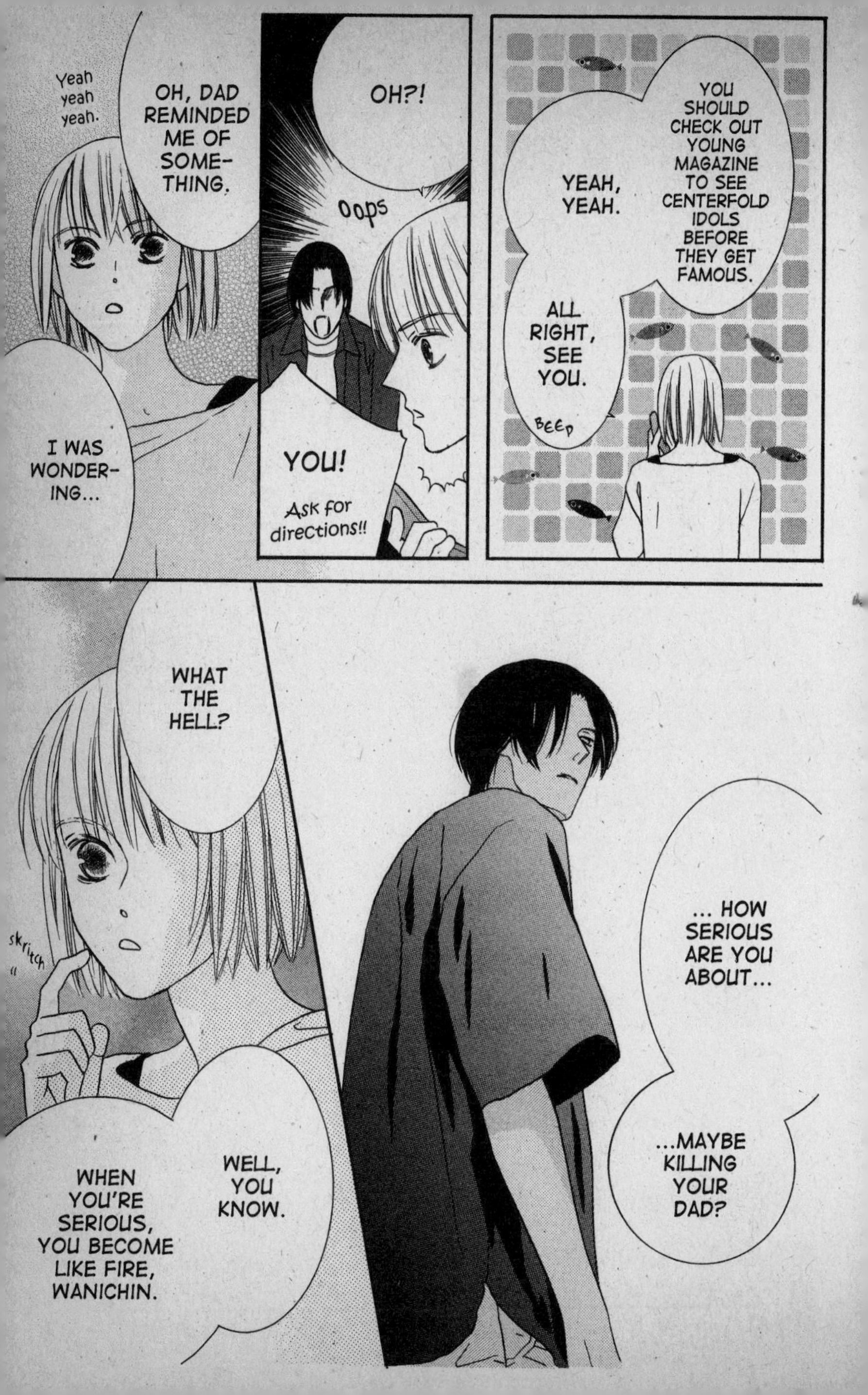
YOU SHOULD CHECK OUT YOUNG MAGAZINE TO SEE CENTERFOLD IDOLS BEFORE THEY GET FAMOUS.
YEAH, YEAH.
ALL RIGHT, SEE YOU.
BEEP
OH?!
Oops
YOU!
Ask for directions!!
Yeah yeah yeah.
OH, DAD REMINDED ME OF SOMETHING.
I WAS WONDERING...
... HOW SERIOUS ARE YOU ABOUT...
...MAYBE KILLING YOUR DAD?
WHAT THE HELL?
skritch
WELL, YOU KNOW.
WHEN YOU'RE SERIOUS, YOU BECOME LIKE FIRE, WANICHIN.

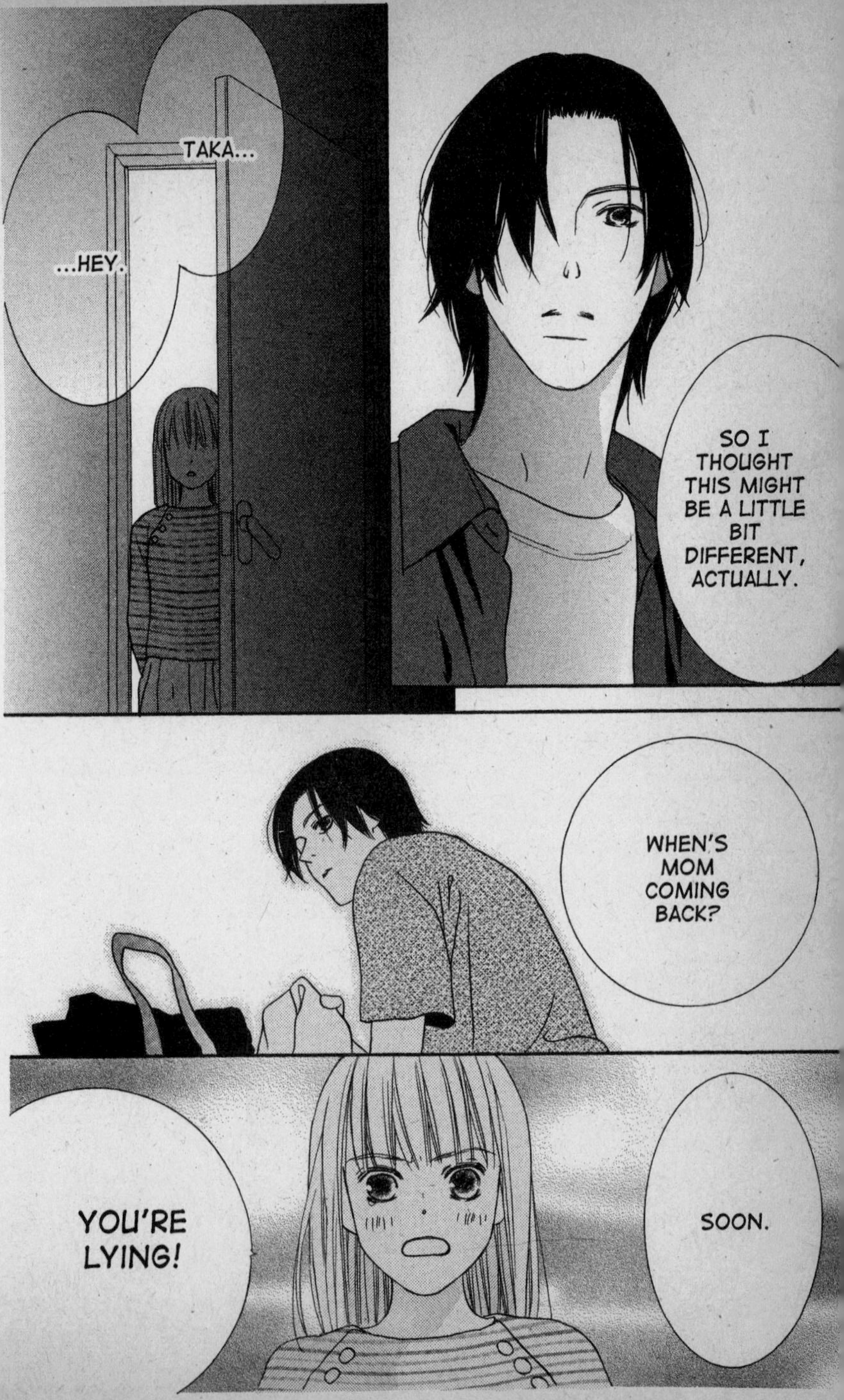
SO I THOUGHT THIS MIGHT BE A LITTLE BIT DIFFERENT, ACTUALLY.
TAKA...
...HEY.
WHEN'S MOM COMING BACK?
SOON.
YOU'RE LYING!

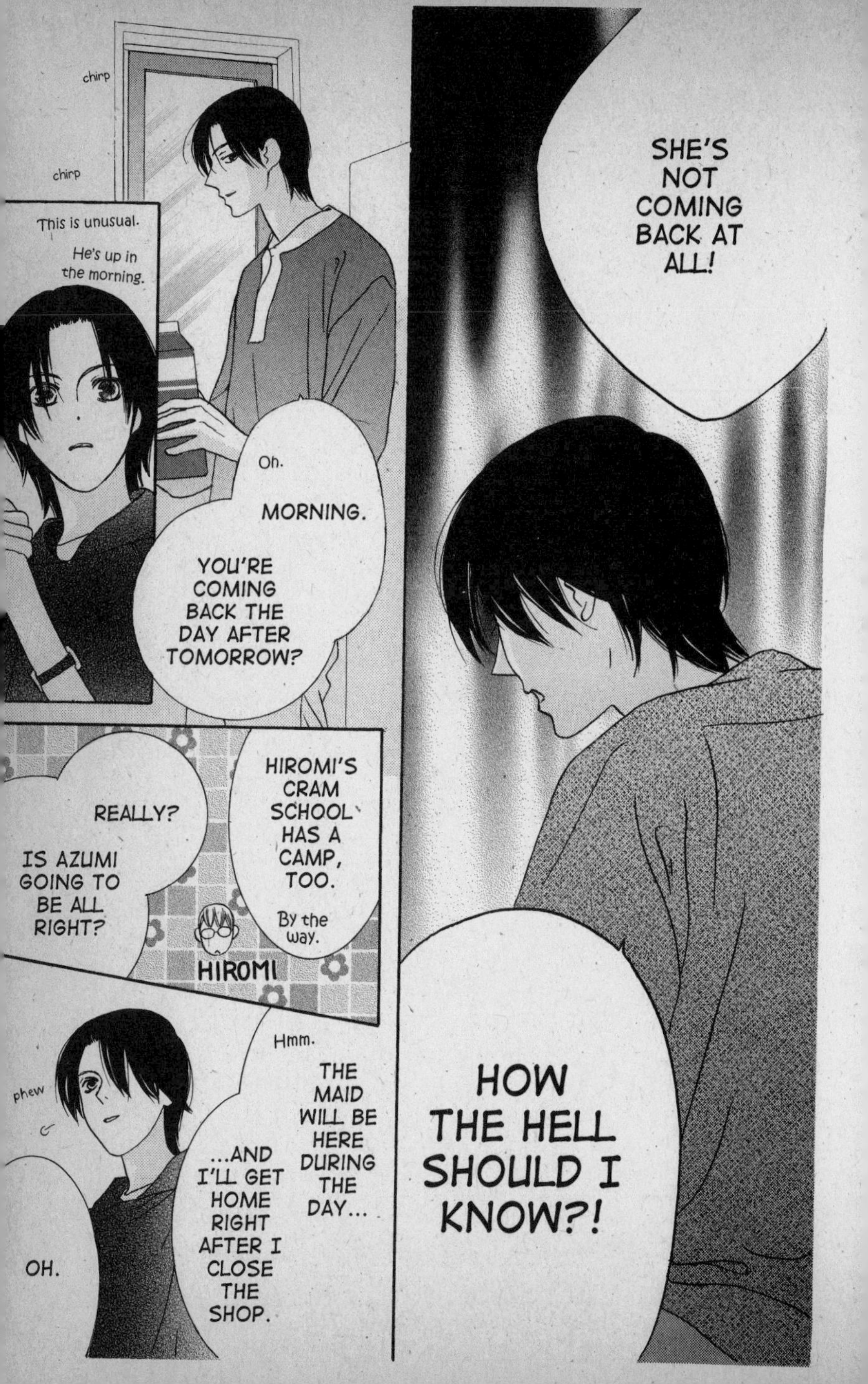
SHE'S NOT COMING BACK AT ALL!
HOW THE HELL SHOULD I KNOW?!
chirp
chirp
This is unusual.
He's up in the morning.
Oh.
MORNING.
YOU'RE COMING BACK THE DAY AFTER TOMORROW?
HIROMI'S CRAM SCHOOL HAS A CAMP, TOO.
By the way.
REALLY?
IS AZUMI GOING TO BE ALL RIGHT?
HIROMI
Hmm.
THE MAID WILL BE HERE DURING THE DAY...
...AND I'LL GET HOME RIGHT AFTER I CLOSE THE SHOP.
phew
OH.

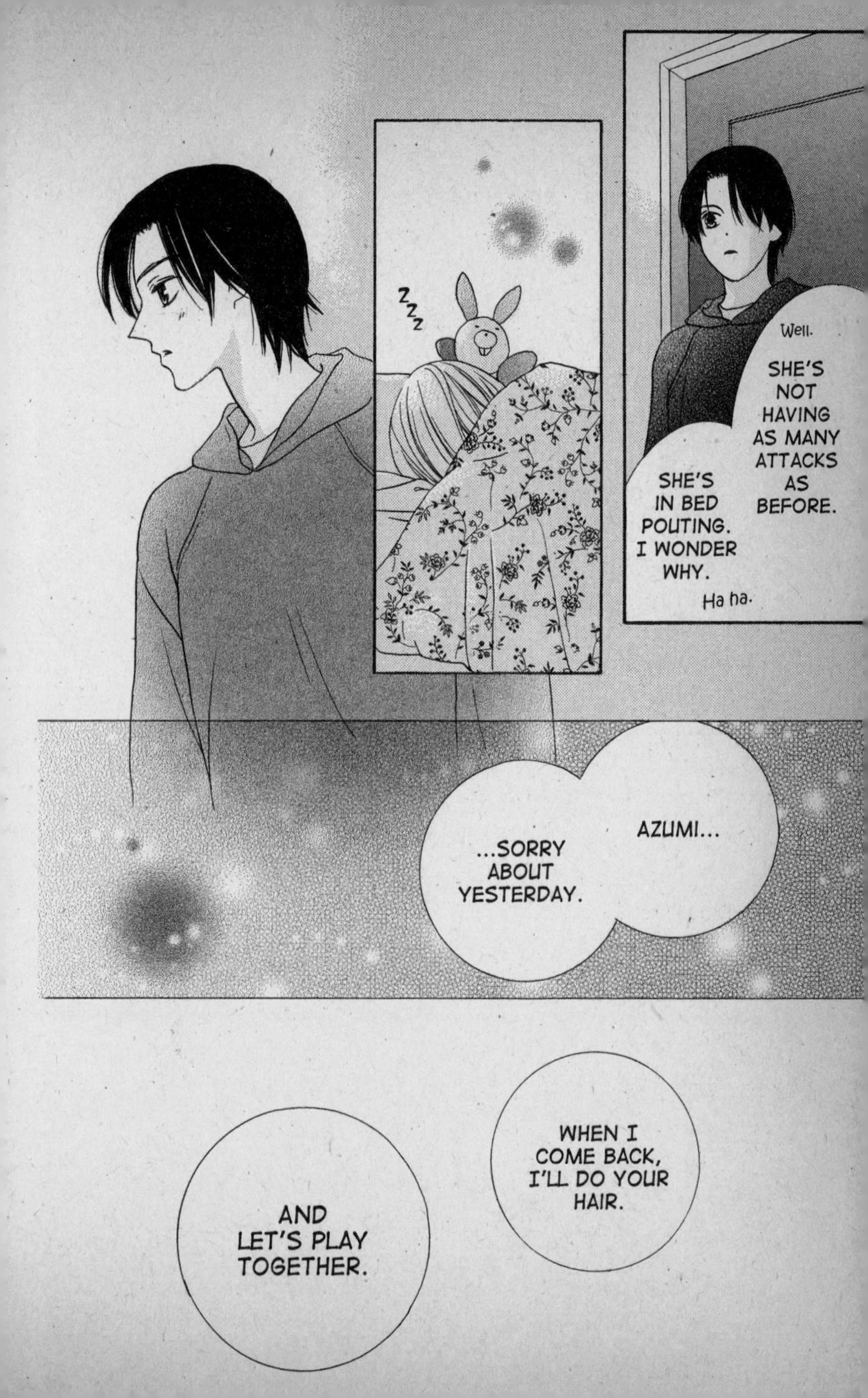
Well.
SHE'S NOT HAVING AS MANY ATTACKS AS BEFORE.
SHE'S IN BED POUTING. I WONDER WHY.
Ha ha.
Z Z Z
AZUMI...
...SORRY ABOUT YESTERDAY.
WHEN I COME BACK, I'LL DO YOUR HAIR.
AND LET'S PLAY TOGETHER.

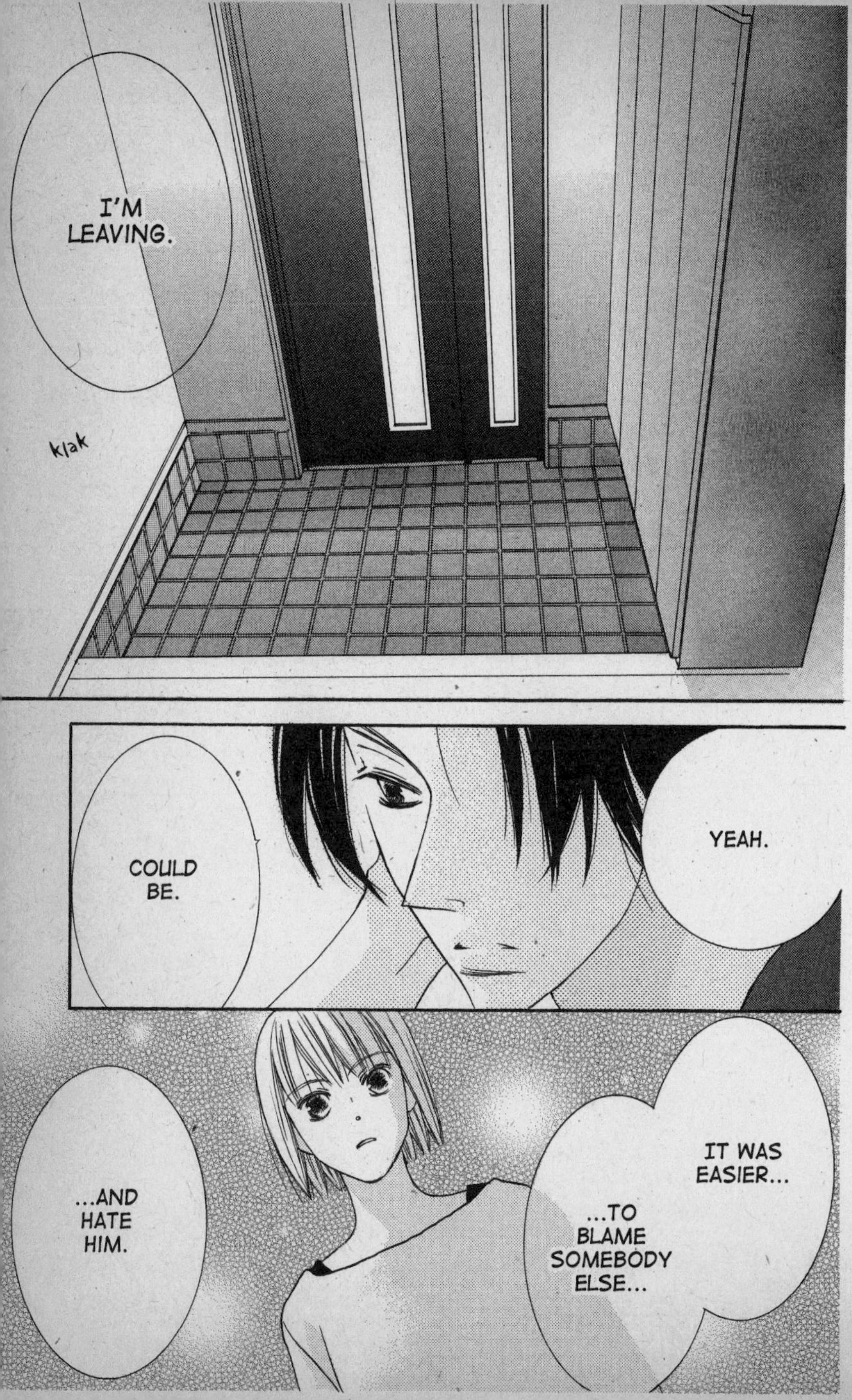
I'M LEAVING.
klak
YEAH.
COULD BE.
IT WAS EASIER...
...TO BLAME SOMEBODY ELSE...
...AND HATE HIM.

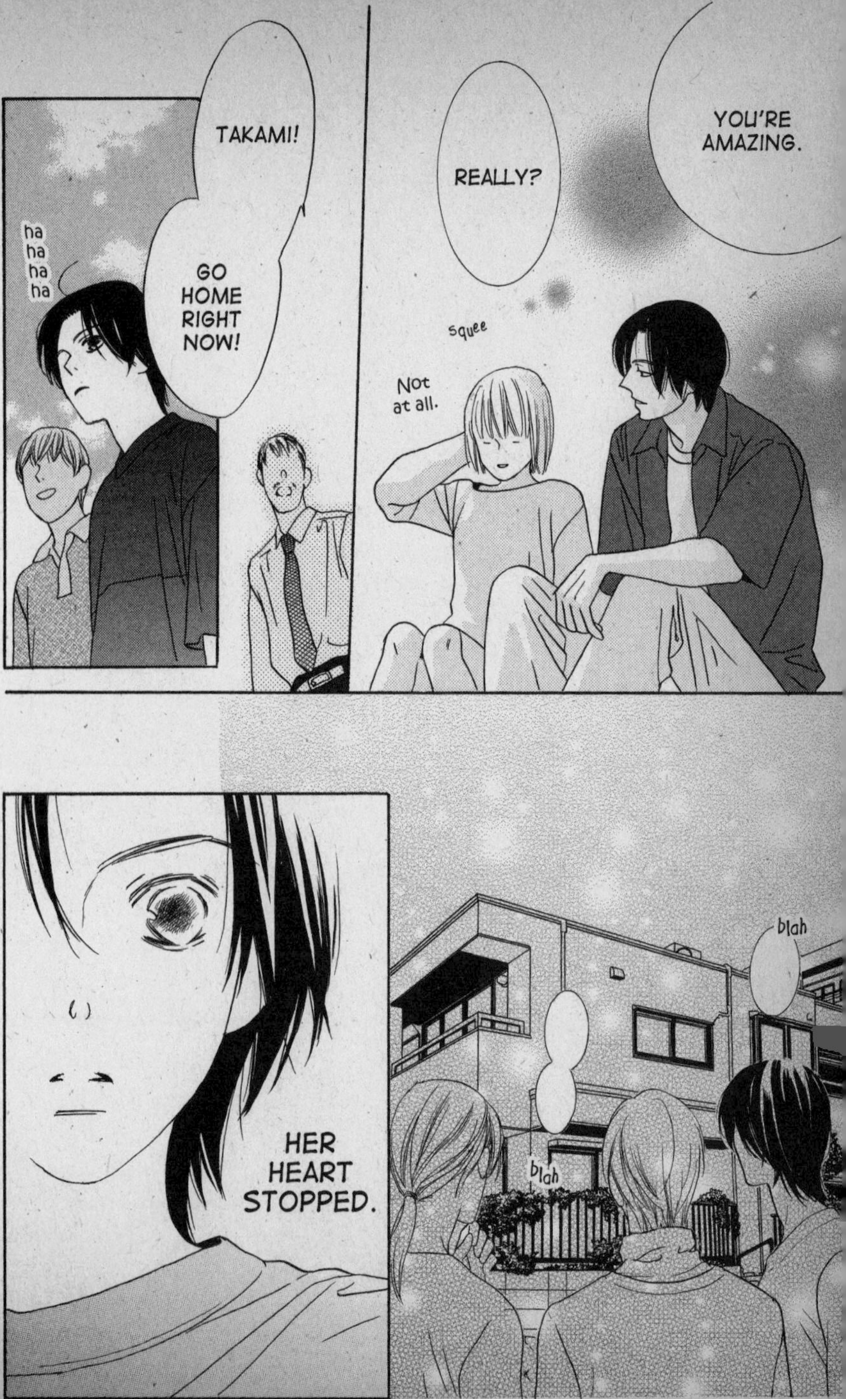
YOU'RE AMAZING.
REALLY?
squee
Not at all.
TAKAMI!
GO HOME RIGHT NOW!
ha ha ha ha
blah
blah
HER HEART STOPPED.

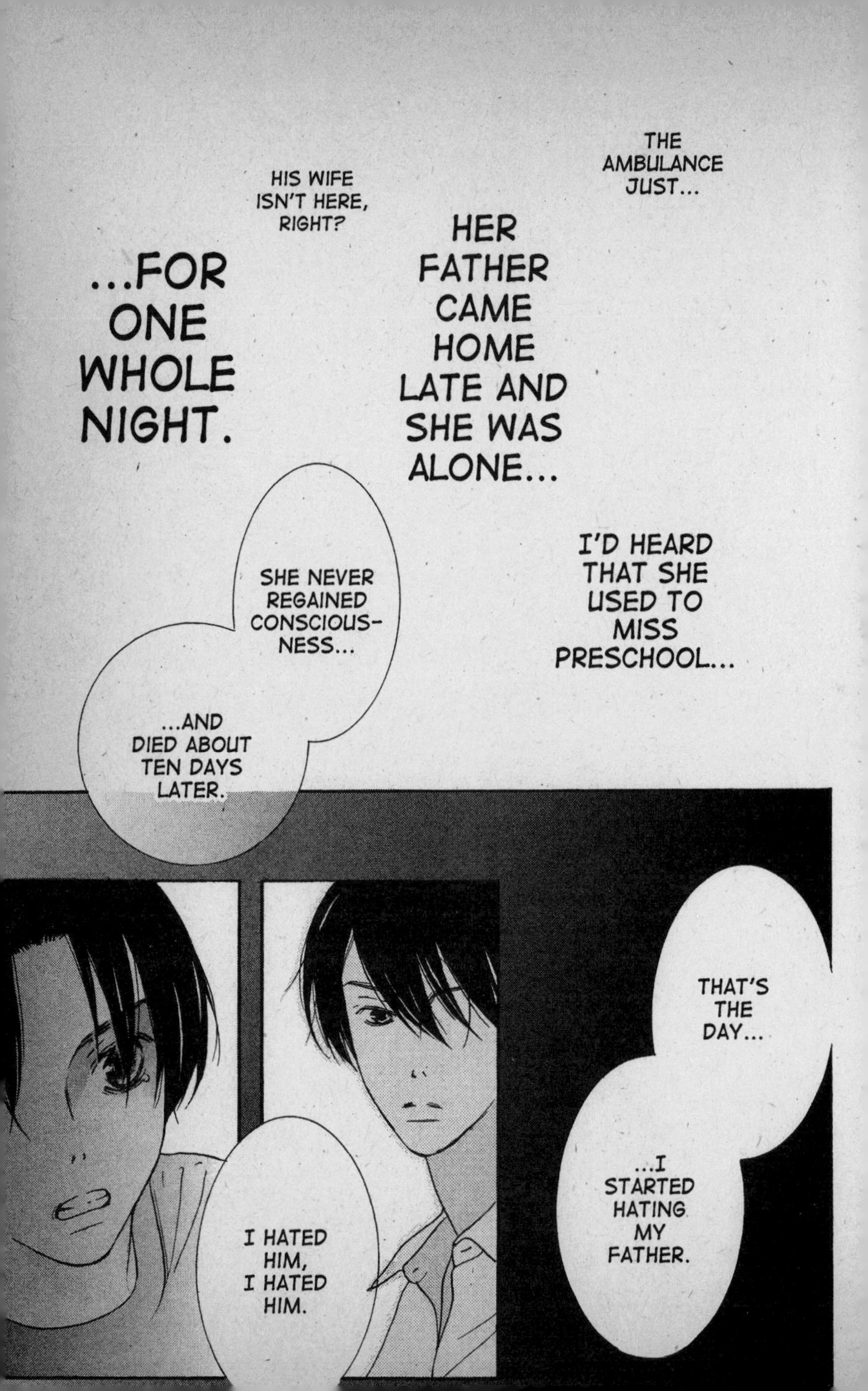
THE AMBULANCE JUST...
HER FATHER CAME HOME LATE AND SHE WAS ALONE...
HIS WIFE ISN'T HERE, RIGHT?
...FOR ONE WHOLE NIGHT.
I'D HEARD THAT SHE USED TO MISS PRESCHOOL...
SHE NEVER REGAINED CONSCIOUS-NESS...
...AND DIED ABOUT TEN DAYS LATER.
THAT'S THE DAY...
...I STARTED HATING MY FATHER.
I HATED HIM, I HATED HIM.

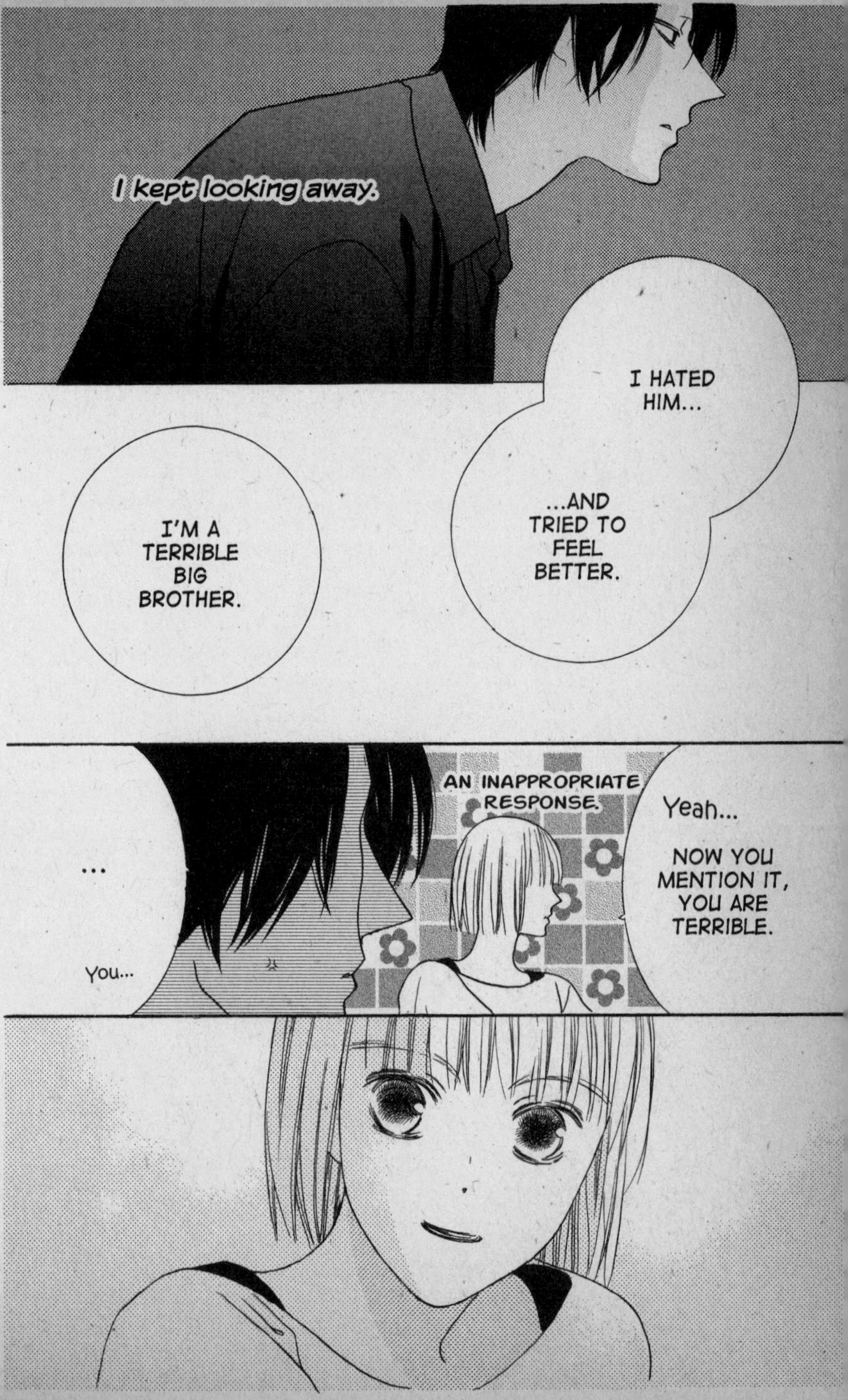
I kept looking away.
I HATED HIM...
...AND TRIED TO FEEL BETTER.
I'M A TERRIBLE BIG BROTHER.
Yeah...
NOW YOU MENTION IT, YOU ARE TERRIBLE.
AN INAPPROPRIATE RESPONSE.
...
You...

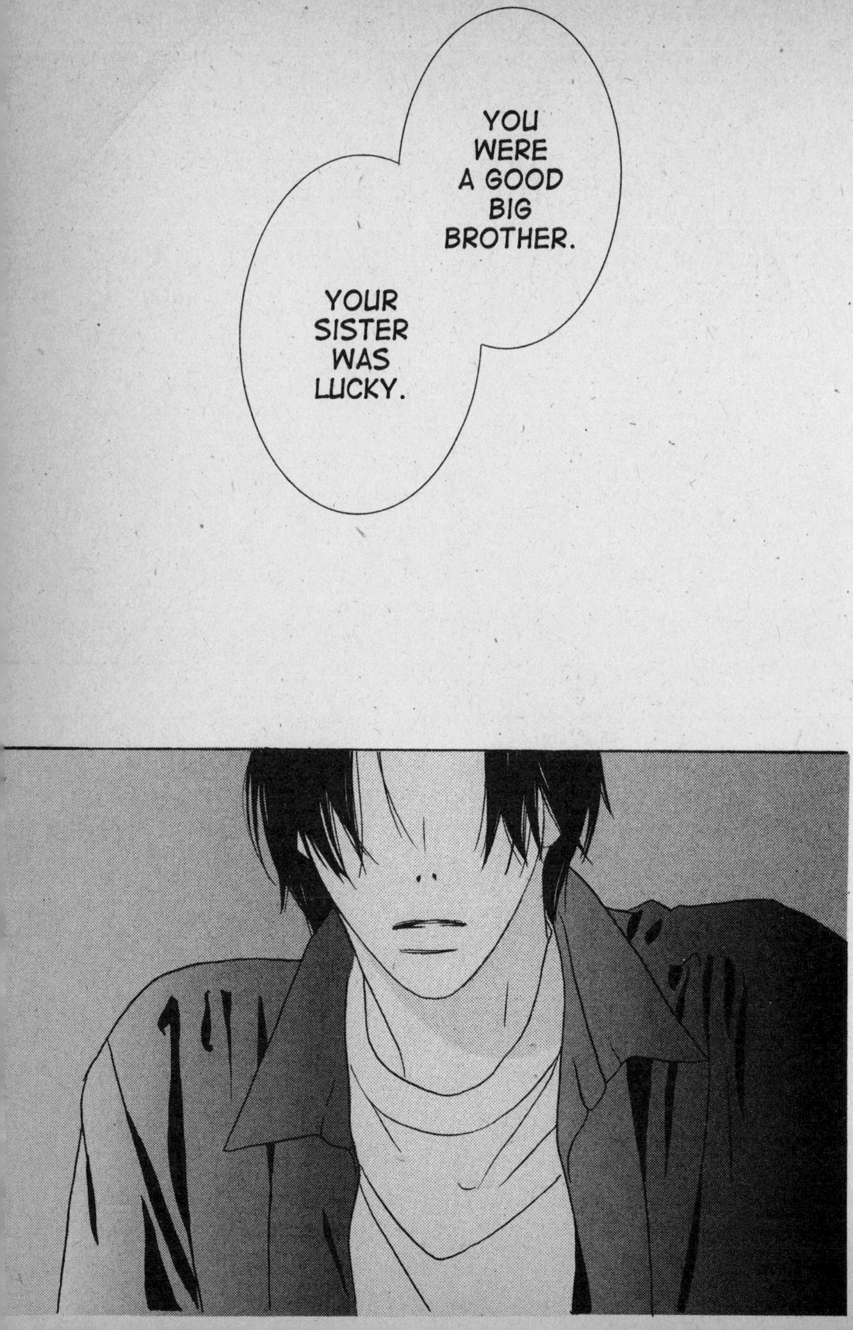
YOU WERE A GOOD BIG BROTHER.
YOUR SISTER WAS LUCKY.

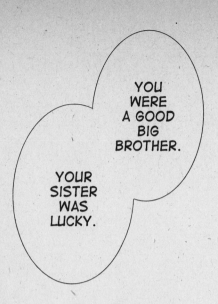

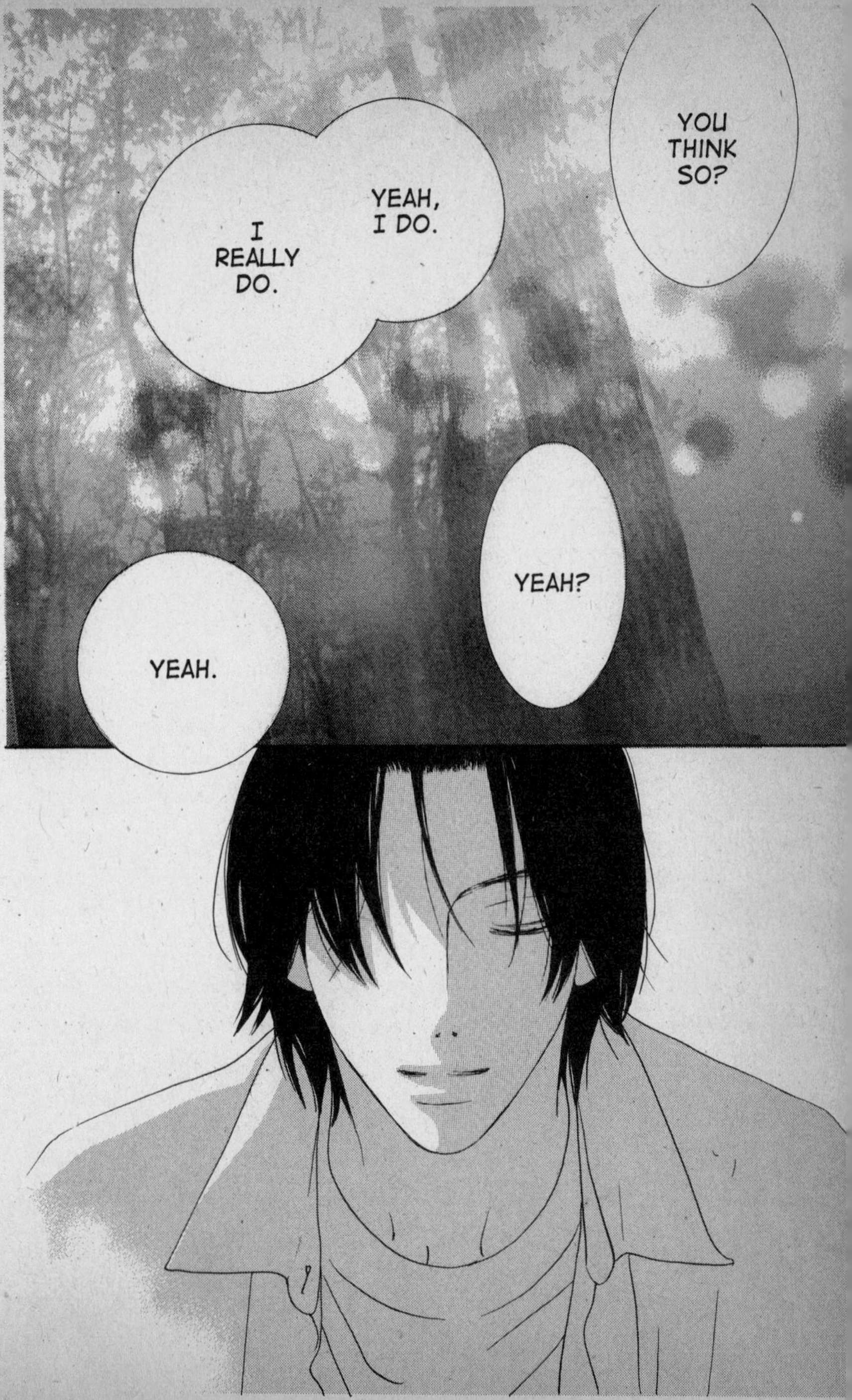
YOU THINK SO?
YEAH, I DO.
I REALLY DO.
YEAH?
YEAH.

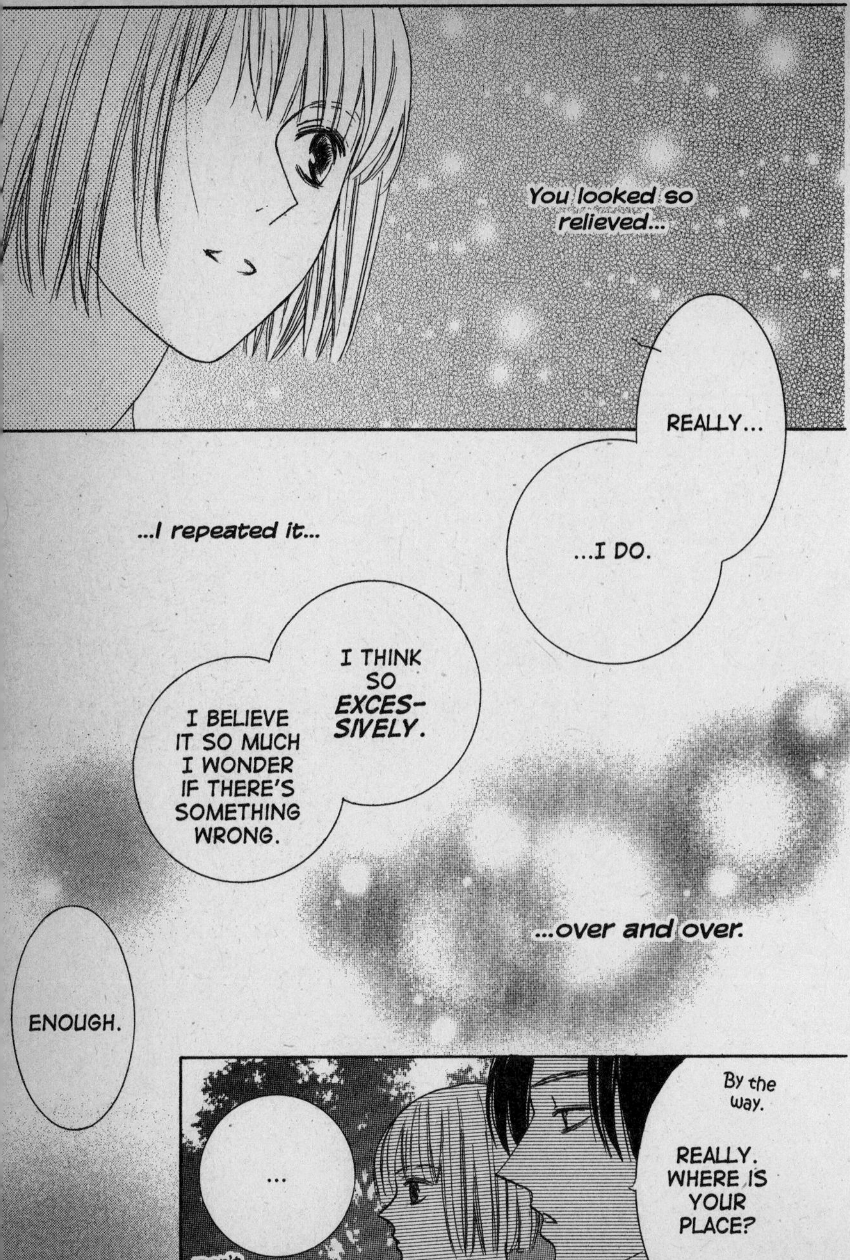

You looked so relieved...
REALLY... ...I DO.
...I repeated it...
I THINK SO *EXCESSIVELY*.
I BELIEVE IT SO MUCH I WONDER IF THERE'S SOMETHING WRONG.
...over and over.
ENOUGH.
By the way.
REALLY. WHERE IS YOUR PLACE?
...
Don't know...

BEAUTY IS THE BEAST

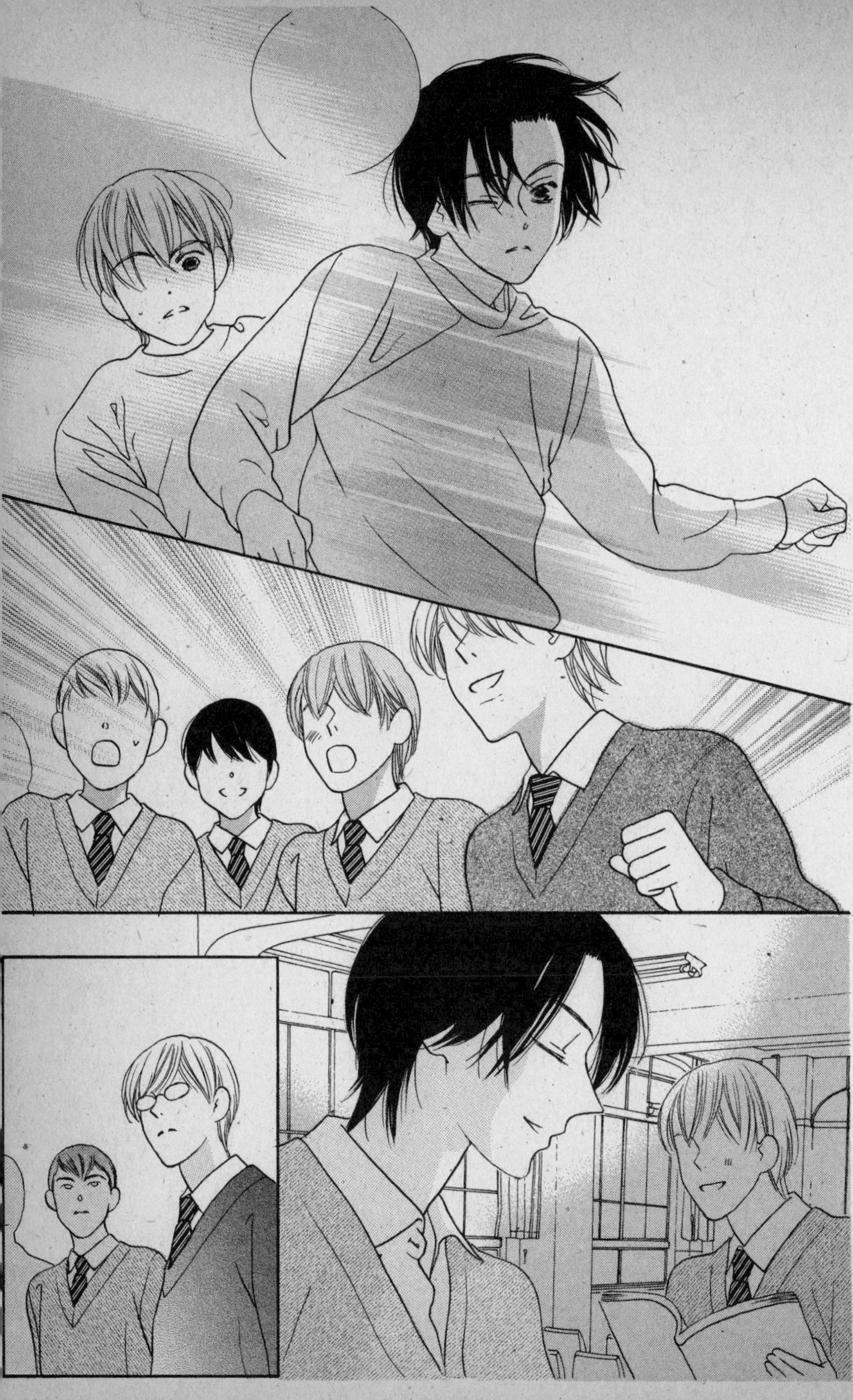

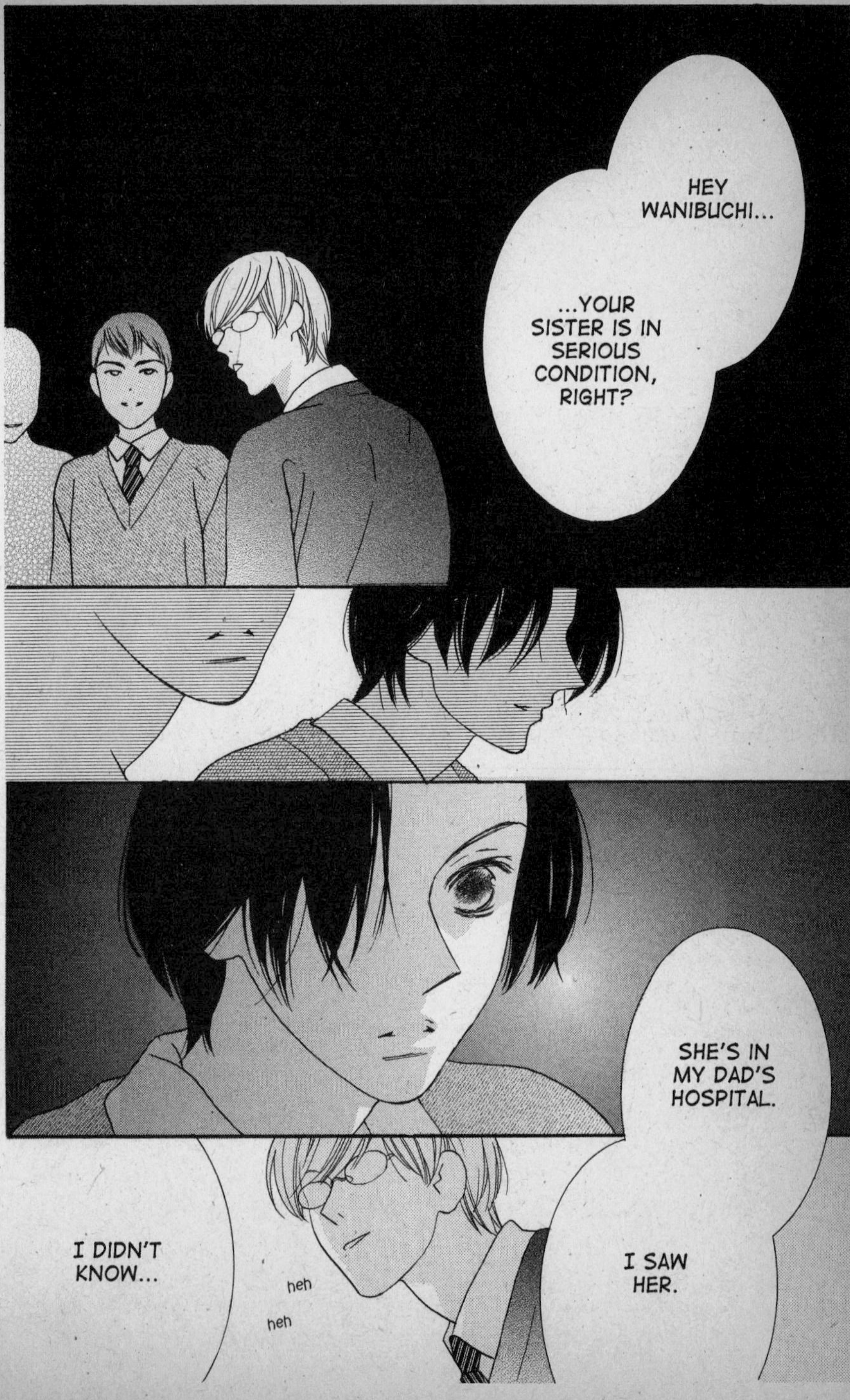
HEY WANIBUCHI...
...YOUR SISTER IS IN SERIOUS CONDITION, RIGHT?
SHE'S IN MY DAD'S HOSPITAL.
I SAW HER.
heh
heh
I DIDN'T KNOW...

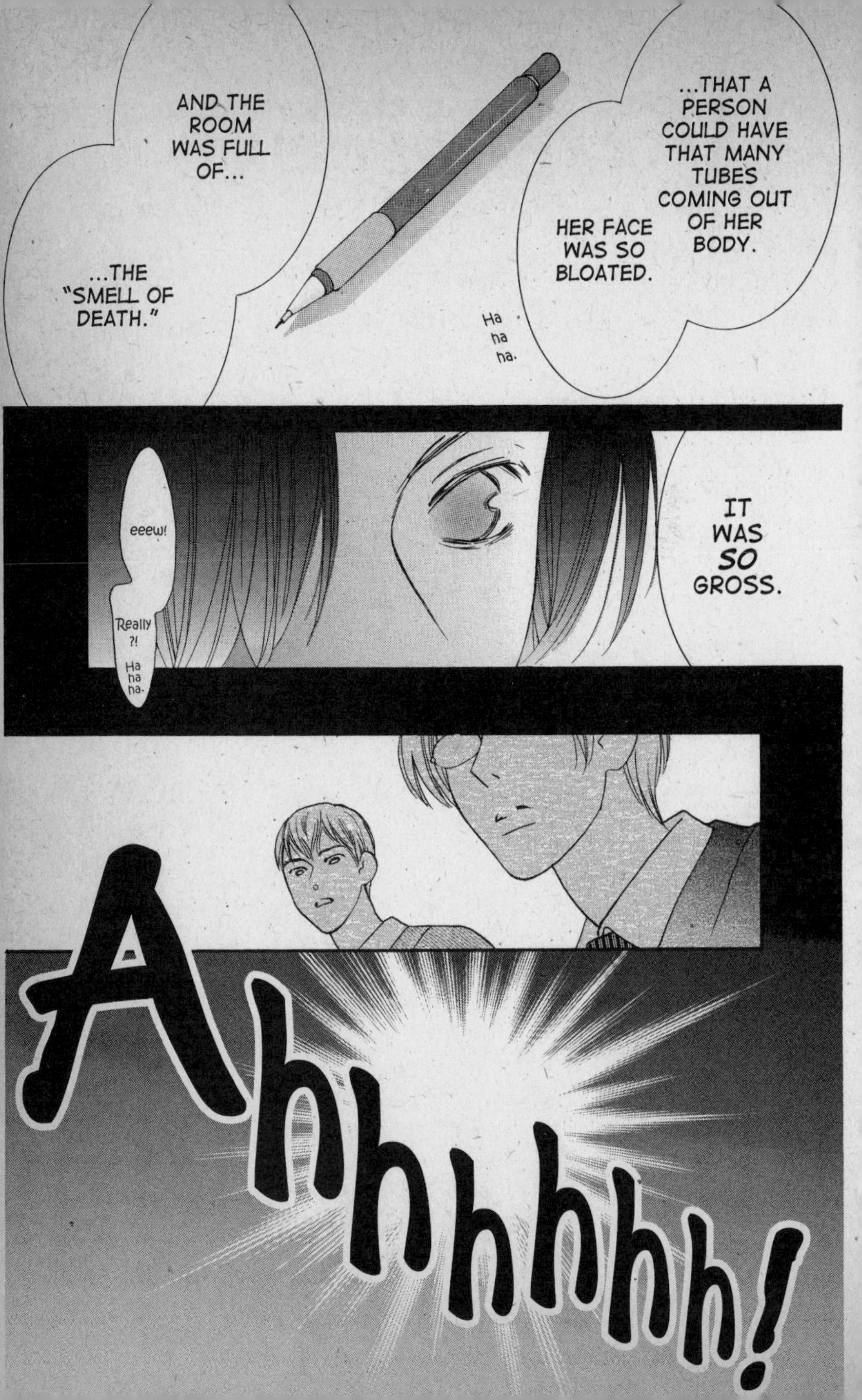
AND THE ROOM WAS FULL OF...
...THE "SMELL OF DEATH."
...THAT A PERSON COULD HAVE THAT MANY TUBES COMING OUT OF HER BODY.
HER FACE WAS SO BLOATED.
Ha ha ha.
eeew!
Really?!
Ha ha ha.
IT WAS SO GROSS.
Ahhhhhh!

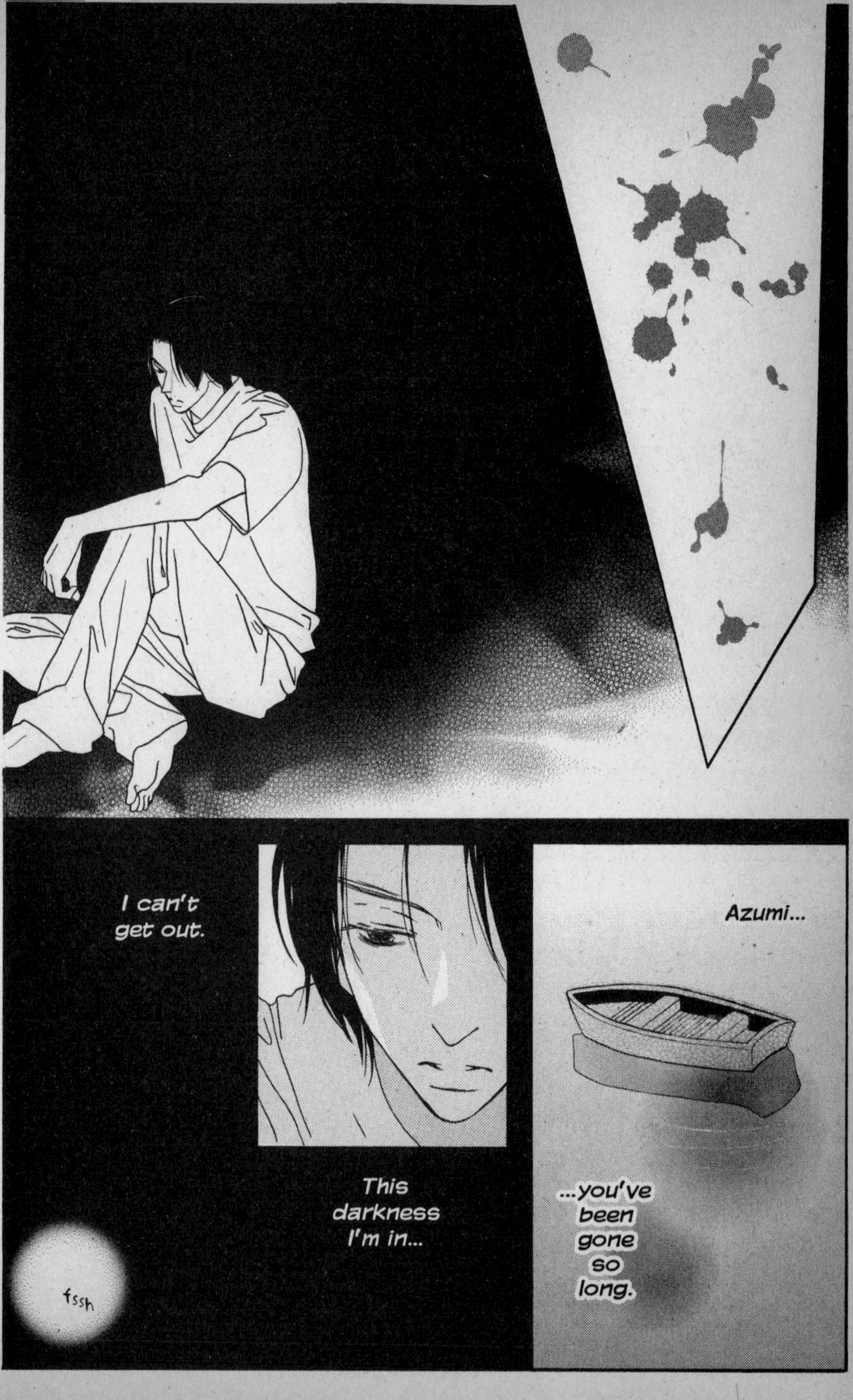
Azumi...
...you've been gone so long.
This darkness I'm in...
I can't get out.
fssh

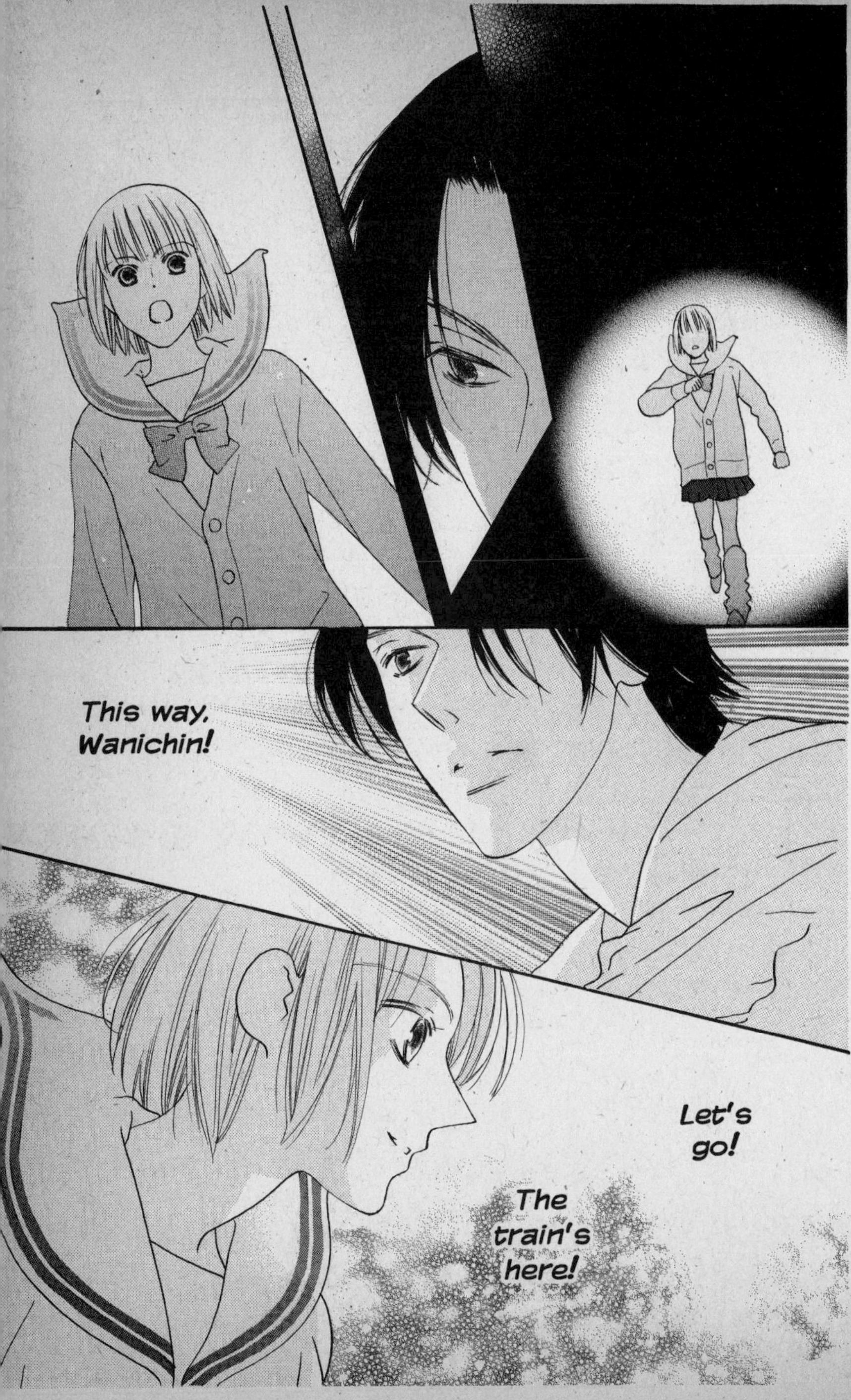
This way, Wanichin!
Let's go!
The train's here!

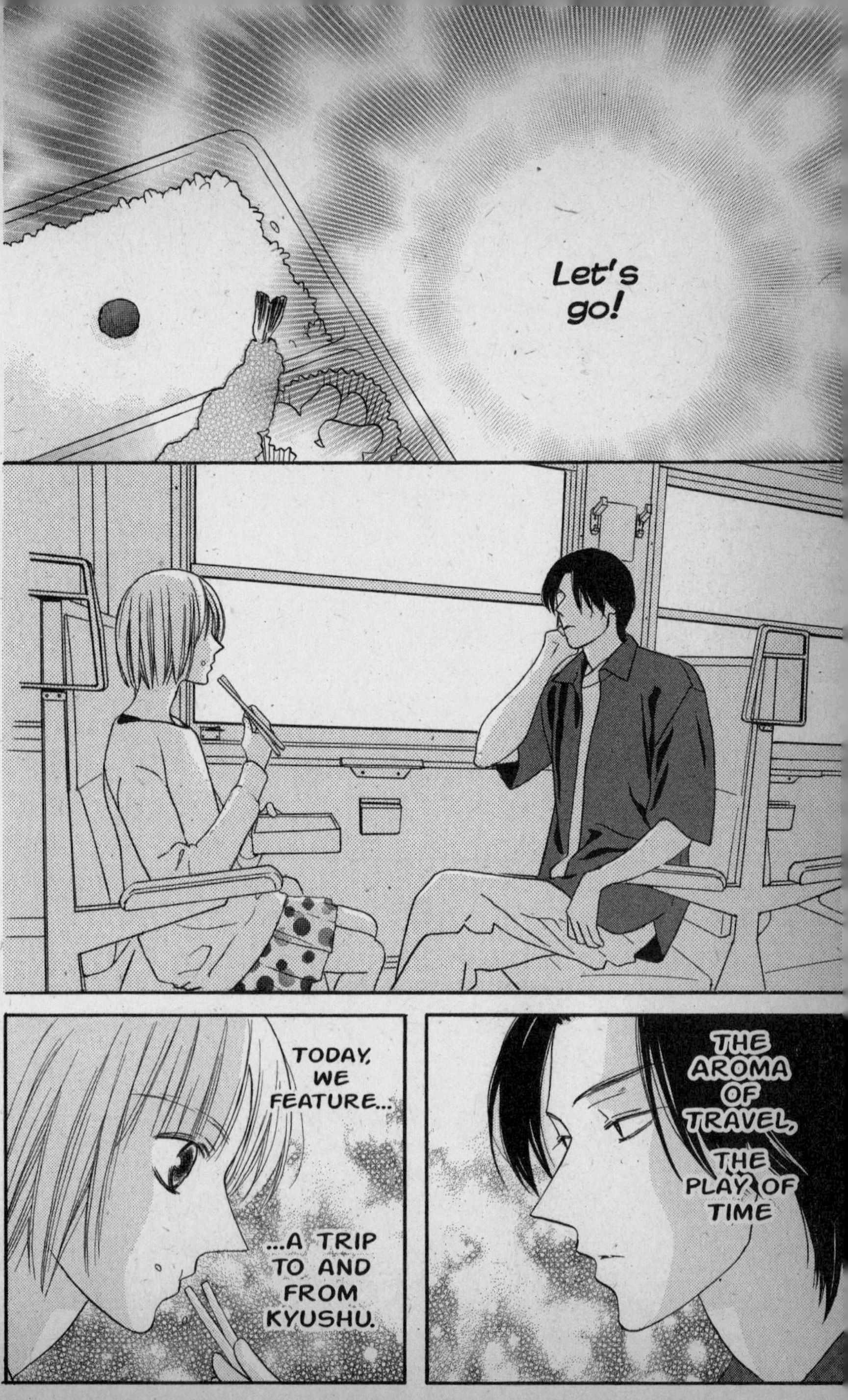
Let's go!
THE AROMA OF TRAVEL,
THE PLAY OF TIME
TODAY, WE FEATURE...
...A TRIP TO AND FROM KYUSHU.

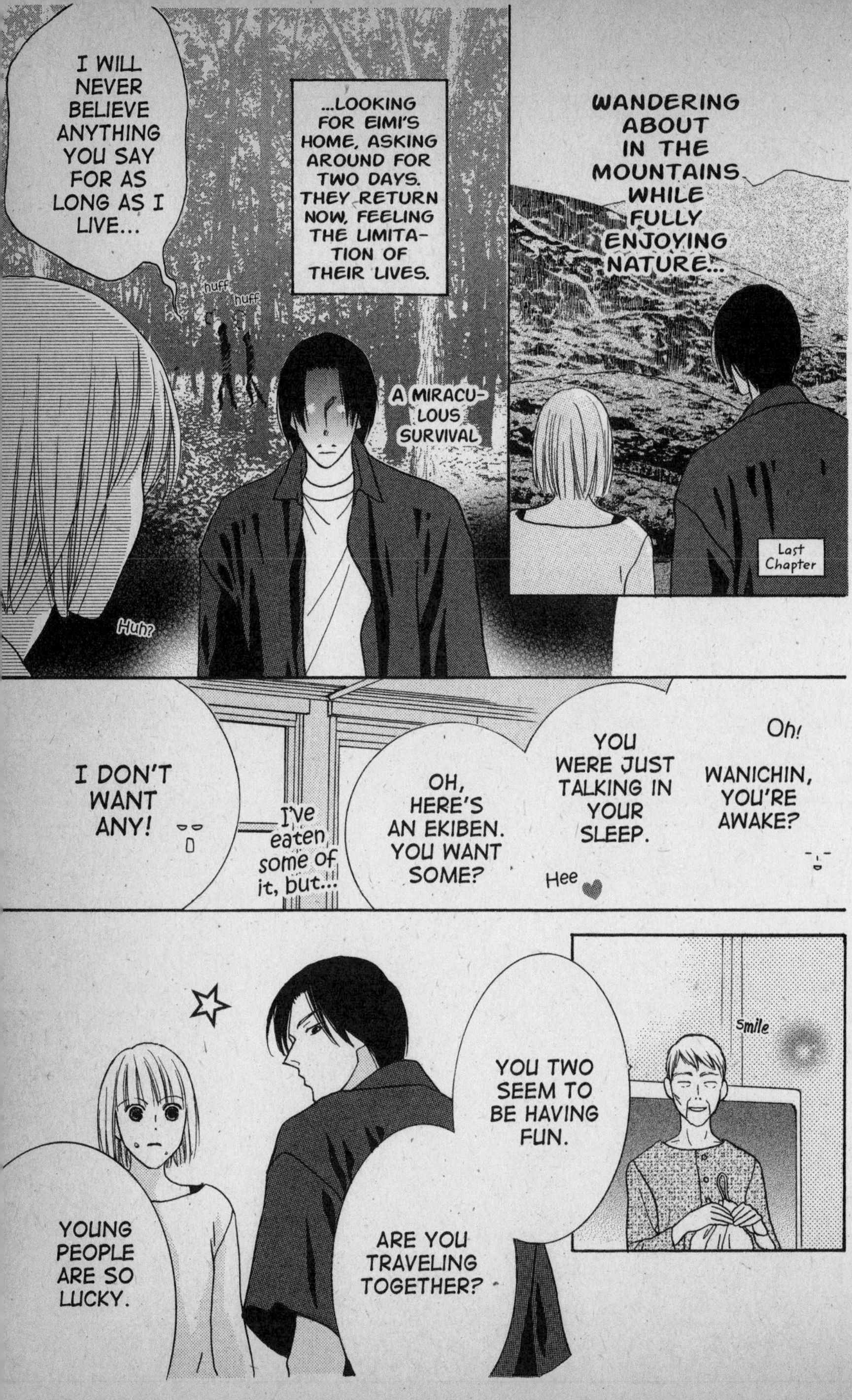
WANDERING ABOUT IN THE MOUNTAINS WHILE FULLY ENJOYING NATURE...
Last Chapter
...LOOKING FOR EIMI'S HOME, ASKING AROUND FOR TWO DAYS. THEY RETURN NOW, FEELING THE LIMITATION OF THEIR LIVES.
I WILL NEVER BELIEVE ANYTHING YOU SAY FOR AS LONG AS I LIVE...
huff huff
A MIRACULOUS SURVIVAL
Huh?
Oh!
WANICHIN, YOU'RE AWAKE?
YOU WERE JUST TALKING IN YOUR SLEEP.
Hee
OH, HERE'S AN EKIBEN. YOU WANT SOME?
I've eaten some of it, but...
I DON'T WANT ANY!
Smile
YOU TWO SEEM TO BE HAVING FUN.
ARE YOU TRAVELING TOGETHER?
YOUNG PEOPLE ARE SO LUCKY.

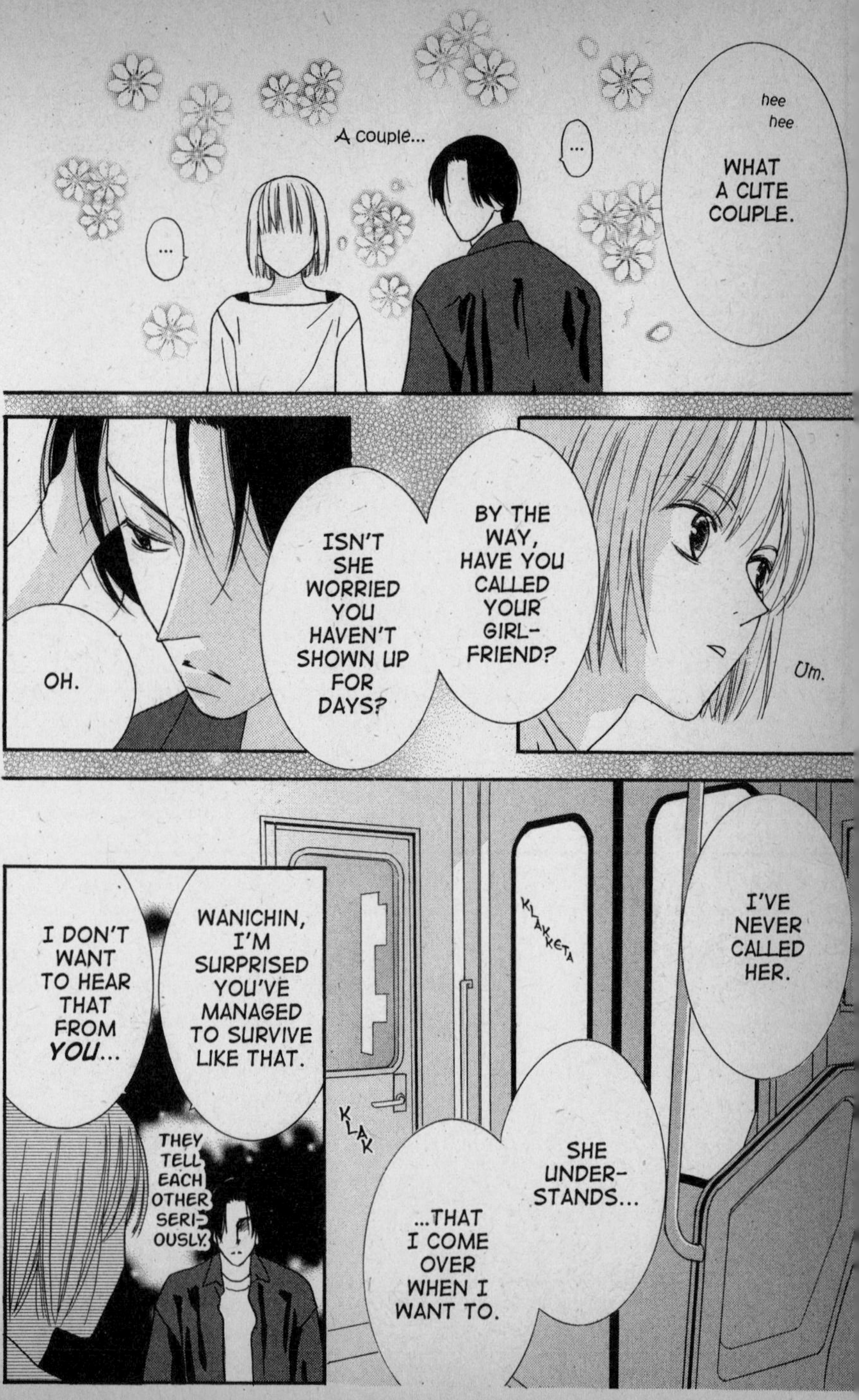
hee hee
WHAT A CUTE COUPLE.
...
A couple...
...
Um.
BY THE WAY, HAVE YOU CALLED YOUR GIRL-FRIEND?
ISN'T SHE WORRIED YOU HAVEN'T SHOWN UP FOR DAYS?
OH.
I'VE NEVER CALLED HER.
KLAKKETA
SHE UNDER-STANDS...
...THAT I COME OVER WHEN I WANT TO.
KLAK
WANICHIN, I'M SURPRISED YOU'VE MANAGED TO SURVIVE LIKE THAT.
I DON'T WANT TO HEAR THAT FROM *YOU*...
THEY TELL EACH OTHER SERI-OUSLY.

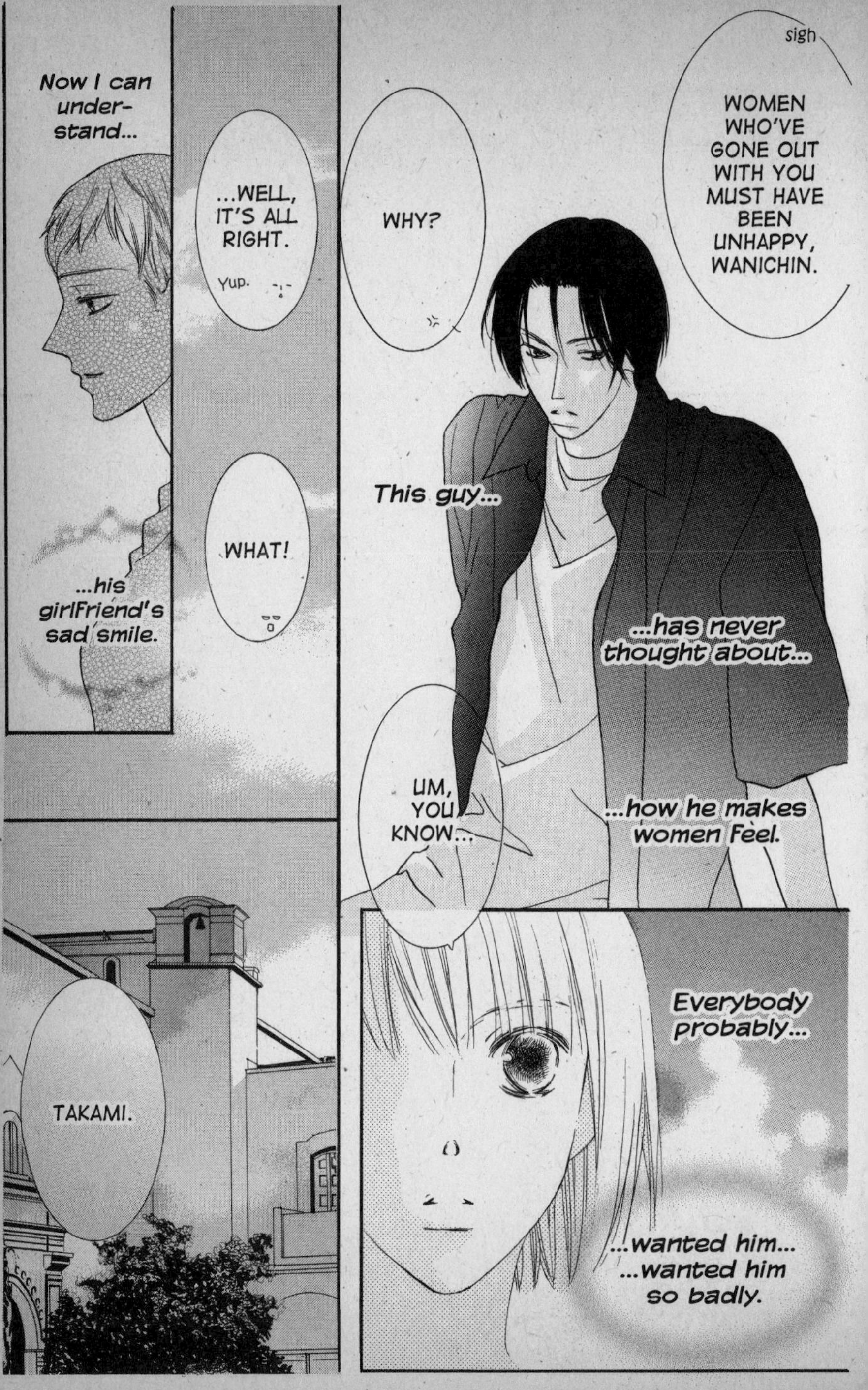
sigh
WOMEN WHO'VE GONE OUT WITH YOU MUST HAVE BEEN UNHAPPY, WANICHIN.
WHY?
This guy...
...has never thought about...
...how he makes women feel.
...WELL, IT'S ALL RIGHT.
Yup.
WHAT!
Now I can understand...
...his girlfriend's sad smile.
UM, YOU KNOW...
Everybody probably...
...wanted him... ...wanted him so badly.
TAKAMI.

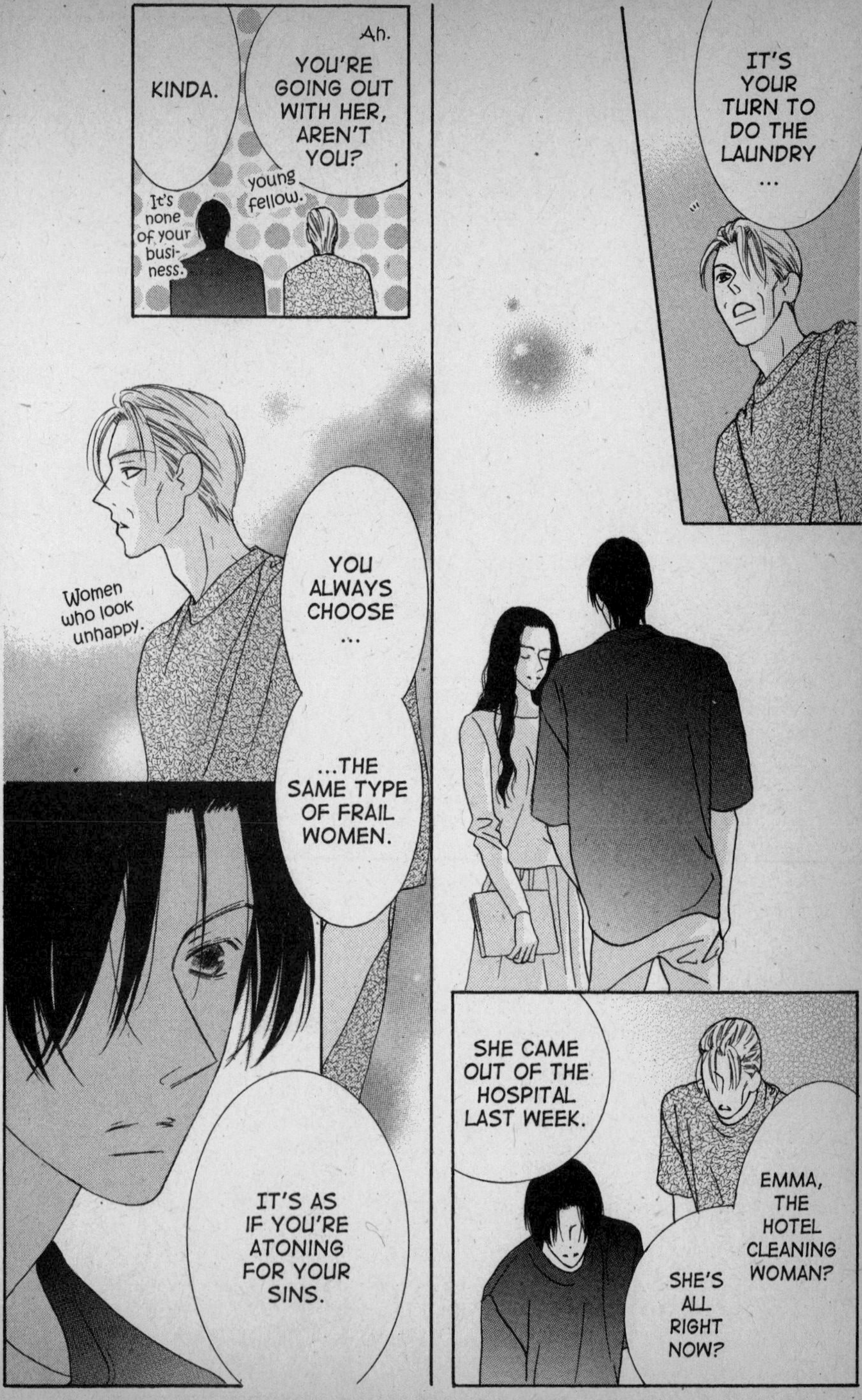
IT'S YOUR TURN TO DO THE LAUNDRY ...
EMMA, THE HOTEL CLEANING WOMAN?
SHE'S ALL RIGHT NOW?
SHE CAME OUT OF THE HOSPITAL LAST WEEK.
Ah. YOU'RE GOING OUT WITH HER, AREN'T YOU?
young fellow.
KINDA.
It's none of your busi-ness.
YOU ALWAYS CHOOSE ...
...THE SAME TYPE OF FRAIL WOMEN.
Women who look unhappy.
IT'S AS IF YOU'RE ATONING FOR YOUR SINS.

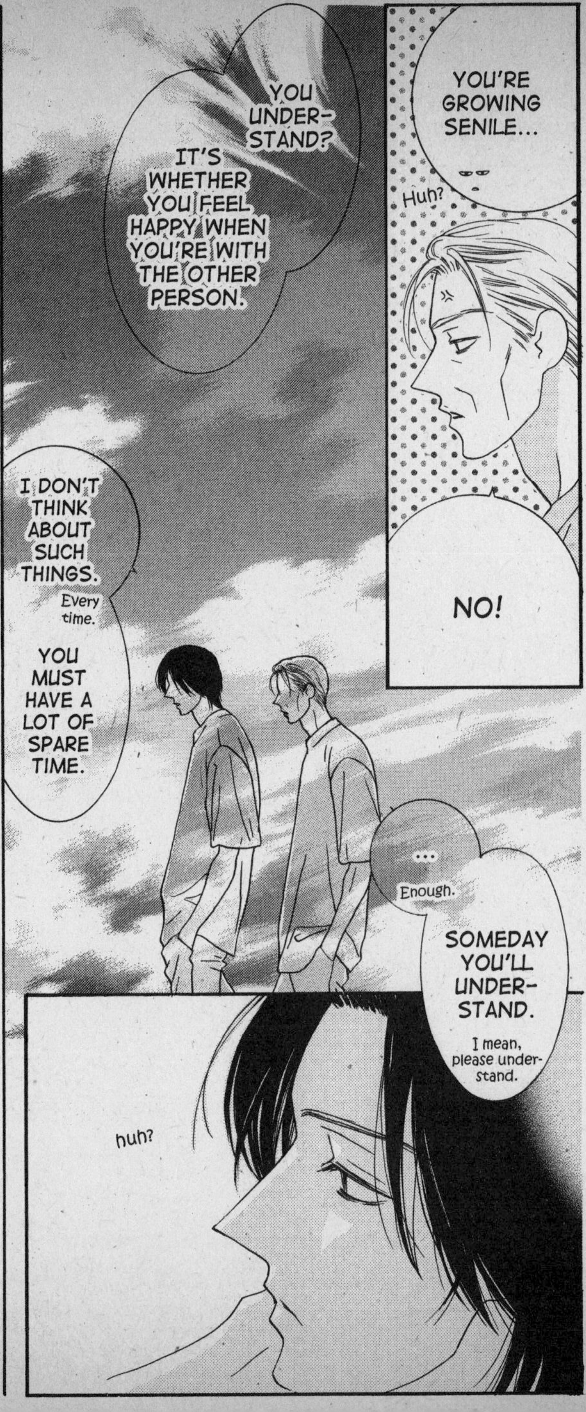
YOU'RE GROWING SENILE...
Huh?
NO!
YOU UNDERSTAND?
IT'S WHETHER YOU FEEL HAPPY WHEN YOU'RE WITH THE OTHER PERSON.
I DON'T THINK ABOUT SUCH THINGS.
Every time.
YOU MUST HAVE A LOT OF SPARE TIME.
...
Enough.
SOMEDAY YOU'LL UNDER-STAND.
I mean, please under-stand.
huh?

③

I was going to talk about this before, but I completely forgot. Mango is actually my favorite favorite fruit. I hadn't eaten a lot of tropical fruit before, but when I was really tired before my deadline, it was shockingly delicious...and I've loved them since.

Philippine mangoes are famous, but Mexican ones are my favorite! They smell so good. I feel that they are very effective!! (For what?) Domestic ones don't have strong characteristics. They have a delicate flavor and are easy to eat. It's fun to make people who aren't used to peeling mangoes peel one, and make them flustered. (There's a big seed right in the middle, so it's a little difficult.)

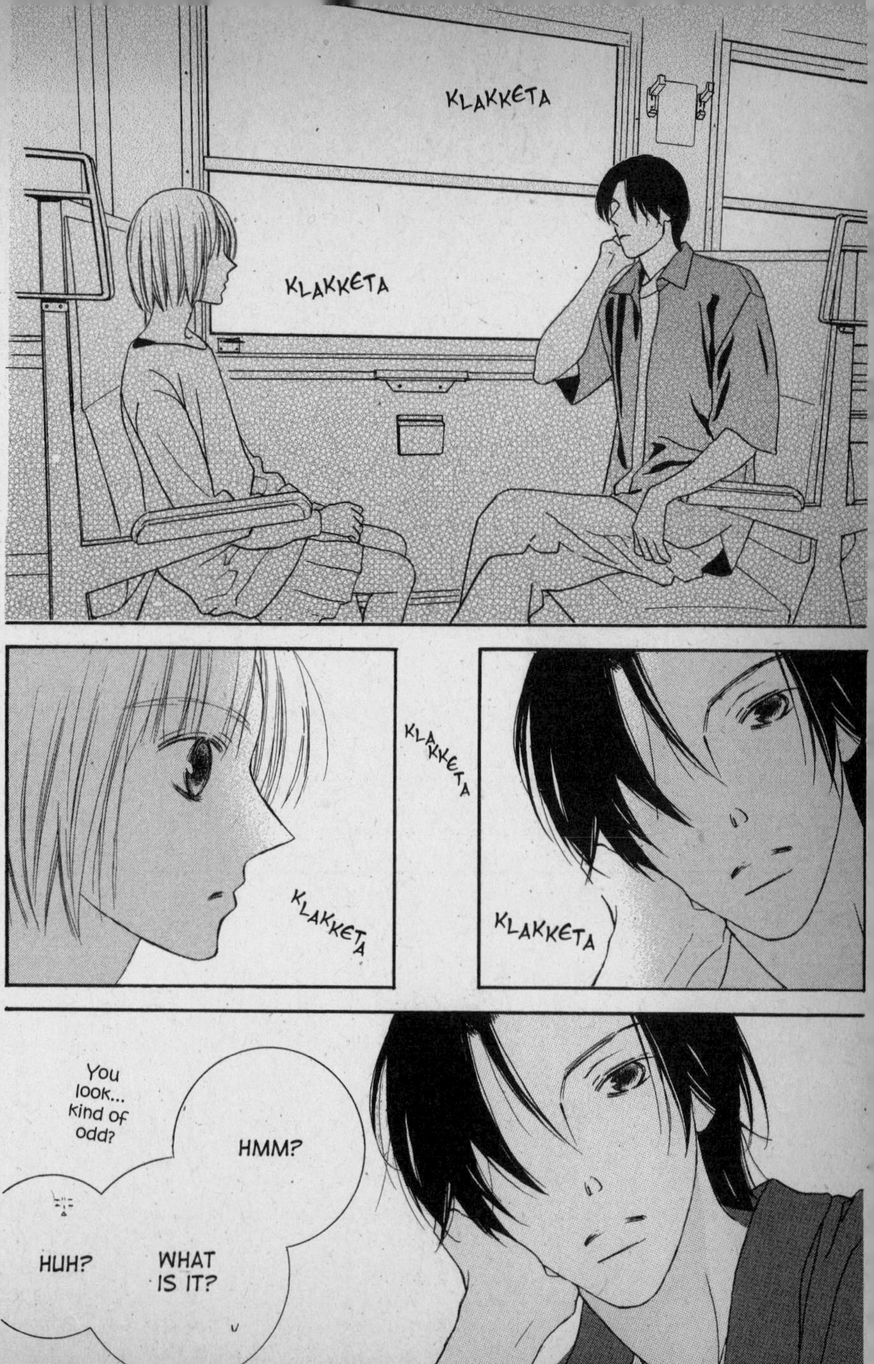
KLAKKETA
KLAKKETA
KLAKKETA
KLAKKETA
KLAKKETA
HMM?
You look... kind of odd?
WHAT IS IT?
HUH?

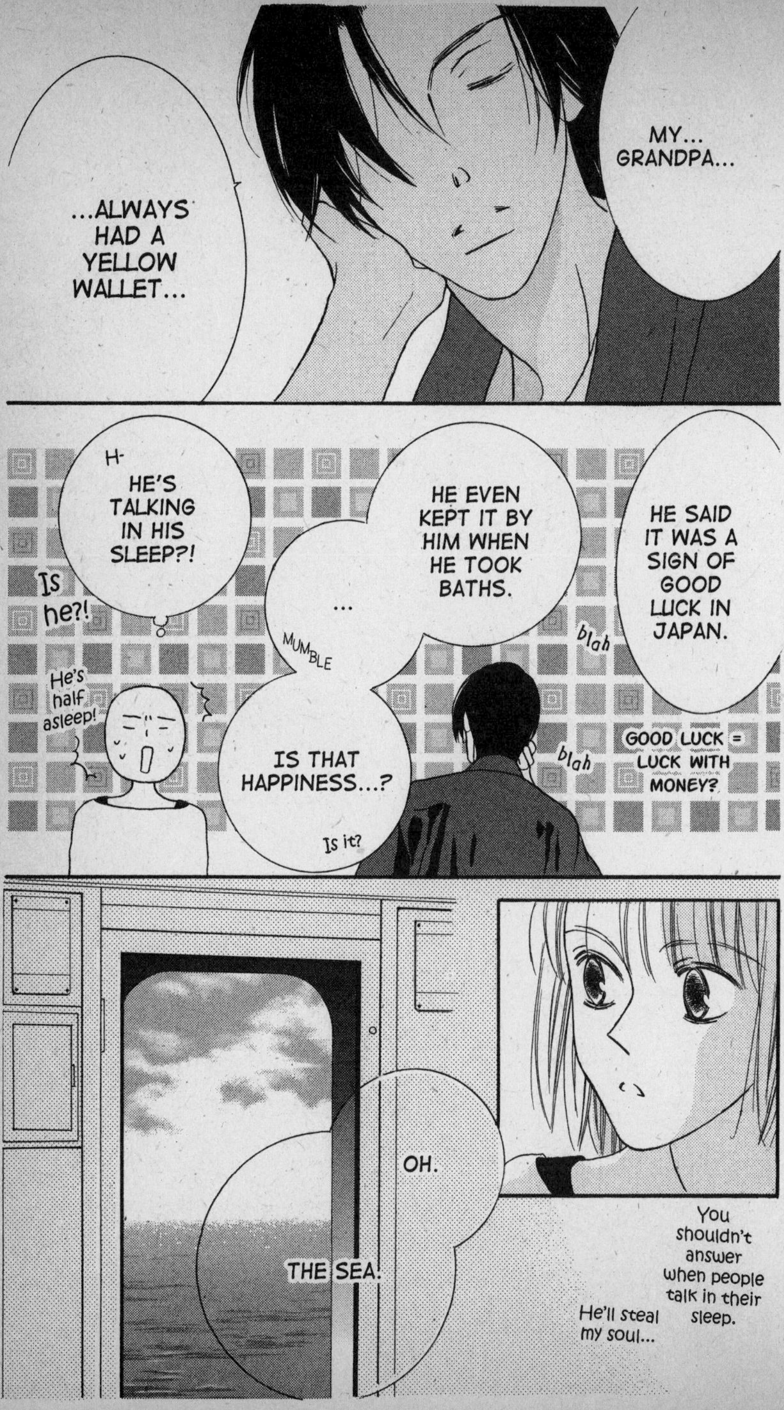
MY... GRANDPA...
...ALWAYS HAD A YELLOW WALLET...
HE SAID IT WAS A SIGN OF GOOD LUCK IN JAPAN.
blah
GOOD LUCK = LUCK WITH MONEY?
blah
HE EVEN KEPT IT BY HIM WHEN HE TOOK BATHS.
...
MUMBLE
IS THAT HAPPINESS...?
Is it?
H- HE'S TALKING IN HIS SLEEP?!
Is he?!
He's half asleep!
OH.
THE SEA.
You shouldn't answer when people talk in their sleep.
He'll steal my soul...

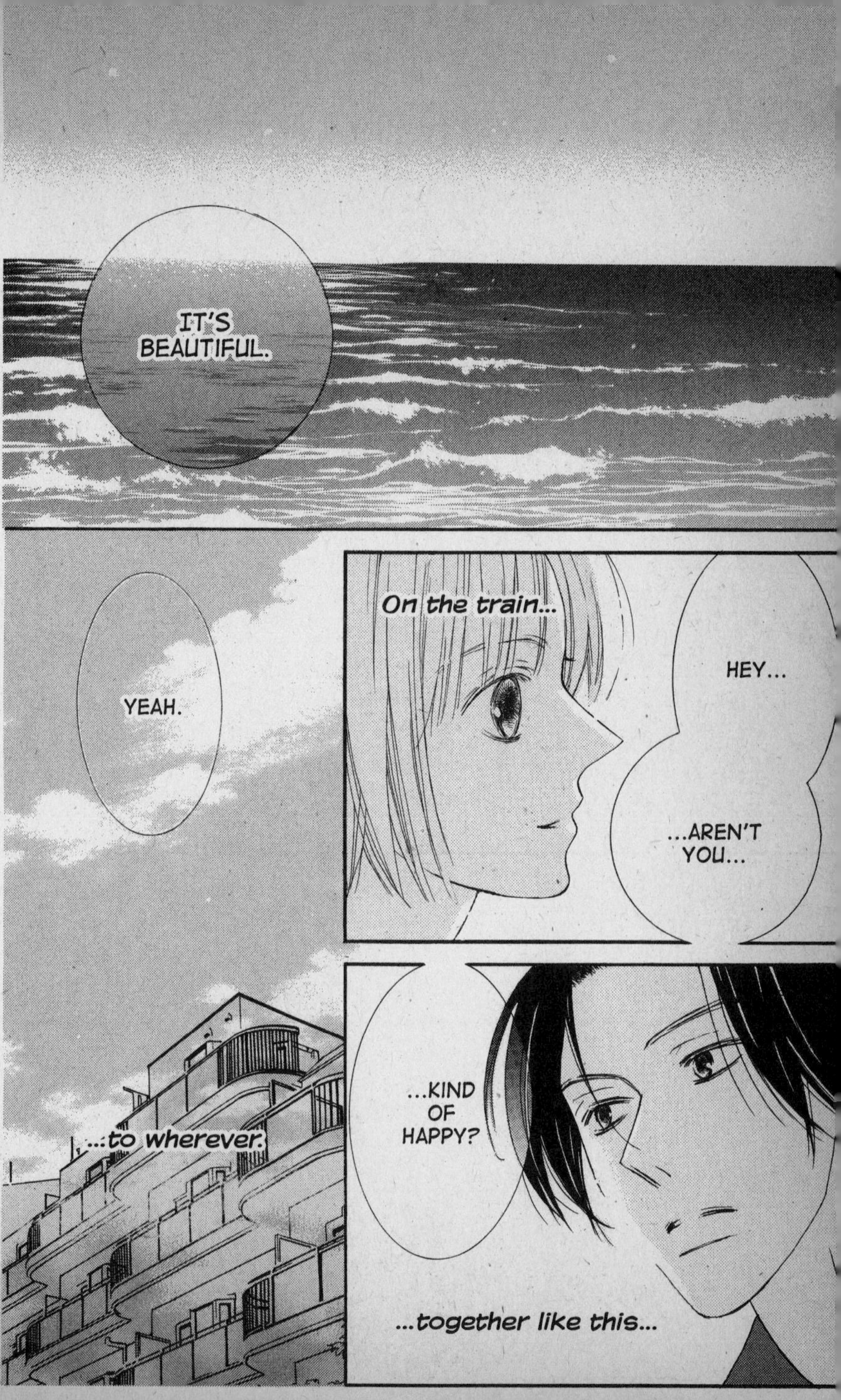
IT'S BEAUTIFUL.
On the train...
HEY...
...AREN'T YOU...
...KIND OF HAPPY?
...together like this...
YEAH.
...to wherever.

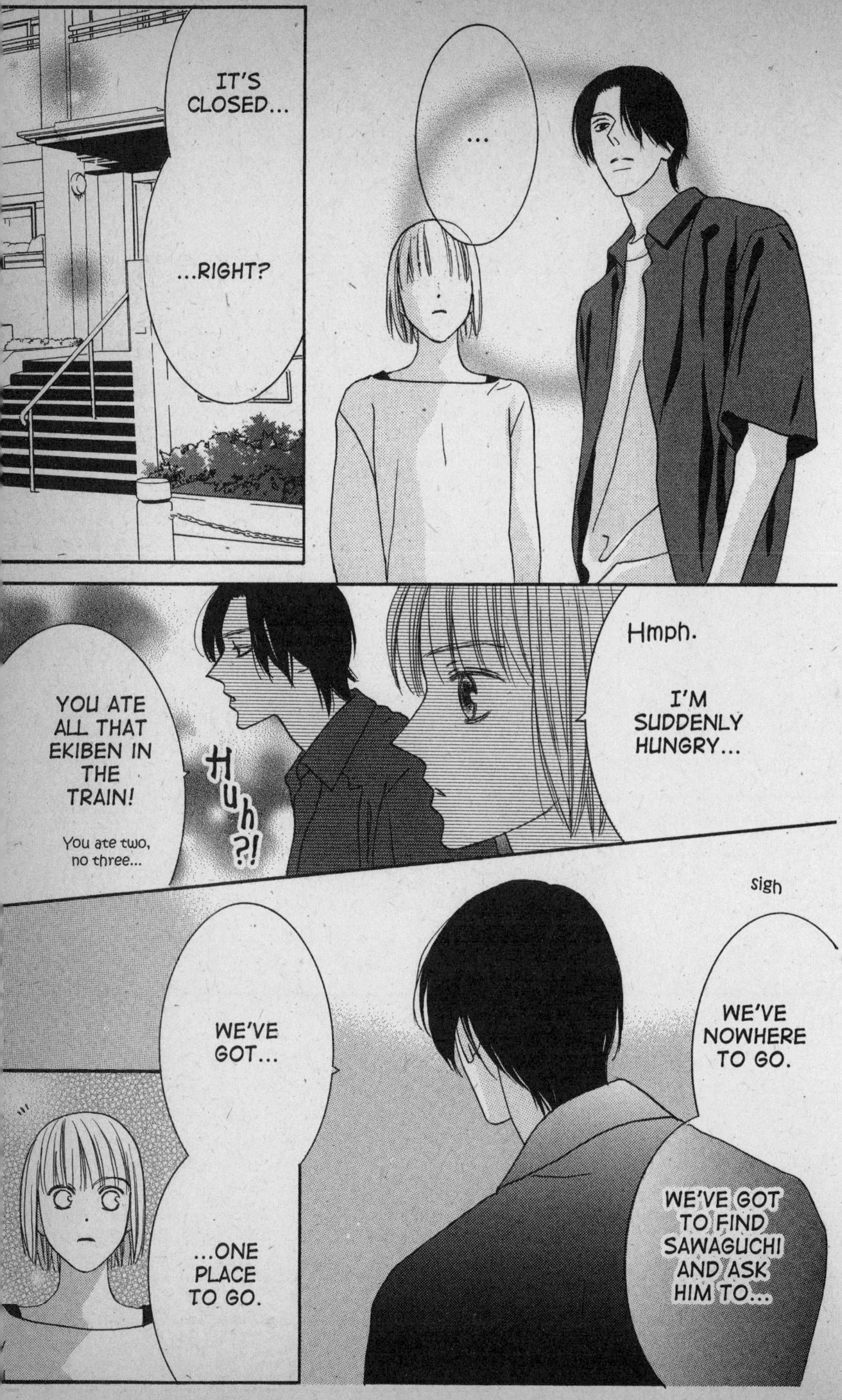
...
IT'S CLOSED...
...RIGHT?
Hmph.
I'M SUDDENLY HUNGRY...
Huh?!
YOU ATE ALL THAT EKIBEN IN THE TRAIN!
You ate two, no three...
sigh
WE'VE NOWHERE TO GO.
WE'VE GOT TO FIND SAWAGUCHI AND ASK HIM TO...
WE'VE GOT...
...ONE PLACE TO GO.

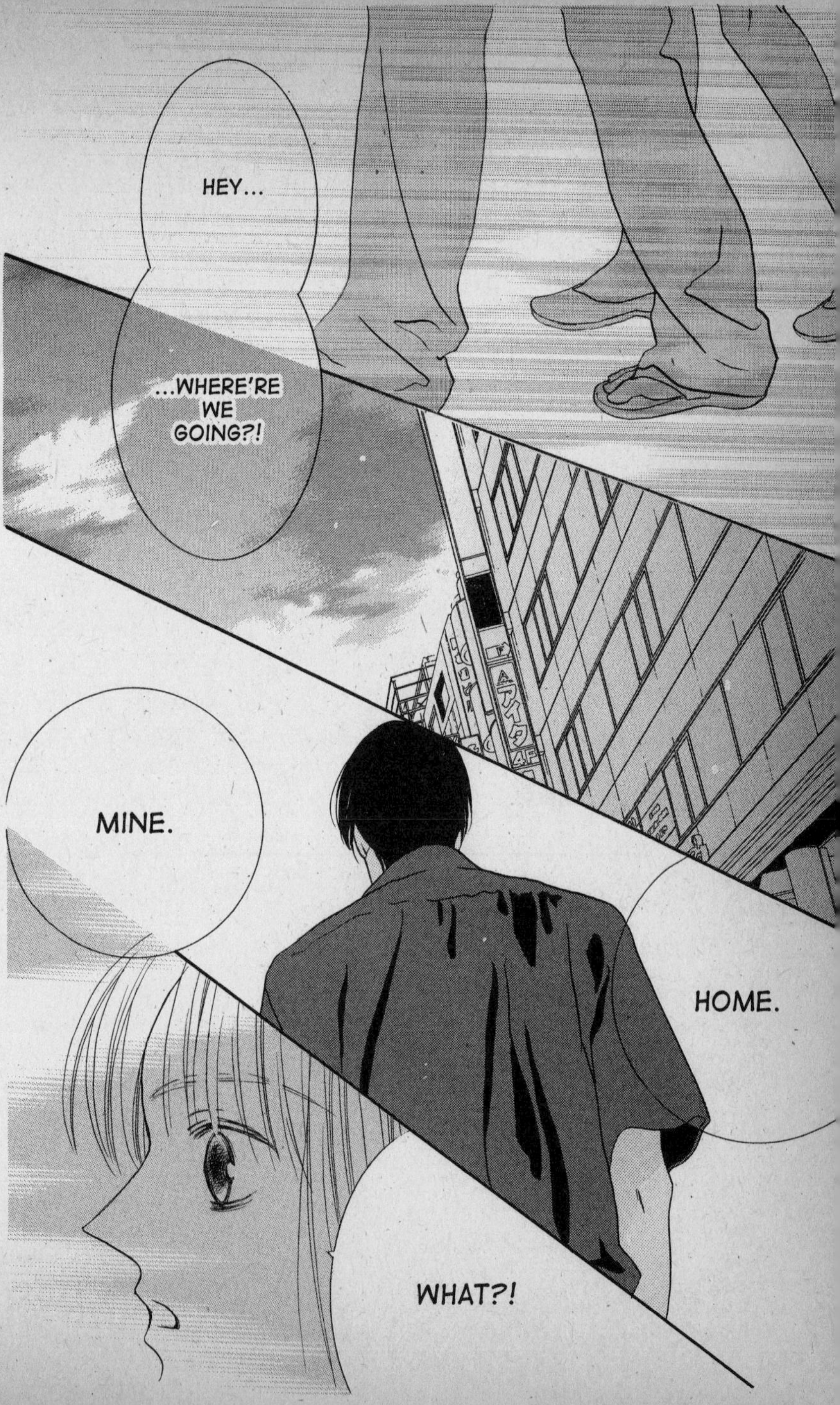
HEY...
...WHERE'RE WE GOING?!
HOME.
MINE.
WHAT?!

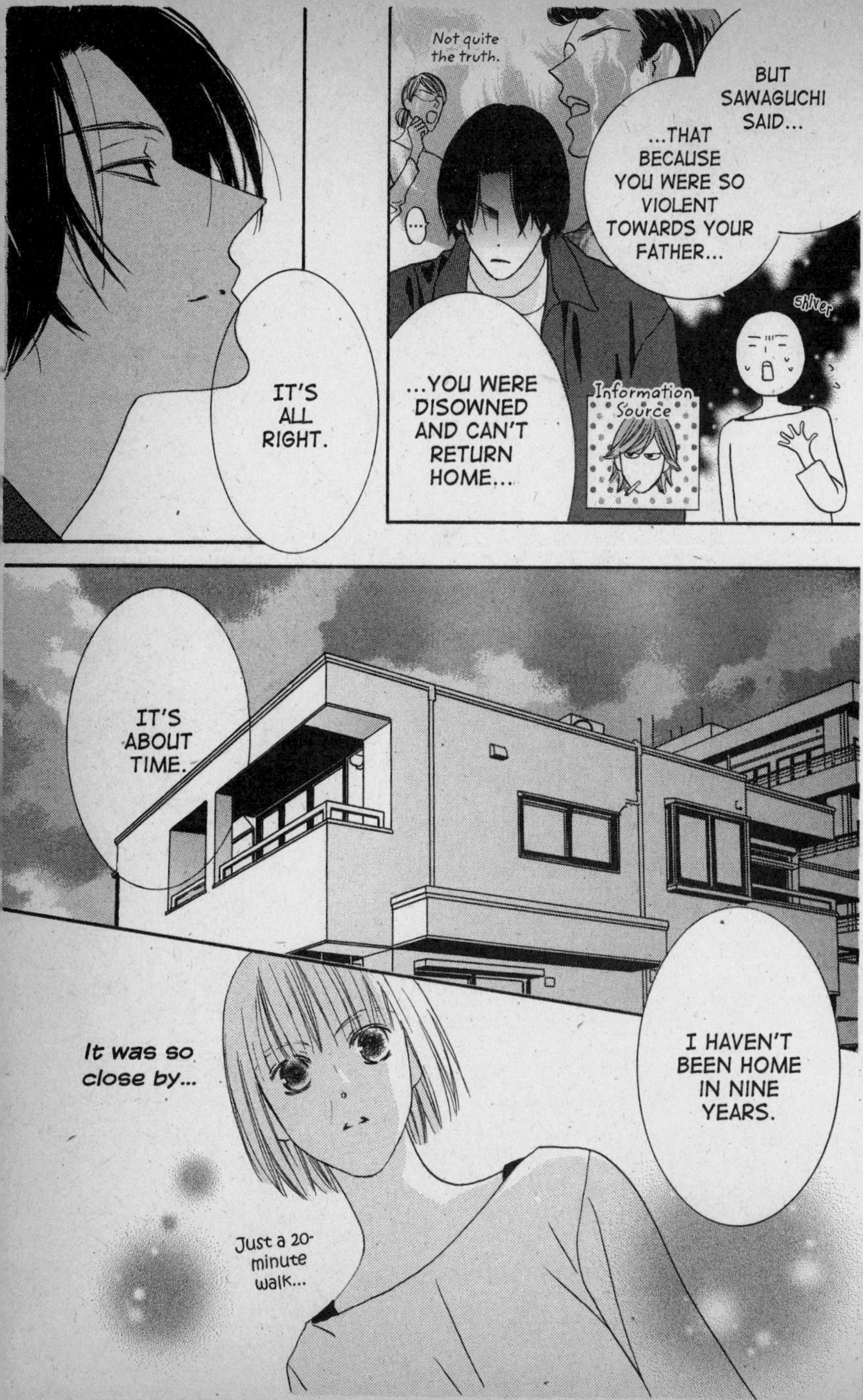
BUT SAWAGUCHI SAID...
...THAT BECAUSE YOU WERE SO VIOLENT TOWARDS YOUR FATHER...
Not quite the truth.
shiver
...
...YOU WERE DISOWNED AND CAN'T RETURN HOME...
Information Source
IT'S ALL RIGHT.
IT'S ABOUT TIME.
I HAVEN'T BEEN HOME IN NINE YEARS.
It was so close by...
Just a 20-minute walk...

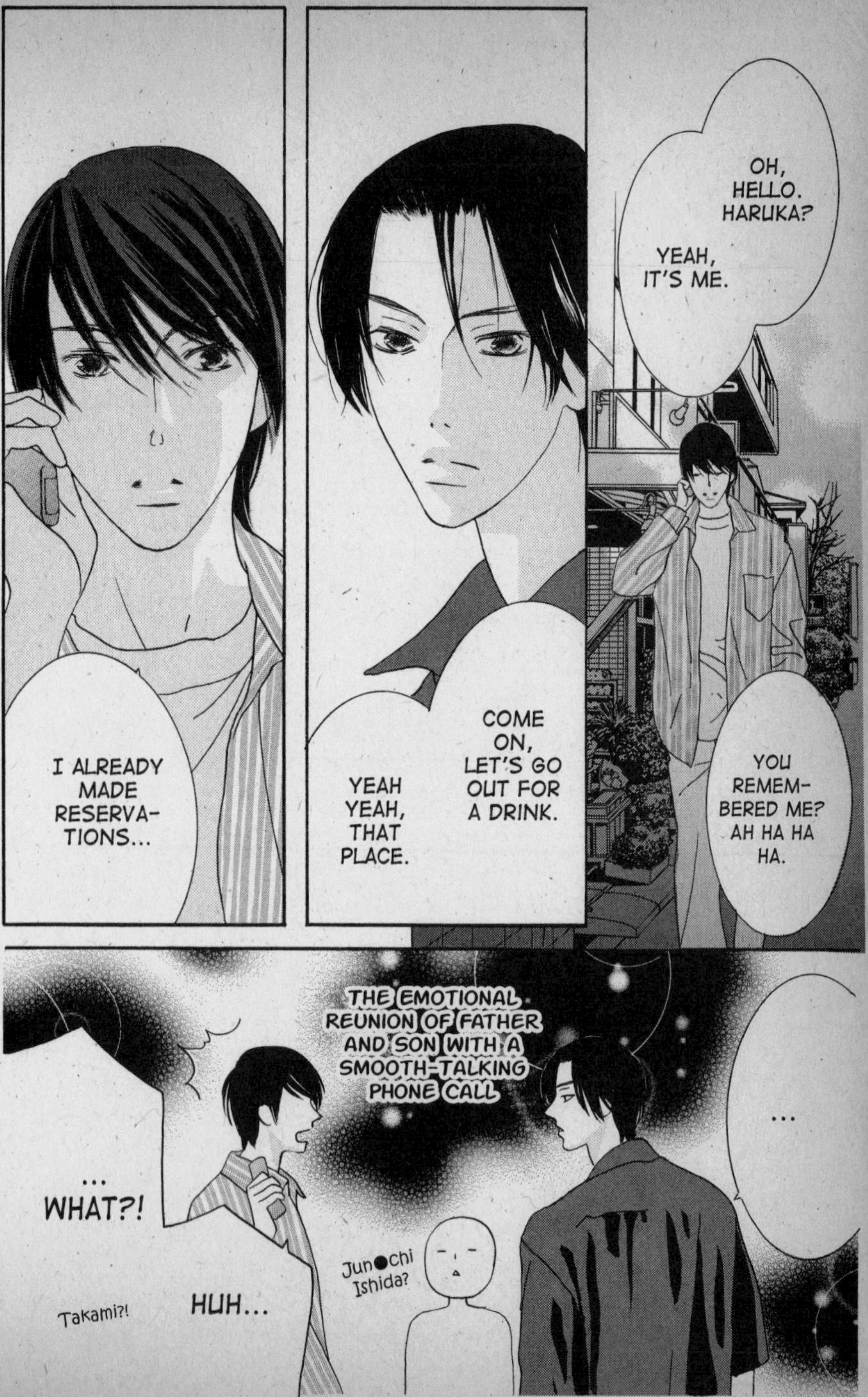
OH, HELLO. HARUKA?
YEAH, IT'S ME.
YOU REMEMBERED ME? AH HA HA HA.
COME ON, LET'S GO OUT FOR A DRINK.
YEAH YEAH, THAT PLACE.
I ALREADY MADE RESERVATIONS...
...
THE EMOTIONAL REUNION OF FATHER AND SON WITH A SMOOTH-TALKING PHONE CALL
... WHAT?!
Jun●chi Ishida?
HUH...
Takami?!

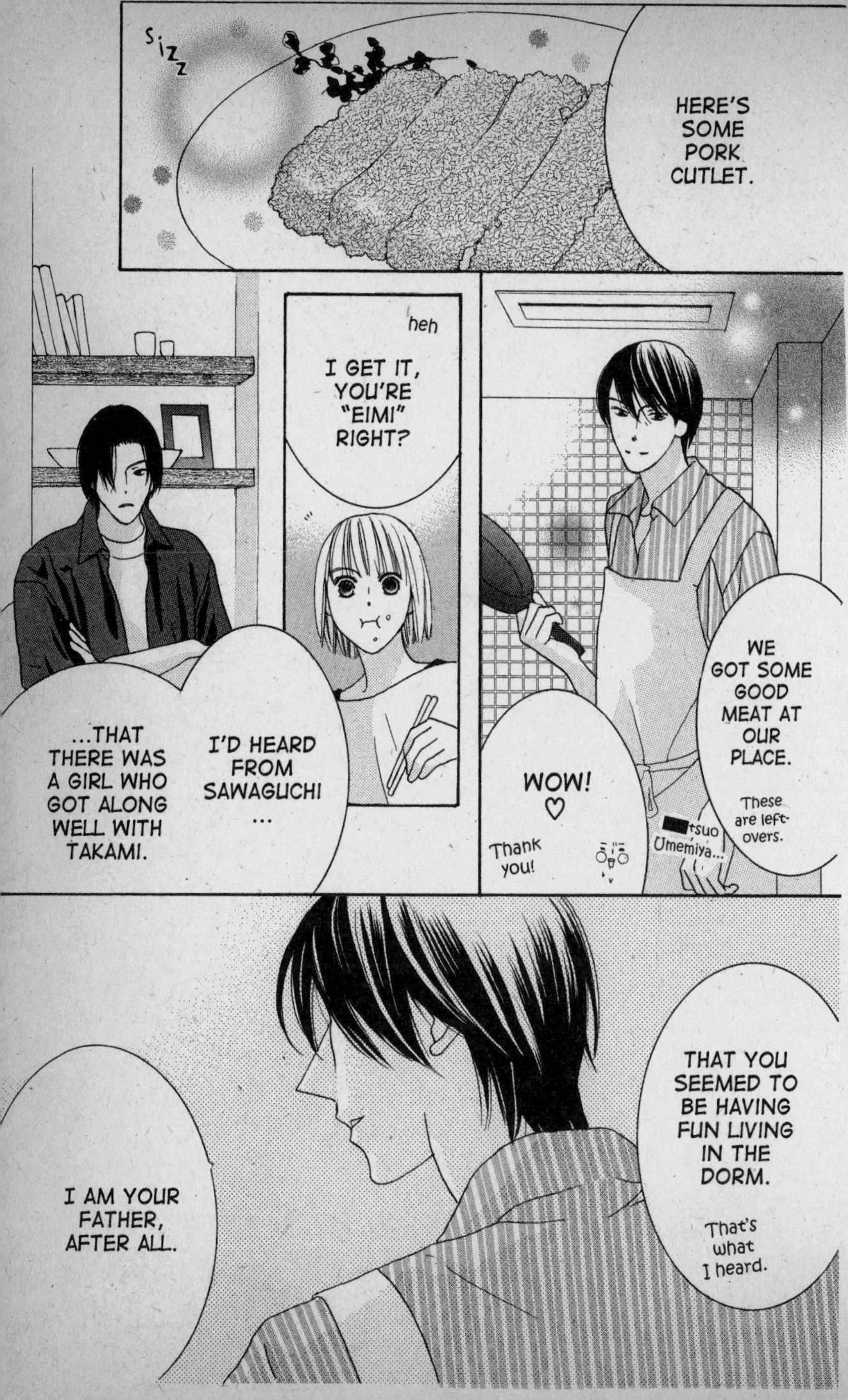
sizz
HERE'S SOME PORK CUTLET.
WE GOT SOME GOOD MEAT AT OUR PLACE.
These are left-overs.
[redacted]tsuo Umemiya...
WOW! ♡
Thank you!
heh
I GET IT, YOU'RE "EIMI" RIGHT?
I'D HEARD FROM SAWAGUCHI ...
...THAT THERE WAS A GIRL WHO GOT ALONG WELL WITH TAKAMI.
THAT YOU SEEMED TO BE HAVING FUN LIVING IN THE DORM.
That's what I heard.
I AM YOUR FATHER, AFTER ALL.

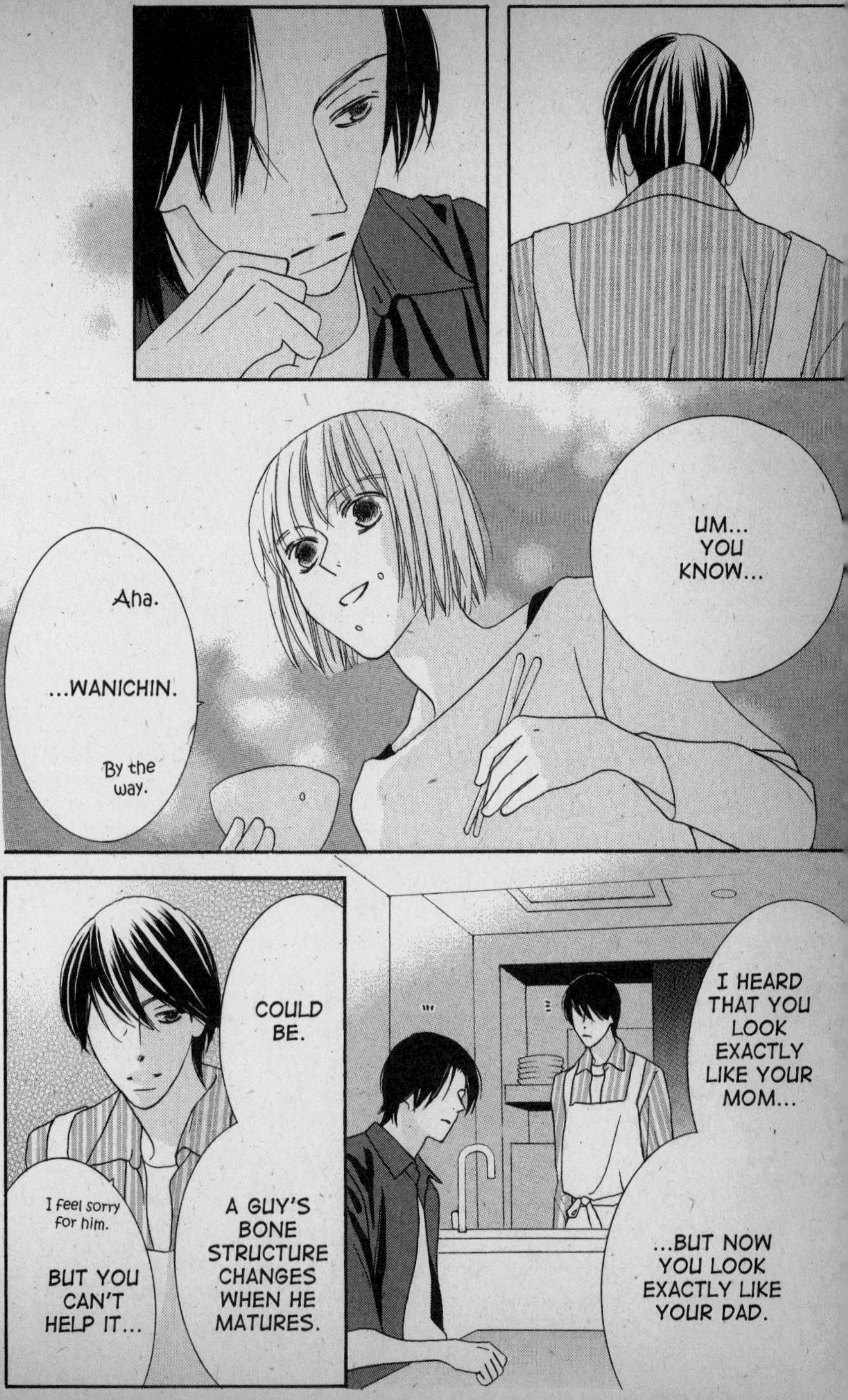
UM... YOU KNOW...
Aha.
...WANICHIN.
By the way.
I HEARD THAT YOU LOOK EXACTLY LIKE YOUR MOM...
...BUT NOW YOU LOOK EXACTLY LIKE YOUR DAD.
COULD BE.
A GUY'S BONE STRUCTURE CHANGES WHEN HE MATURES.
I feel sorry for him.
BUT YOU CAN'T HELP IT...

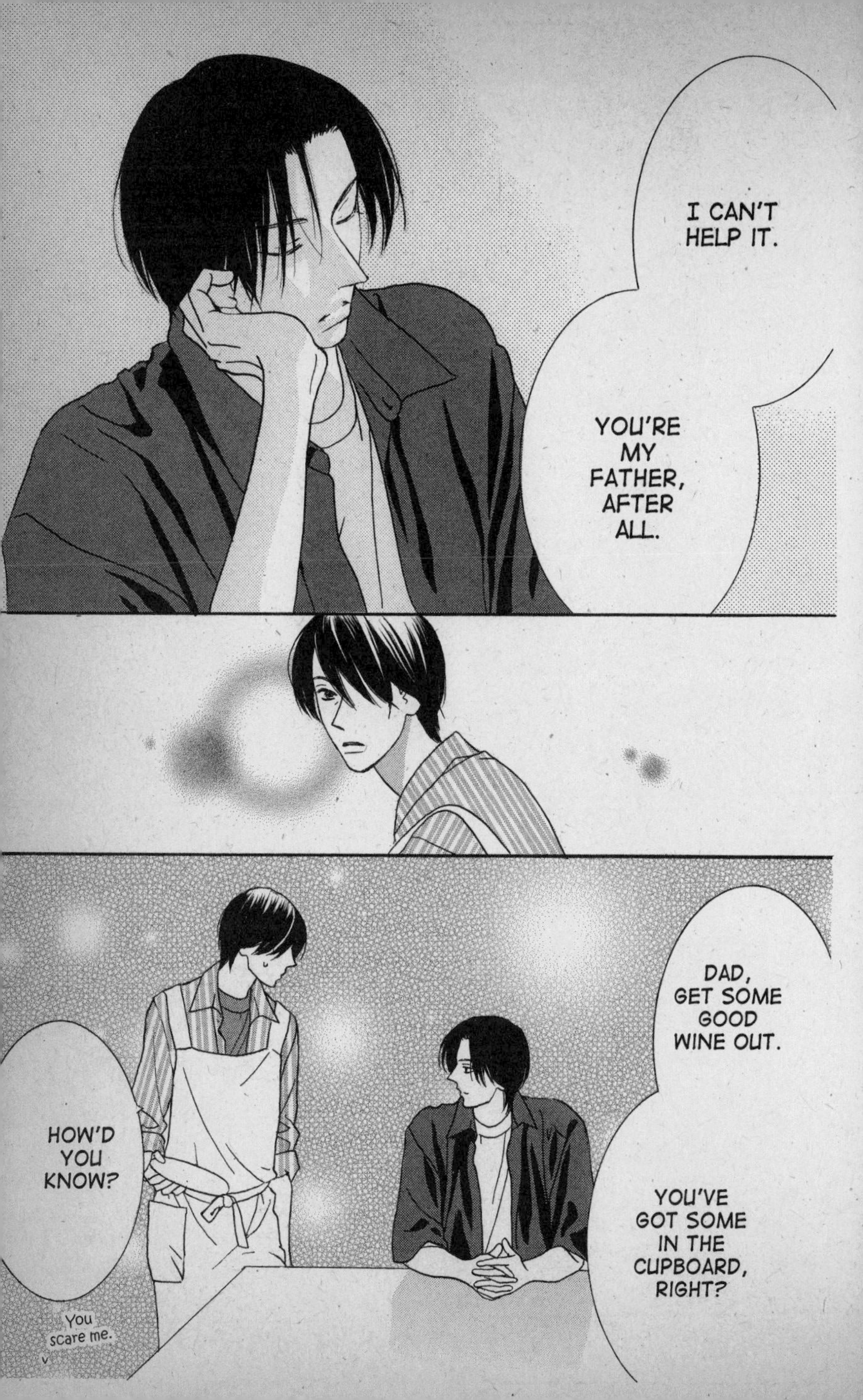
I CAN'T HELP IT.
YOU'RE MY FATHER, AFTER ALL.
DAD, GET SOME GOOD WINE OUT.
YOU'VE GOT SOME IN THE CUPBOARD, RIGHT?
HOW'D YOU KNOW?
You scare me.

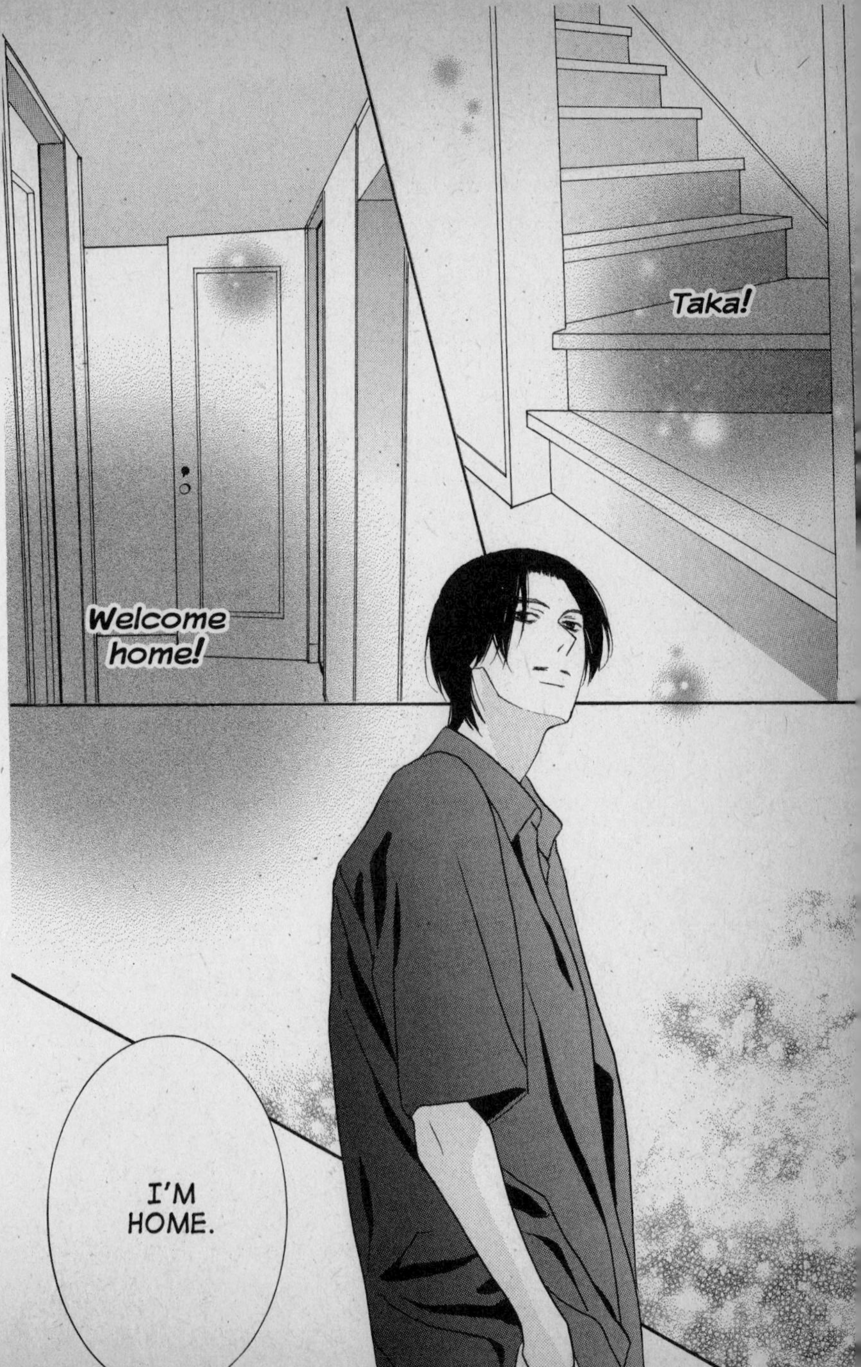
Taka!
Welcome home!
I'M HOME.

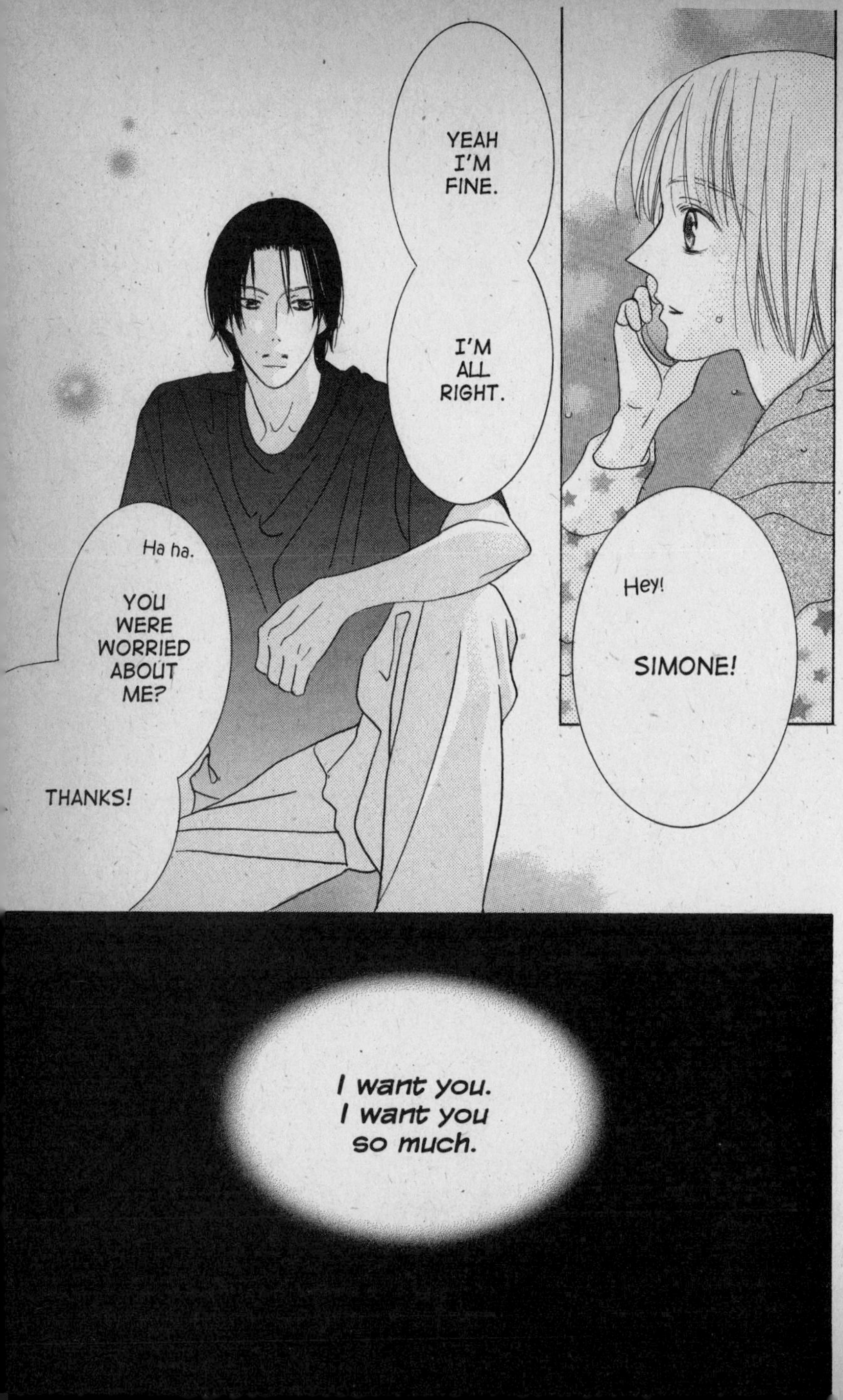
Hey!
SIMONE!
YEAH I'M FINE.
I'M ALL RIGHT.
Ha ha.
YOU WERE WORRIED ABOUT ME?
THANKS!
I want you. I want you so much.

BEAUTY IS THE BEAST

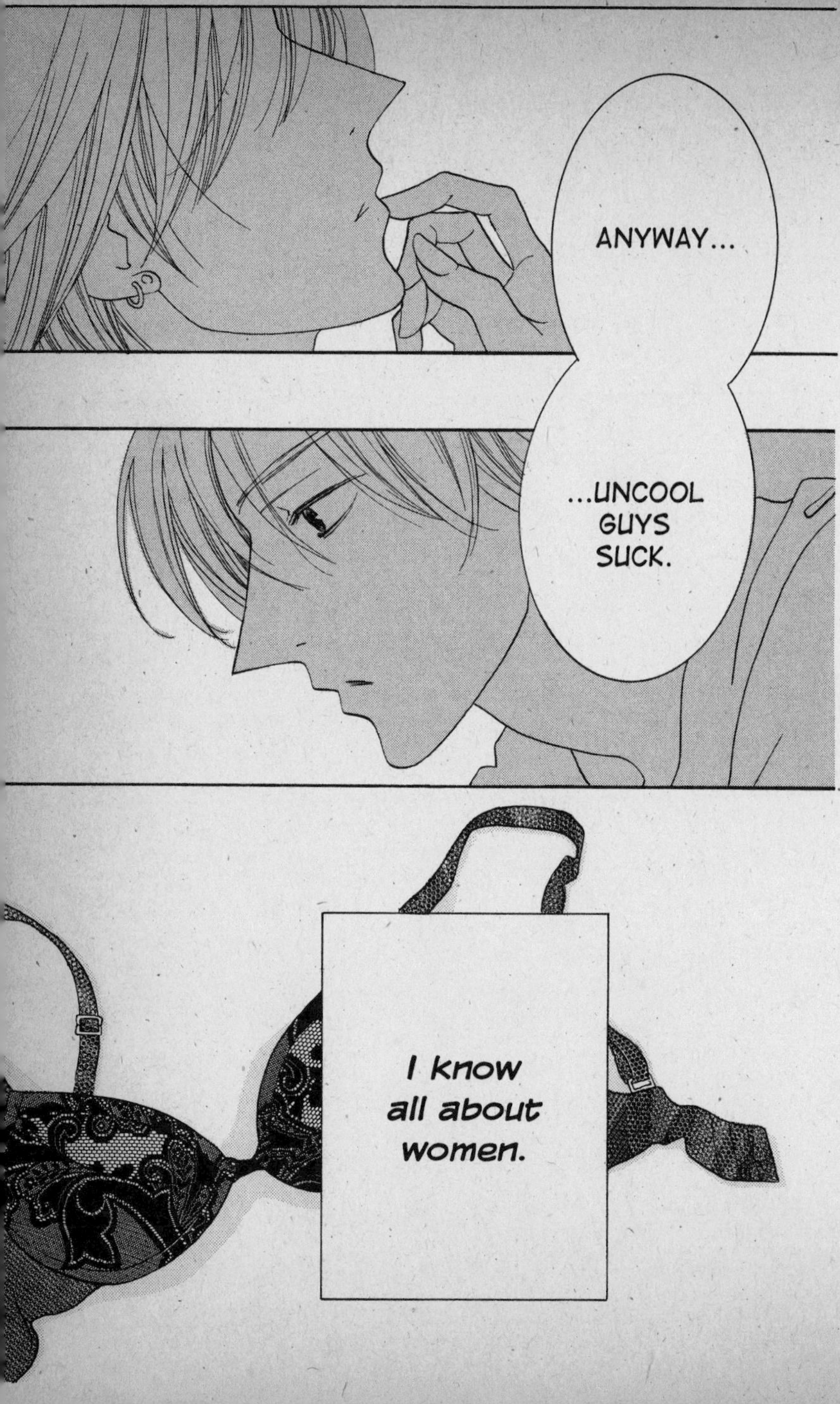
ANYWAY...
...UNCOOL GUYS SUCK.
I know all about women.

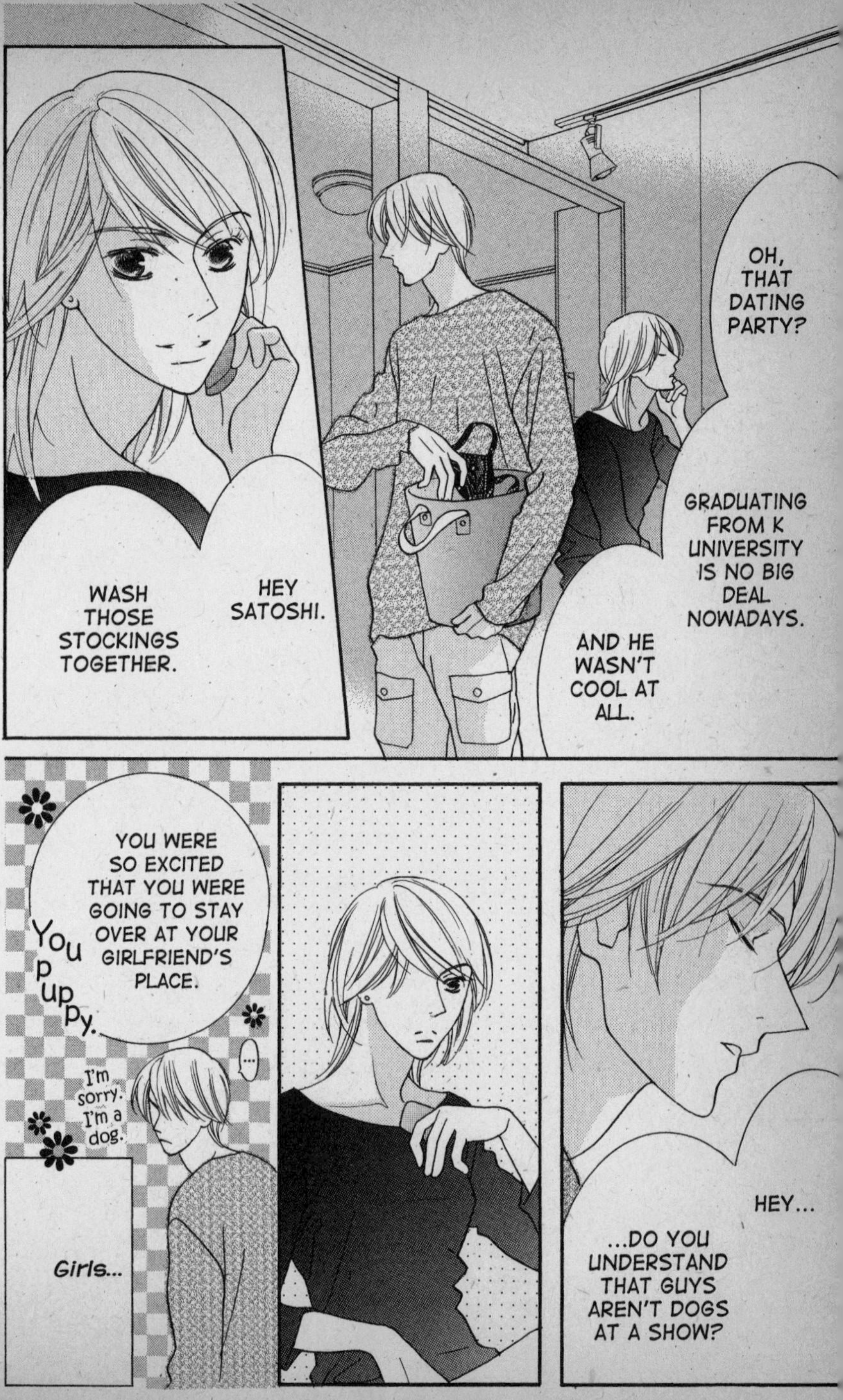
OH, THAT DATING PARTY?
GRADUATING FROM K UNIVERSITY IS NO BIG DEAL NOWADAYS.
AND HE WASN'T COOL AT ALL.
HEY SATOSHI.
WASH THOSE STOCKINGS TOGETHER.
HEY...
...DO YOU UNDERSTAND THAT GUYS AREN'T DOGS AT A SHOW?
YOU WERE SO EXCITED THAT YOU WERE GOING TO STAY OVER AT YOUR GIRLFRIEND'S PLACE.
You puppy.
...
I'm sorry. I'm a dog.
Girls...

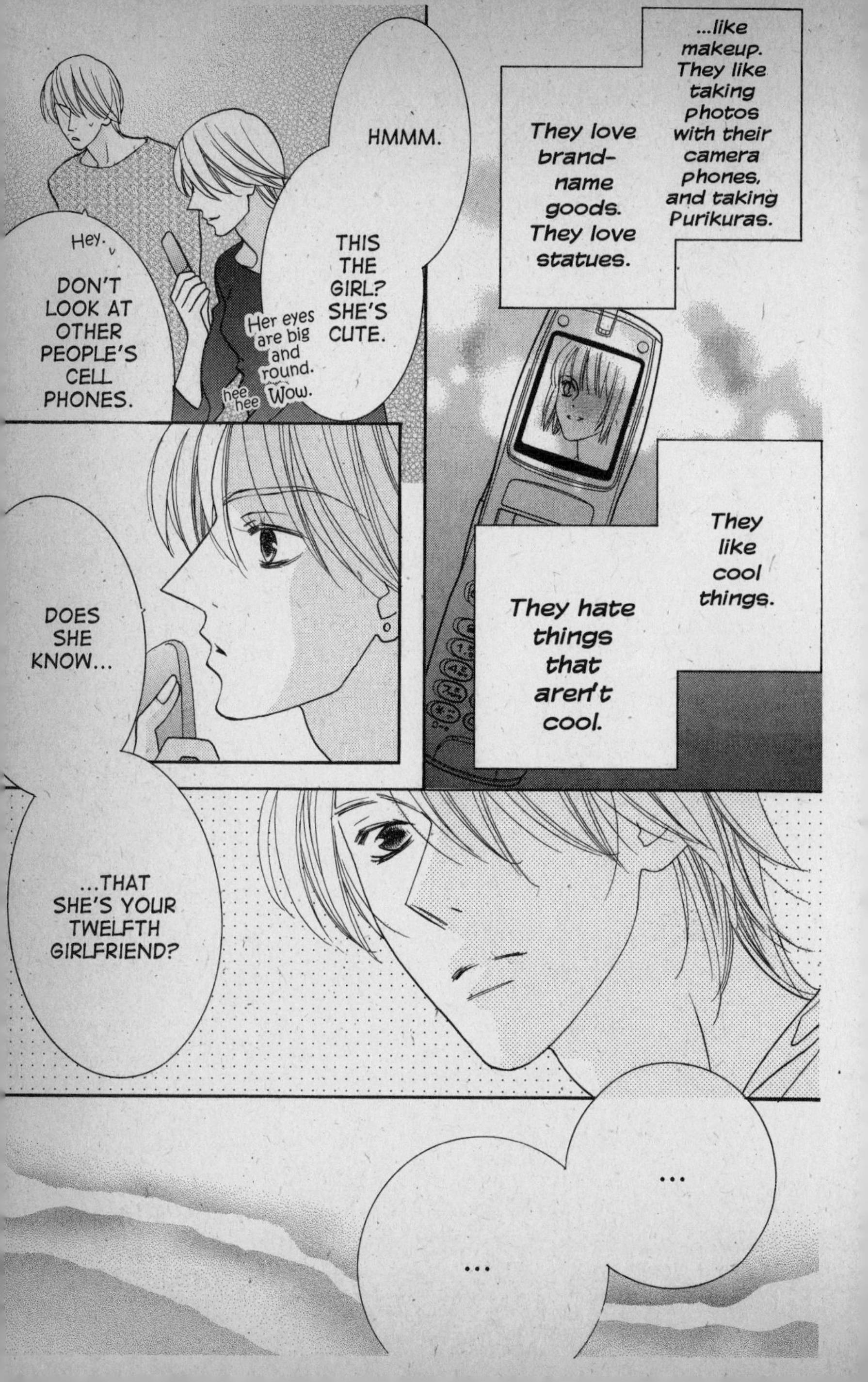

...like makeup. They like taking photos with their camera phones, and taking Purikuras.
They love brand-name goods. They love statues.
They like cool things.
They hate things that aren't cool.
HMMM.
THIS THE GIRL? SHE'S CUTE.
Her eyes are big and round. Wow.
hee hee
Hey.
DON'T LOOK AT OTHER PEOPLE'S CELL PHONES.
DOES SHE KNOW...
...THAT SHE'S YOUR TWELFTH GIRLFRIEND?
...
...

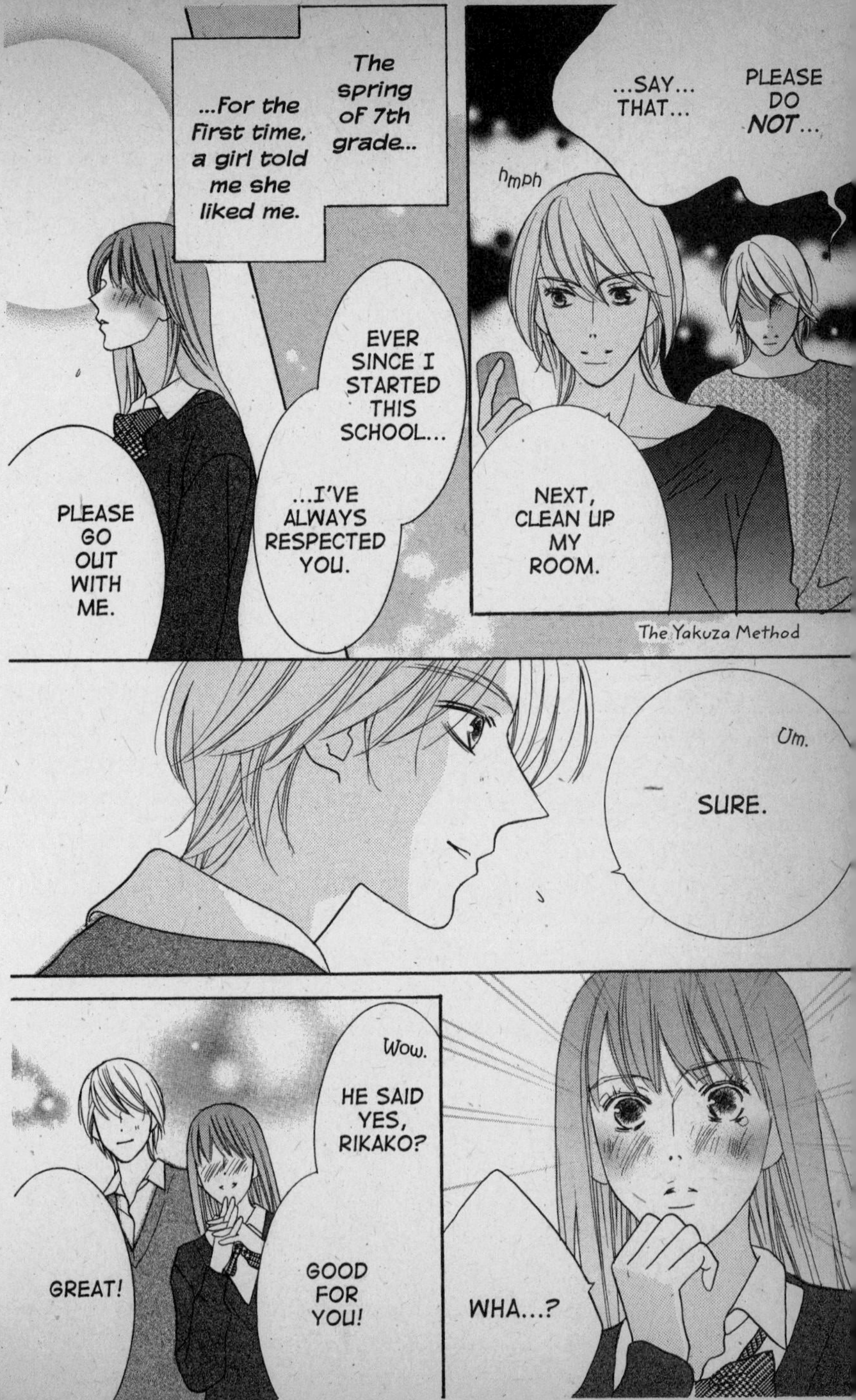
PLEASE DO NOT...
...SAY... THAT...
hmph
NEXT, CLEAN UP MY ROOM.
The Yakuza Method
The spring of 7th grade...
...For the first time, a girl told me she liked me.
EVER SINCE I STARTED THIS SCHOOL...
...I'VE ALWAYS RESPECTED YOU.
PLEASE GO OUT WITH ME.
Um.
SURE.
WHA...?
Wow.
HE SAID YES, RIKAKO?
GOOD FOR YOU!
GREAT!

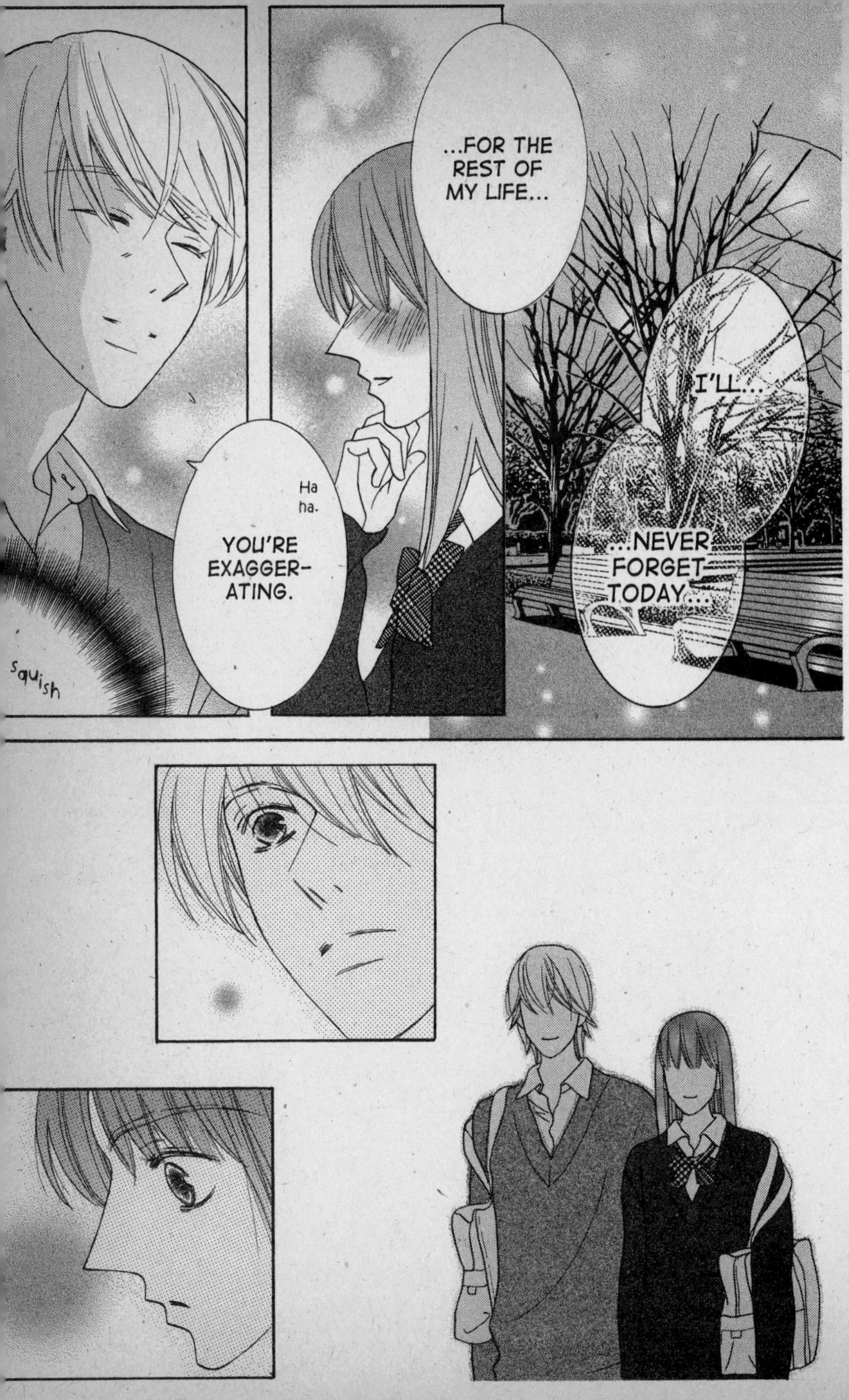
I'LL...
...NEVER FORGET TODAY...
...FOR THE REST OF MY LIFE...
Ha ha.
YOU'RE EXAGGER-ATING.
squish

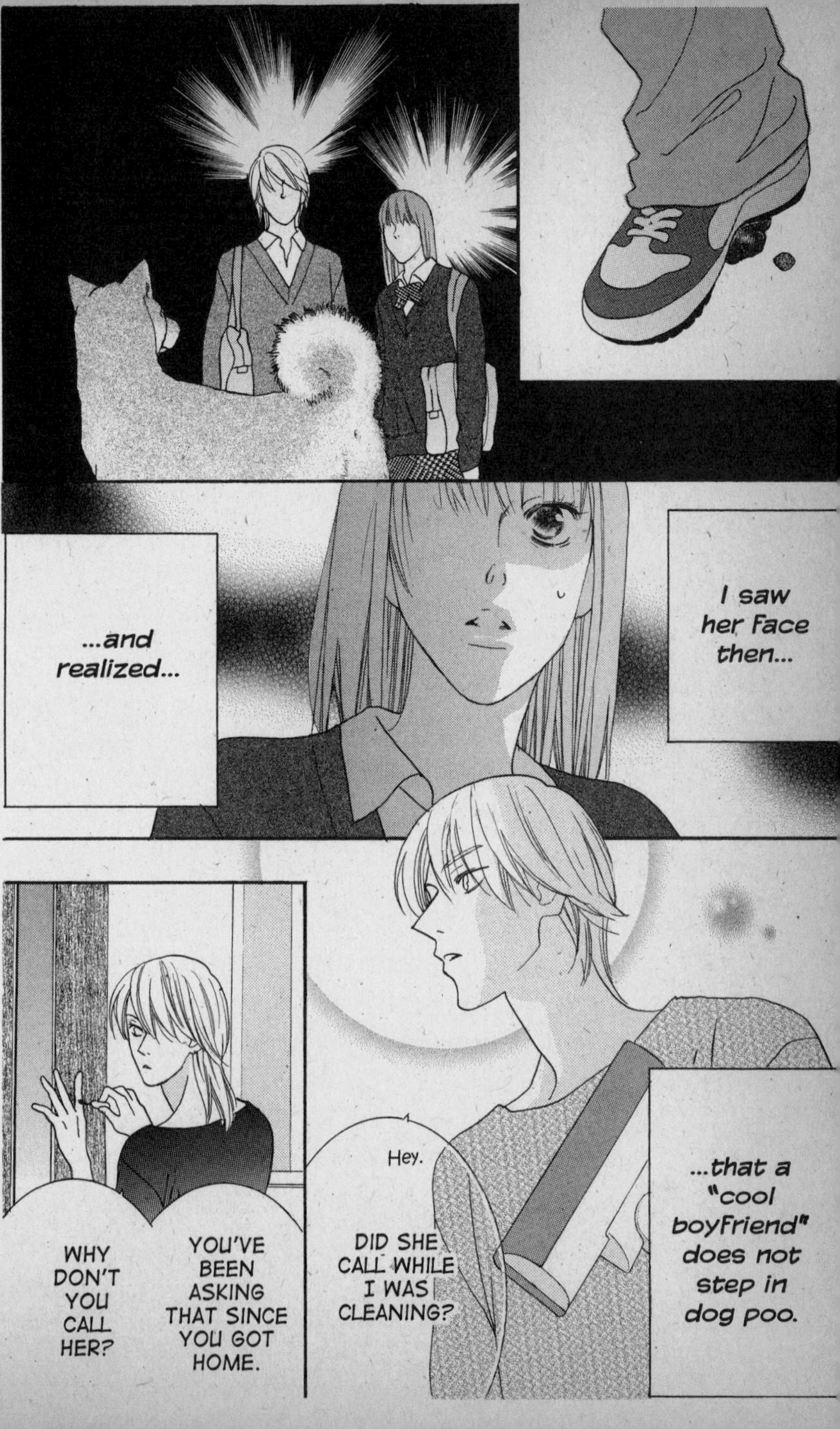
I saw her face then...
...and realized...
...that a "cool boyfriend" does not step in dog poo.
Hey.
DID SHE CALL WHILE I WAS CLEANING?
YOU'VE BEEN ASKING THAT SINCE YOU GOT HOME.
WHY DON'T YOU CALL HER?

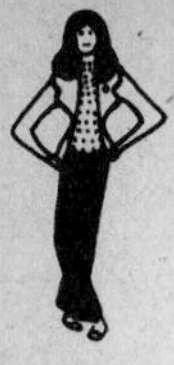

④

When I watch TV or videos and suddenly think of something, I tend to write it down on whatever paper is around me. It may be because of my work. I just do it. And I'm careless, so I don't keep track of those papers, and soon lose them. When I was cleaning the other day, I found many of those papers... I looked at them, and I'd written "A lewd Suke-san." ...What the...? What was I thinking...? I'm embarrassed to say I wrote this because of my work. I hate cleaning up my room because such things turn up.

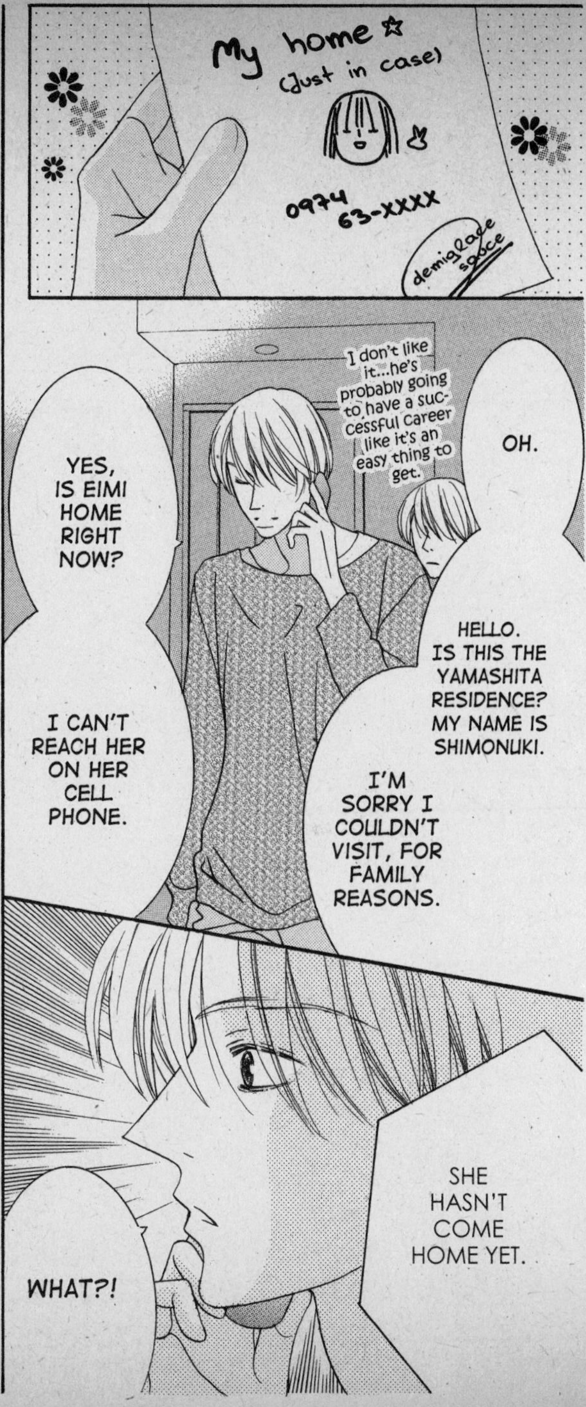
My home ☆
(Just in case)
0974
63-XXXX
demiglace sauce
OH.
I don't like it...he's probably going to have a successful career like it's an easy thing to get.
HELLO. IS THIS THE YAMASHITA RESIDENCE? MY NAME IS SHIMONUKI.
I'M SORRY I COULDN'T VISIT, FOR FAMILY REASONS.
YES, IS EIMI HOME RIGHT NOW?
I CAN'T REACH HER ON HER CELL PHONE.
SHE HASN'T COME HOME YET.
WHAT?!

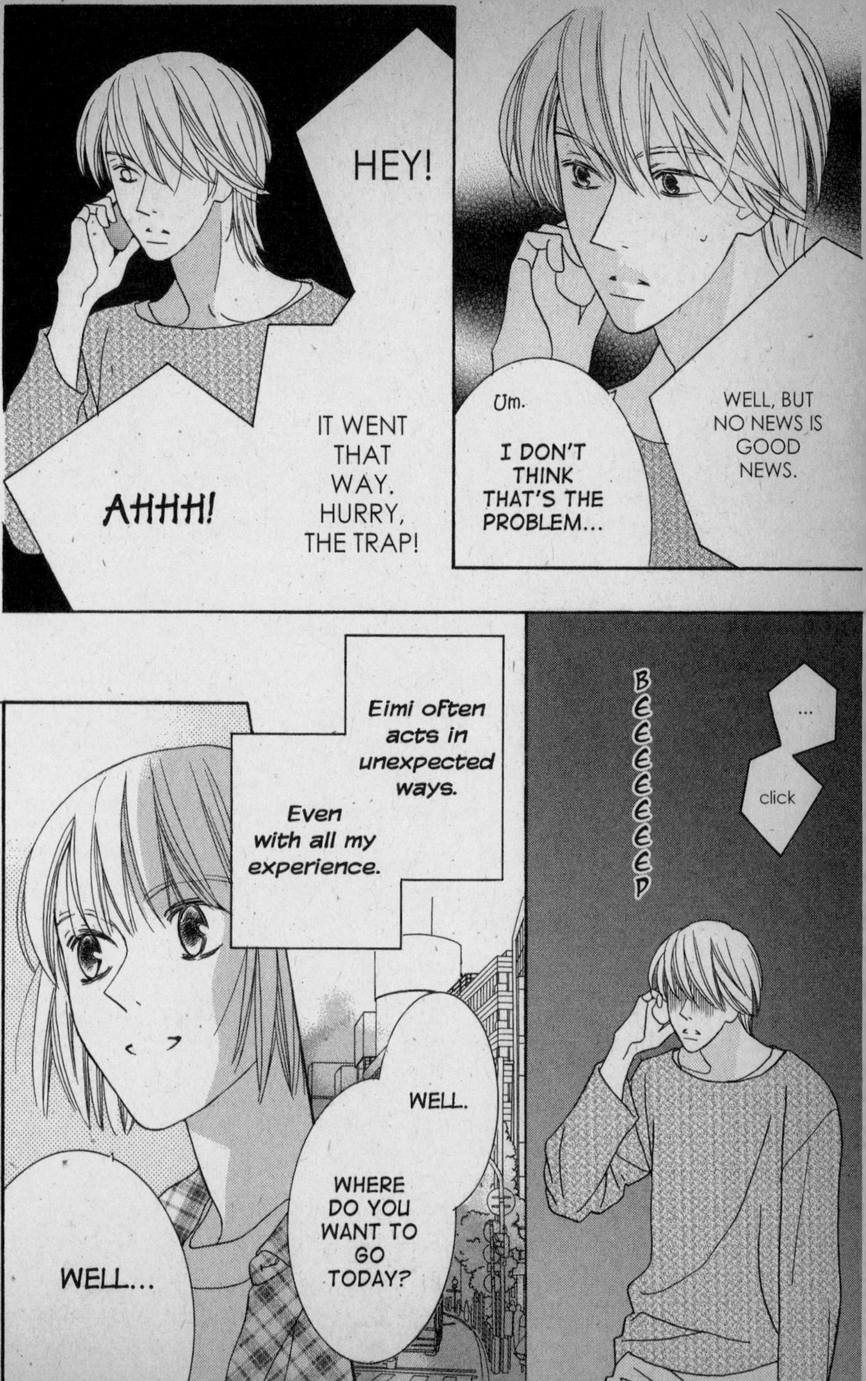
WELL, BUT NO NEWS IS GOOD NEWS.
Um.
I DON'T THINK THAT'S THE PROBLEM...
HEY!
IT WENT THAT WAY. HURRY, THE TRAP!
AHHH!
BEEEEEEEEP
...
click
Eimi often acts in unexpected ways.
Even with all my experience.
WELL.
WHERE DO YOU WANT TO GO TODAY?
WELL...

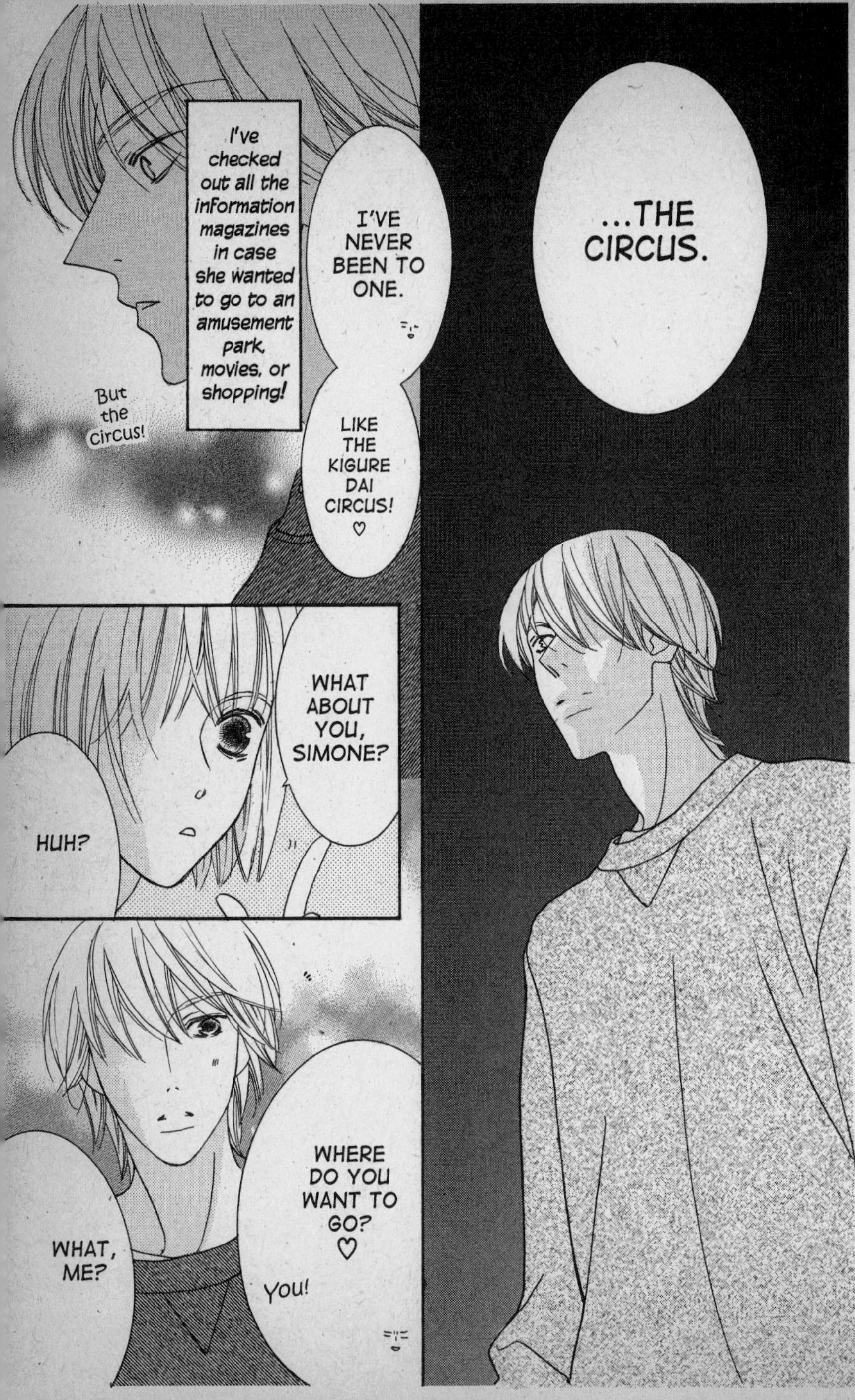
...THE CIRCUS.
I'VE NEVER BEEN TO ONE.
LIKE THE KIGURE DAI CIRCUS! ♡
I've checked out all the information magazines in case she wanted to go to an amusement park, movies, or shopping!
But the circus!
WHAT ABOUT YOU, SIMONE?
HUH?
WHERE DO YOU WANT TO GO? ♡
WHAT, ME?
YOU!

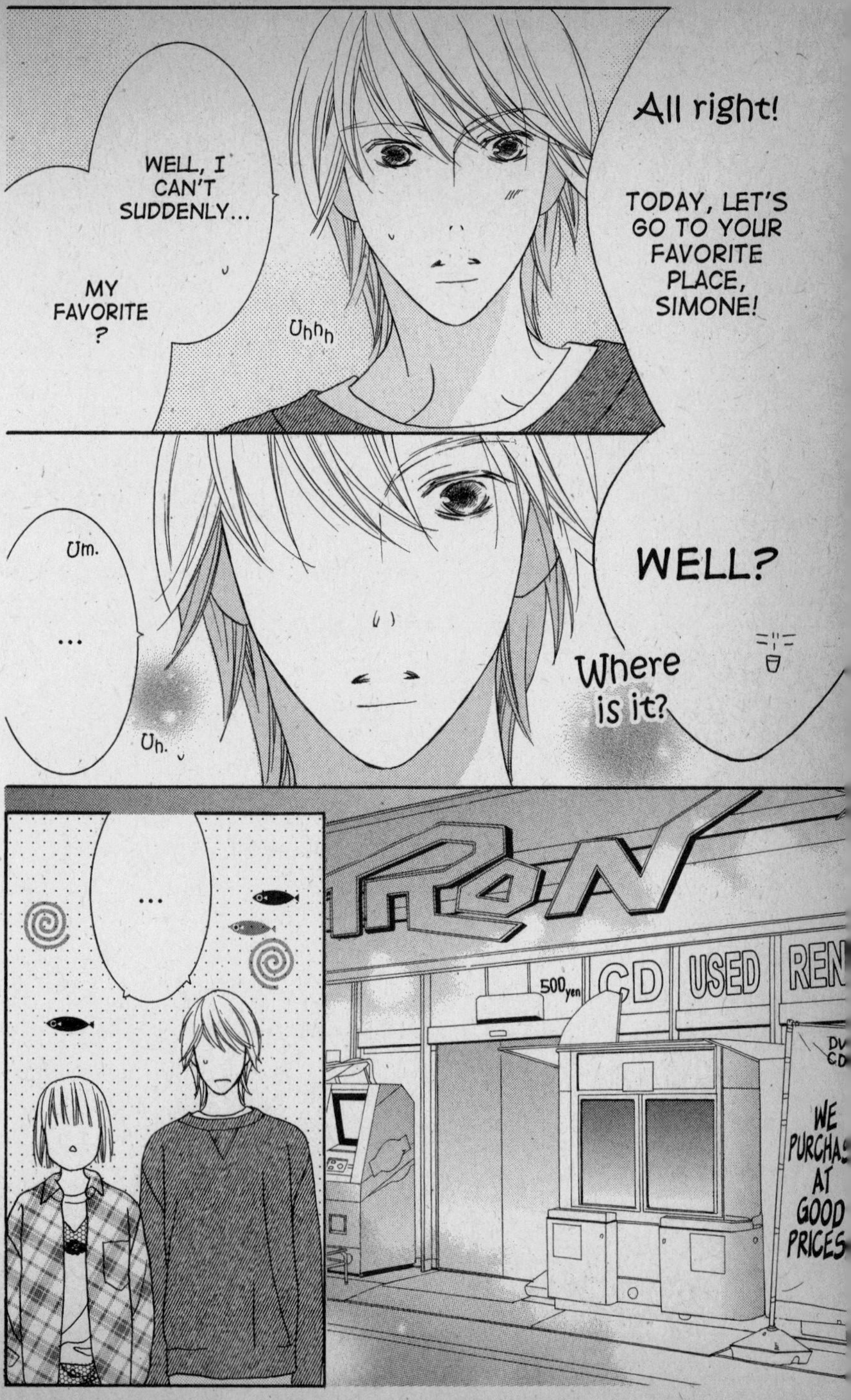
All right!
TODAY, LET'S GO TO YOUR FAVORITE PLACE, SIMONE!
WELL, I CAN'T SUDDENLY...
Uhhh
MY FAVORITE ?
WELL?
Where is it?
Um.
...
Uh.
...
500yen
CD
USED
REN
WE PURCHAS AT GOOD PRICES

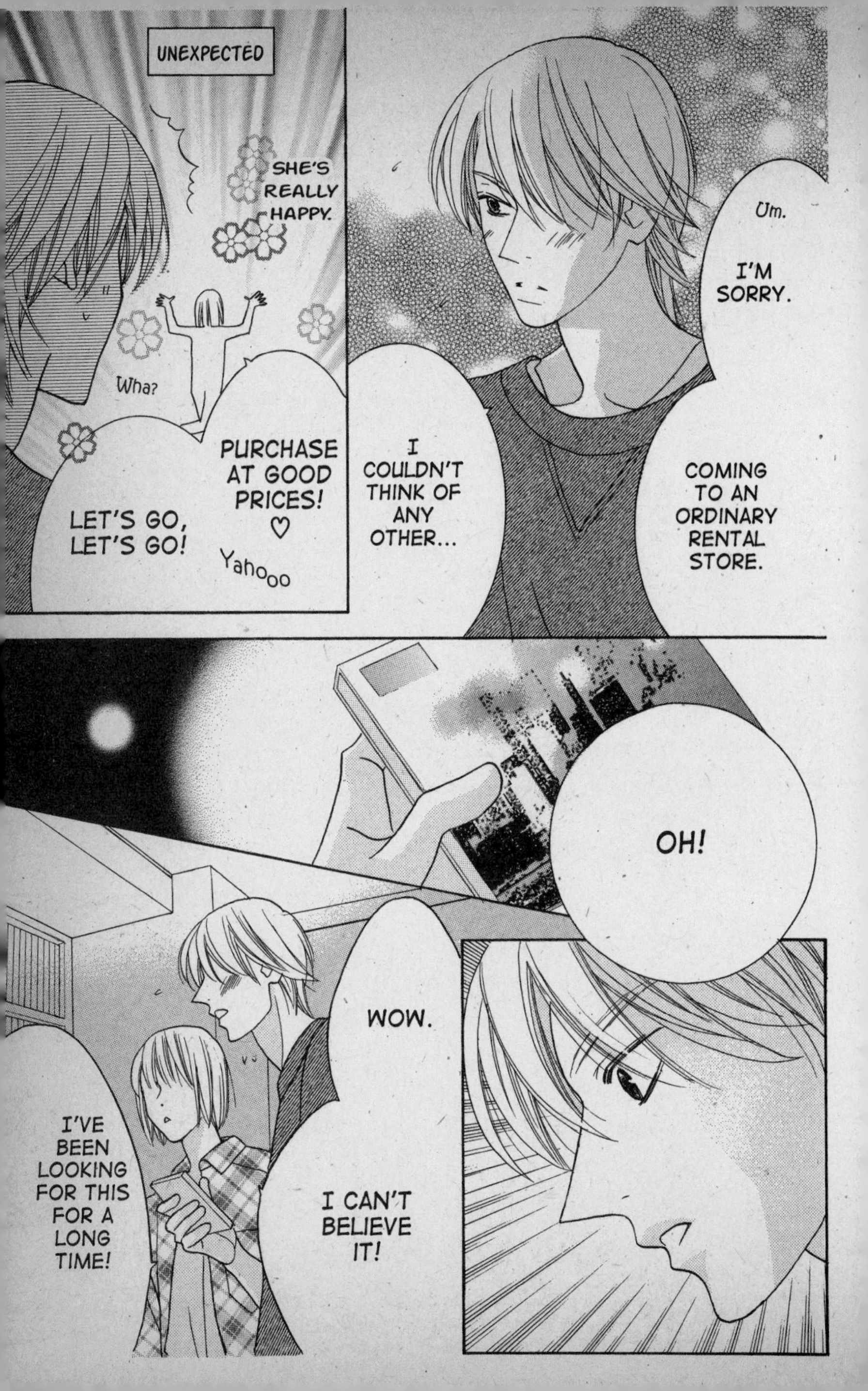
Um.
I'M SORRY.
COMING TO AN ORDINARY RENTAL STORE.
I COULDN'T THINK OF ANY OTHER...
UNEXPECTED
SHE'S REALLY HAPPY.
PURCHASE AT GOOD PRICES! ♡
Wha?
Yahooo
LET'S GO, LET'S GO!
OH!
WOW.
I CAN'T BELIEVE IT!
I'VE BEEN LOOKING FOR THIS FOR A LONG TIME!

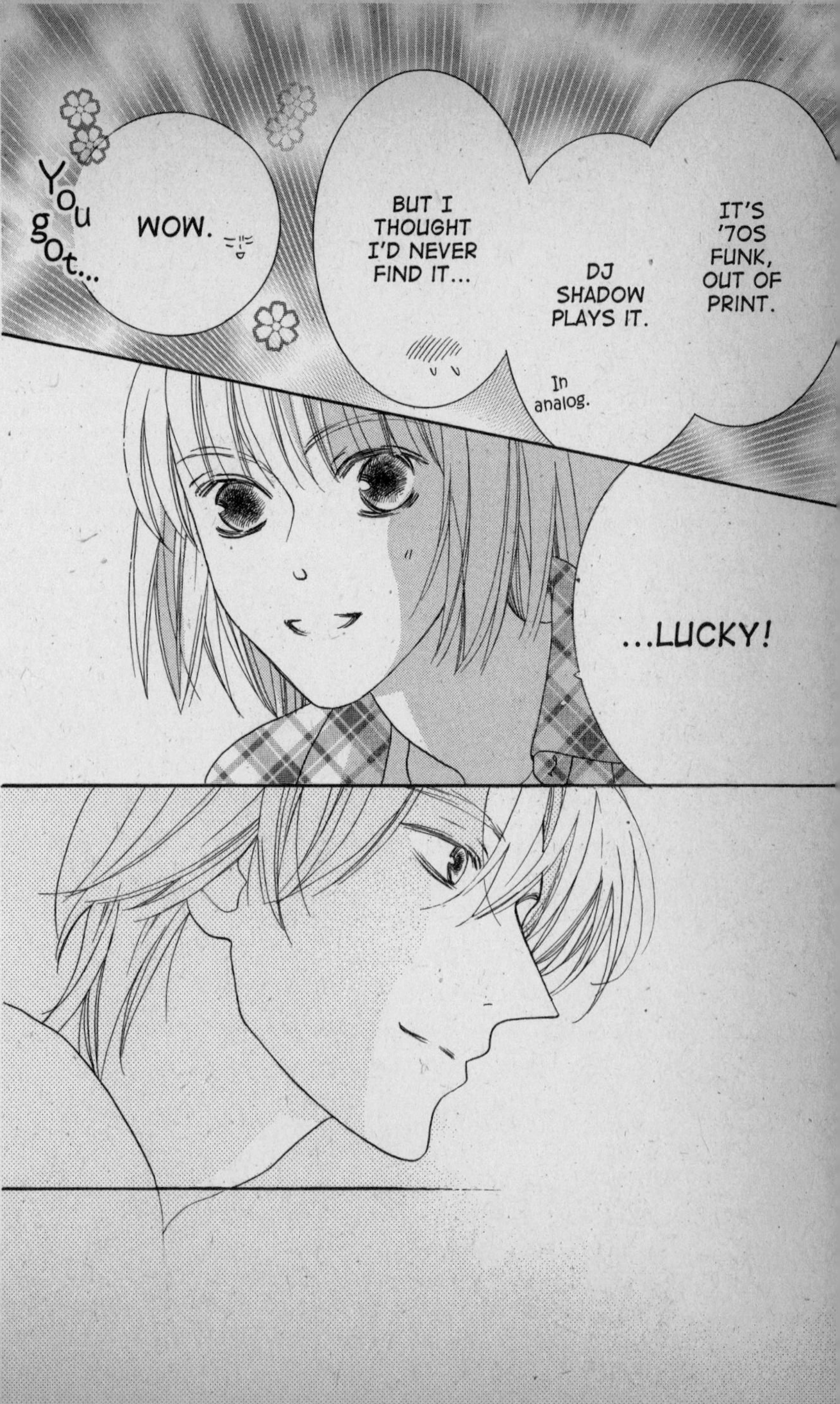
IT'S '70S FUNK, OUT OF PRINT.
DJ SHADOW PLAYS IT.
In analog.
BUT I THOUGHT I'D NEVER FIND IT...
WOW.
You got...
...LUCKY!

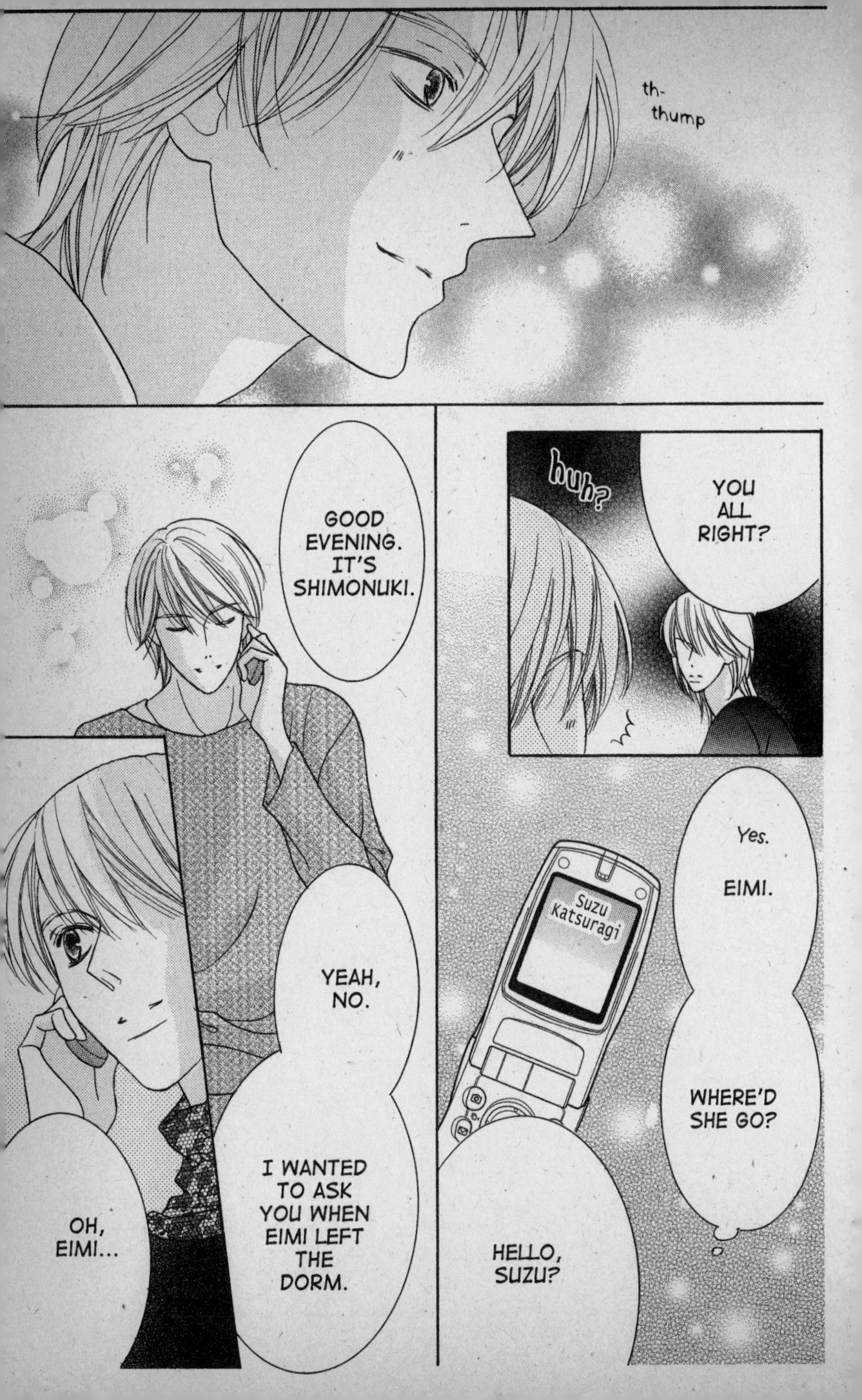
th-
thump
huh?
YOU ALL RIGHT?
Suzu Katsuragi
Yes.
EIMI.
WHERE'D SHE GO?
HELLO, SUZU?
GOOD EVENING. IT'S SHIMONUKI.
YEAH, NO.
I WANTED TO ASK YOU WHEN EIMI LEFT THE DORM.
OH, EIMI...

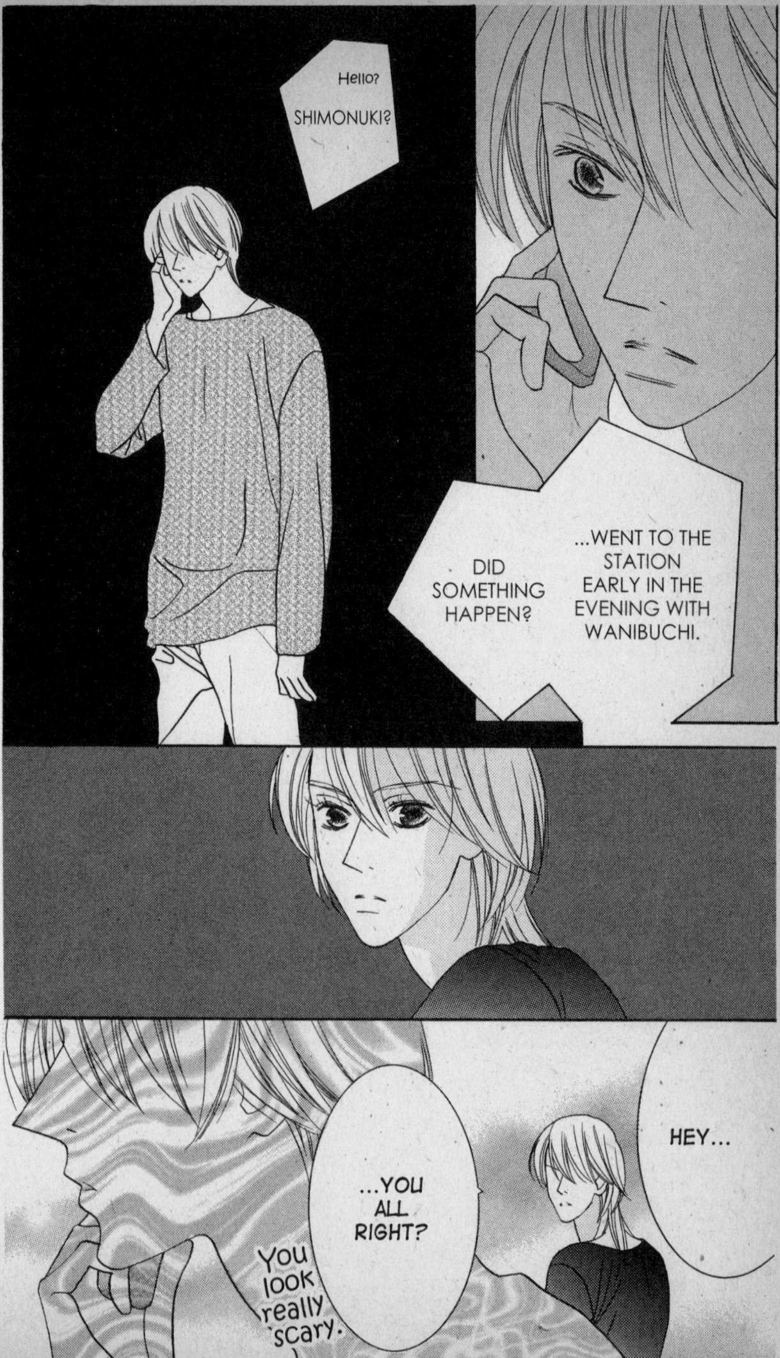
...WENT TO THE STATION EARLY IN THE EVENING WITH WANIBUCHI.
DID SOMETHING HAPPEN?
Hello?
SHIMONUKI?
HEY...
...YOU ALL RIGHT?
You look really scary.

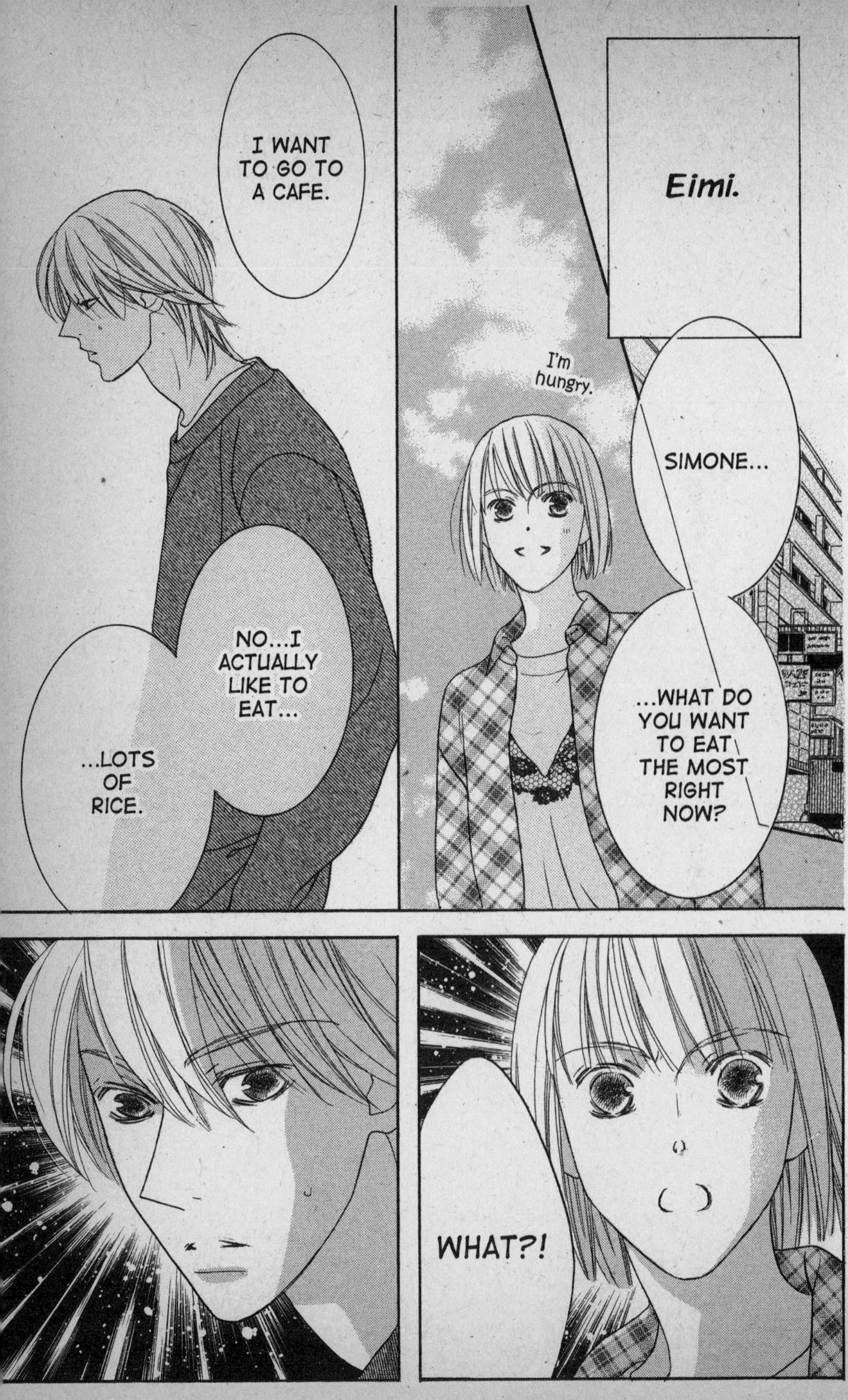
Eimi.
I'm hungry.
SIMONE...
...WHAT DO YOU WANT TO EAT THE MOST RIGHT NOW?
I WANT TO GO TO A CAFE.
NO...I ACTUALLY LIKE TO EAT...
...LOTS OF RICE.
WHAT?!

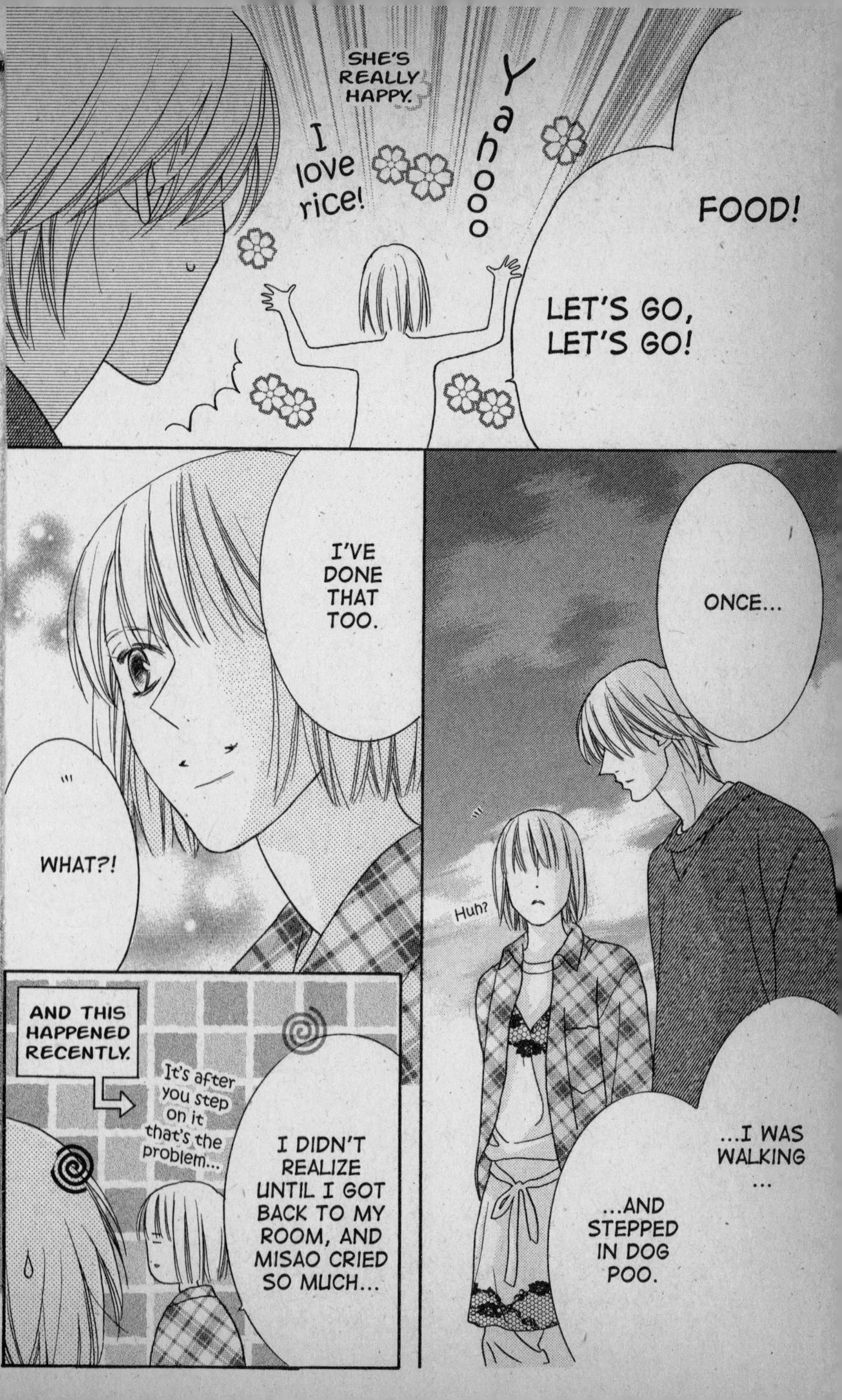
FOOD!
LET'S GO, LET'S GO!
Yahooo
I love rice!
SHE'S REALLY HAPPY.
ONCE...
Huh?
...I WAS WALKING ...
...AND STEPPED IN DOG POO.
I'VE DONE THAT TOO.
WHAT?!
AND THIS HAPPENED RECENTLY.
I DIDN'T REALIZE UNTIL I GOT BACK TO MY ROOM, AND MISAO CRIED SO MUCH...
It's after you step on it that's the problem...

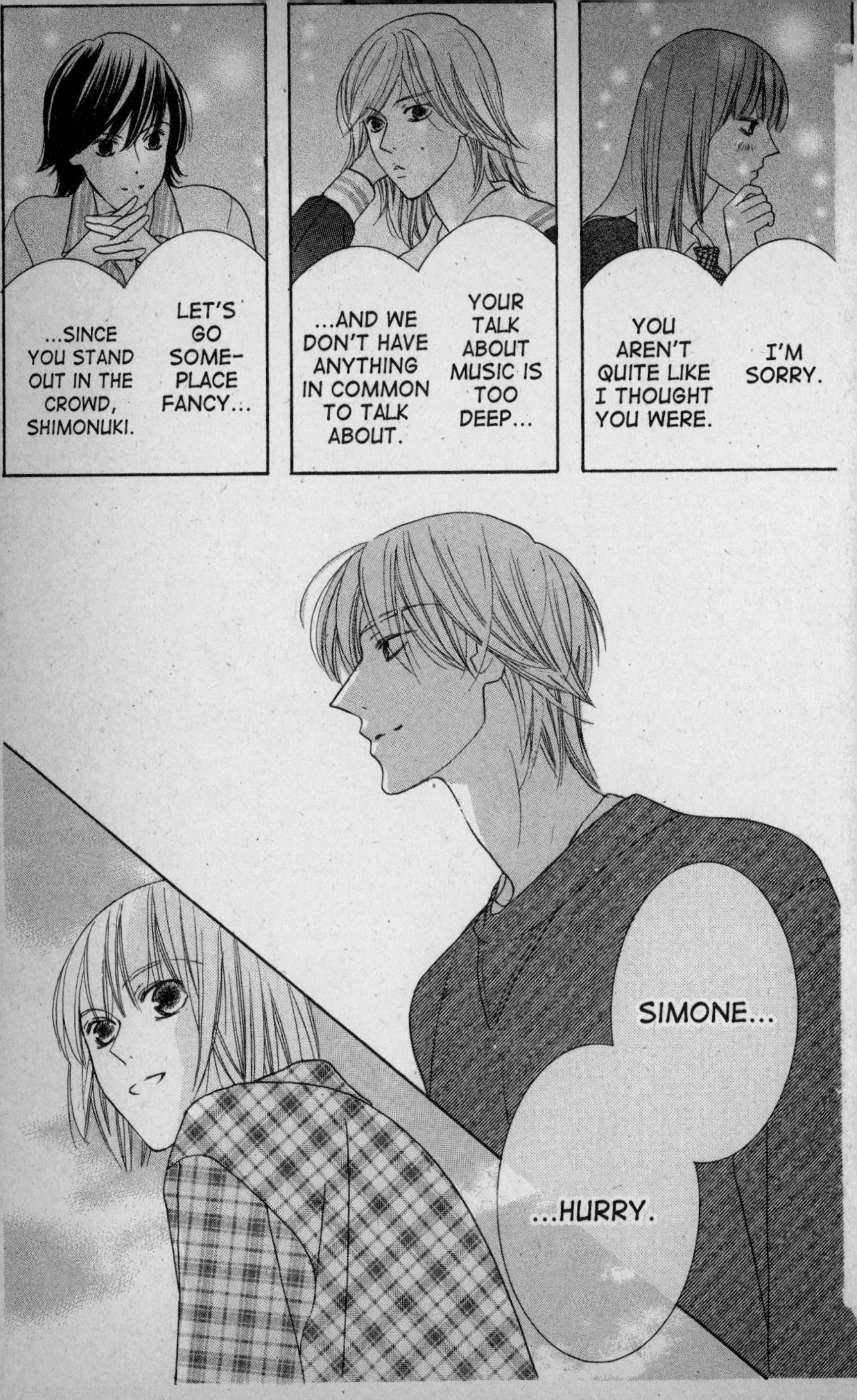
I'M SORRY.
YOU AREN'T QUITE LIKE I THOUGHT YOU WERE.
YOUR TALK ABOUT MUSIC IS TOO DEEP...
...AND WE DON'T HAVE ANYTHING IN COMMON TO TALK ABOUT.
LET'S GO SOME-PLACE FANCY...
...SINCE YOU STAND OUT IN THE CROWD, SHIMONUKI.
SIMONE...
...HURRY.

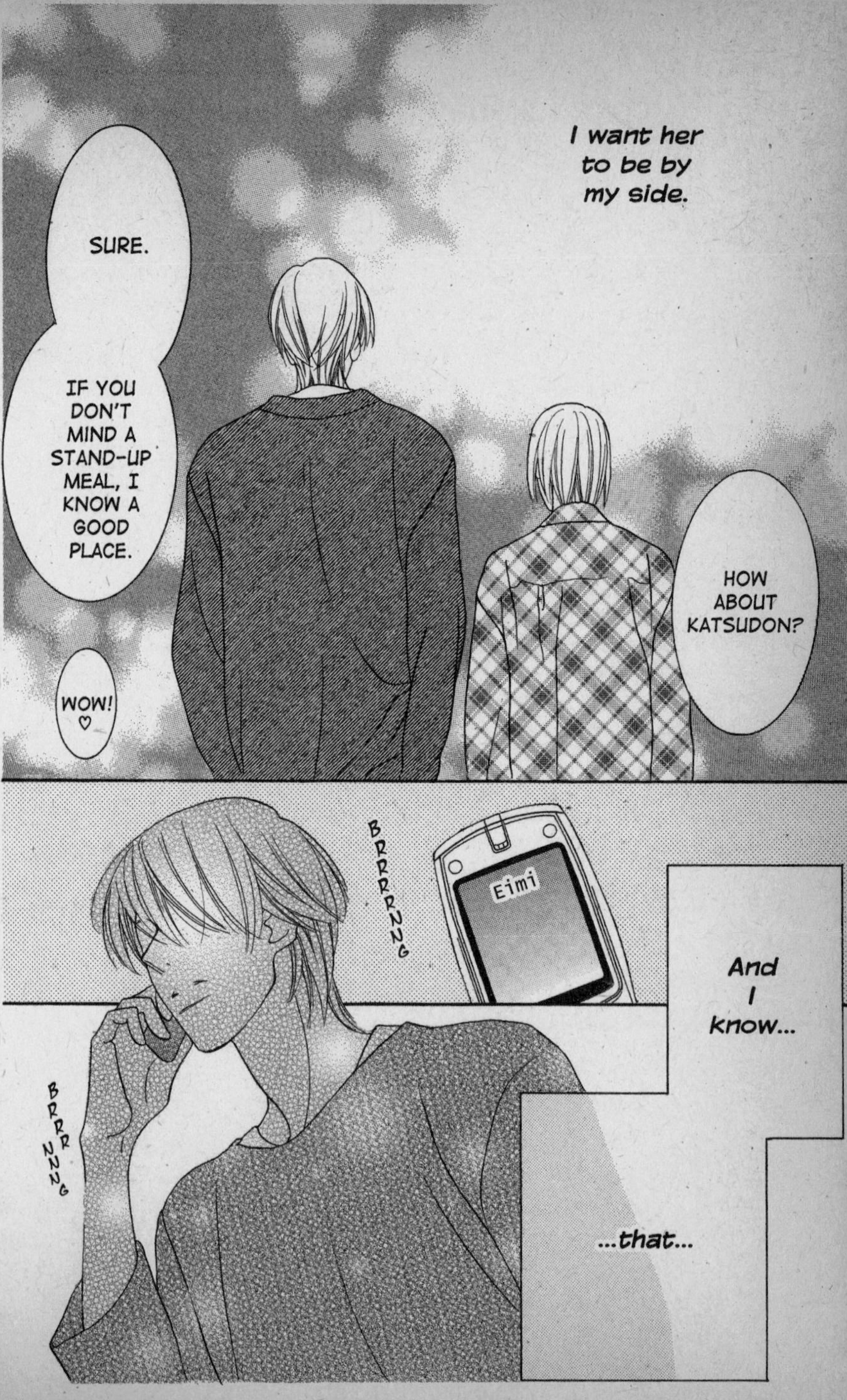
I want her to be by my side.
HOW ABOUT KATSUDON?
SURE.
IF YOU DON'T MIND A STAND-UP MEAL, I KNOW A GOOD PLACE.
WOW! ♡
Eimi
BRRRRRNNG
And I know...
BRRRNNNG
...that...

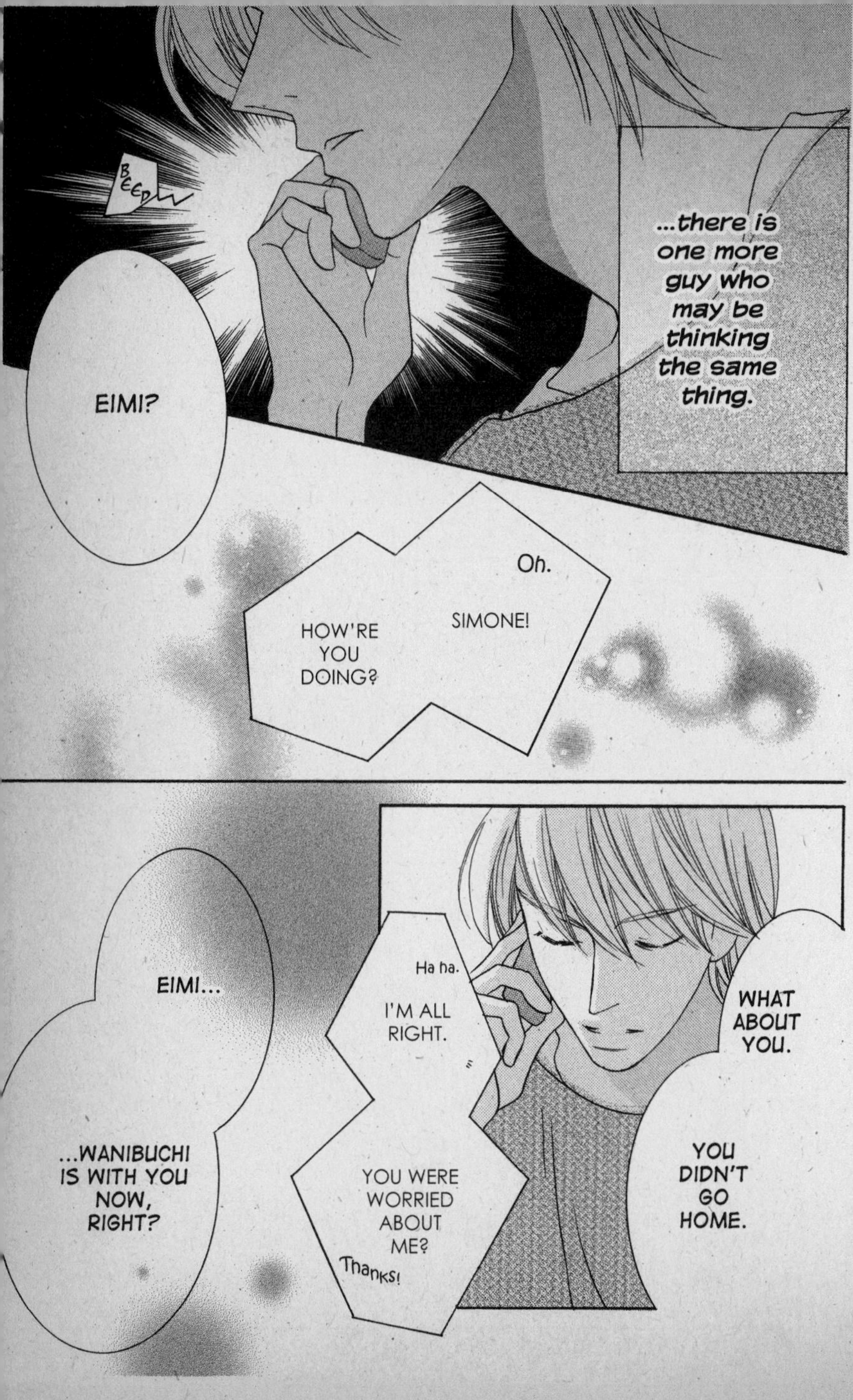
...there is one more guy who may be thinking the same thing.
BEEP
EIMI?
Oh.
SIMONE!
HOW'RE YOU DOING?
WHAT ABOUT YOU.
YOU DIDN'T GO HOME.
Ha ha.
I'M ALL RIGHT.
YOU WERE WORRIED ABOUT ME?
Thanks!
EIMI...
...WANIBUCHI IS WITH YOU NOW, RIGHT?

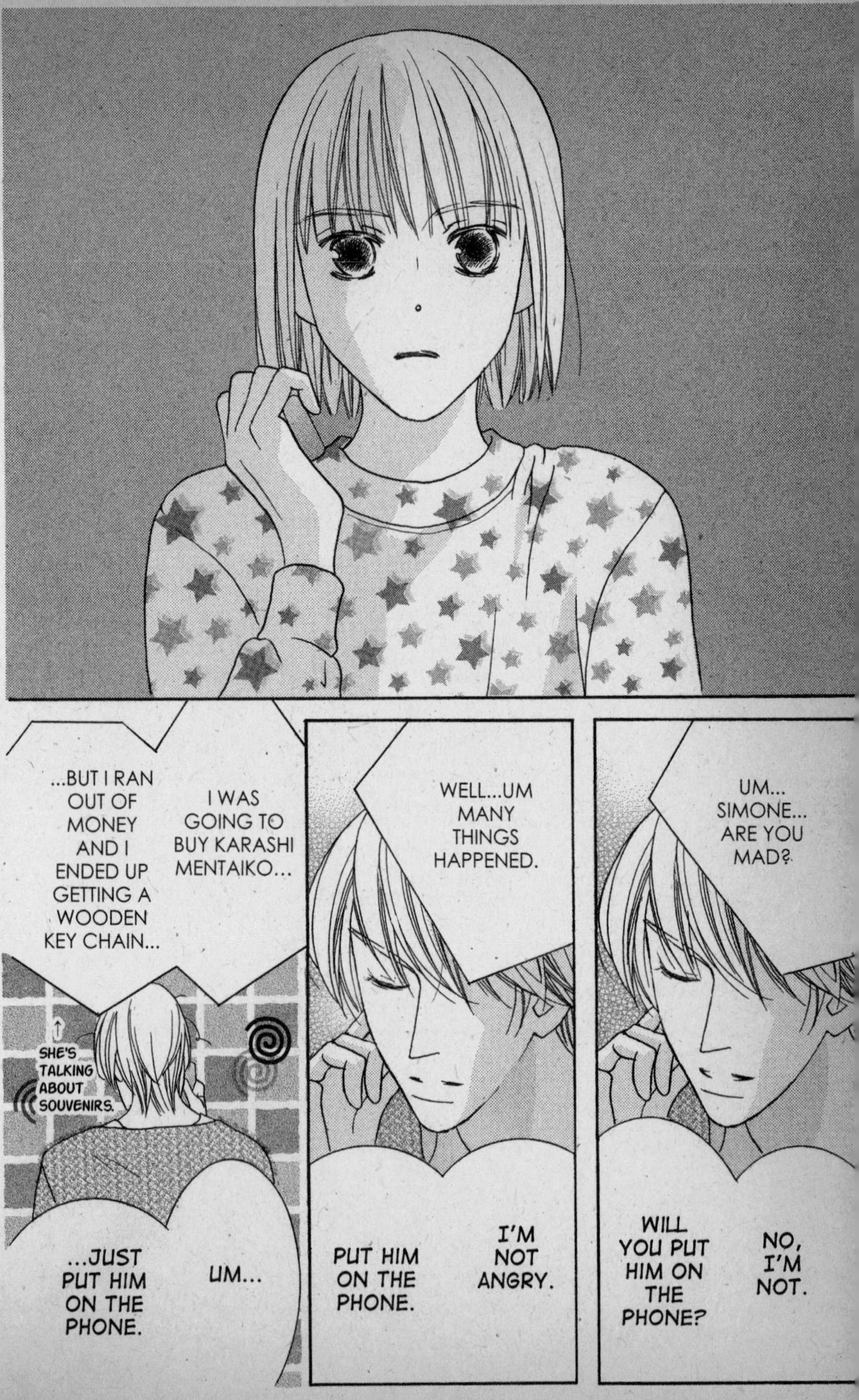
UM... SIMONE... ARE YOU MAD?
NO, I'M NOT.
WILL YOU PUT HIM ON THE PHONE?
WELL...UM MANY THINGS HAPPENED.
I'M NOT ANGRY.
PUT HIM ON THE PHONE.
I WAS GOING TO BUY KARASHI MENTAIKO...
...BUT I RAN OUT OF MONEY AND I ENDED UP GETTING A WOODEN KEY CHAIN...
SHE'S TALKING ABOUT SOUVENIRS.
UM...
...JUST PUT HIM ON THE PHONE.

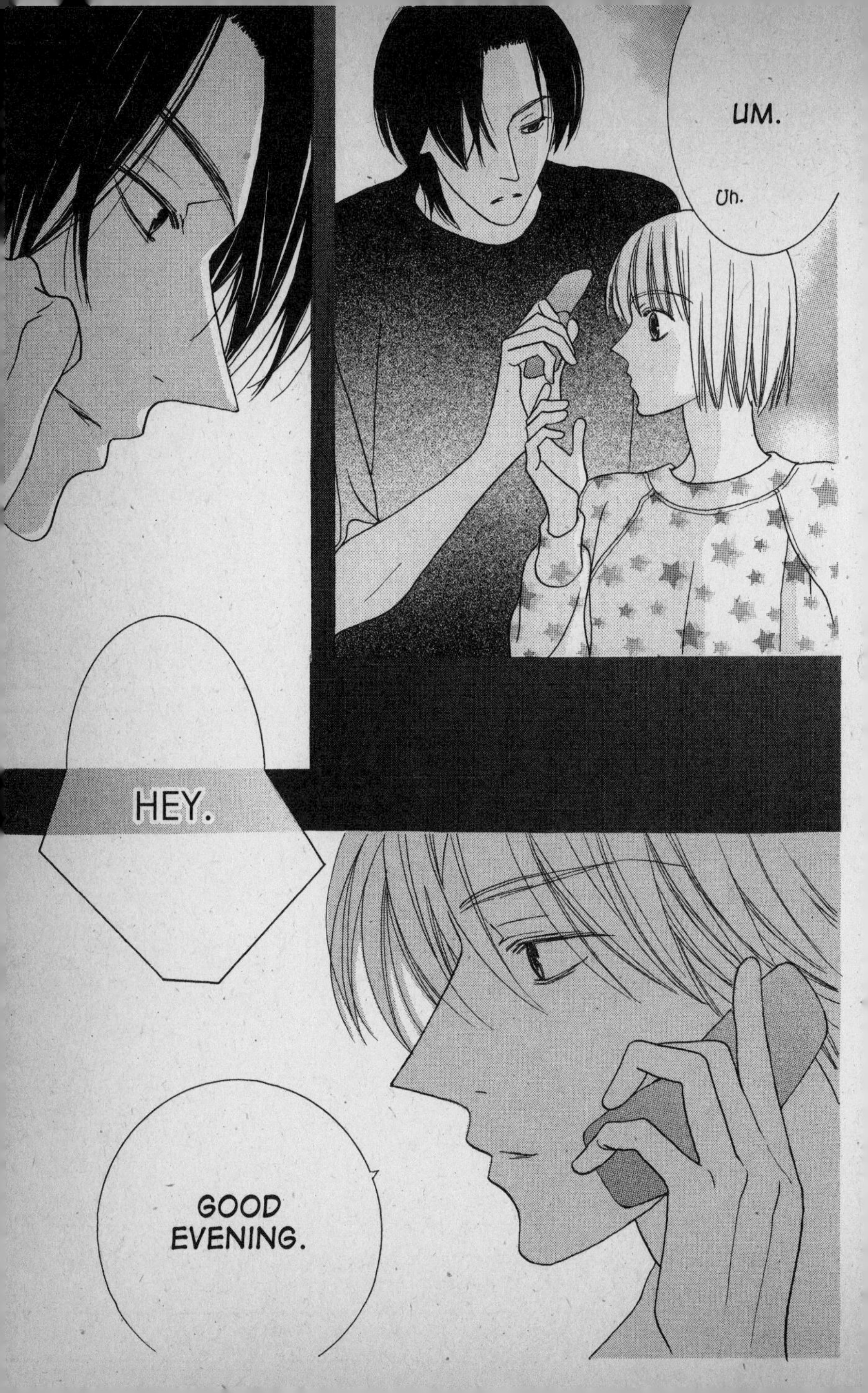
UM.
Uh.
HEY.
GOOD EVENING.

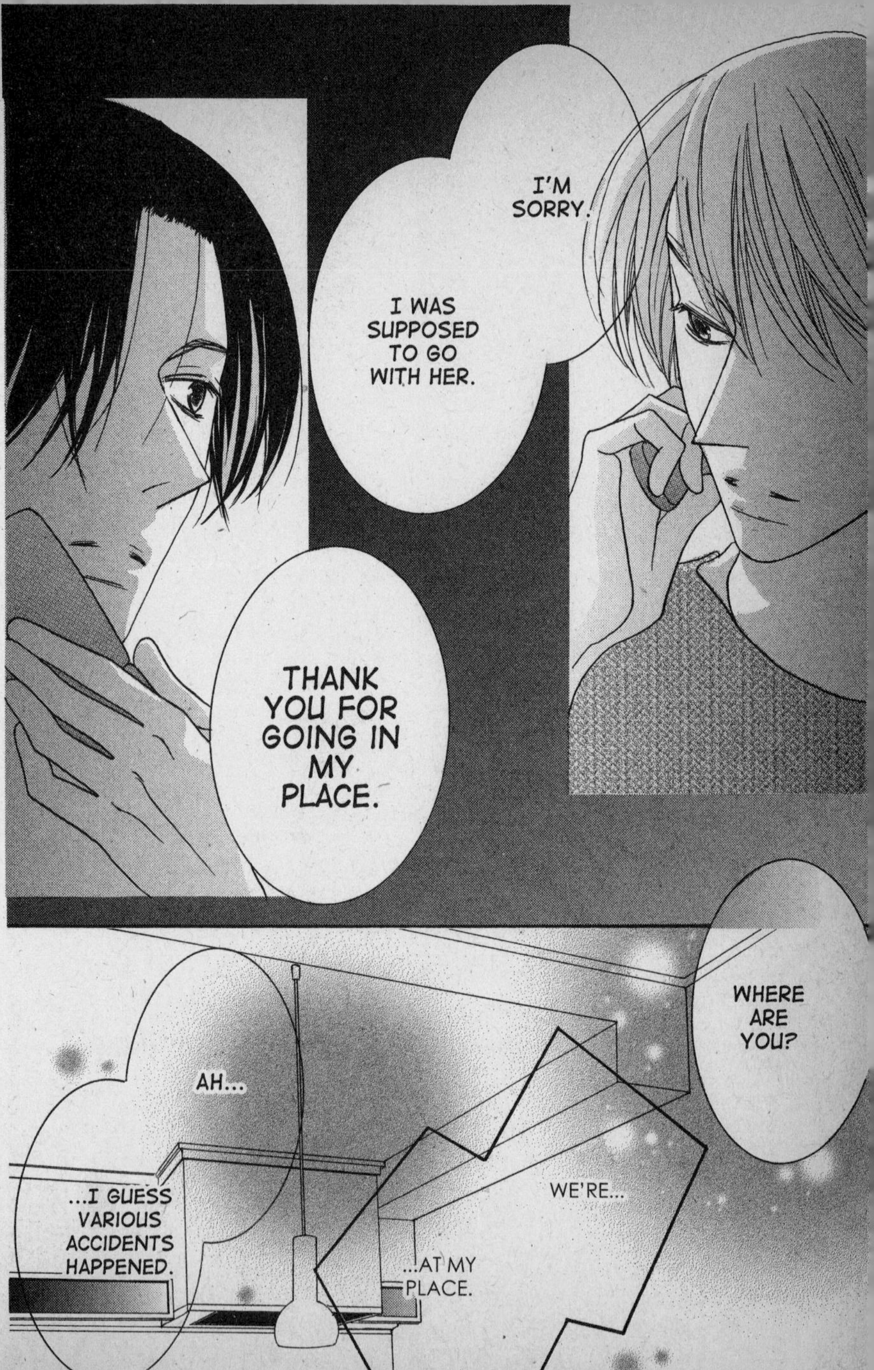
I'M SORRY.
I WAS SUPPOSED TO GO WITH HER.
THANK YOU FOR GOING IN MY PLACE.
WHERE ARE YOU?
WE'RE...
...AT MY PLACE.
AH...
...I GUESS VARIOUS ACCIDENTS HAPPENED.

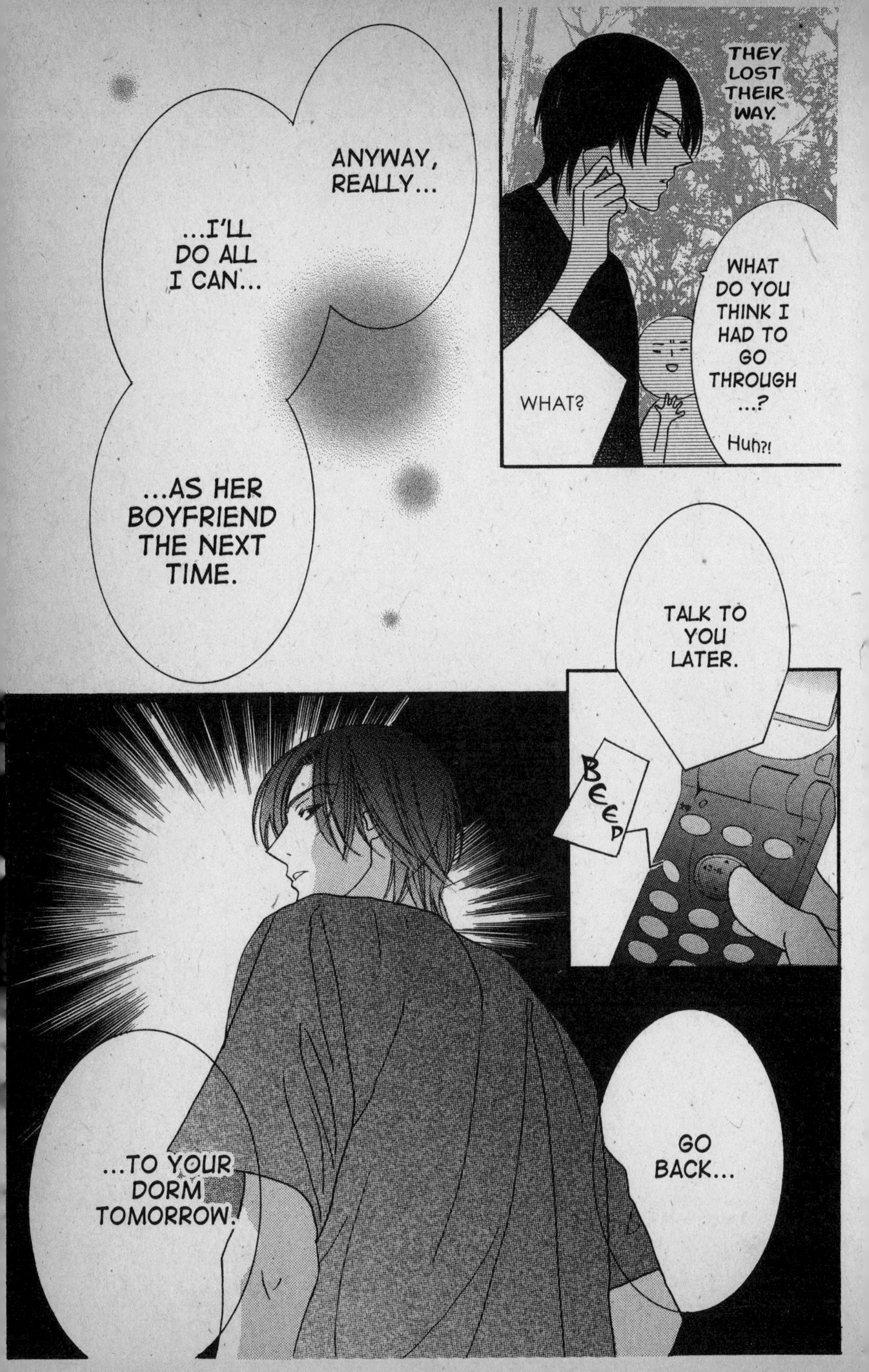
THEY LOST THEIR WAY.
WHAT DO YOU THINK I HAD TO GO THROUGH ...?
Huh?!
WHAT?
ANYWAY, REALLY...
...I'LL DO ALL I CAN...
...AS HER BOYFRIEND THE NEXT TIME.
TALK TO YOU LATER.
BEEP
GO BACK...
...TO YOUR DORM TOMORROW.

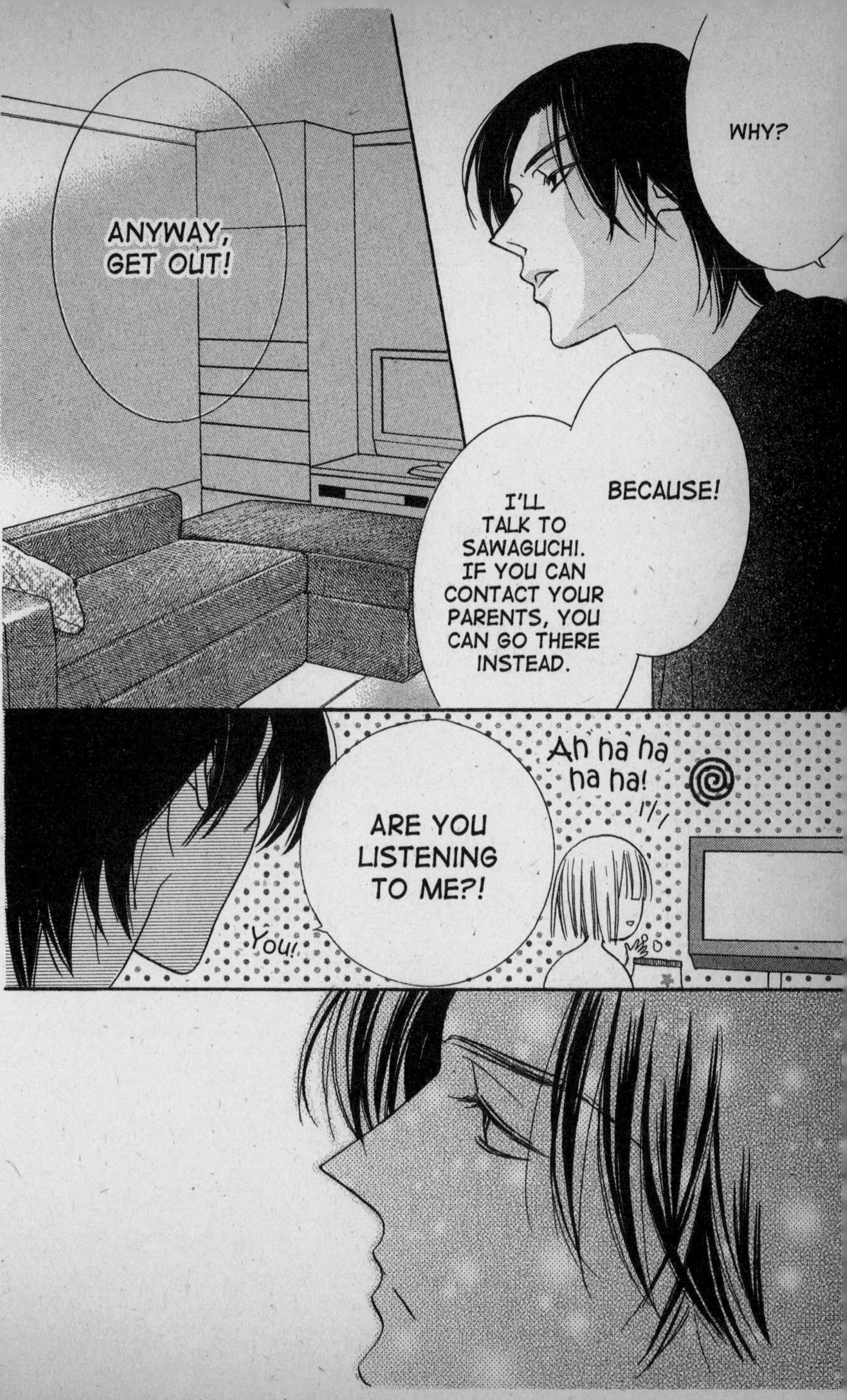
WHY?
BECAUSE!
I'LL TALK TO SAWAGUCHI. IF YOU CAN CONTACT YOUR PARENTS, YOU CAN GO THERE INSTEAD.
ANYWAY, GET OUT!
Ah ha ha ha ha!
ARE YOU LISTENING TO ME?!
You!

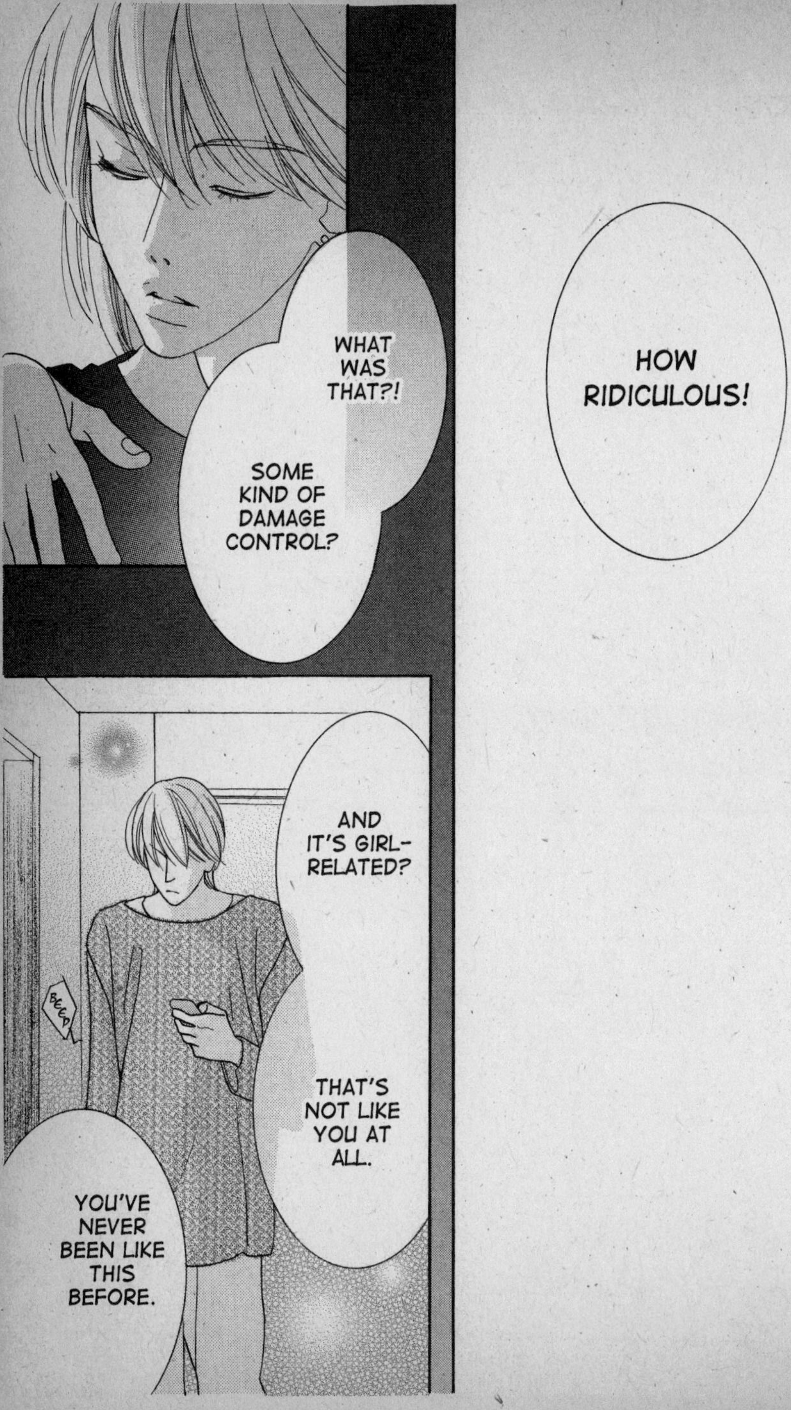
HOW RIDICULOUS!
WHAT WAS THAT?!
SOME KIND OF DAMAGE CONTROL?
AND IT'S GIRL-RELATED?
THAT'S NOT LIKE YOU AT ALL.
BEEP
YOU'VE NEVER BEEN LIKE THIS BEFORE.

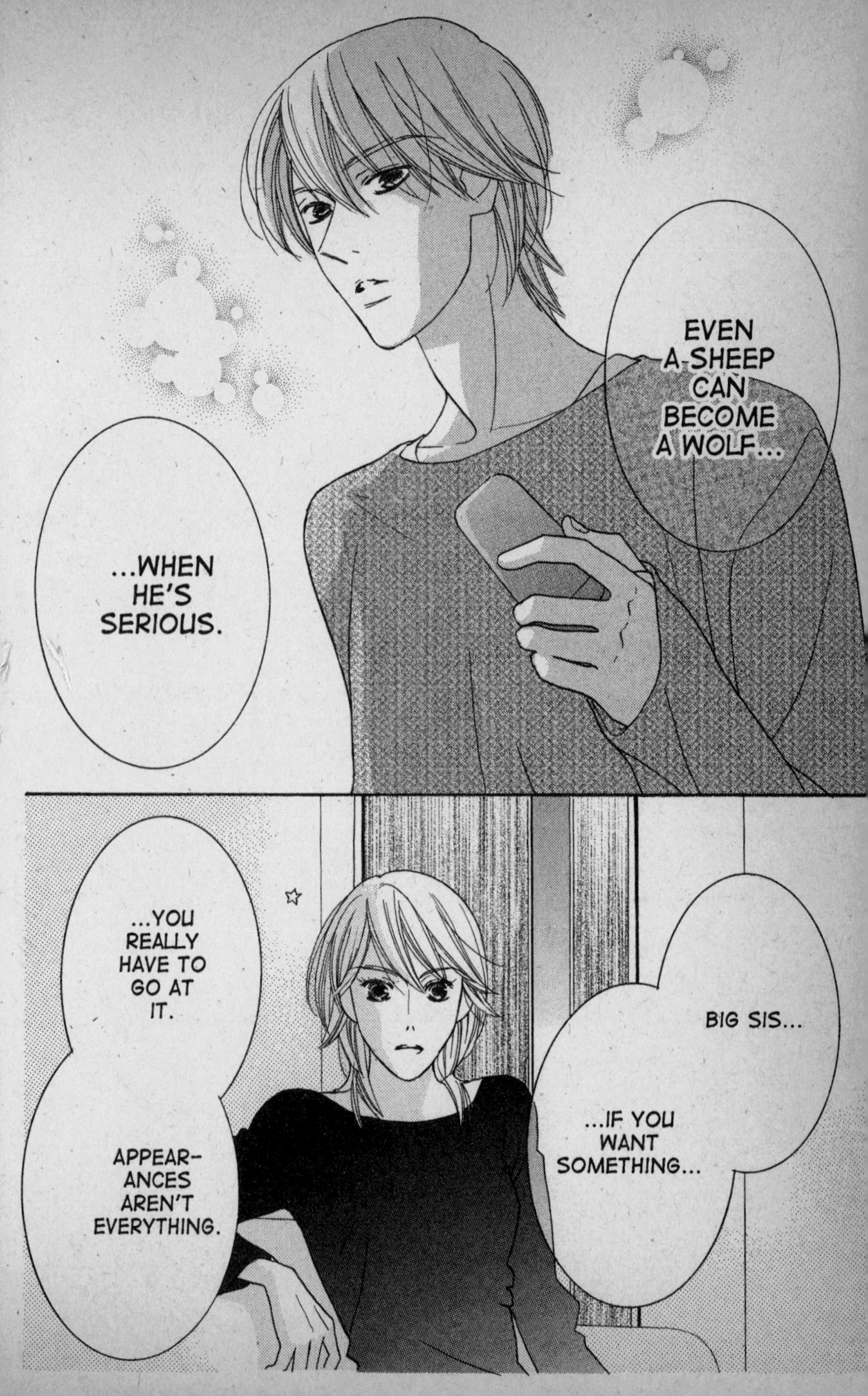
EVEN A SHEEP CAN BECOME A WOLF...
...WHEN HE'S SERIOUS.
BIG SIS...
...IF YOU WANT SOMETHING...
...YOU REALLY HAVE TO GO AT IT.
APPEAR-ANCES AREN'T EVERYTHING.

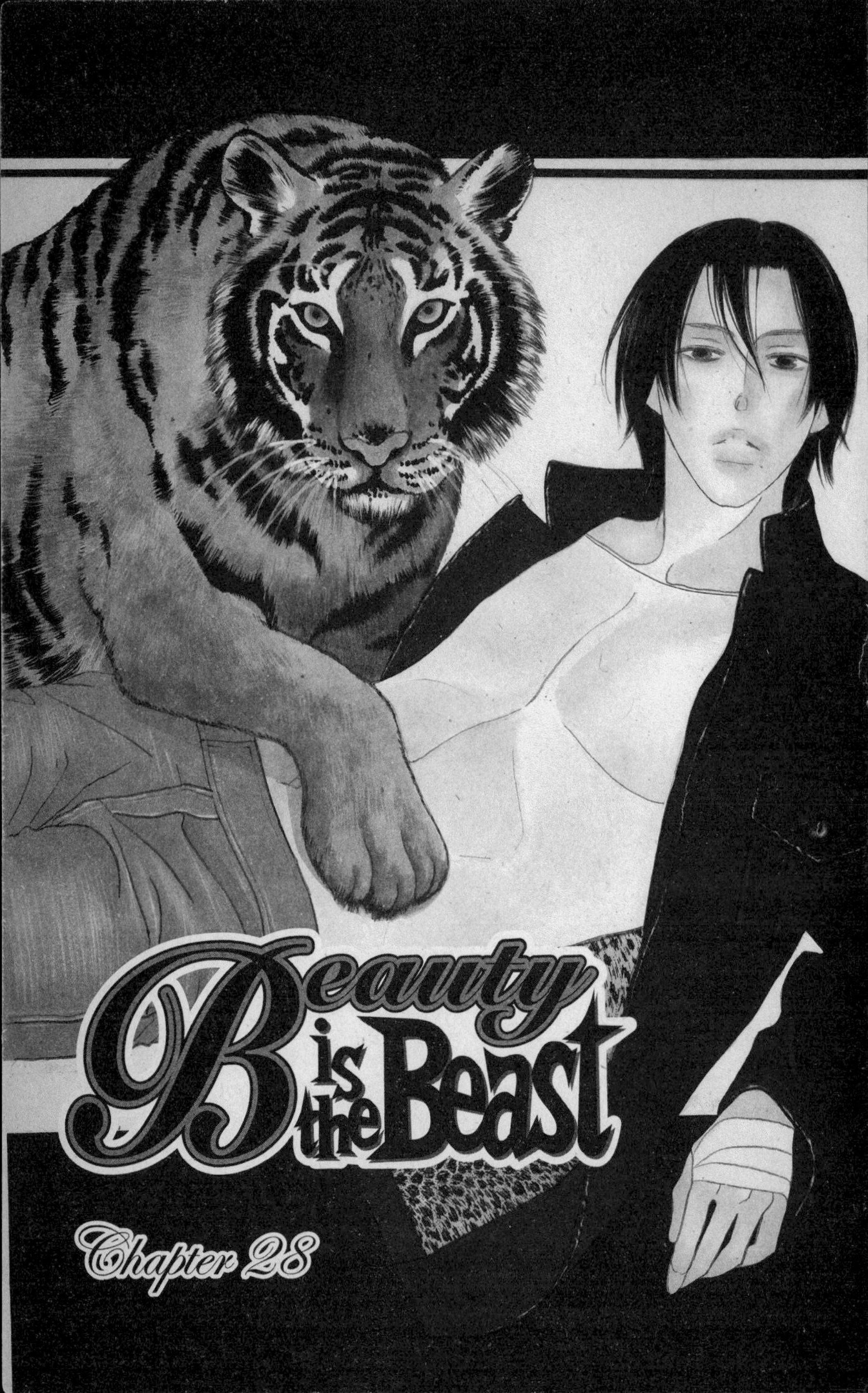
Beauty is the Beast
Chapter 28

My name is Kei Akase.

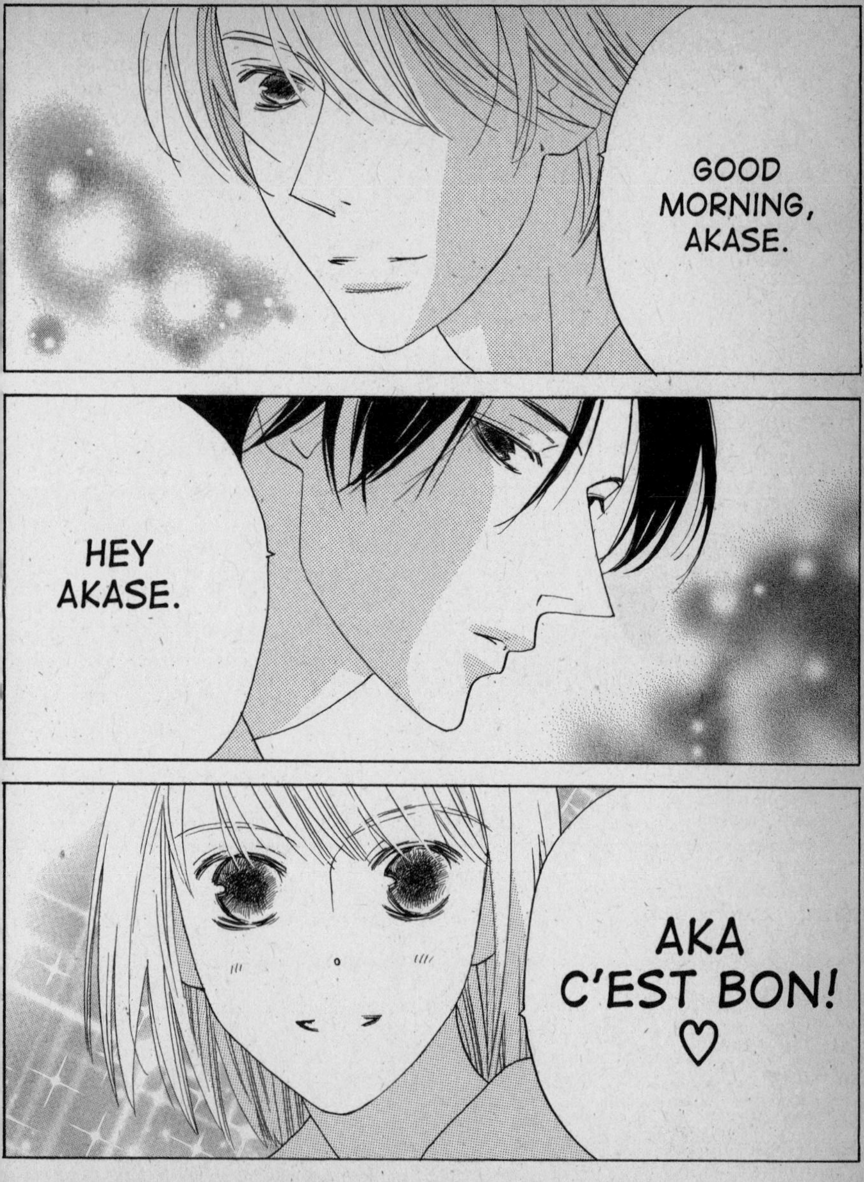
GOOD MORNING, AKASE.
HEY AKASE.
AKA C'EST BON! ♡

Her skill is not being called by nicknames. (except by Eimi).

⬅ Continued on Page 156.

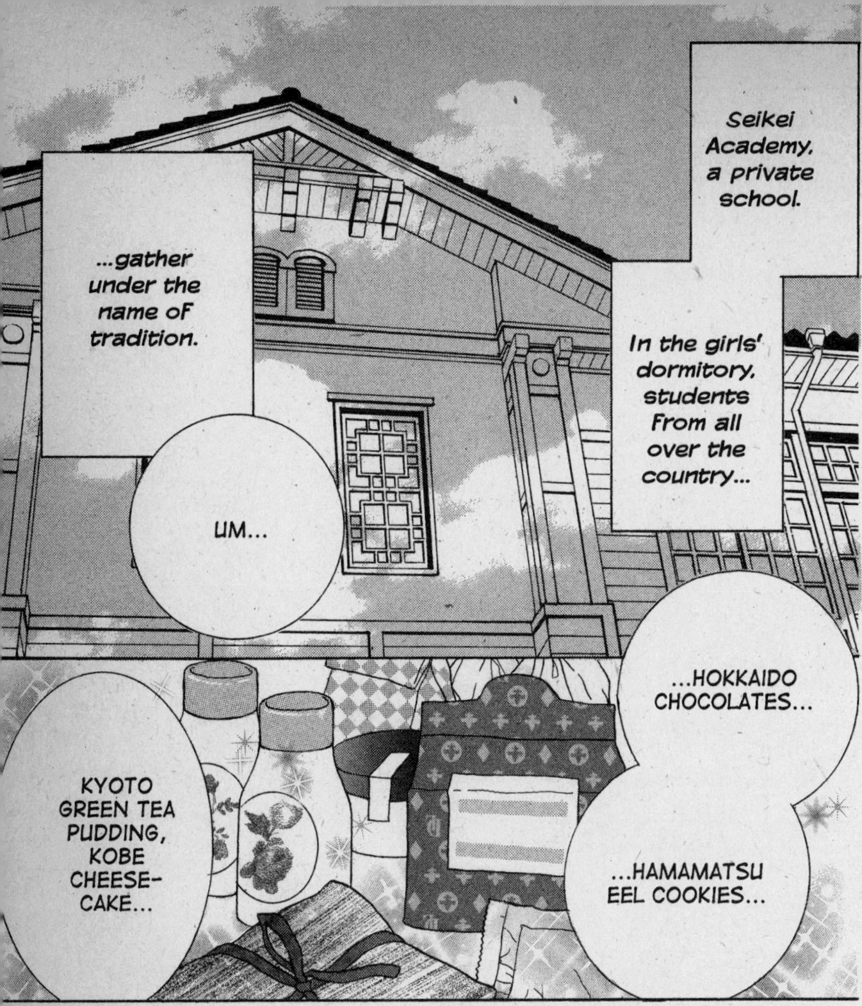
Seikei Academy, a private school.
In the girls' dormitory, students from all over the country...
...gather under the name of tradition.
UM...
...HOKKAIDO CHOCOLATES...
...HAMAMATSU EEL COOKIES...
KYOTO GREEN TEA PUDDING, KOBE CHEESE-CAKE...

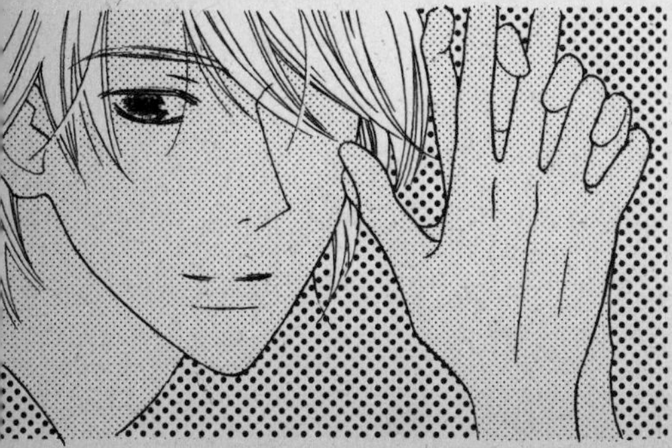

Shimonuki

After graduating from Tokyo University, he started working for a national newspaper. He is going full speed on the fast track. He is popular with women, but is not quite satisfied. He is still friends with Eimi. In a sense, his life is unhappy. He is carrying a lot of baggage from his past.

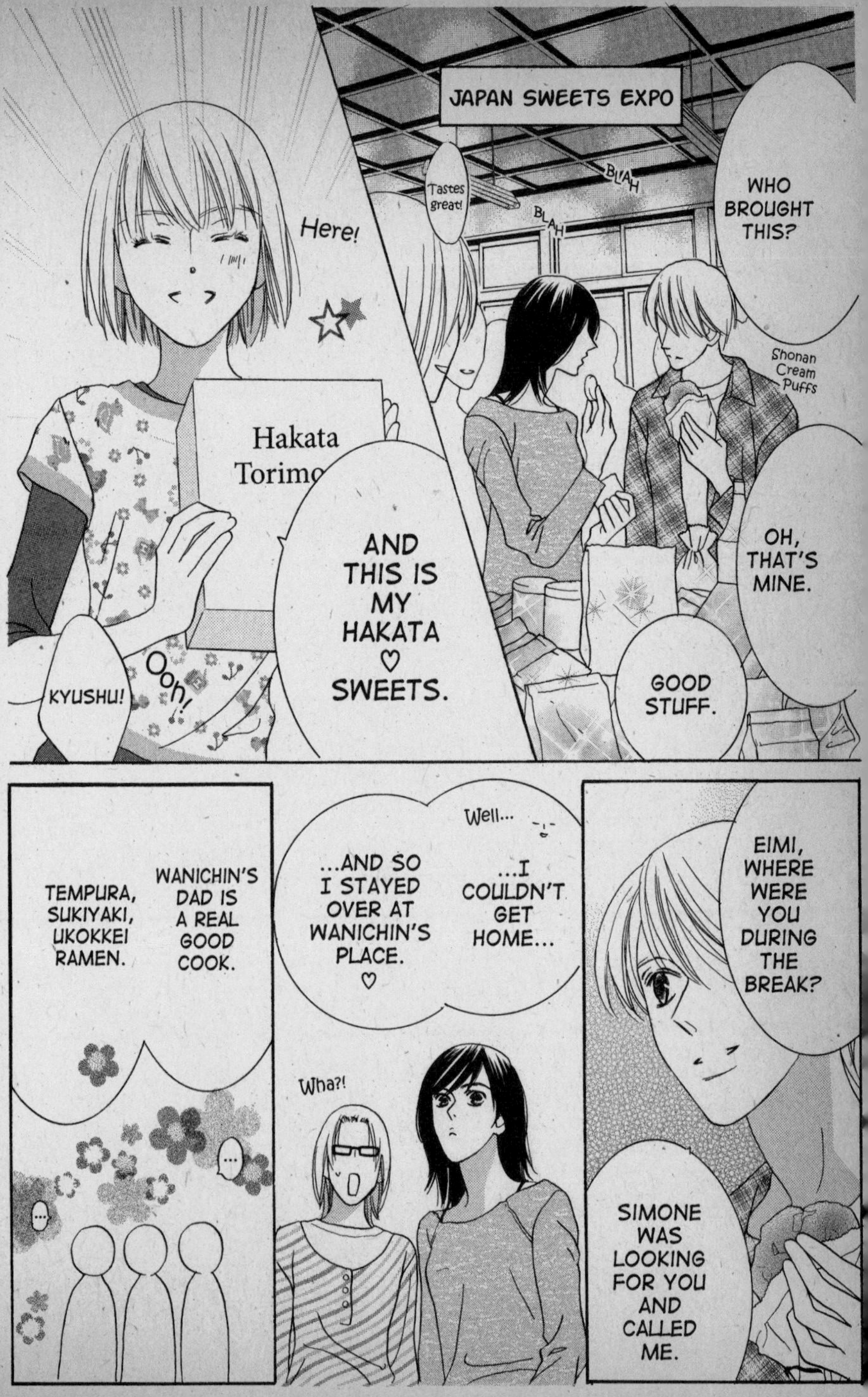
JAPAN SWEETS EXPO
WHO BROUGHT THIS?
Tastes great!
BLAH
BLAH
Shonan Cream Puffs
OH, THAT'S MINE.
GOOD STUFF.
Here!
Hakata Torimo
AND THIS IS MY HAKATA ♡ SWEETS.
Ooh!
KYUSHU!
EIMI, WHERE WERE YOU DURING THE BREAK?
SIMONE WAS LOOKING FOR YOU AND CALLED ME.
Well...
...I COULDN'T GET HOME...
...AND SO I STAYED OVER AT WANICHIN'S PLACE. ♡
Wha?!
WANICHIN'S DAD IS A REAL GOOD COOK.
TEMPURA, SUKIYAKI, UKOKKEI RAMEN.
...
...

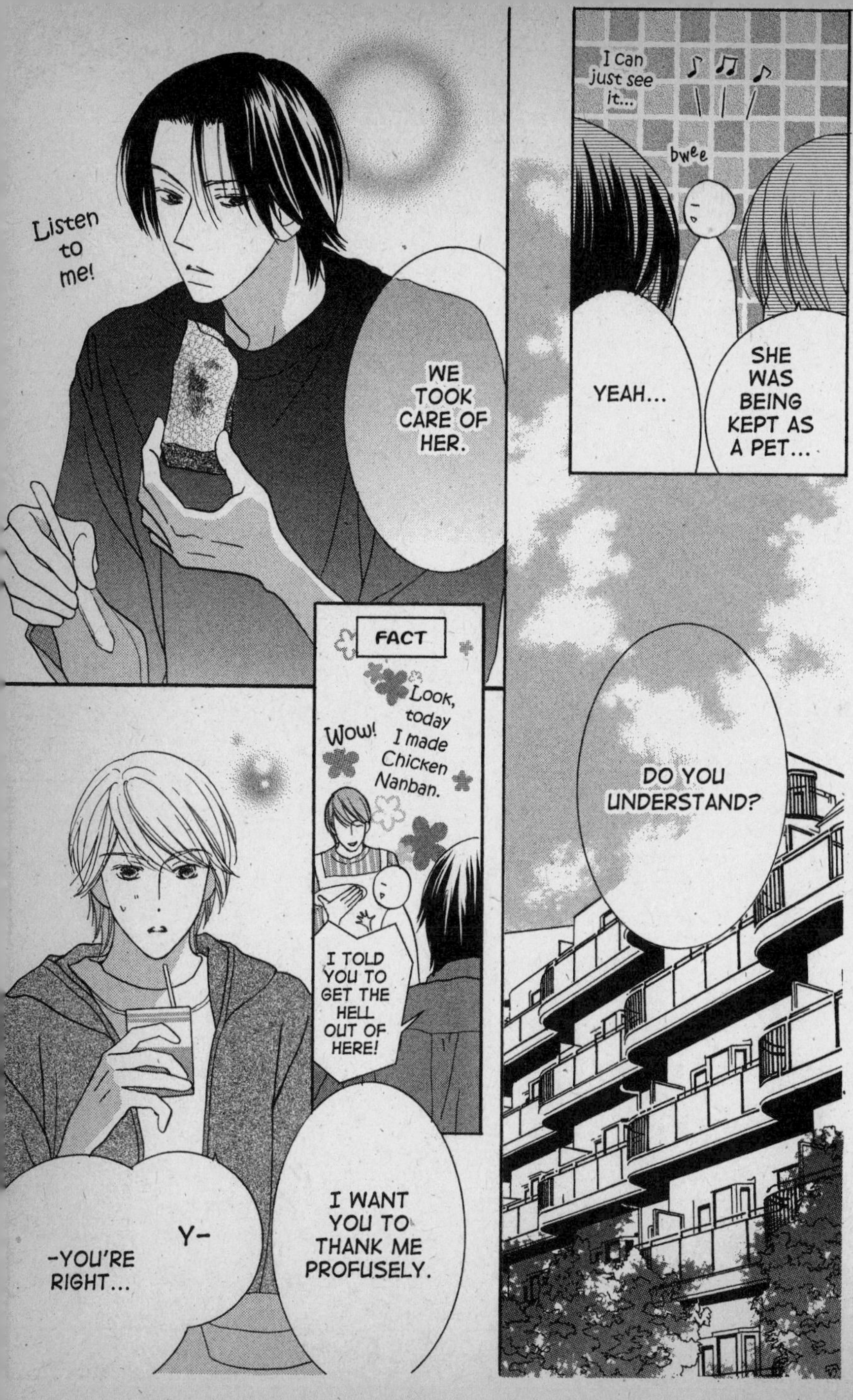
I can just see it...
bwee
SHE WAS BEING KEPT AS A PET...
YEAH...
WE TOOK CARE OF HER.
Listen to me!
DO YOU UNDERSTAND?
FACT
Look, today I made Chicken Nanban.
Wow!
I TOLD YOU TO GET THE HELL OUT OF HERE!
I WANT YOU TO THANK ME PROFUSELY.
Y-
-YOU'RE RIGHT...

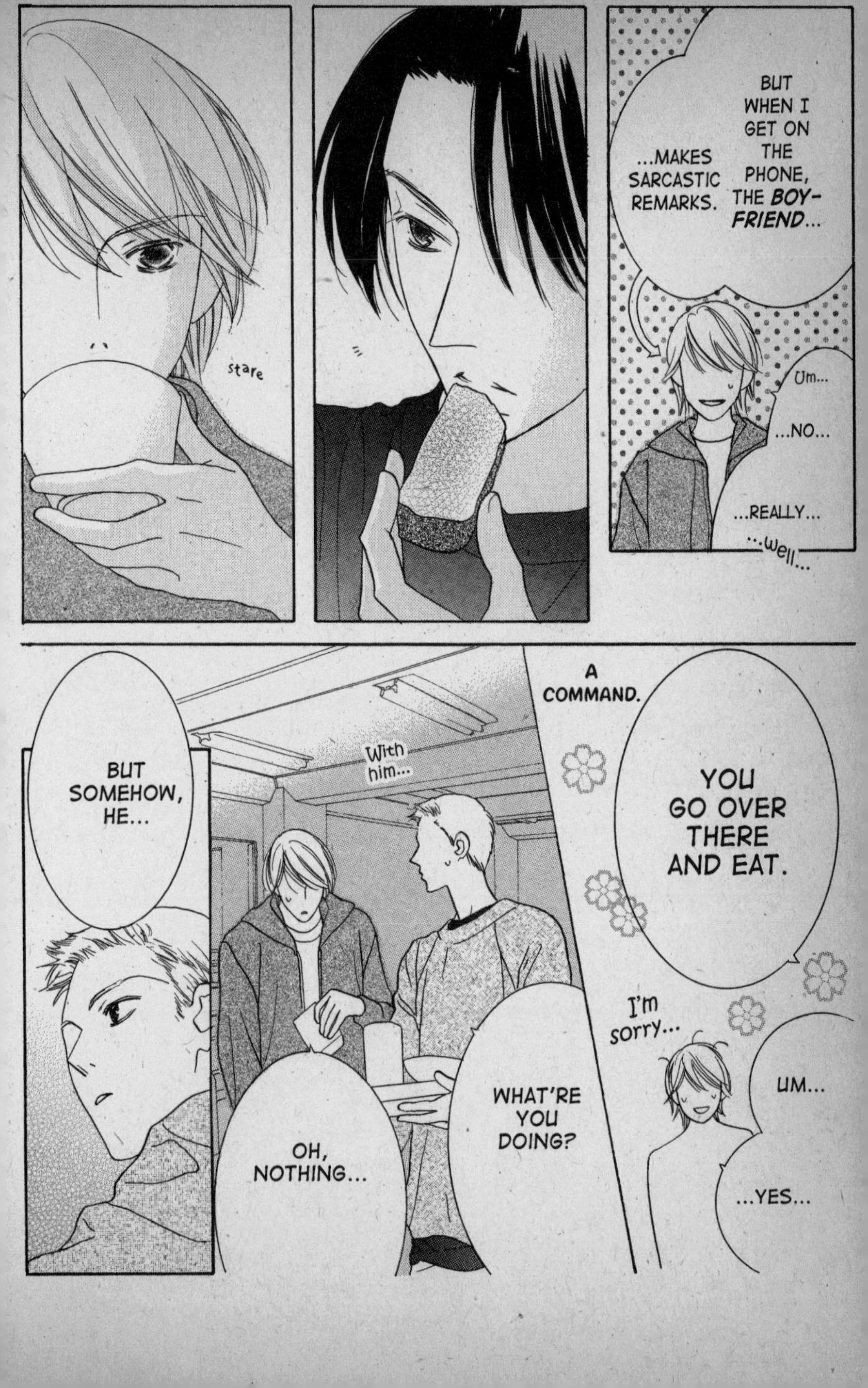
BUT WHEN I GET ON THE PHONE, THE *BOY-FRIEND*...
...MAKES SARCASTIC REMARKS.
Um...
...NO...
...REALLY...
...well...
stare
A COMMAND.
YOU GO OVER THERE AND EAT.
I'm sorry...
UM...
...YES...
BUT SOMEHOW, HE...
With him...
WHAT'RE YOU DOING?
OH, NOTHING...

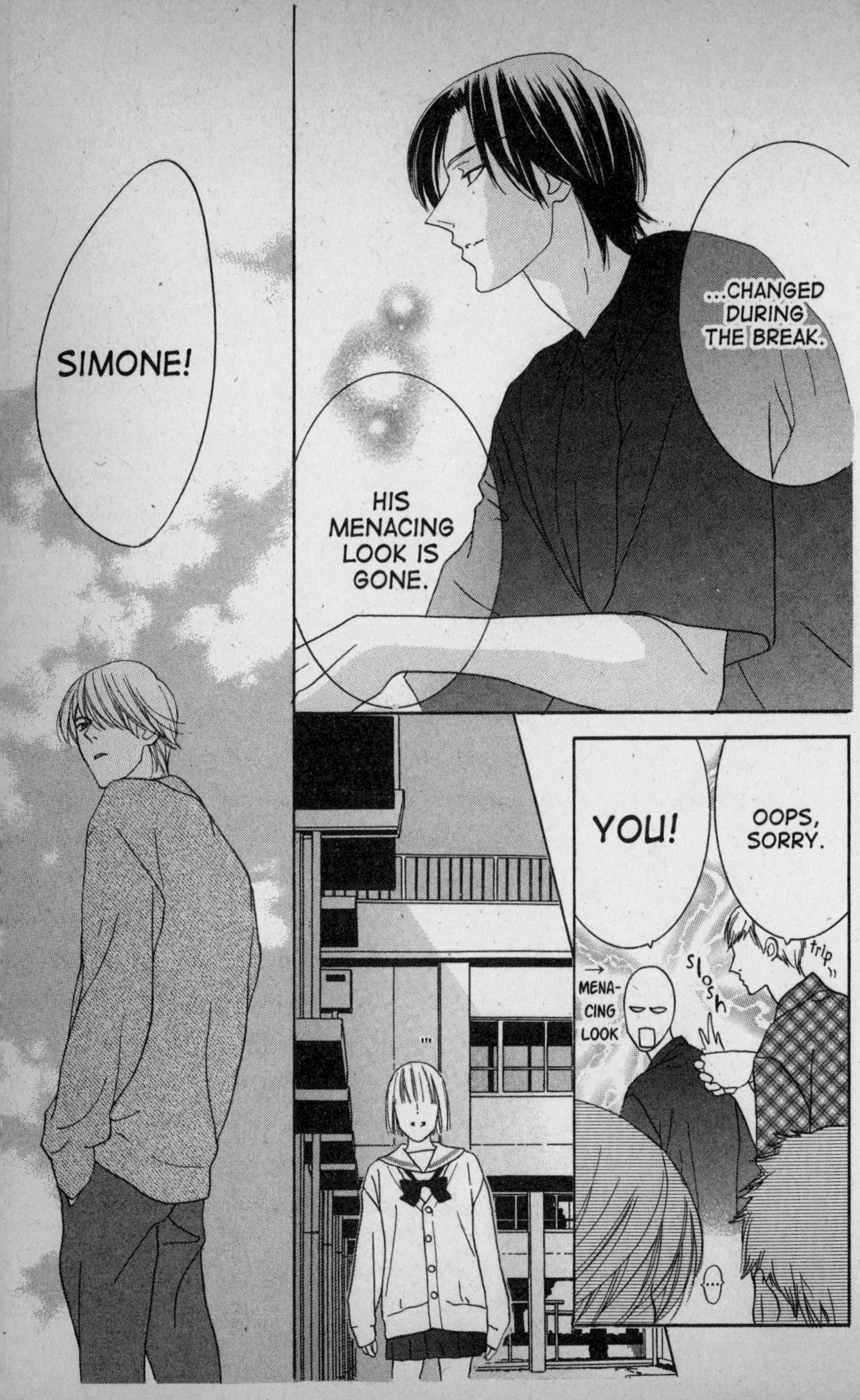
...CHANGED DURING THE BREAK.
HIS MENACING LOOK IS GONE.
OOPS, SORRY.
YOU!
trip
slosh
MENA-CING LOOK
SIMONE!

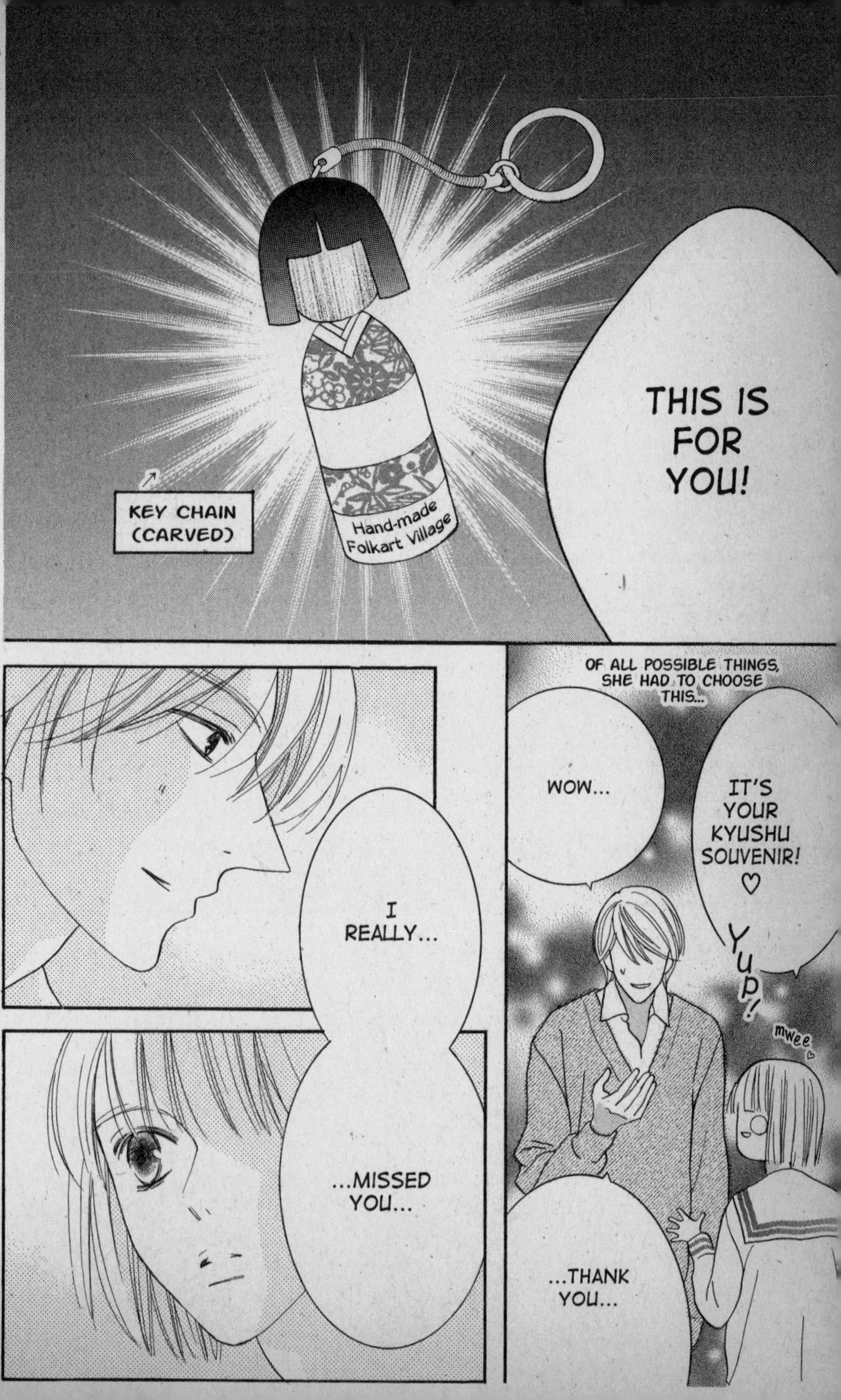
THIS IS FOR YOU!
KEY CHAIN (CARVED)
Hand-made Folkart Village
OF ALL POSSIBLE THINGS, SHE HAD TO CHOOSE THIS...
IT'S YOUR KYUSHU SOUVENIR! ♡
WOW...
Yup!
mwee ♡
...THANK YOU...
I REALLY...
...MISSED YOU...

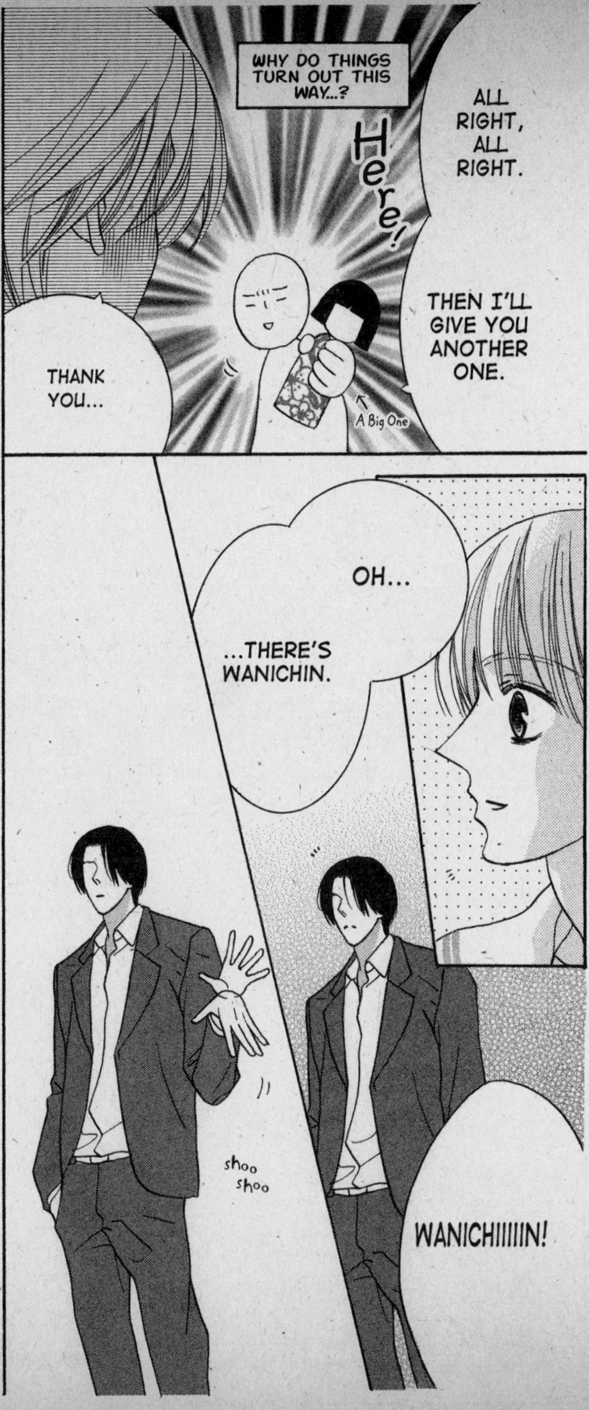
WHY DO THINGS TURN OUT THIS WAY...?
ALL RIGHT, ALL RIGHT.
Here!
THEN I'LL GIVE YOU ANOTHER ONE.
A Big One
THANK YOU...
OH...
...THERE'S WANICHIN.
WANICHIIIIIN!
shoo shoo

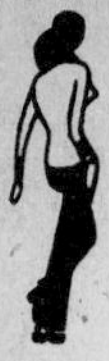

⑤

In the previous volume, I used the lyrics for "A Natural Woman" but there was an error*. It said "You make me fell..." but it should be "feel."

By the way, fell is the past tense of the verb fall, so then the meaning becomes fall or sink or weaken...what are you going to do by weakening!!! I-I'm sorry.

It was a serious love story, so it's even more laugh-able. Excuse me.

*Corrected for the English version.

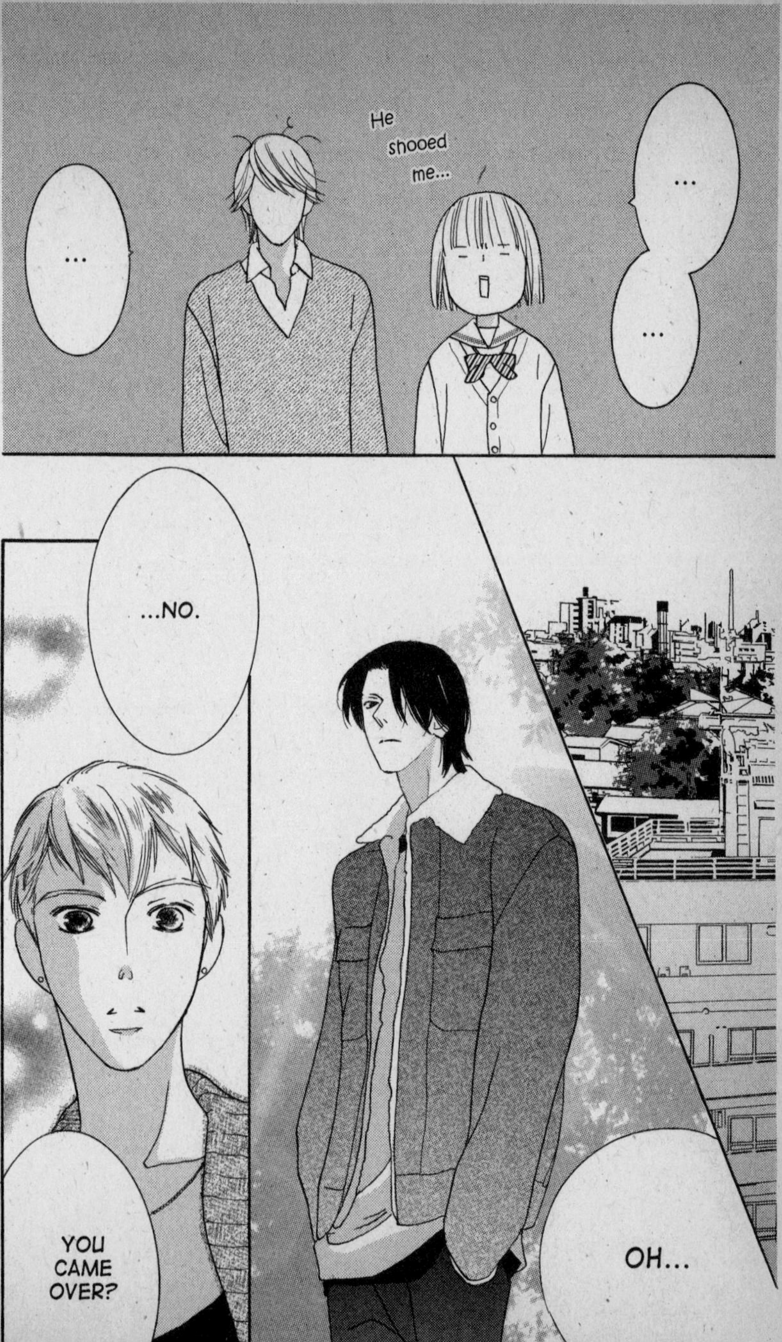
...
...
He shooed me...
...
...NO.
OH...
YOU CAME OVER?

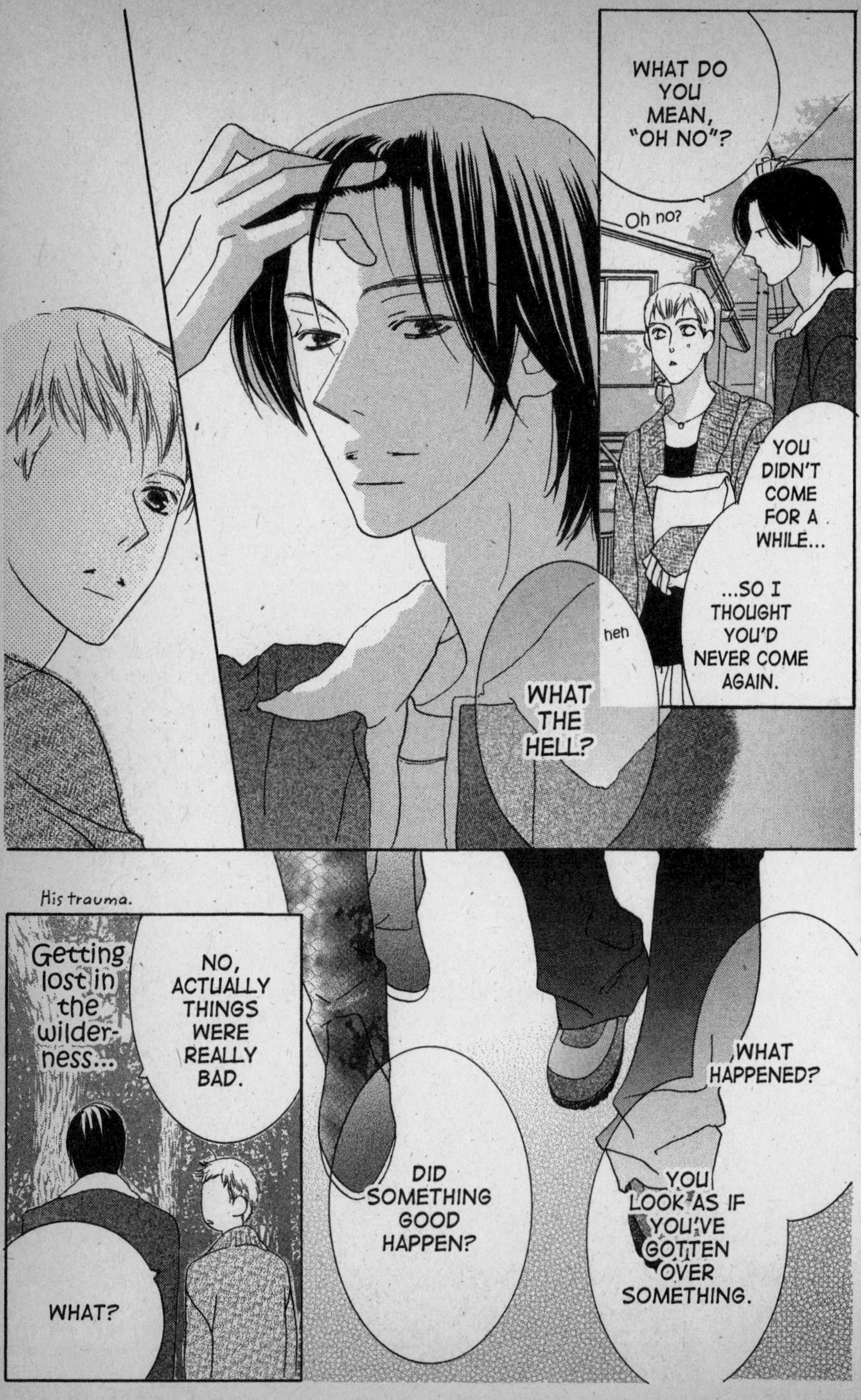
WHAT DO YOU MEAN, "OH NO"?
Oh no?
YOU DIDN'T COME FOR A WHILE...
...SO I THOUGHT YOU'D NEVER COME AGAIN.
heh
WHAT THE HELL?
WHAT HAPPENED?
YOU LOOK AS IF YOU'VE GOTTEN OVER SOMETHING.
DID SOMETHING GOOD HAPPEN?
His trauma.
NO, ACTUALLY THINGS WERE REALLY BAD.
Getting lost in the wilderness...
WHAT?

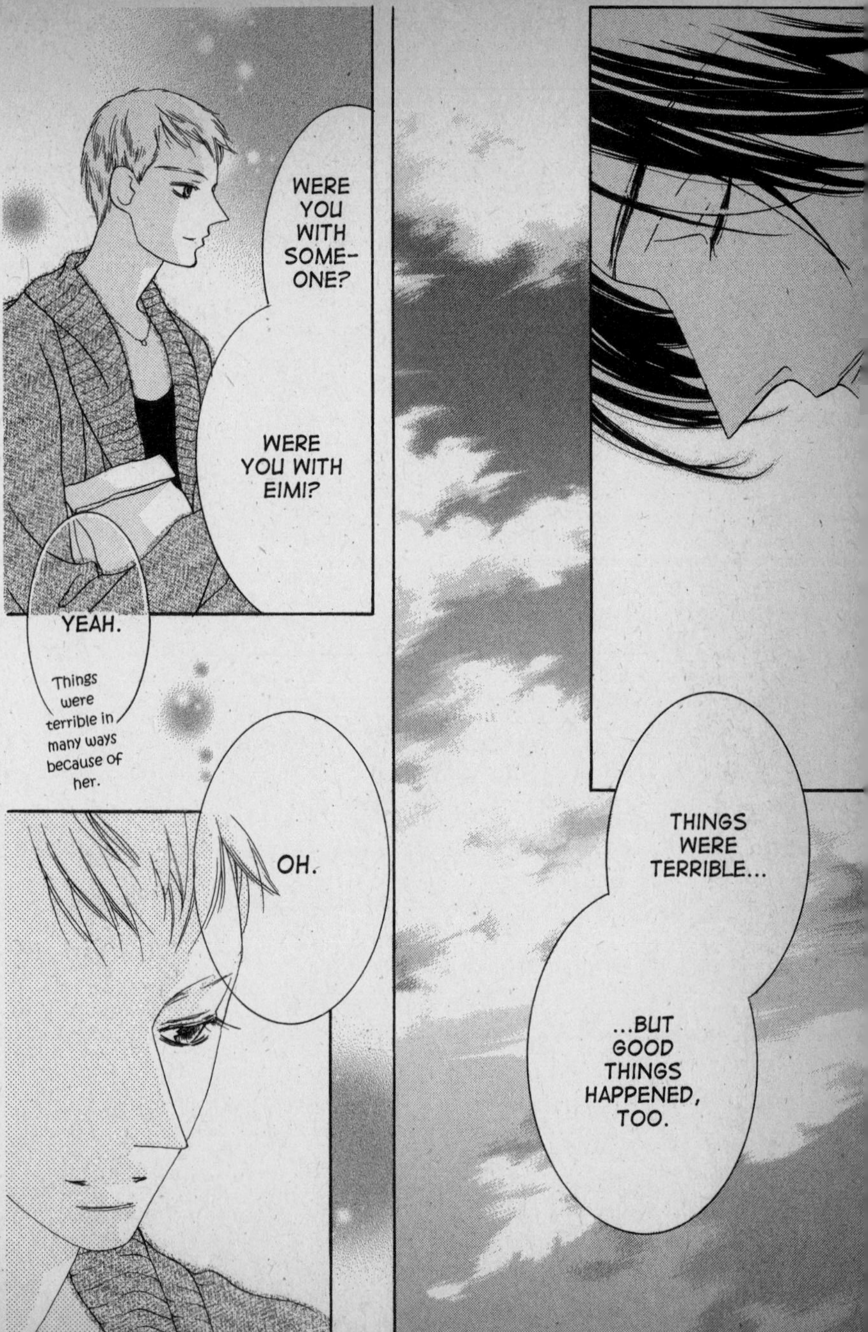
THINGS WERE TERRIBLE...
...BUT GOOD THINGS HAPPENED, TOO.
WERE YOU WITH SOMEONE?
WERE YOU WITH EIMI?
YEAH.
Things were terrible in many ways because of her.
OH.

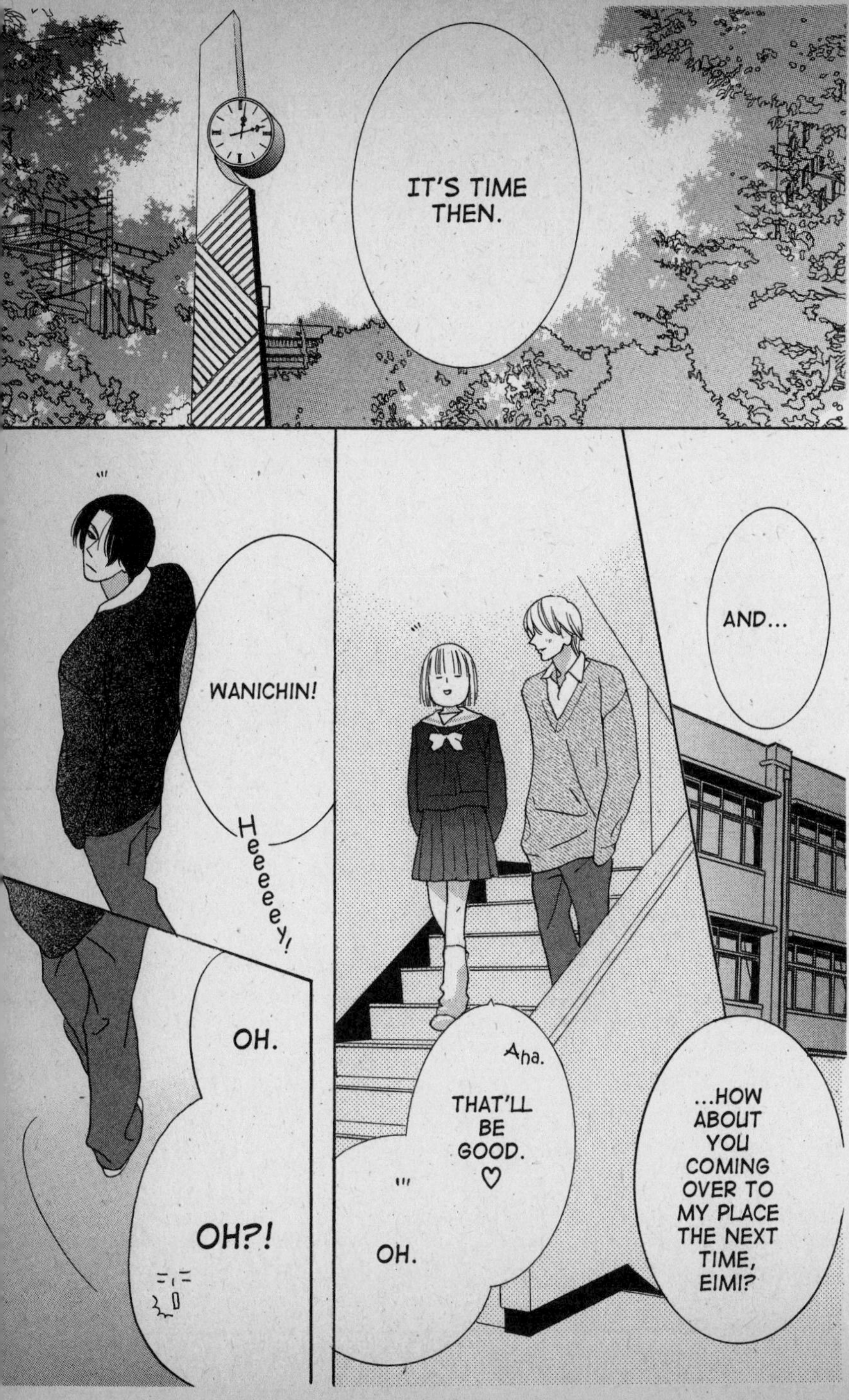
IT'S TIME THEN.
AND...
...HOW ABOUT YOU COMING OVER TO MY PLACE THE NEXT TIME, EIMI?
Aha.
THAT'LL BE GOOD. ♡
OH.
WANICHIN!
Heeeeey!
OH.
OH?!

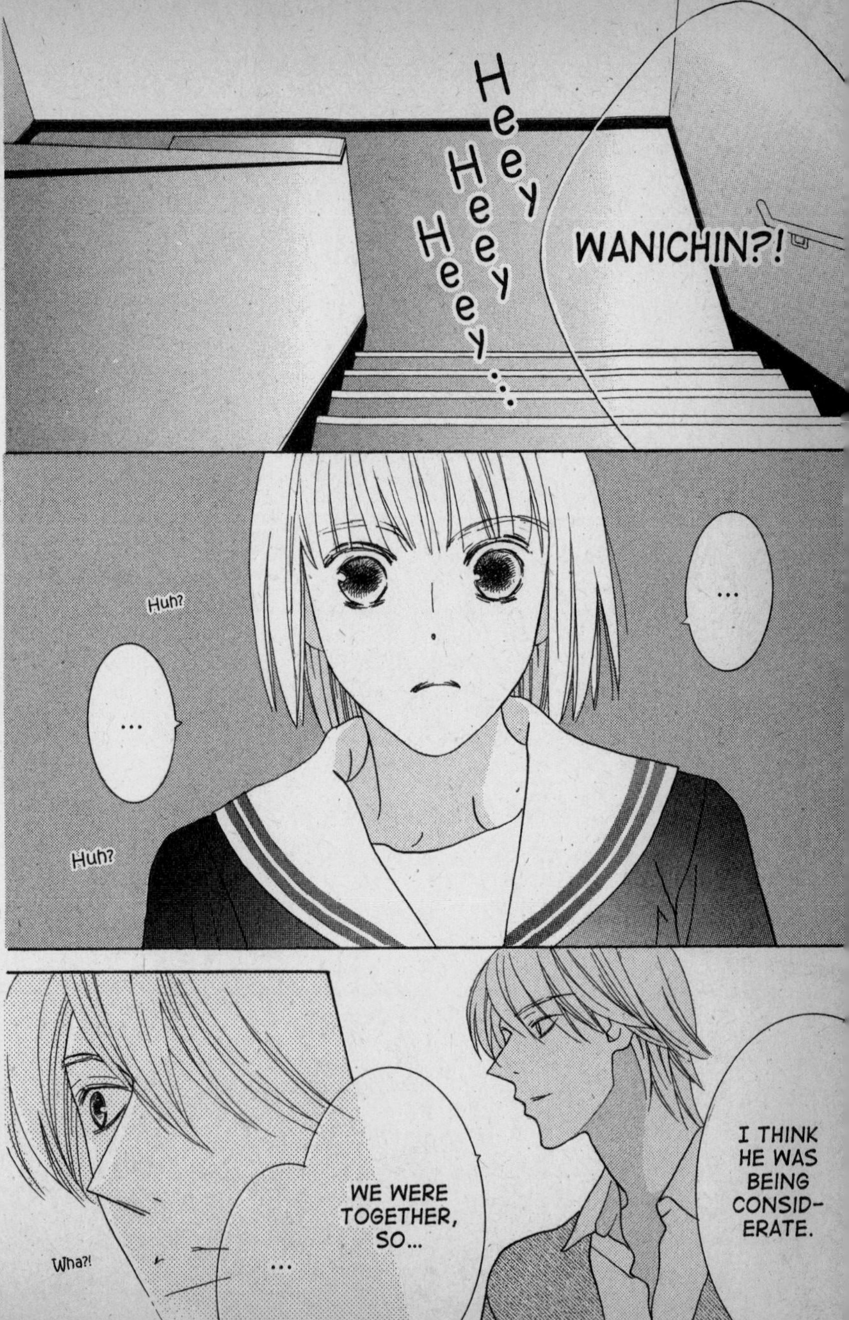
WANICHIN?!
Heey
Heey
Heey...
...
Huh?
...
Huh?
I THINK HE WAS BEING CONSIDERATE.
WE WERE TOGETHER, SO...
...
Wha?!

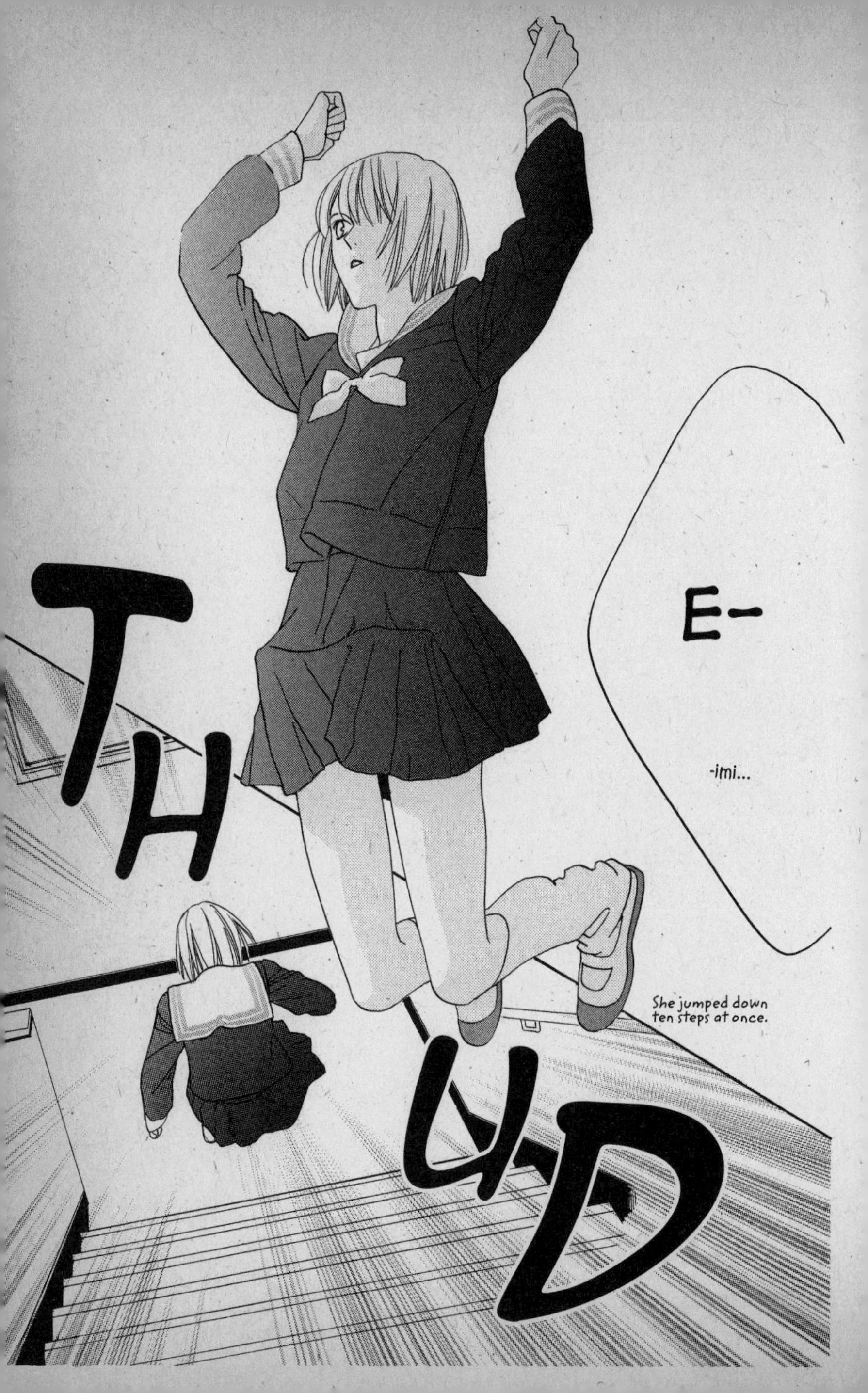
E-
-imi...
THUD
She jumped down ten steps at once.

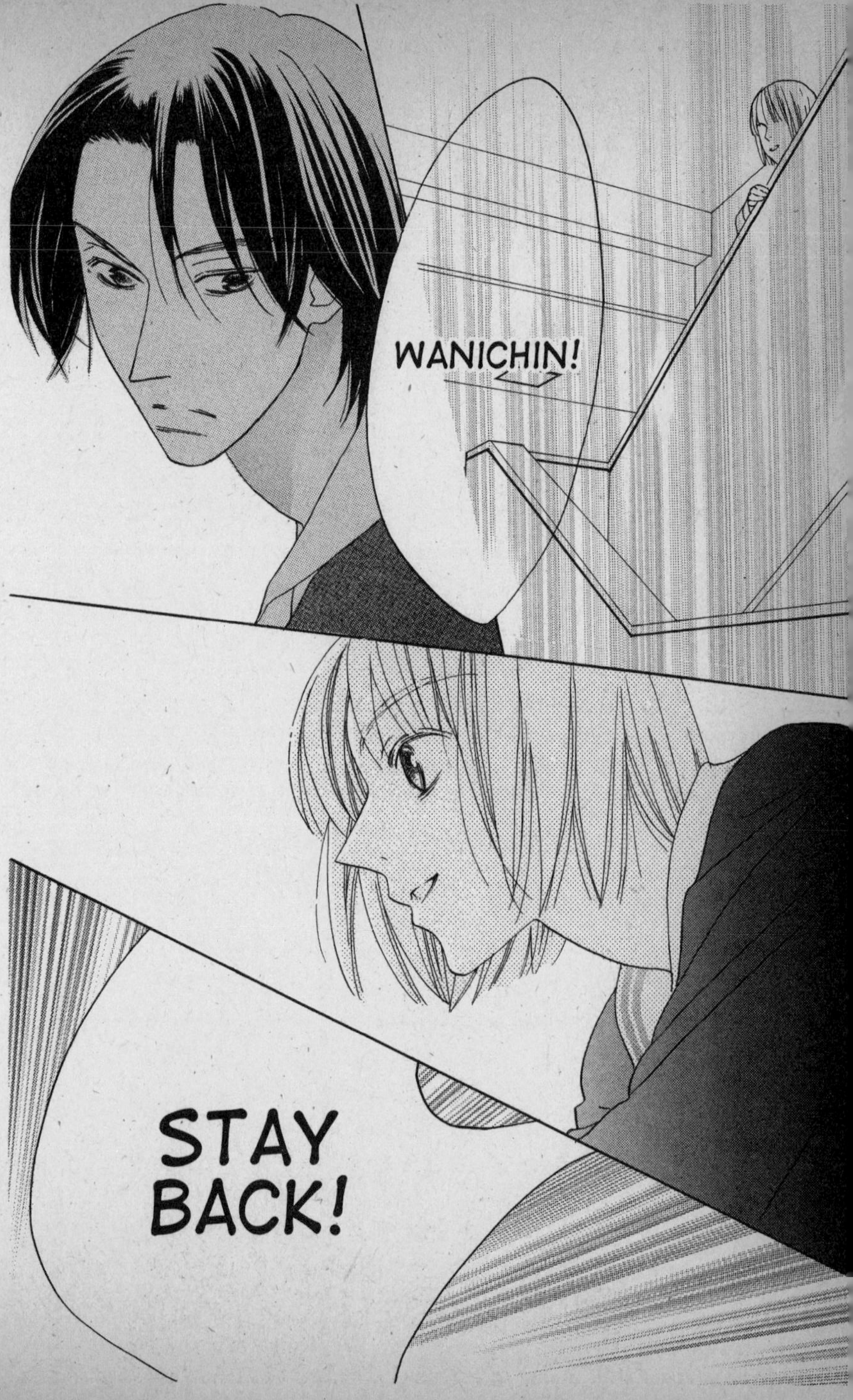
WANICHIN!
STAY BACK!

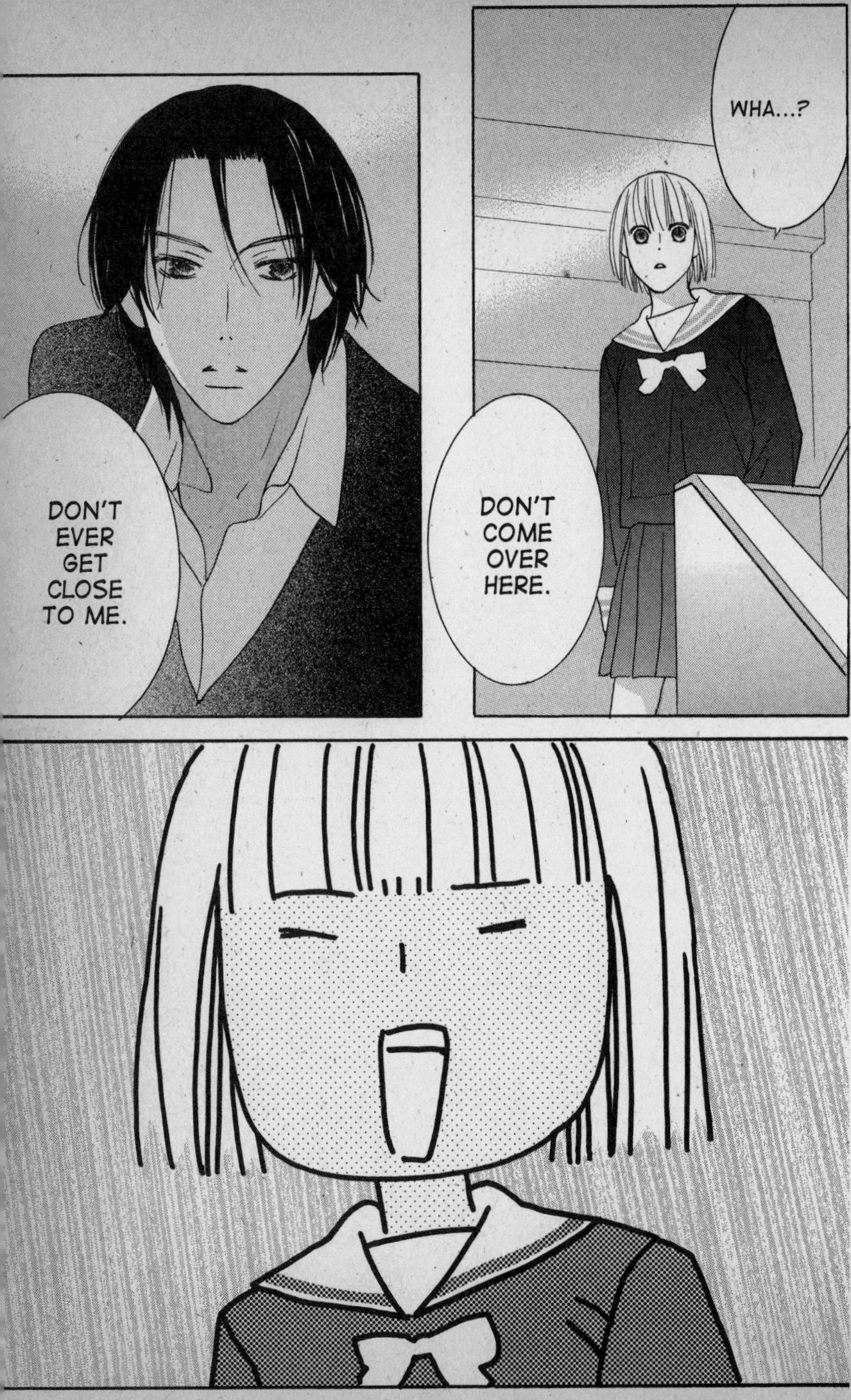
WHA...?
DON'T COME OVER HERE.
DON'T EVER GET CLOSE TO ME.

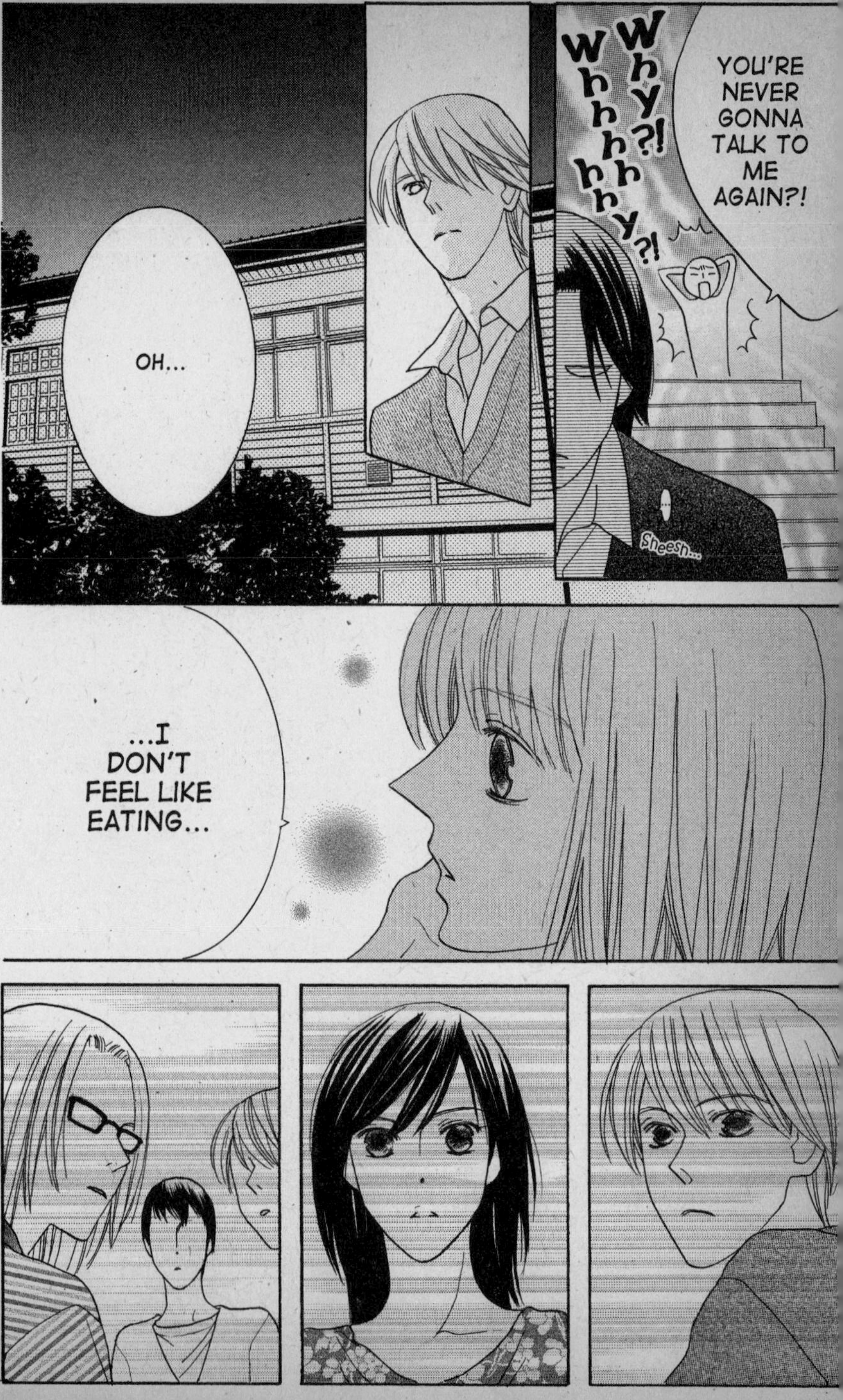
YOU'RE NEVER GONNA TALK TO ME AGAIN?!
Why?!
Whhhhhhy?!
...
Sheesh...
OH...
...I DON'T FEEL LIKE EATING...

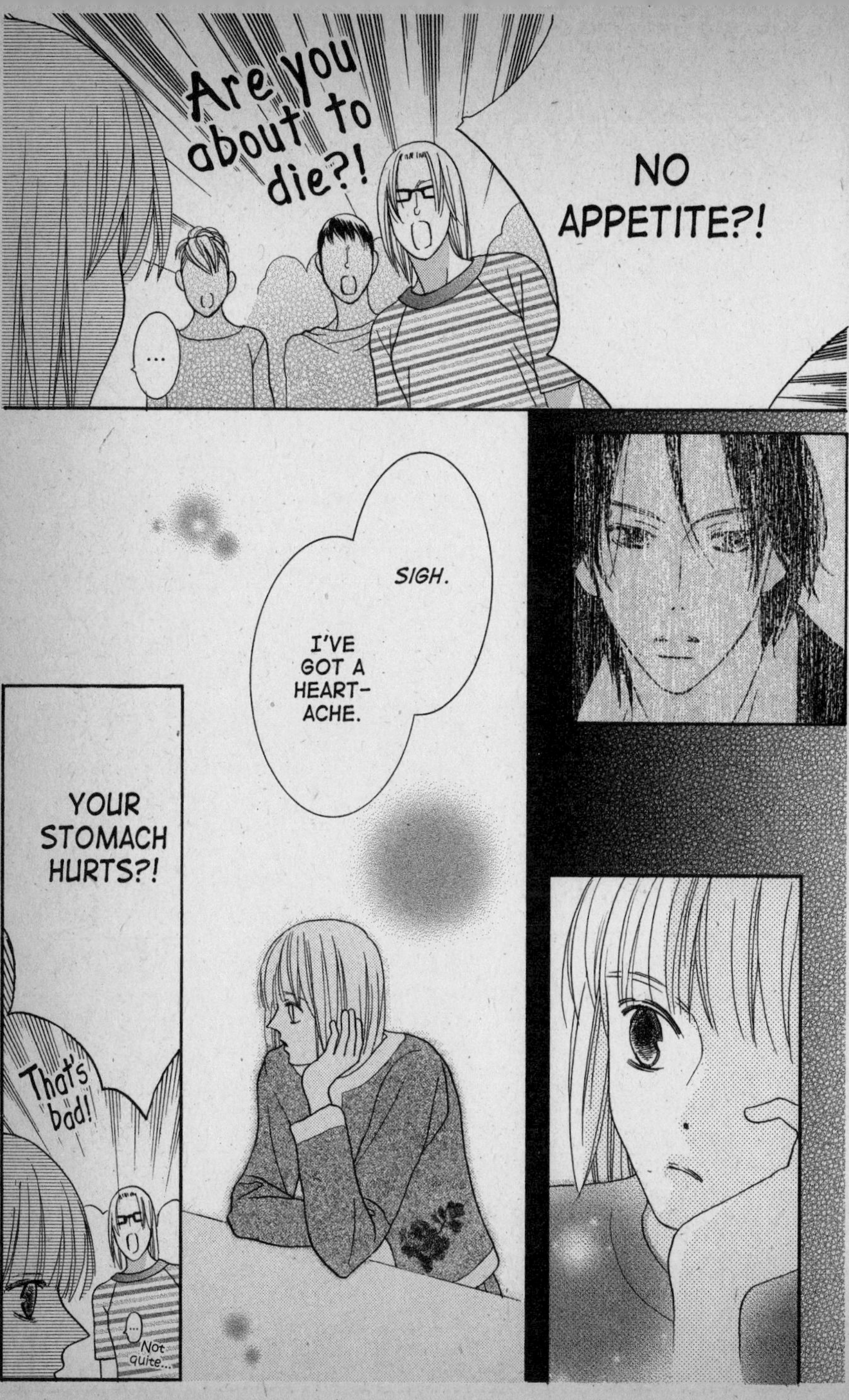
NO APPETITE?!
Are you about to die?!
...
SIGH.
I'VE GOT A HEART-ACHE.
YOUR STOMACH HURTS?!
That's bad!
...
Not quite...

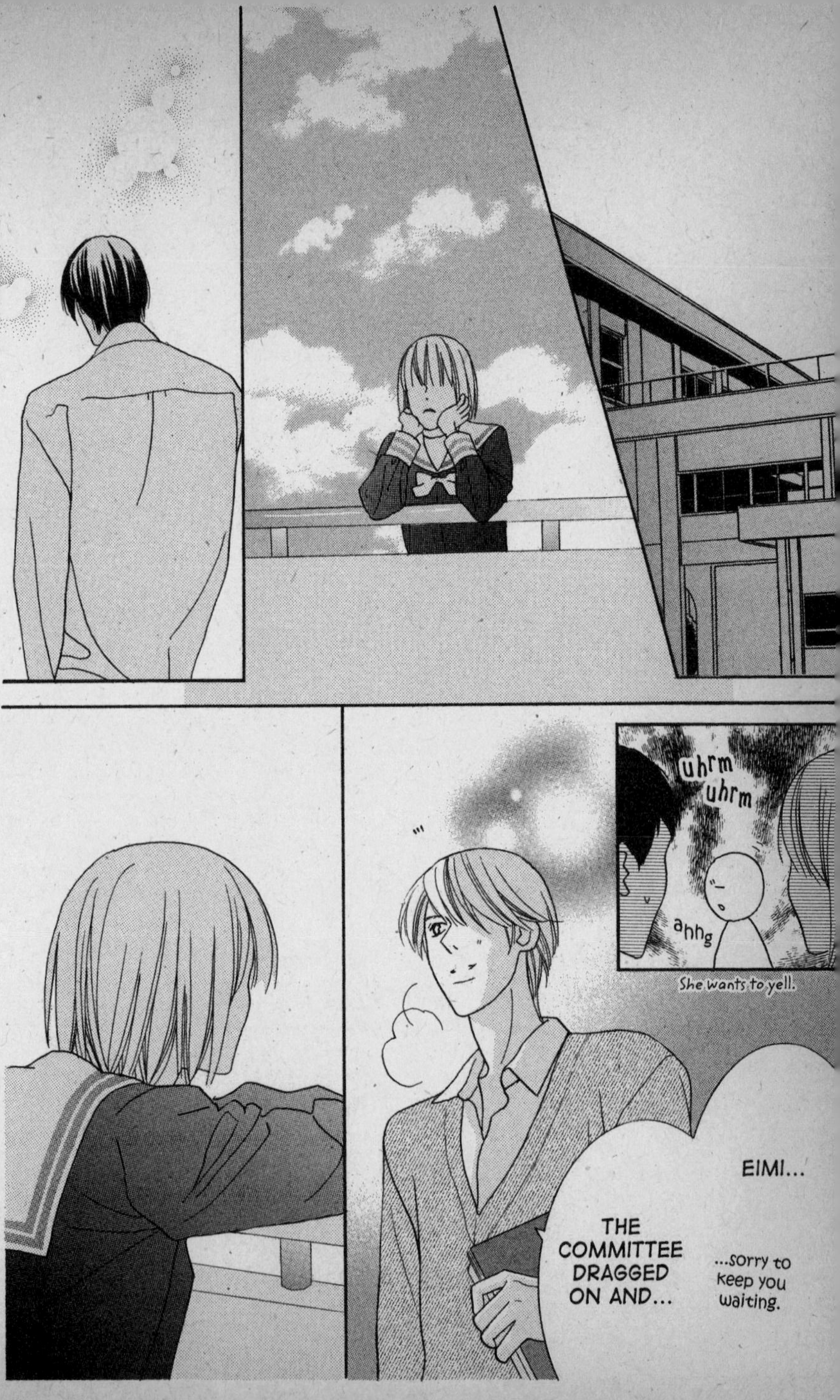
uhrm
uhrm
ahhg
She wants to yell.
EIMI...
...sorry to keep you waiting.
THE COMMITTEE DRAGGED ON AND...

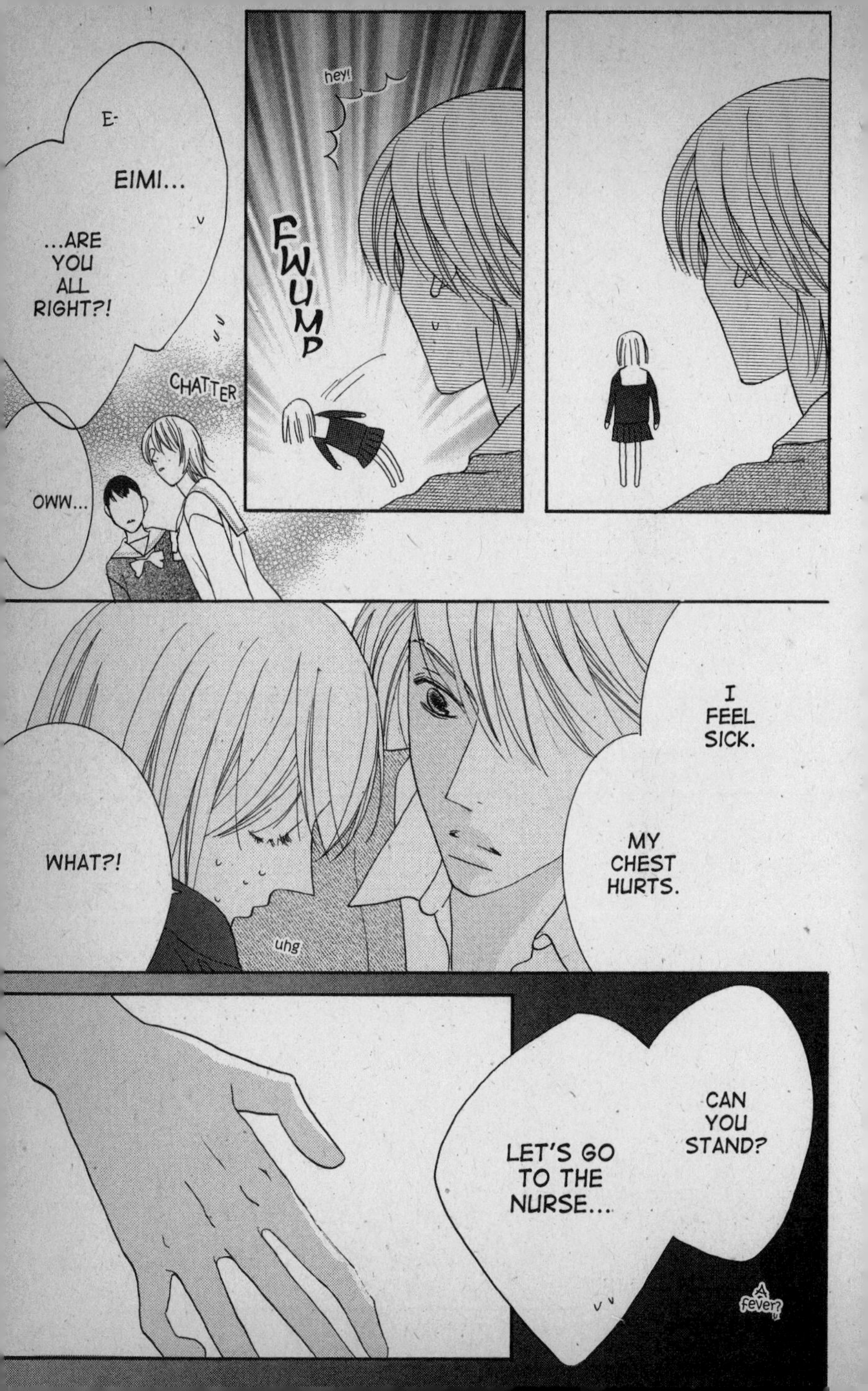
hey!
FWUMP
E-
EIMI...
...ARE YOU ALL RIGHT?!
CHATTER
OWW...
I FEEL SICK.
MY CHEST HURTS.
WHAT?!
uhg
CAN YOU STAND?
LET'S GO TO THE NURSE...
A fever?

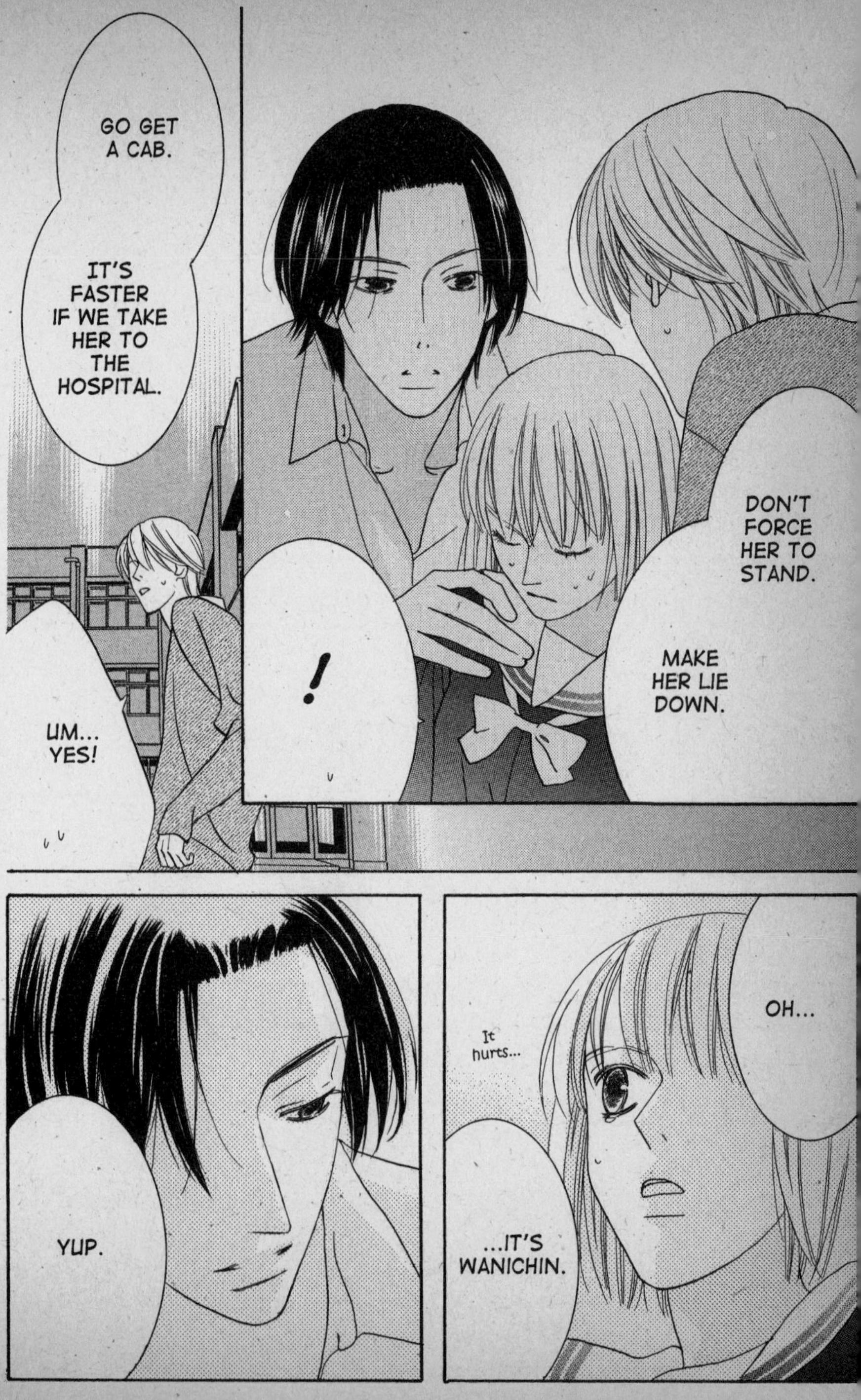
DON'T FORCE HER TO STAND.
MAKE HER LIE DOWN.
!
GO GET A CAB.
IT'S FASTER IF WE TAKE HER TO THE HOSPITAL.
UM... YES!
OH...
It hurts...
...IT'S WANICHIN.
YUP.

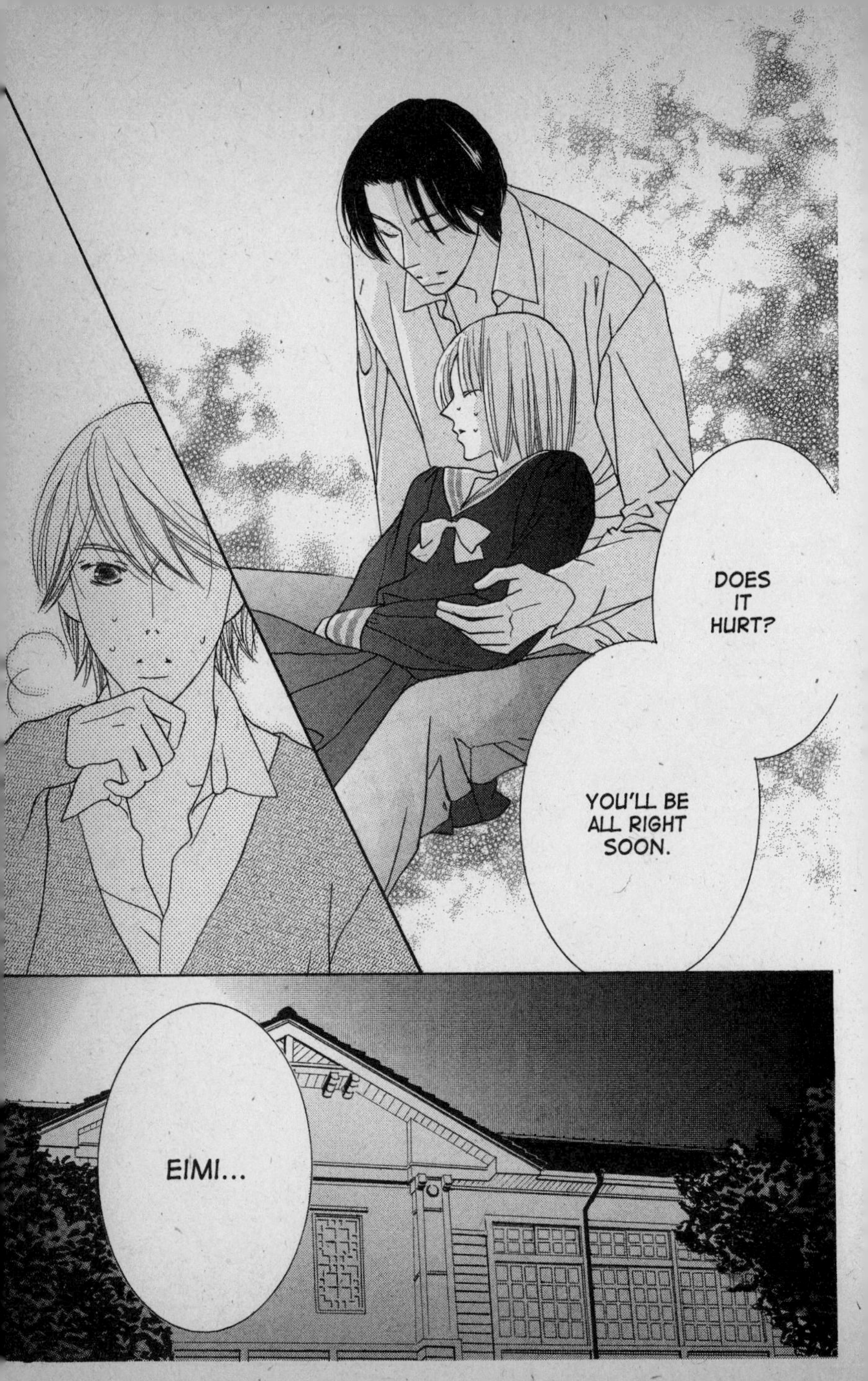
DOES IT HURT?
YOU'LL BE ALL RIGHT SOON.
EIMI...

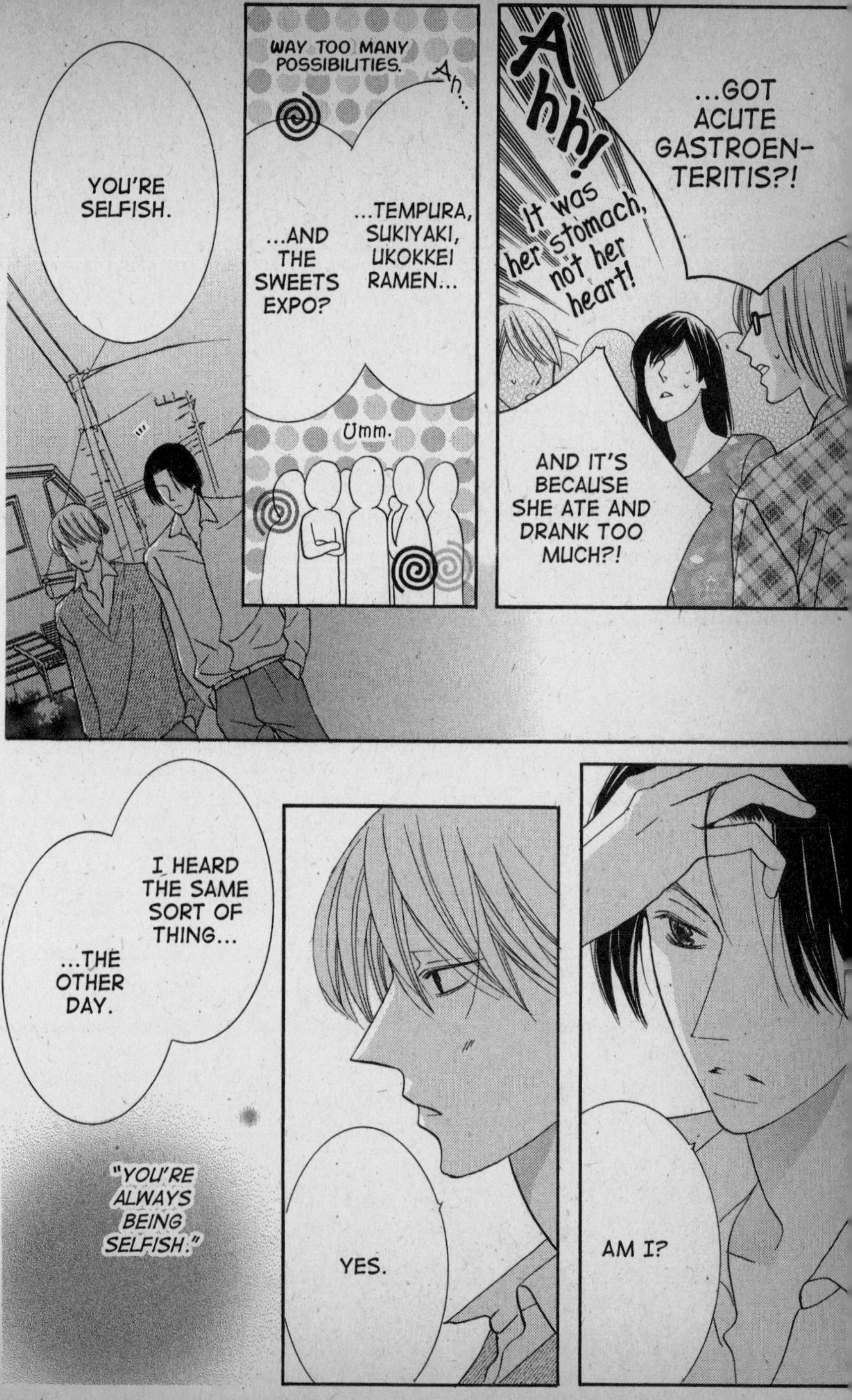
Ahh!
...GOT ACUTE GASTROEN-TERITIS?!
It was her stomach, not her heart!
AND IT'S BECAUSE SHE ATE AND DRANK TOO MUCH?!
WAY TOO MANY POSSIBILITIES.
Ah...
...TEMPURA, SUKIYAKI, UKOKKEI RAMEN...
...AND THE SWEETS EXPO?
Umm.
YOU'RE SELFISH.
AM I?
YES.
I HEARD THE SAME SORT OF THING...
...THE OTHER DAY.
"YOU'RE ALWAYS BEING SELFISH."

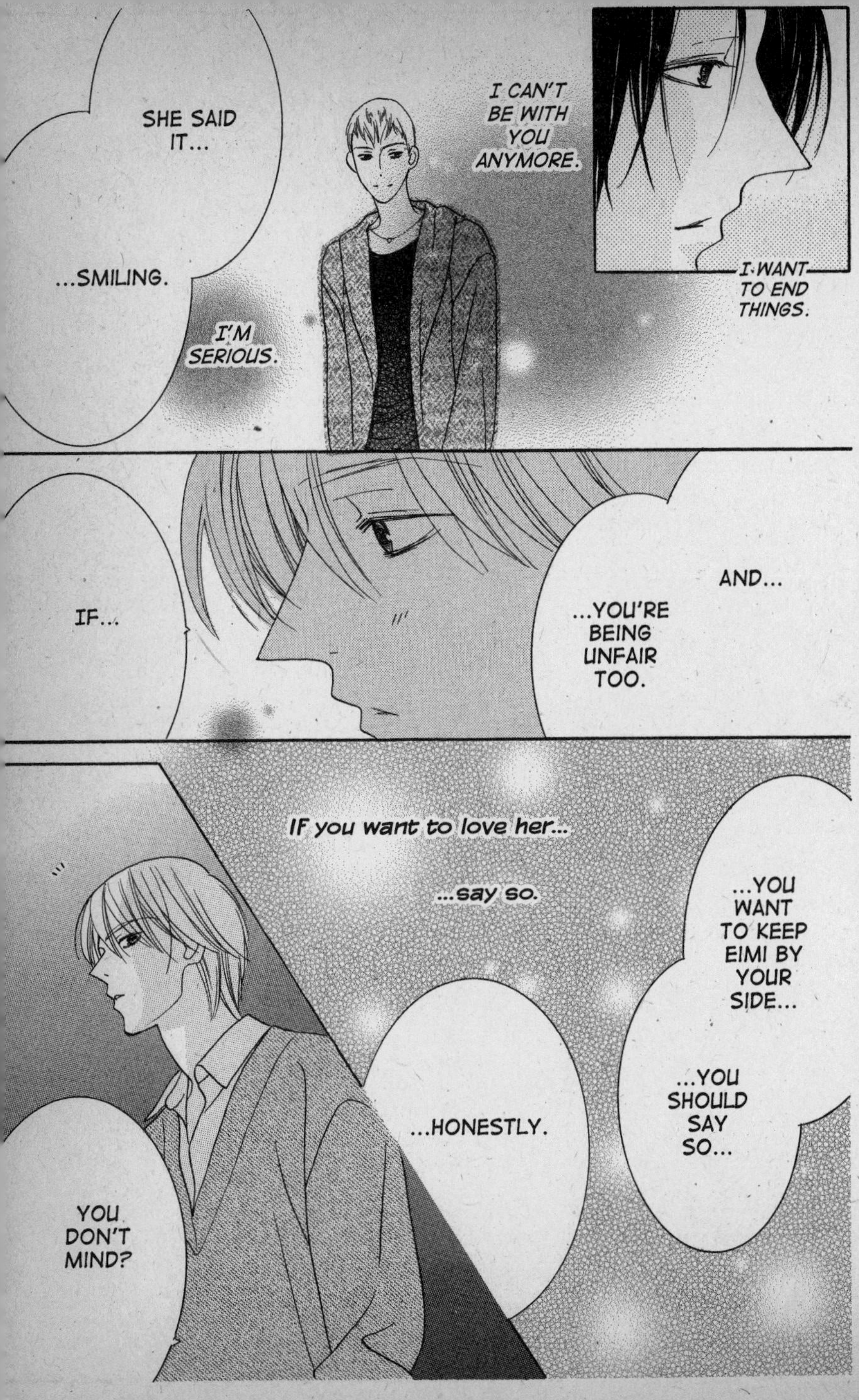
I WANT TO END THINGS.
I CAN'T BE WITH YOU ANYMORE.
SHE SAID IT...
...SMILING.
I'M SERIOUS.
AND...
...YOU'RE BEING UNFAIR TOO.
IF...
IF you want to love her...
...say so.
...YOU WANT TO KEEP EIMI BY YOUR SIDE...
...YOU SHOULD SAY SO...
...HONESTLY.
YOU DON'T MIND?

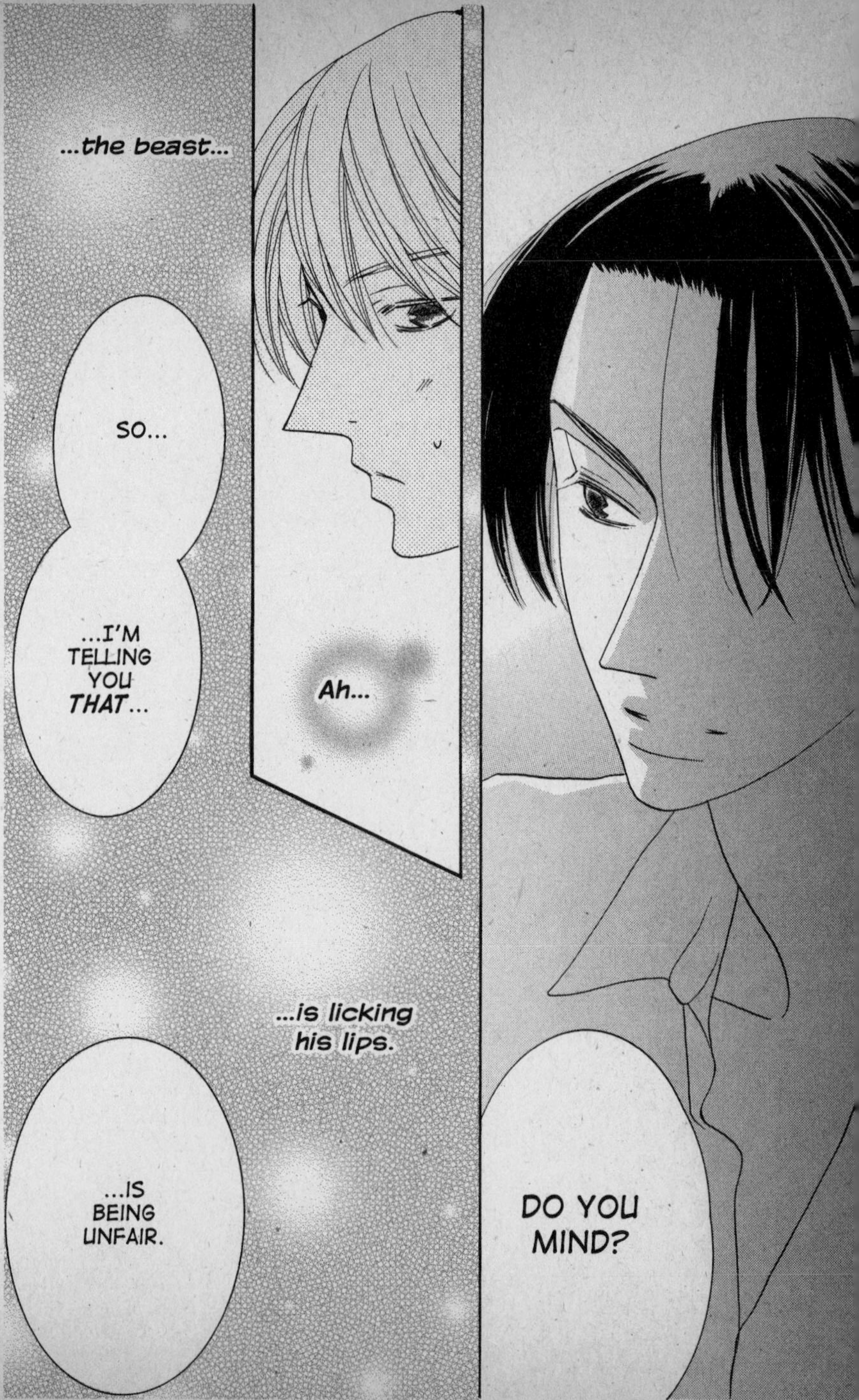
DO YOU MIND?
Ah...
...the beast...
SO...
...I'M TELLING YOU *THAT*...
...is licking his lips.
...IS BEING UNFAIR.

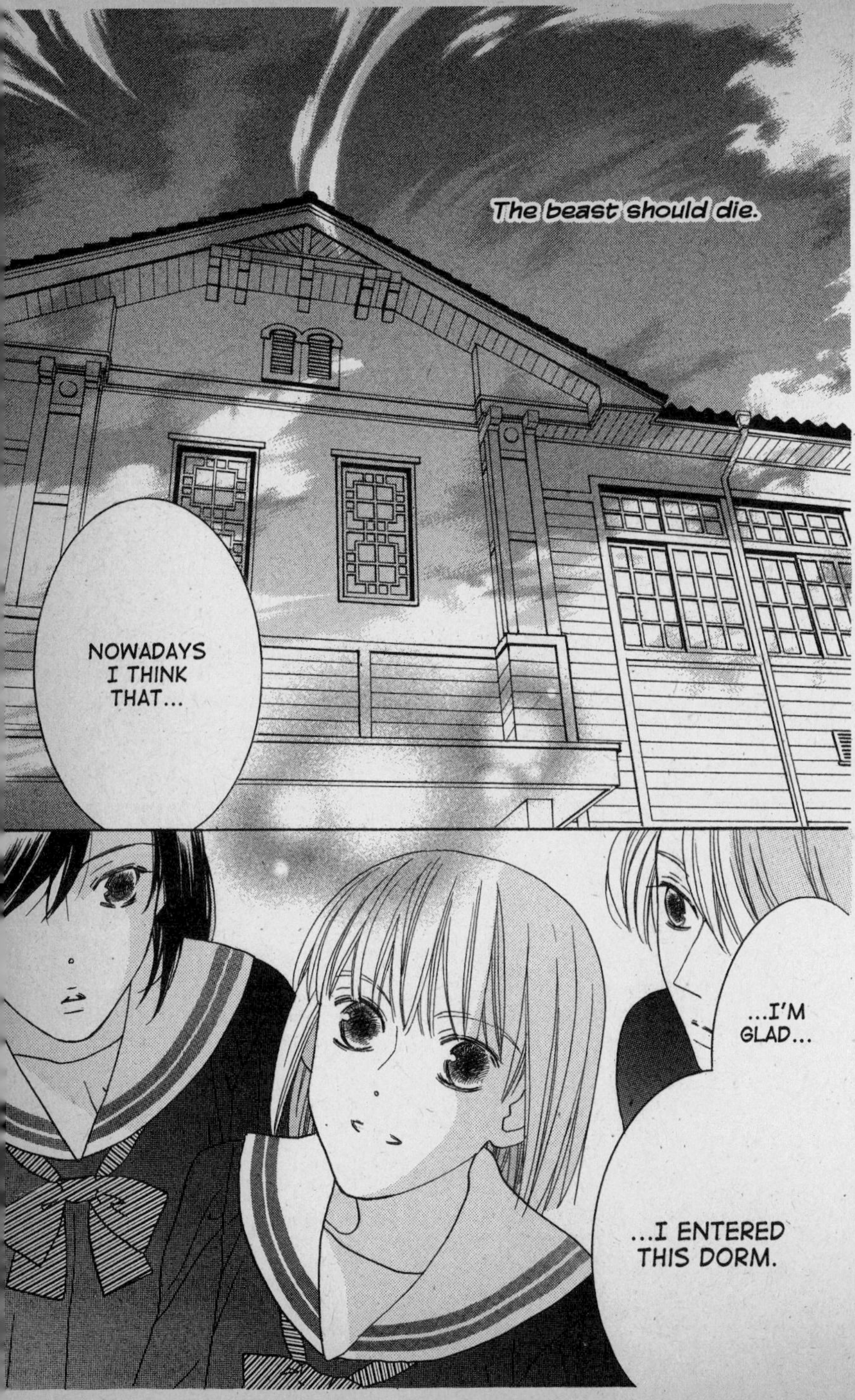
The beast should die.
NOWADAYS I THINK THAT...
...I'M GLAD...
...I ENTERED THIS DORM.

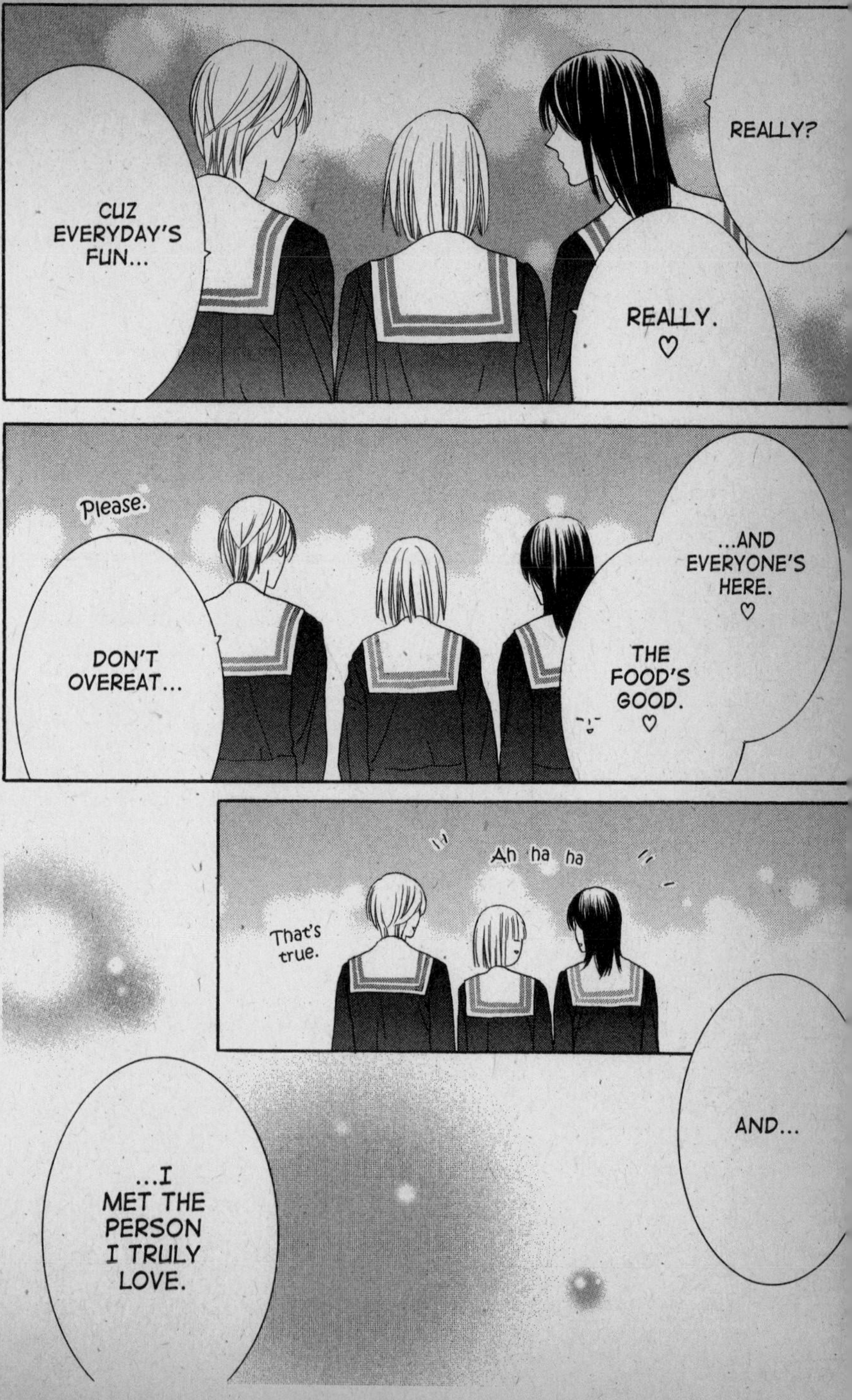
REALLY?
REALLY. ♡
CUZ EVERYDAY'S FUN...
...AND EVERYONE'S HERE. ♡
THE FOOD'S GOOD. ♡
Please.
DON'T OVEREAT...
Ah ha ha
That's true.
AND...
...I MET THE PERSON I TRULY LOVE.

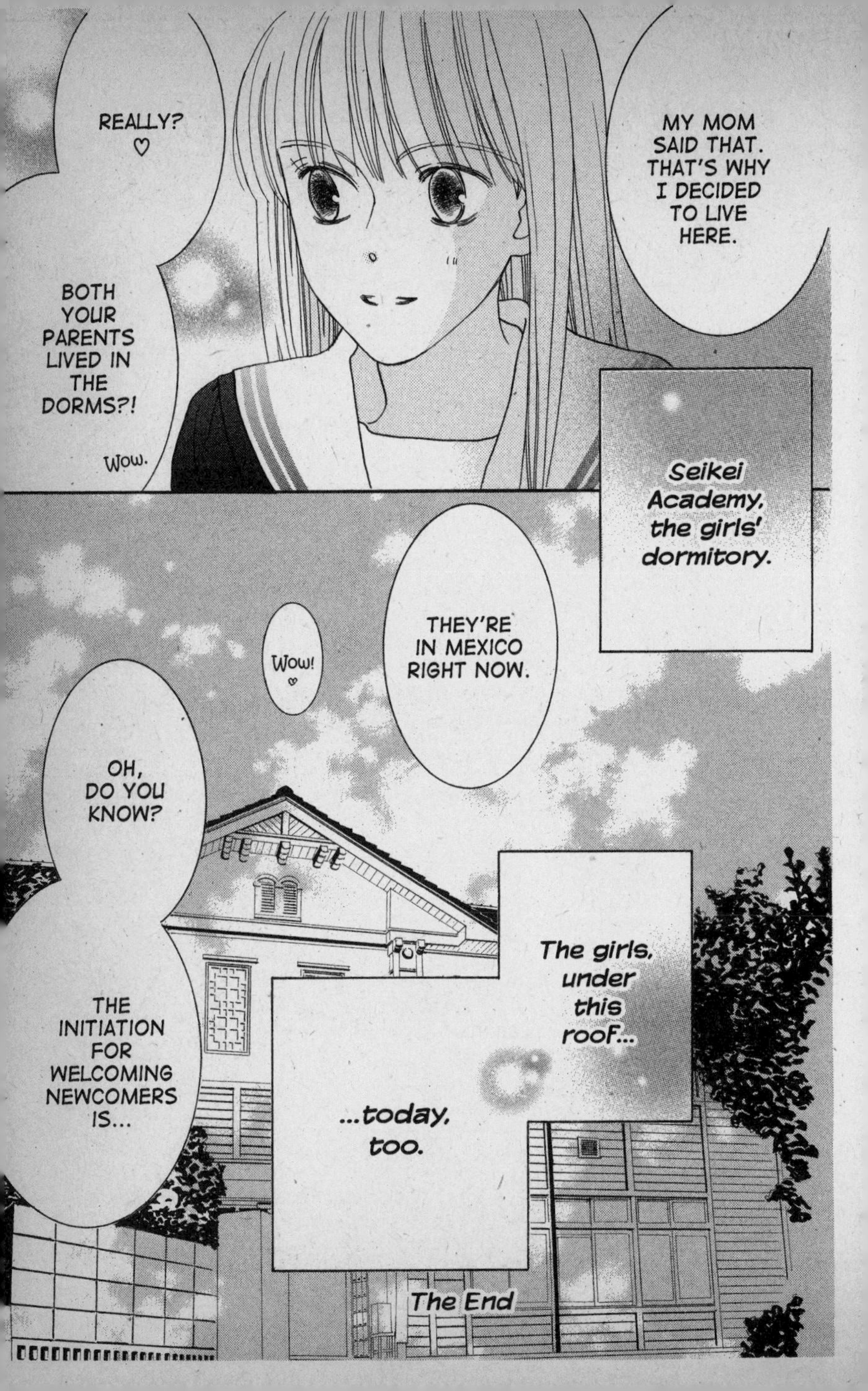
MY MOM SAID THAT. THAT'S WHY I DECIDED TO LIVE HERE.
REALLY? ♡
BOTH YOUR PARENTS LIVED IN THE DORMS?!
Wow.
Seikei Academy, the girls' dormitory.
THEY'RE IN MEXICO RIGHT NOW.
Wow! ♡
OH, DO YOU KNOW?
THE INITIATION FOR WELCOMING NEWCOMERS IS...
The girls, under this roof...
...today, too.
The End

We had people send in their names as candidates for that girl (the girl with the glasses), who has the most presence in the dorm. Below are some excerpts from some of the postcards.
(The candidate names and comments.)

- Naoko Sawayama: "I love this girl.♡ Please use my name!!!!"
- Sayaka Ito: "I want to at least pretend to live in the dorm with Eimi and company!!" (Many people sent in similar comments.)
- Michiko Fukuda: "If Eimi called my name, I may grow to like my name more."
- Sayuri Fujinaga: "If you used my name...I will make every one of my friends buy *Beauty is the Beast*."
- Yukie Kamata: "Fortune-telling using the kanji strokes of my name says it's a really bad-luck name, but..."
- Miwa Minegishi: "People always call me Minami or Miha, so I want to spread the correct way to say my name."
- Kotomi Takeuchi: "I want!! To make my flowers bloom!!!! 4649!"
- Yuka Yasuda: "My nickname is 'Yassan' which is the same as Yasuura-san of Hagure Keiji."
- Kimiko Togami: "I think my personality is exactly the same as her... I burnt out at the year-end big gamble horse race, Arima Kinen..."

(Honorifics abbreviated) etc. etc.

I was surprised that many many people wrote in that "She looks exactly like me!!!" (☺) And people drew glasses on their Purikura photos. (☺)
People wrote in where their names came from, and memories of their names...and many other things.
There were lots of people who thought of names that would suit her well!
It was really fun.
Thank you to everyone who wrote in!

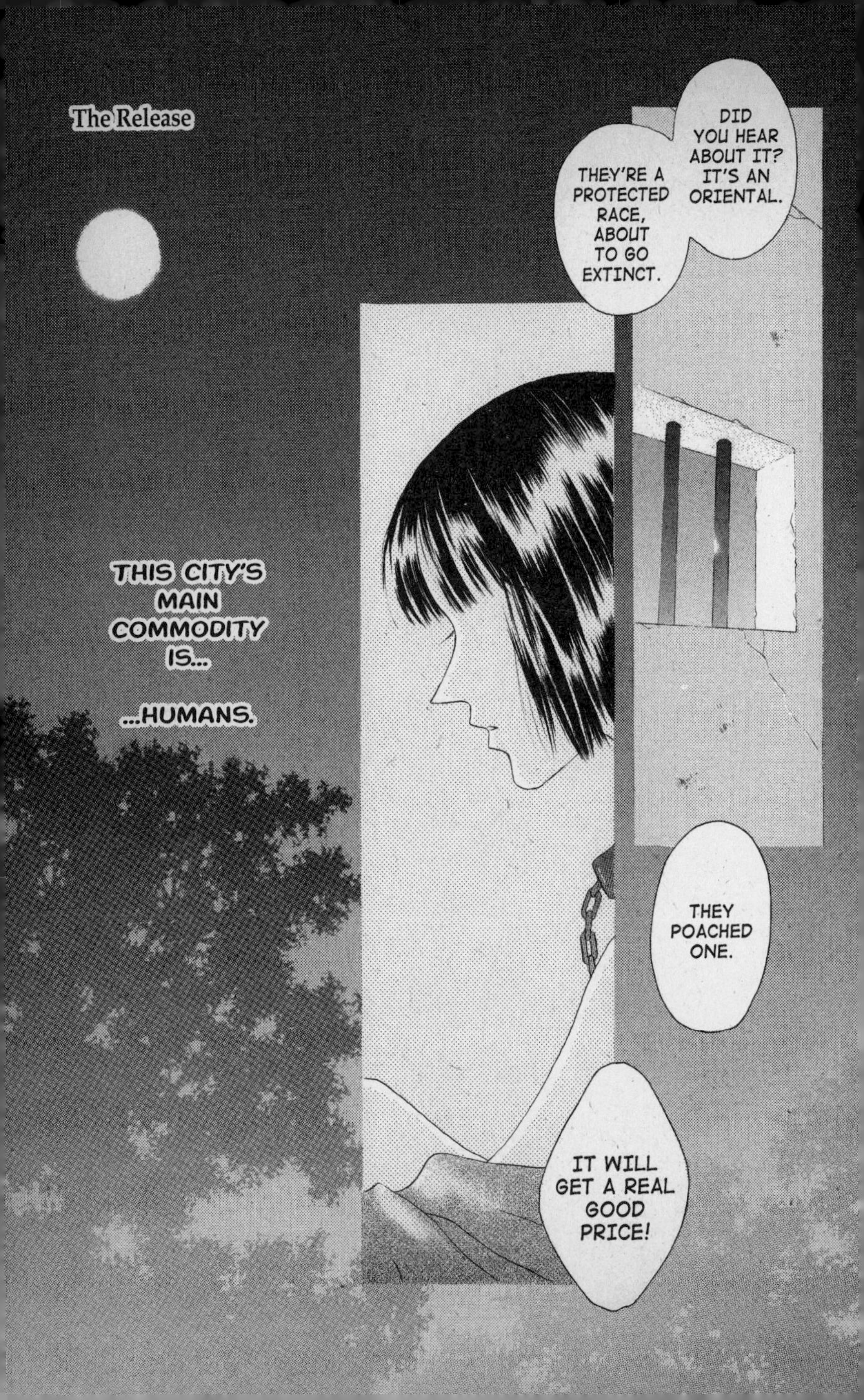
The Release
DID YOU HEAR ABOUT IT? IT'S AN ORIENTAL.
THEY'RE A PROTECTED RACE, ABOUT TO GO EXTINCT.
THEY POACHED ONE.
IT WILL GET A REAL GOOD PRICE!
THIS CITY'S MAIN COMMODITY IS...
...HUMANS.

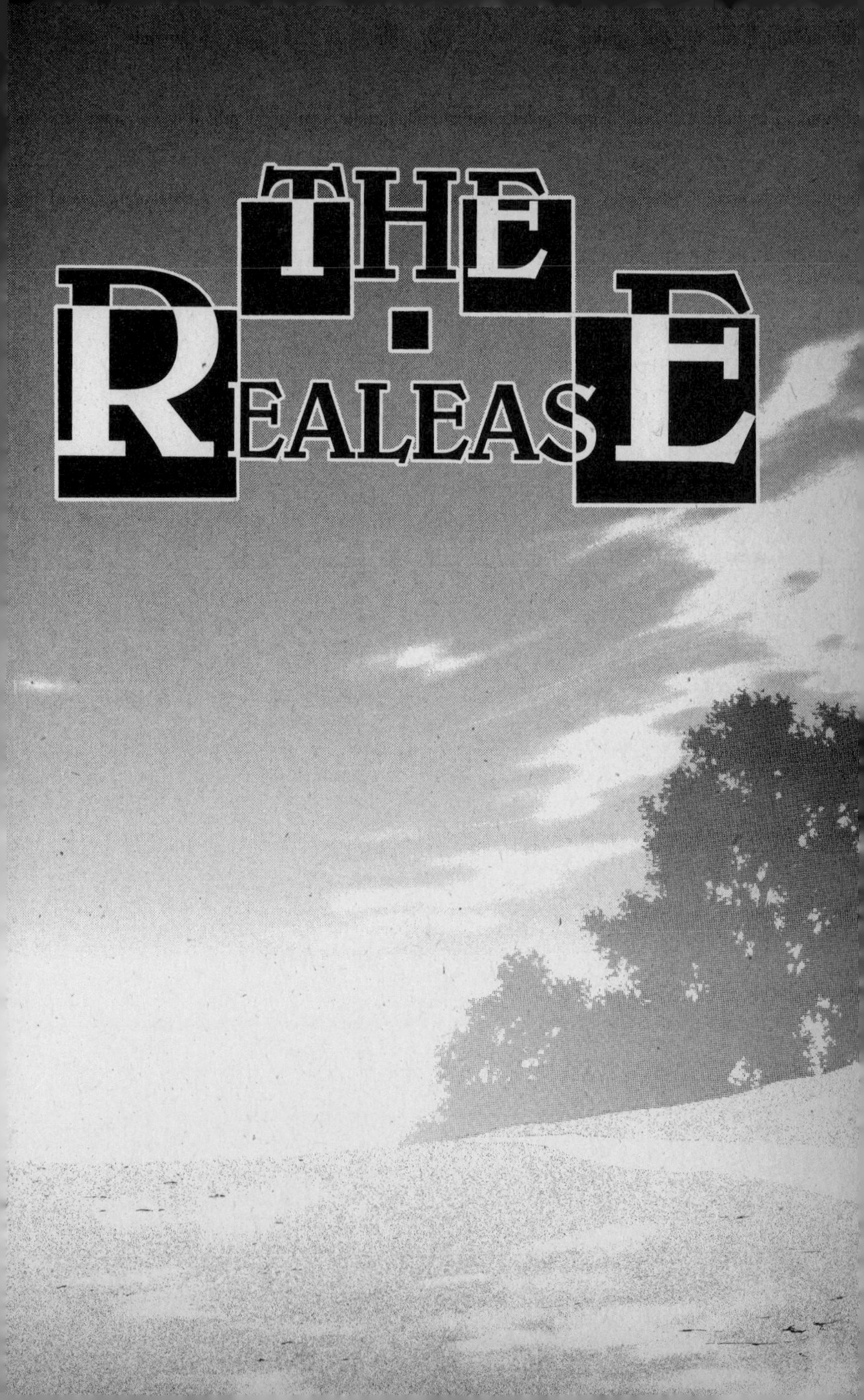
THE
REALEASE

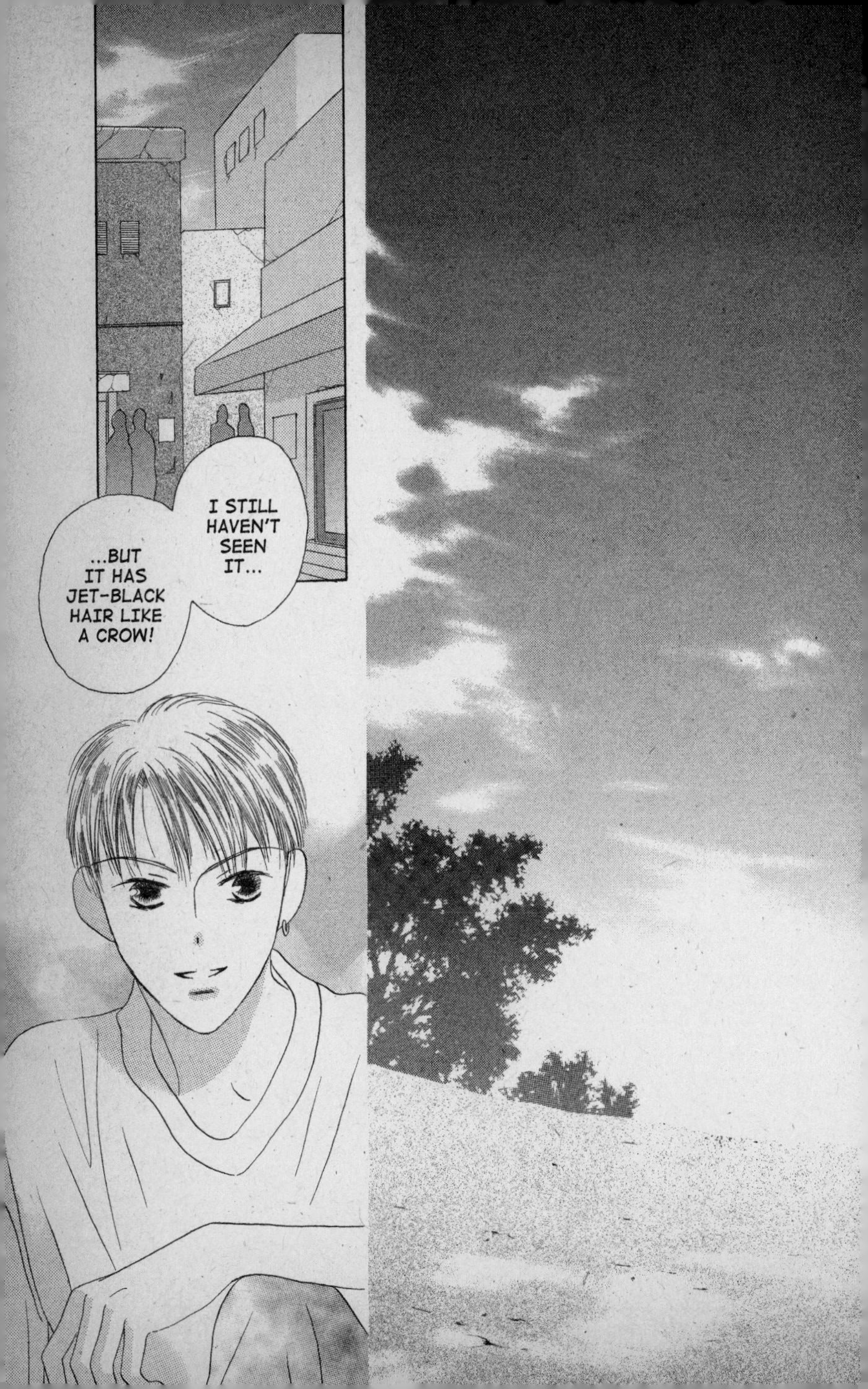
I STILL HAVEN'T SEEN IT...
...BUT IT HAS JET-BLACK HAIR LIKE A CROW!

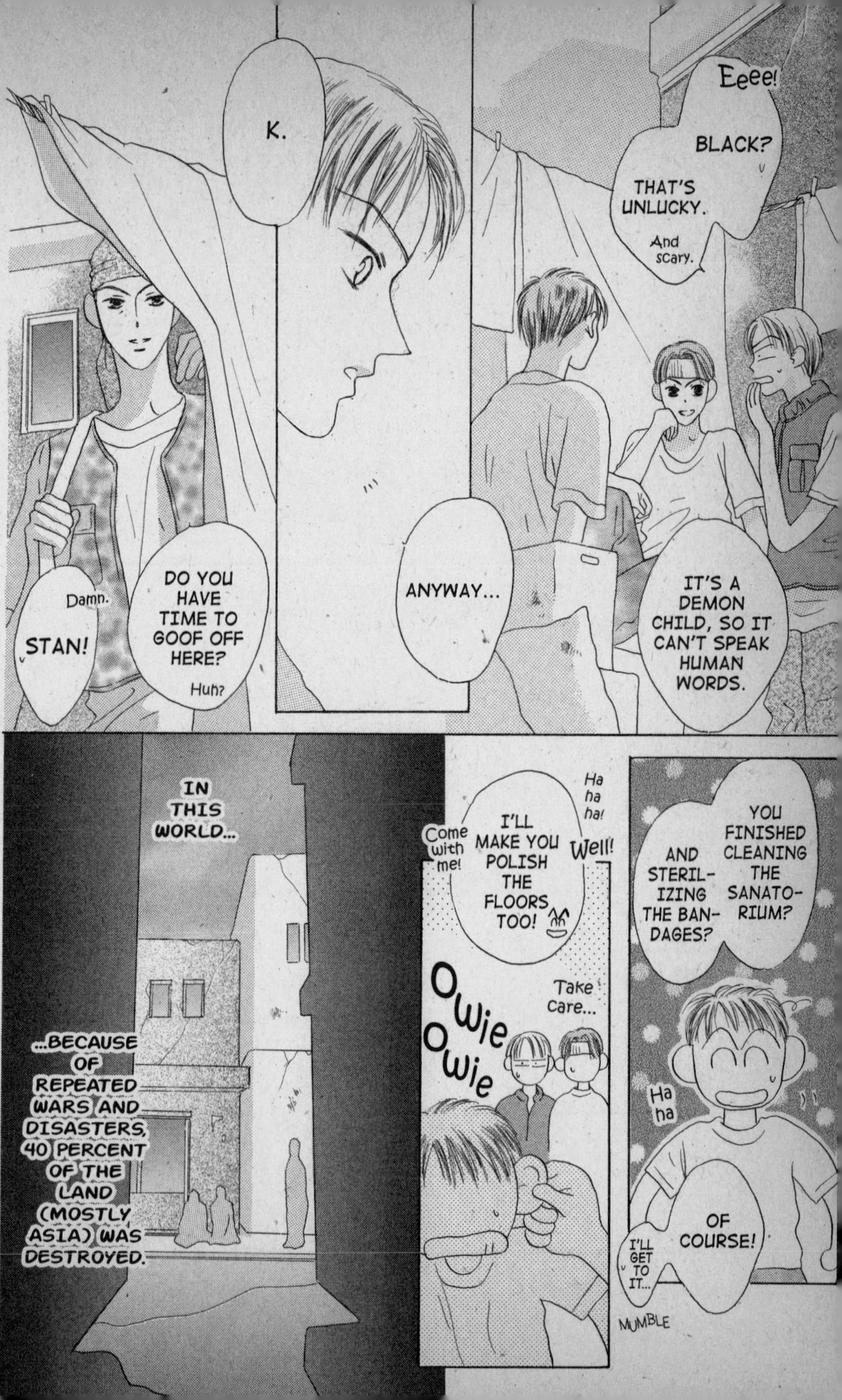
Eeee!
BLACK?
THAT'S UNLUCKY.
And scary.
IT'S A DEMON CHILD, SO IT CAN'T SPEAK HUMAN WORDS.
K.
ANYWAY...
DO YOU HAVE TIME TO GOOF OFF HERE?
Huh?
Damn.
STAN!
YOU FINISHED CLEANING THE SANATORIUM?
AND STERIL-IZING THE BAN-DAGES?
Ha ha
OF COURSE!
I'LL GET TO IT...
MUMBLE
Ha ha ha!
Well!
I'LL MAKE YOU POLISH THE FLOORS TOO!
Come with me!
Take care...
Owie owie
IN THIS WORLD...
...BECAUSE OF REPEATED WARS AND DISASTERS, 40 PERCENT OF THE LAND (MOSTLY ASIA) WAS DESTROYED.

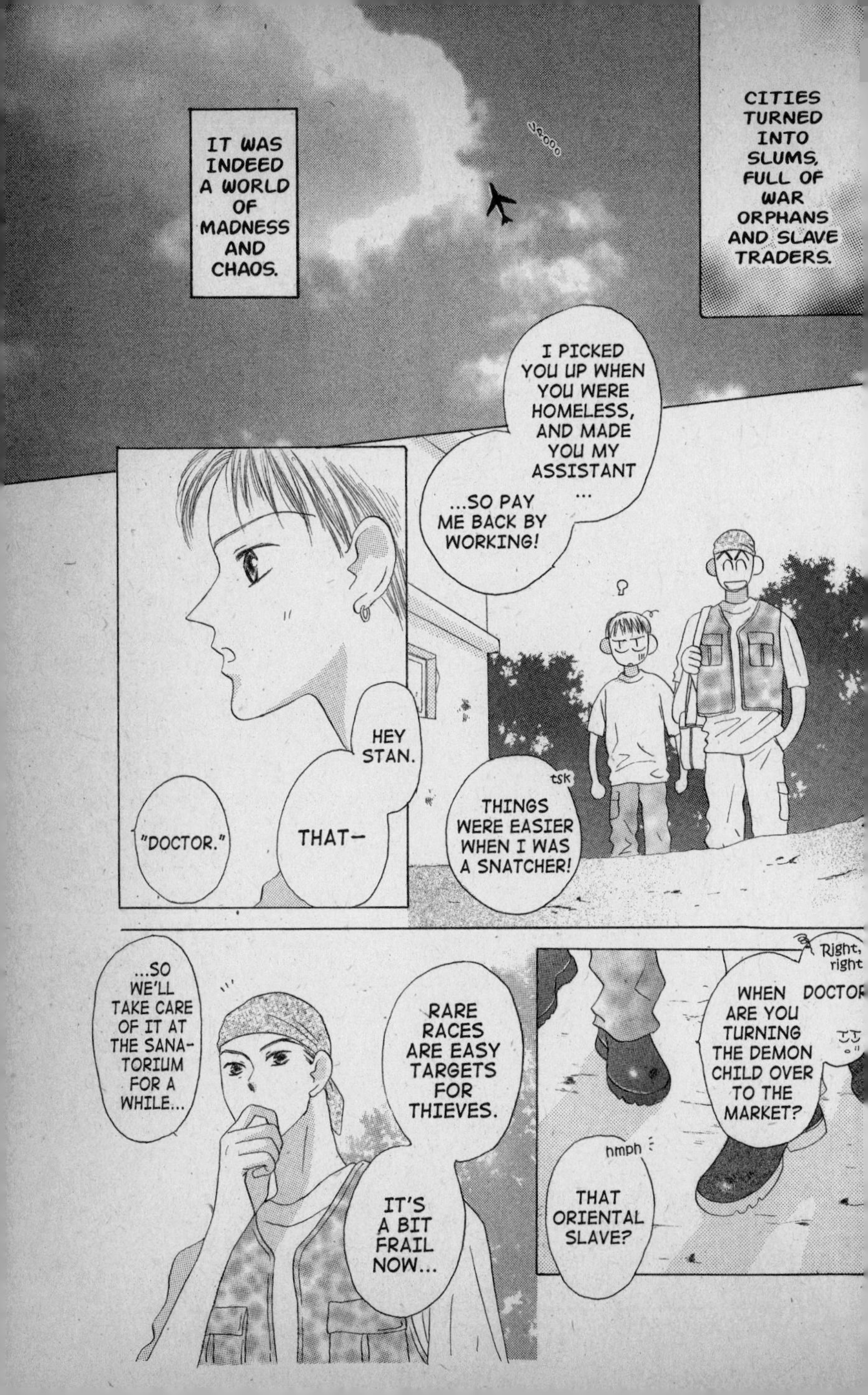
CITIES TURNED INTO SLUMS, FULL OF WAR ORPHANS AND SLAVE TRADERS.
IT WAS INDEED A WORLD OF MADNESS AND CHAOS.
I PICKED YOU UP WHEN YOU WERE HOMELESS, AND MADE YOU MY ASSISTANT ...
...SO PAY ME BACK BY WORKING!
tsk
THINGS WERE EASIER WHEN I WAS A SNATCHER!
HEY STAN.
THAT—
"DOCTOR."
Right, right
DOCTOR
WHEN ARE YOU TURNING THE DEMON CHILD OVER TO THE MARKET?
hmph
THAT ORIENTAL SLAVE?
RARE RACES ARE EASY TARGETS FOR THIEVES.
IT'S A BIT FRAIL NOW...
...SO WE'LL TAKE CARE OF IT AT THE SANATORIUM FOR A WHILE...

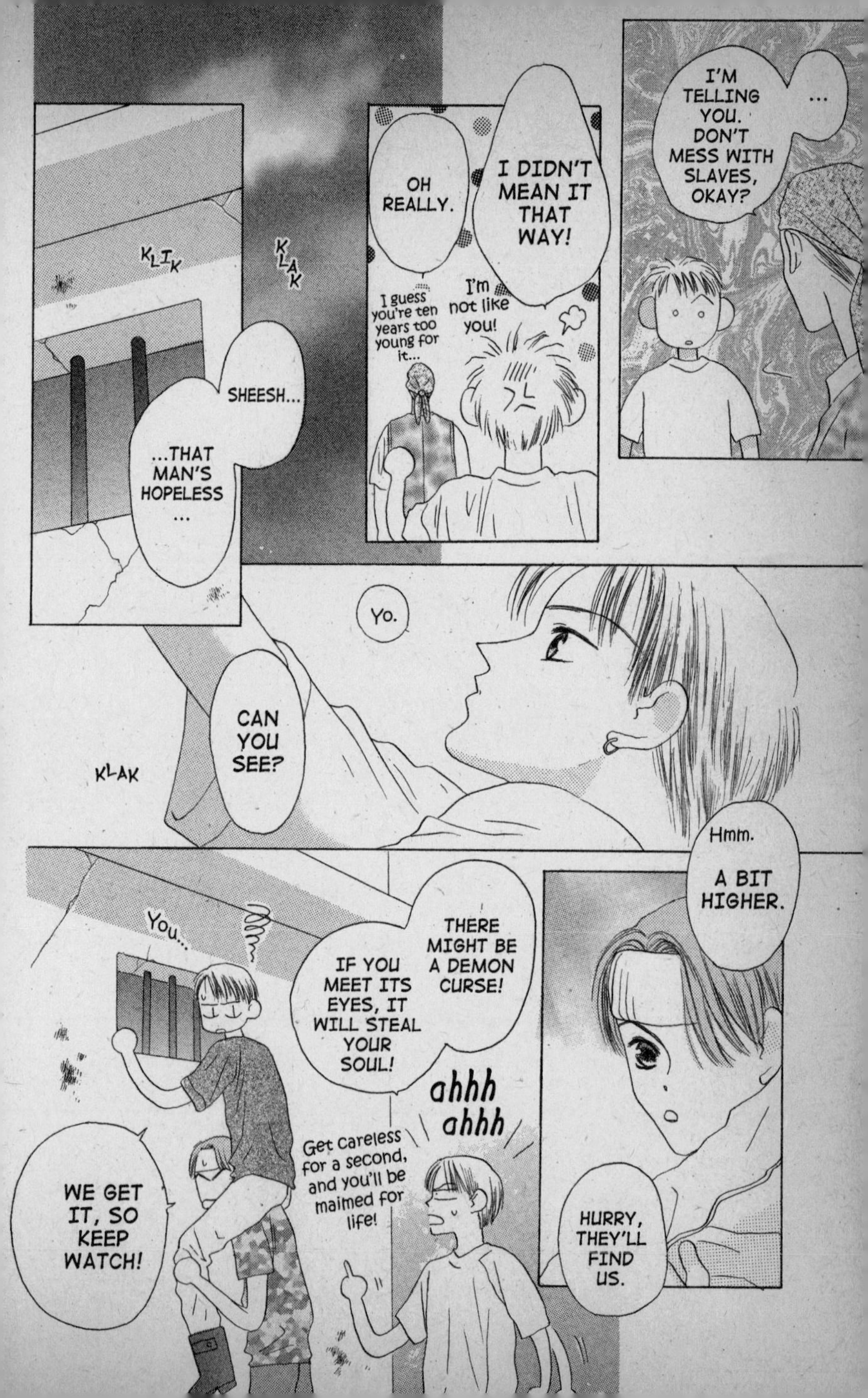
...
I'M TELLING YOU. DON'T MESS WITH SLAVES, OKAY?
I DIDN'T MEAN IT THAT WAY!
OH REALLY.
I'm not like you!
I guess you're ten years too young for it...
KLAK
KLIK
SHEESH...
...THAT MAN'S HOPELESS ...
Yo.
CAN YOU SEE?
KLAK
Hmm.
A BIT HIGHER.
HURRY, THEY'LL FIND US.
THERE MIGHT BE A DEMON CURSE!
IF YOU MEET ITS EYES, IT WILL STEAL YOUR SOUL!
ahhh ahhh
Get careless for a second, and you'll be maimed for life!
You...
WE GET IT, SO KEEP WATCH!

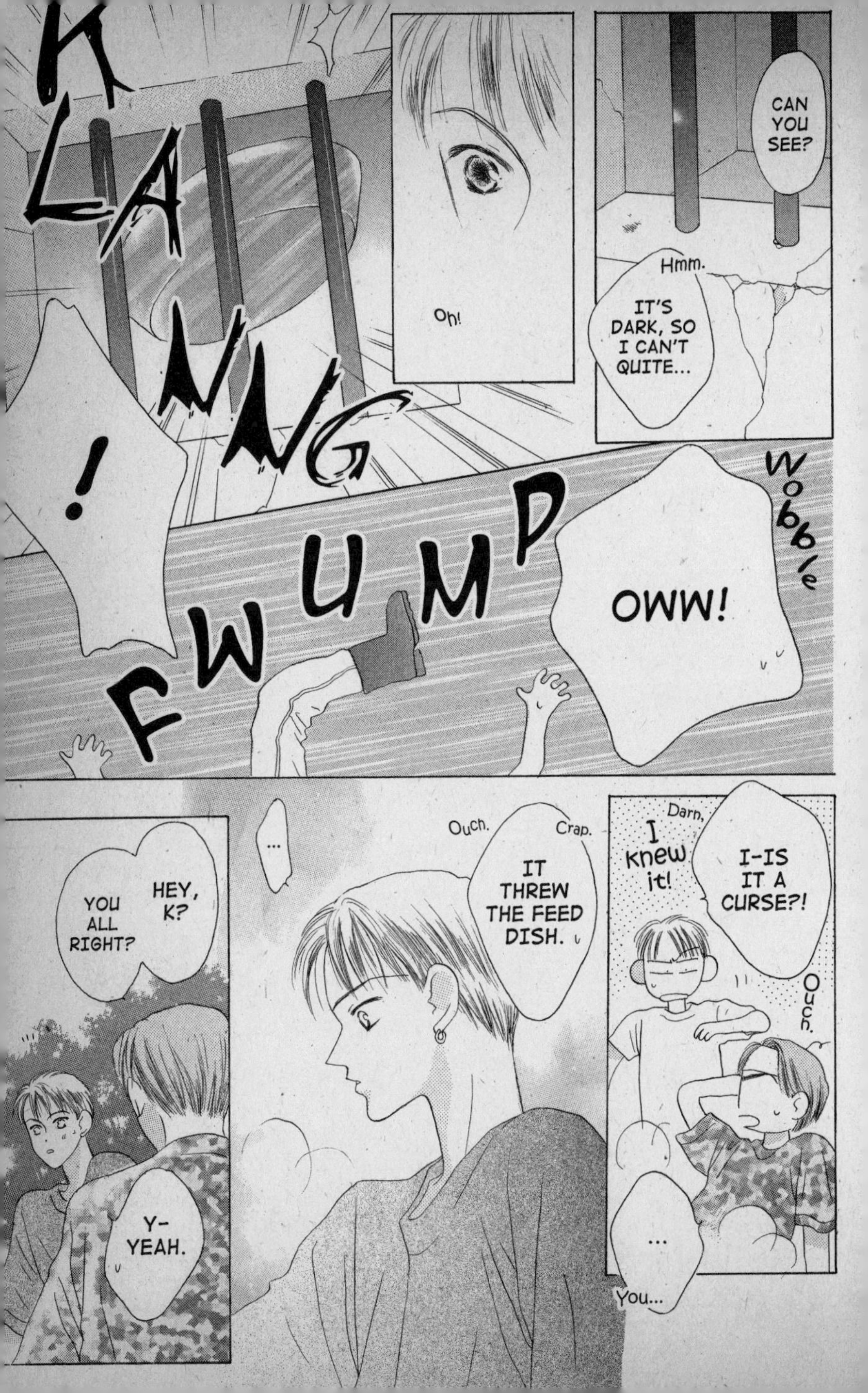
CAN YOU SEE?
Hmm.
IT'S DARK, SO I CAN'T QUITE...
Oh!
KLANNG
!
Wobble
OWW!
FWUMP
I-IS IT A CURSE?!
Darn, I knew it!
Ouch.
...
You...
Crap.
IT THREW THE FEED DISH.
Ouch.
...
HEY, K?
YOU ALL RIGHT?
Y-YEAH.

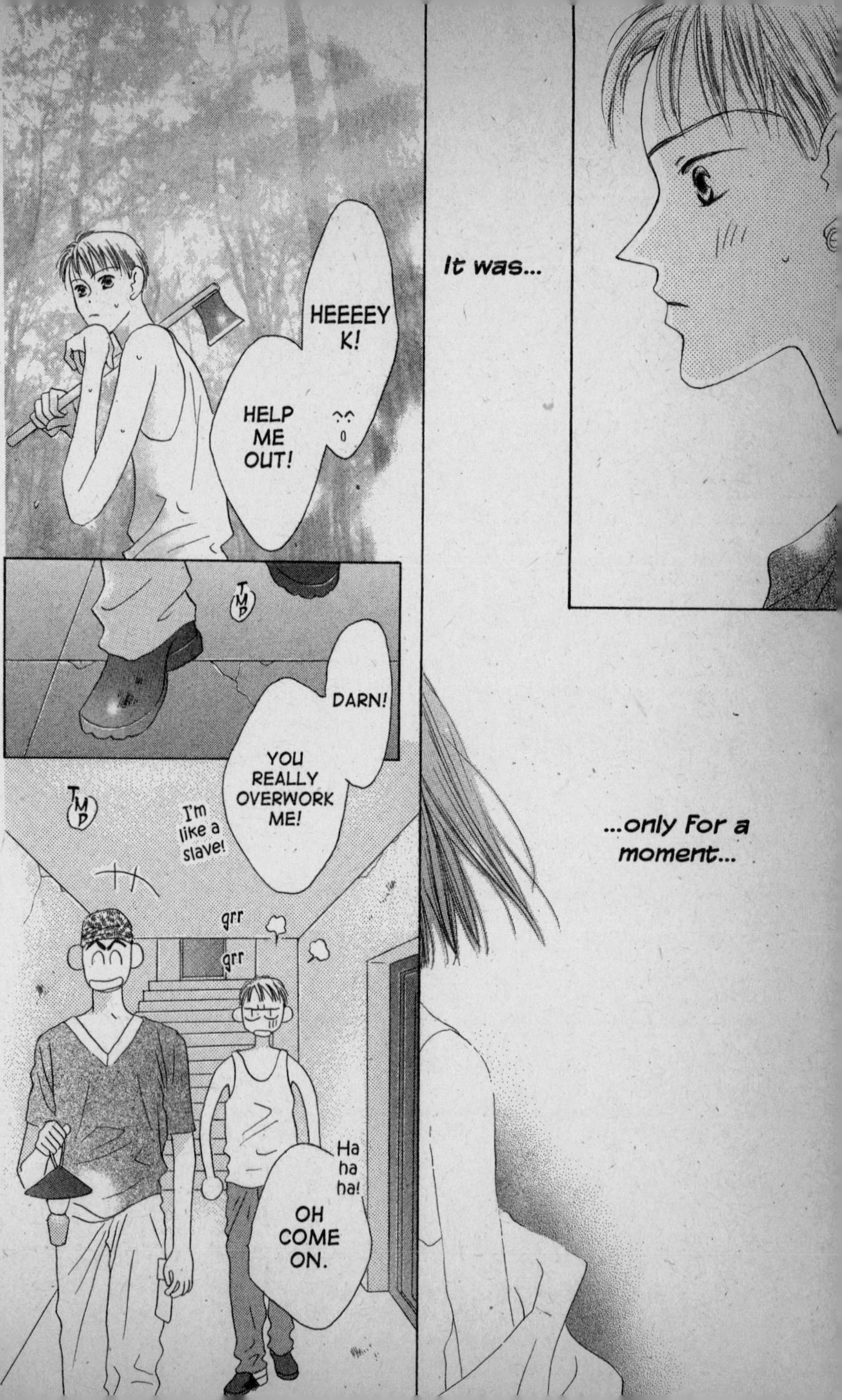
It was...
...only for a moment...
HEEEEY K!
HELP ME OUT!
TMP
DARN!
TMP
YOU REALLY OVERWORK ME!
I'm like a slave!
grr
grr
Ha ha ha!
OH COME ON.

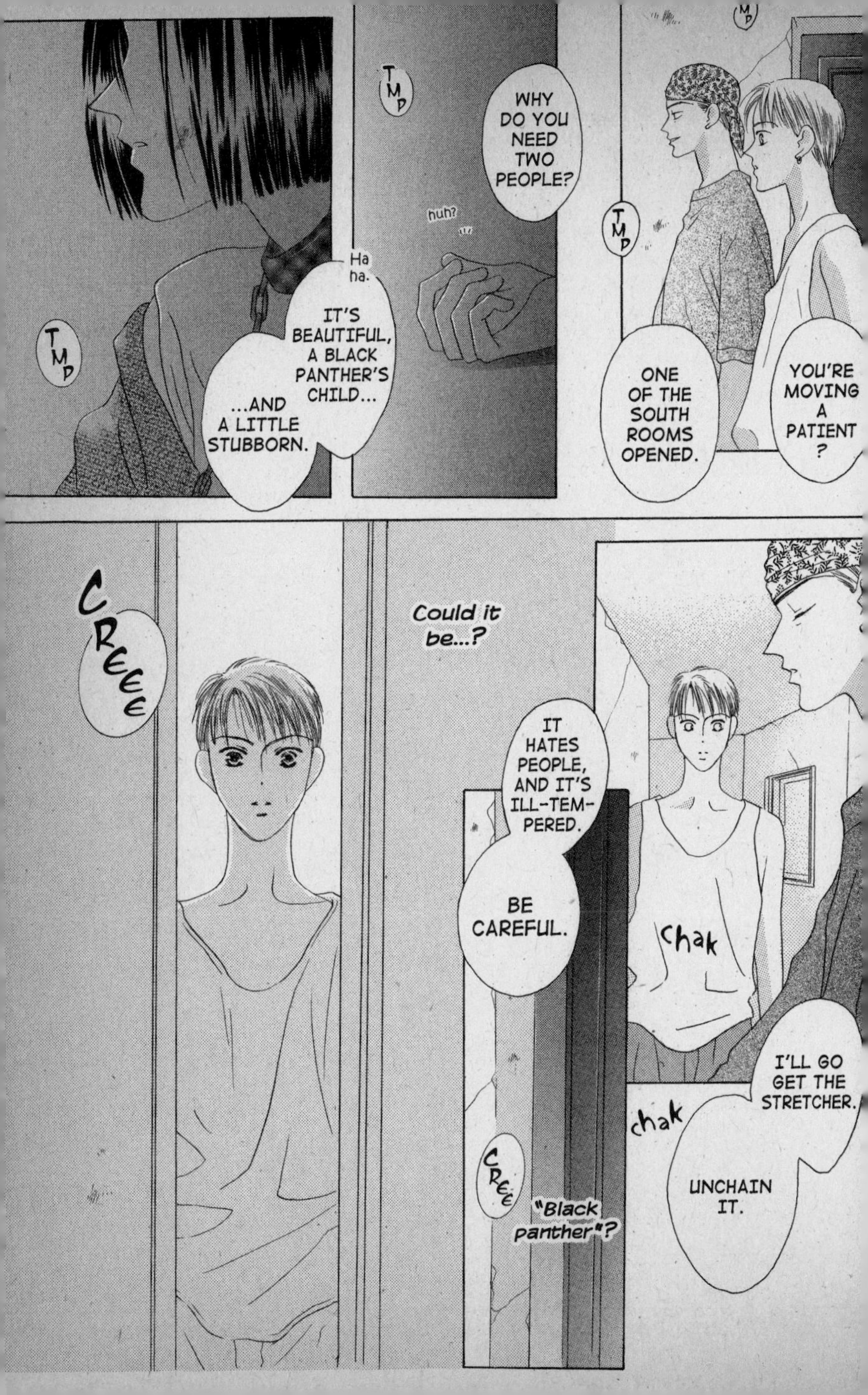
TMP
YOU'RE MOVING A PATIENT?
ONE OF THE SOUTH ROOMS OPENED.
TMP
TMP
WHY DO YOU NEED TWO PEOPLE?
huh?
Ha ha.
IT'S BEAUTIFUL, A BLACK PANTHER'S CHILD...
...AND A LITTLE STUBBORN.
TMP
chak
I'LL GO GET THE STRETCHER.
chak
UNCHAIN IT.
IT HATES PEOPLE, AND IT'S ILL-TEMPERED.
BE CAREFUL.
Could it be...?
"Black panther"?
CREE
CREEE

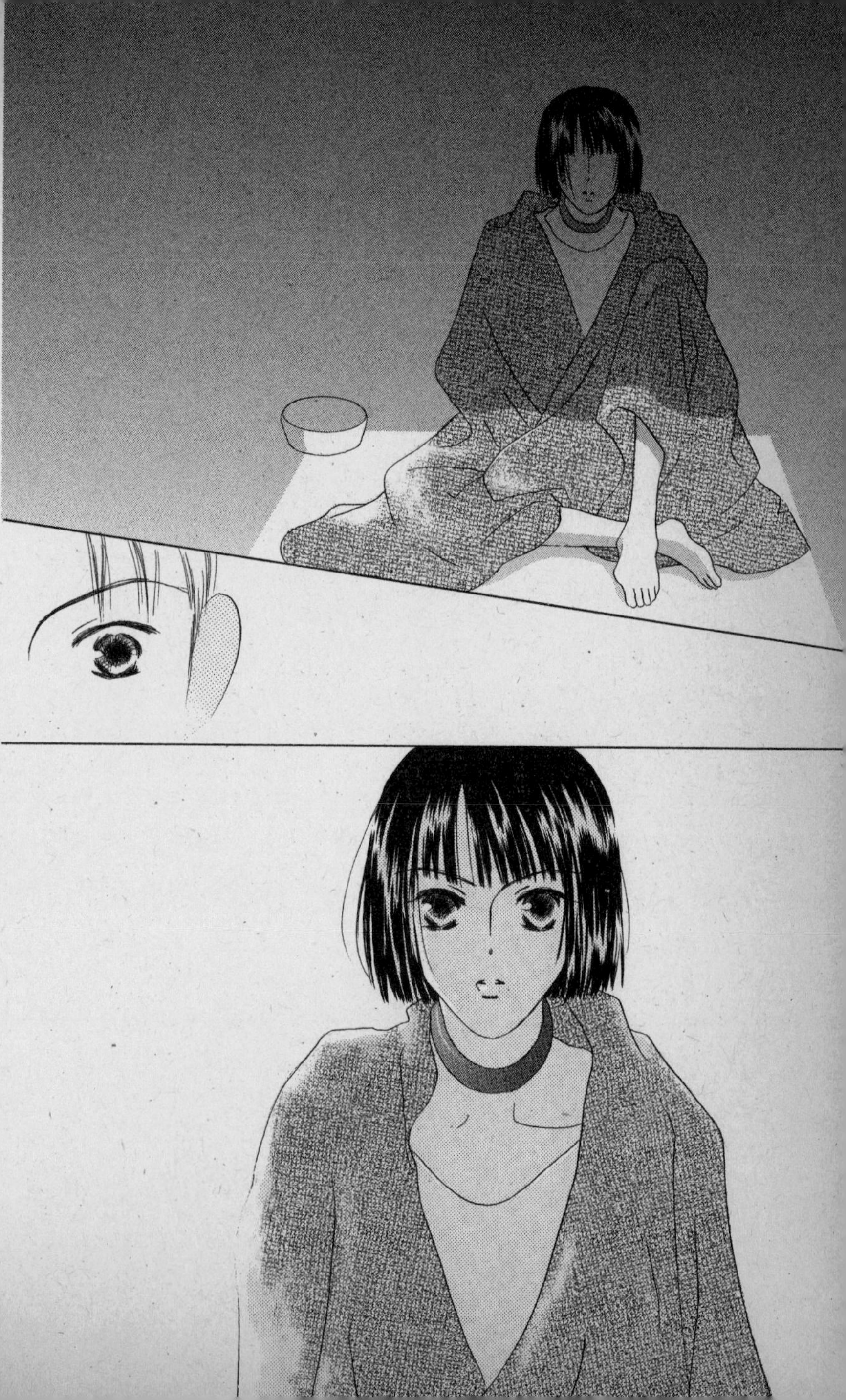

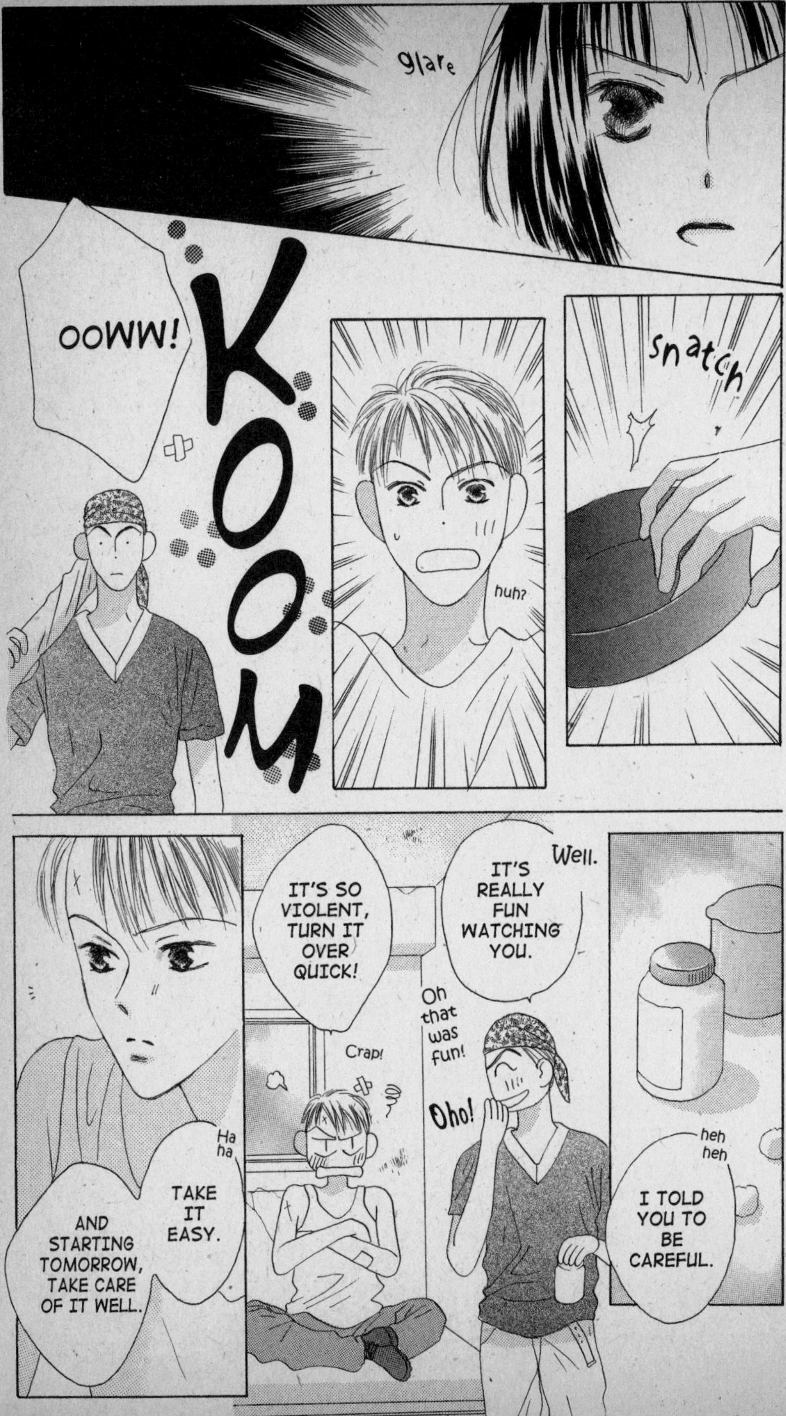
glare
snatch
huh?
OOWW!
KOOM
heh heh
I TOLD YOU TO BE CAREFUL.
Well.
IT'S REALLY FUN WATCHING YOU.
Oh that was fun!
Oho!
IT'S SO VIOLENT, TURN IT OVER QUICK!
Crap!
Ha ha
TAKE IT EASY.
AND STARTING TOMORROW, TAKE CARE OF IT WELL.

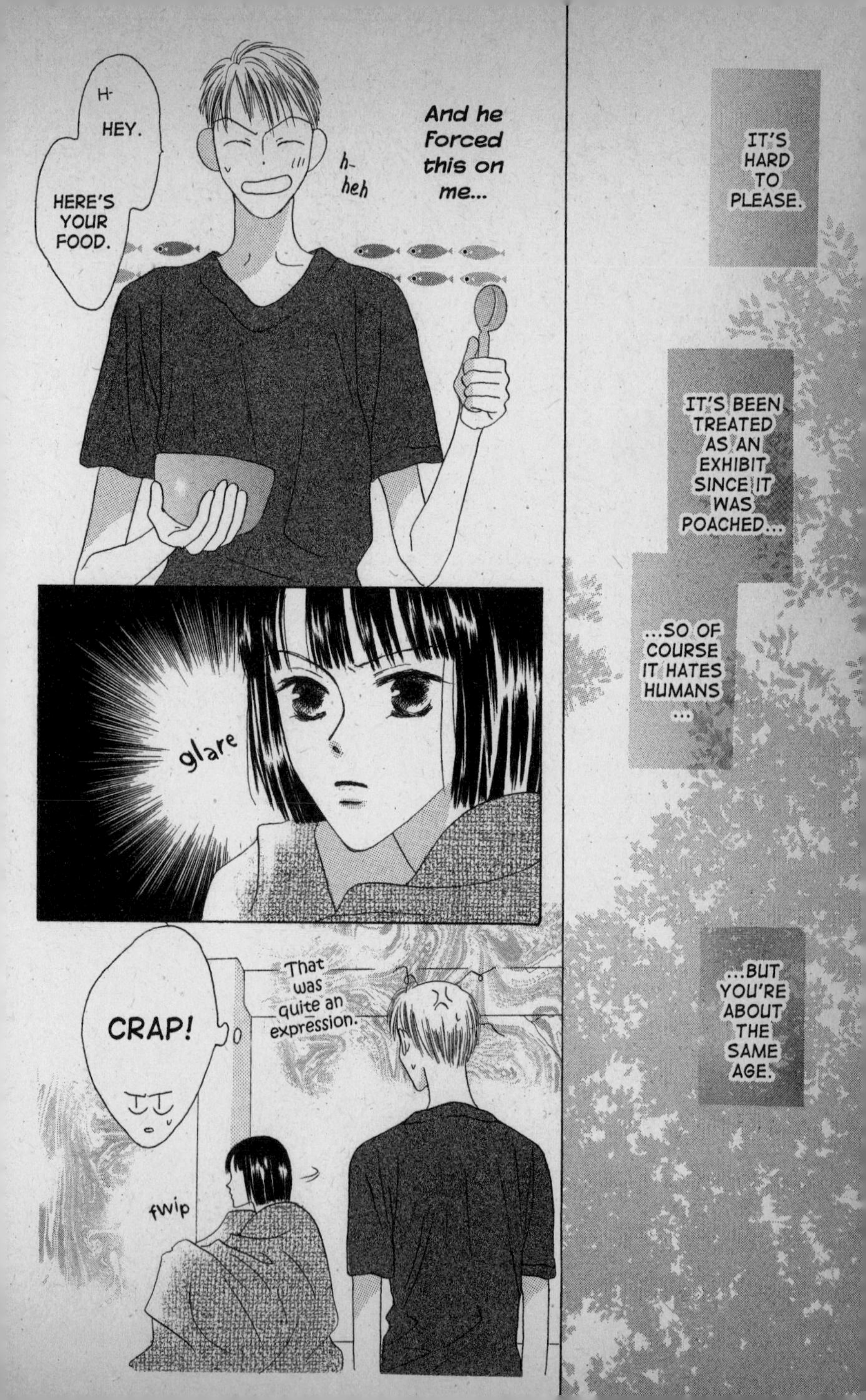
IT'S HARD TO PLEASE.
IT'S BEEN TREATED AS AN EXHIBIT SINCE IT WAS POACHED...
...SO OF COURSE IT HATES HUMANS...
...BUT YOU'RE ABOUT THE SAME AGE.
And he forced this on me...
h-heh
H- HEY. HERE'S YOUR FOOD.
glare
That was quite an expression.
CRAP!
fwip

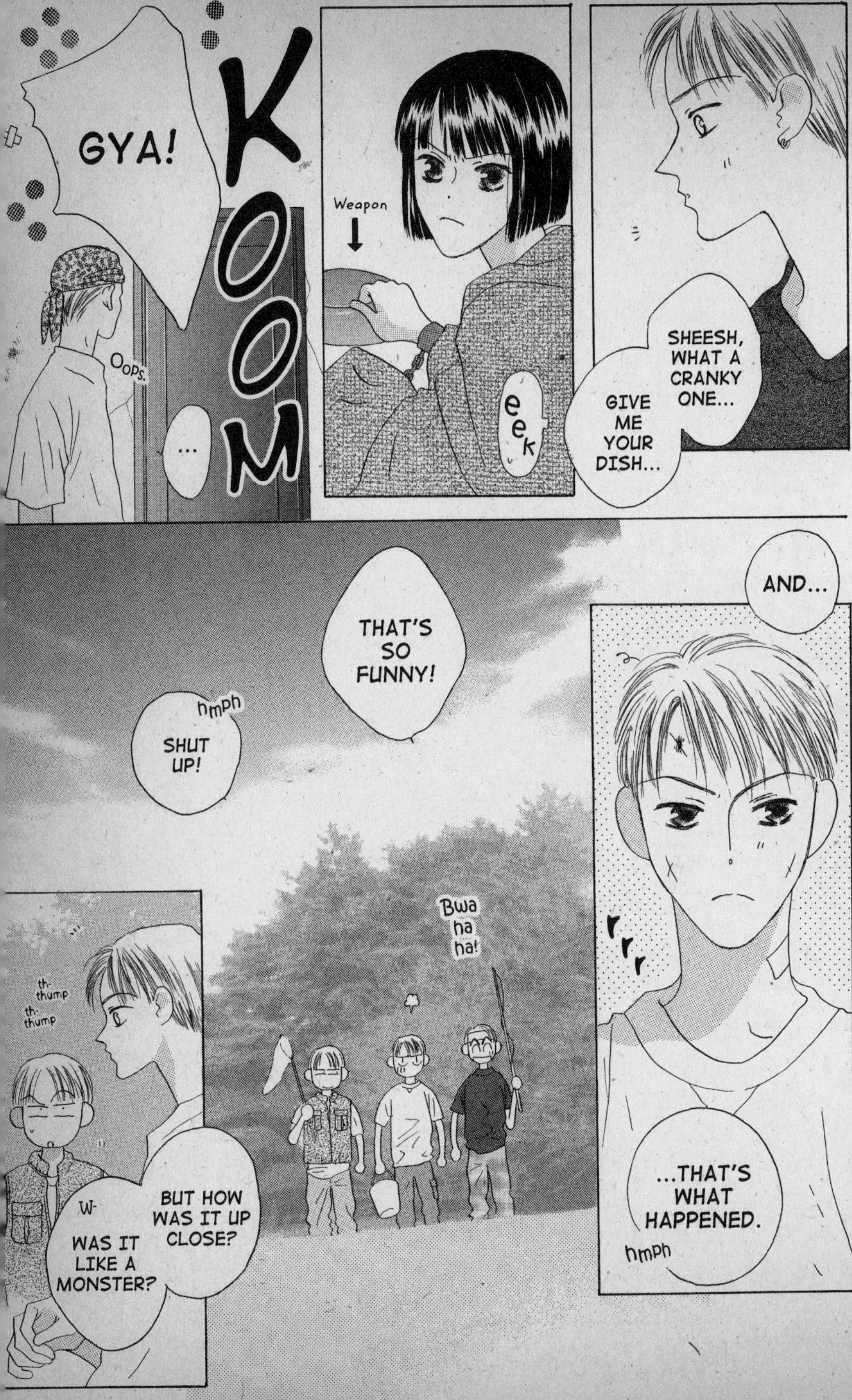
SHEESH, WHAT A CRANKY ONE...
GIVE ME YOUR DISH...
Weapon
eek
KOOOM
GYA!
Oops.
...
AND...
rrr
...THAT'S WHAT HAPPENED.
hmph
THAT'S SO FUNNY!
hmph
SHUT UP!
Bwa ha ha!
th-thump
th-thump
BUT HOW WAS IT UP CLOSE?
W-
WAS IT LIKE A MONSTER?

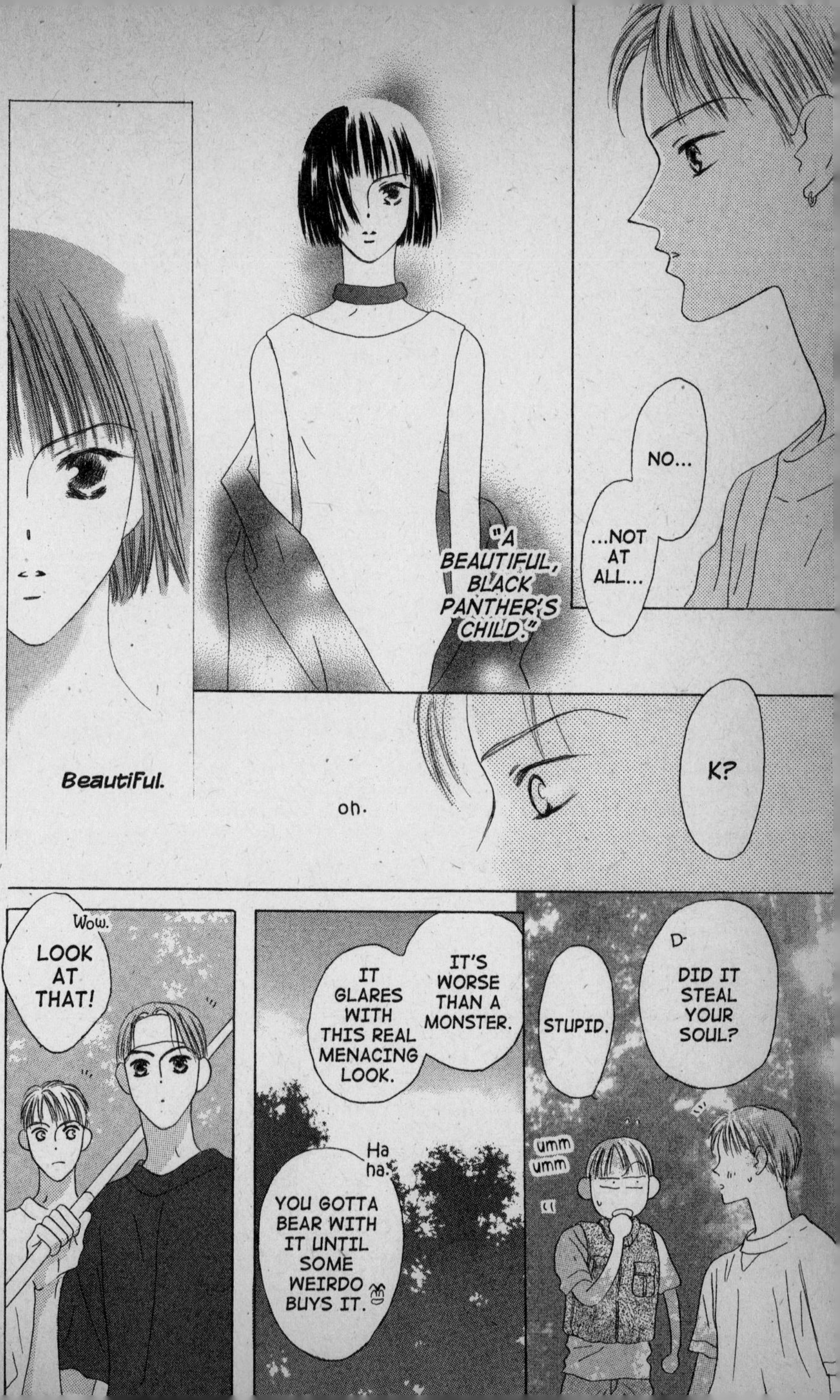
NO...
...NOT AT ALL...
"A BEAUTIFUL, BLACK PANTHER'S CHILD."
K?
oh.
Beautiful.
D- DID IT STEAL YOUR SOUL?
STUPID.
umm umm
IT'S WORSE THAN A MONSTER.
IT GLARES WITH THIS REAL MENACING LOOK.
Ha ha.
YOU GOTTA BEAR WITH IT UNTIL SOME WEIRDO BUYS IT.
Wow.
LOOK AT THAT!

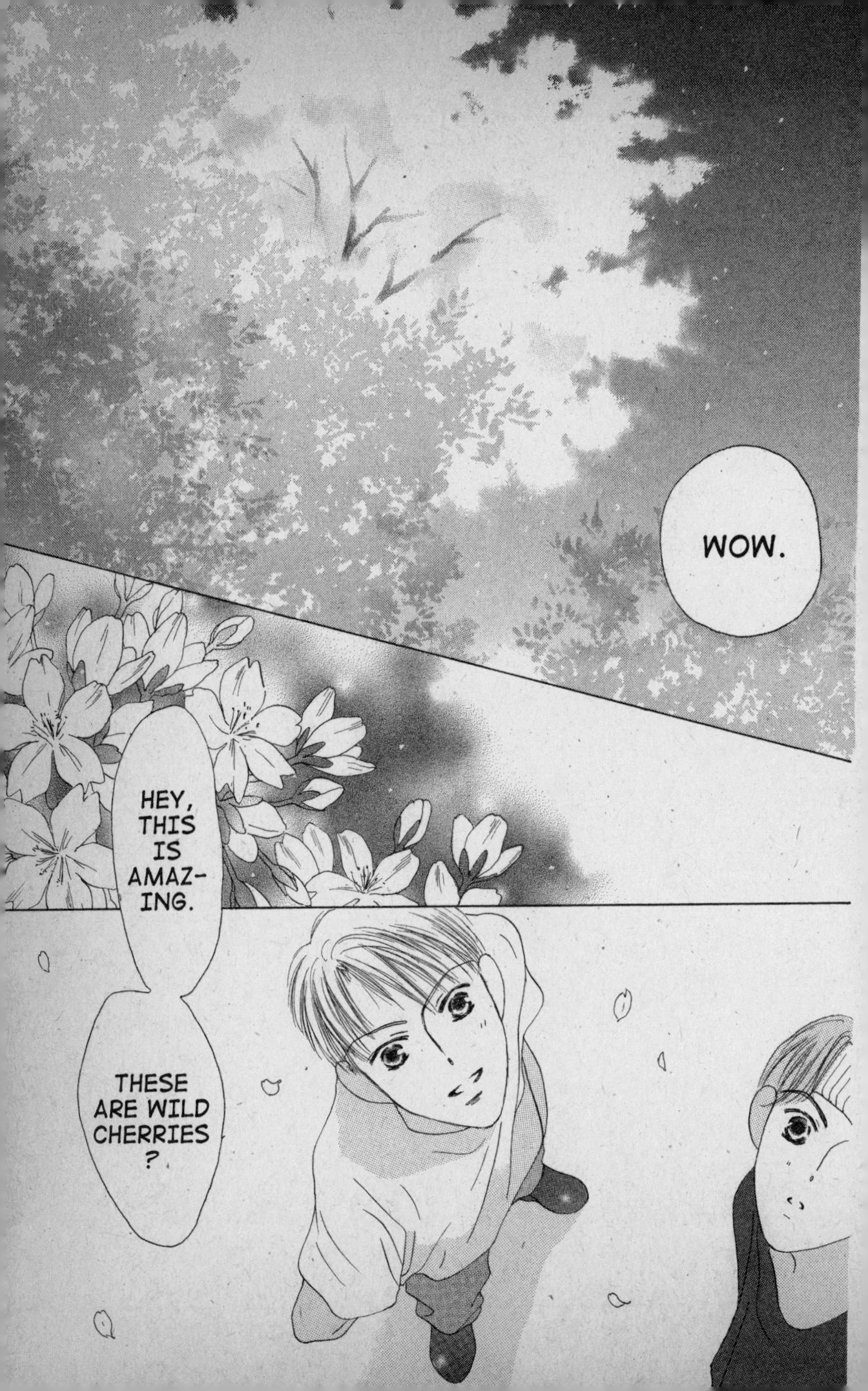
WOW.
HEY, THIS IS AMAZ-ING.
THESE ARE WILD CHERRIES?

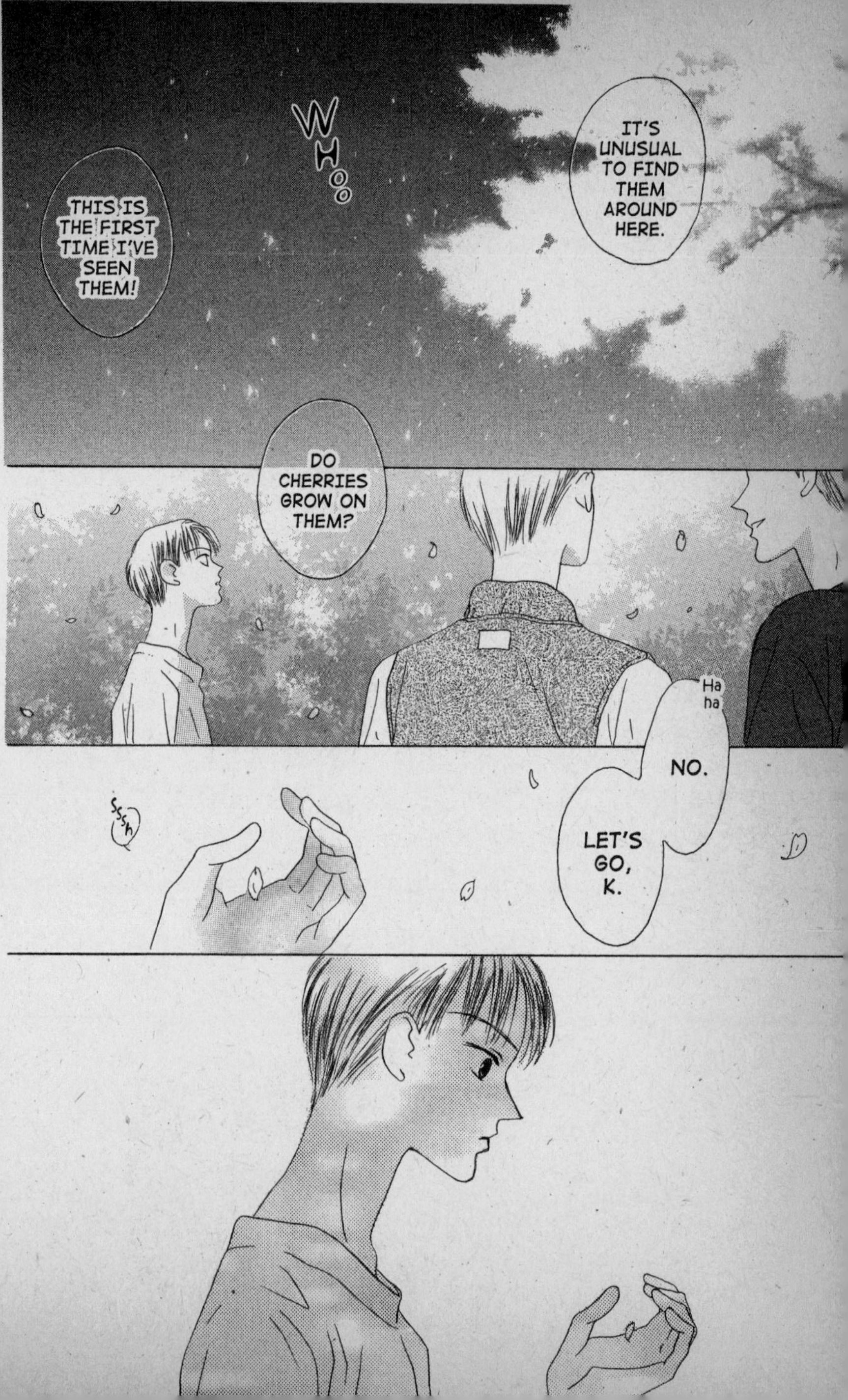
IT'S UNUSUAL TO FIND THEM AROUND HERE.
WHOO
THIS IS THE FIRST TIME I'VE SEEN THEM!
DO CHERRIES GROW ON THEM?
Ha ha
NO.
LET'S GO, K.
sssh

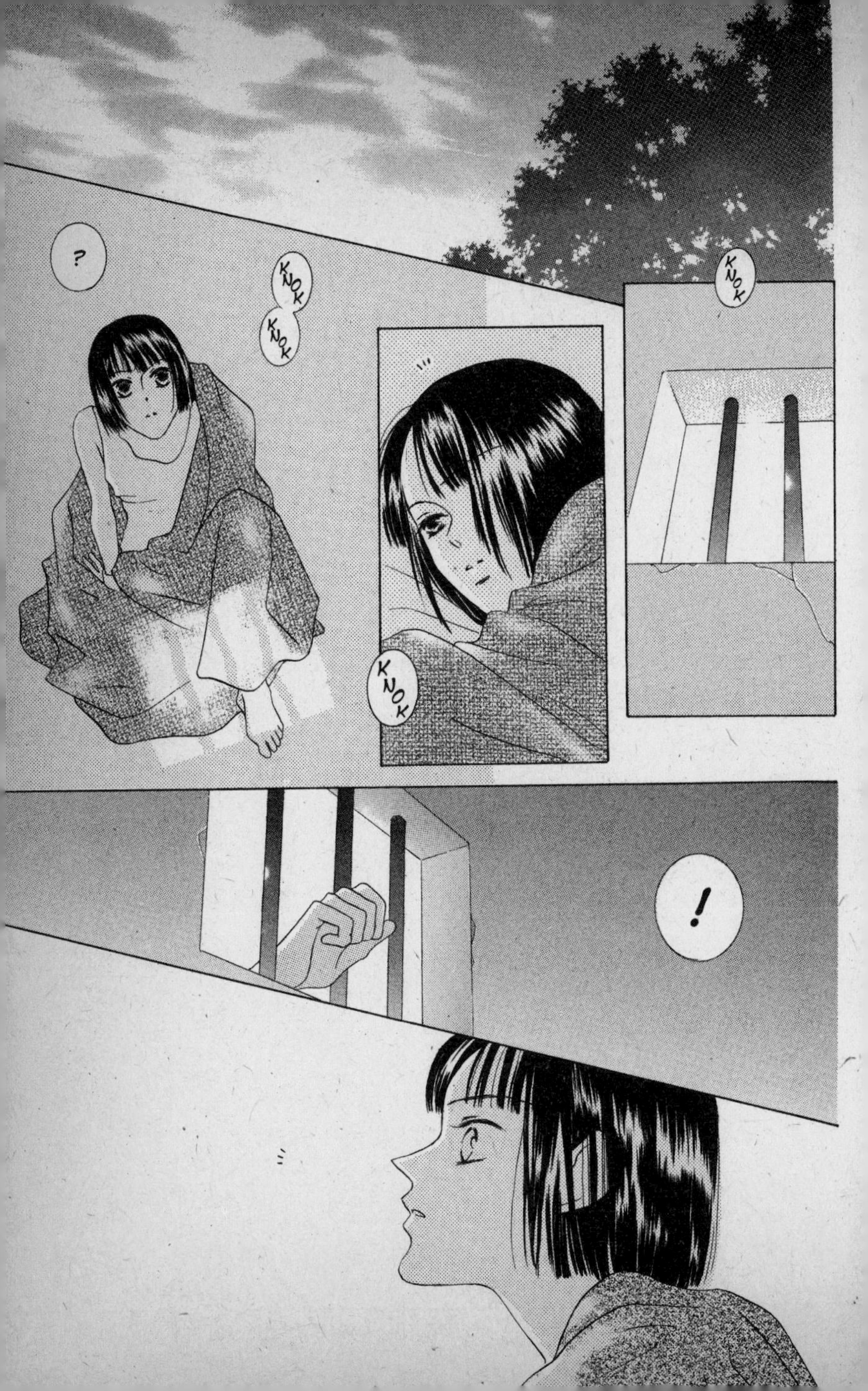
KNOK
KNOK
KNOK
KNOK
?
!

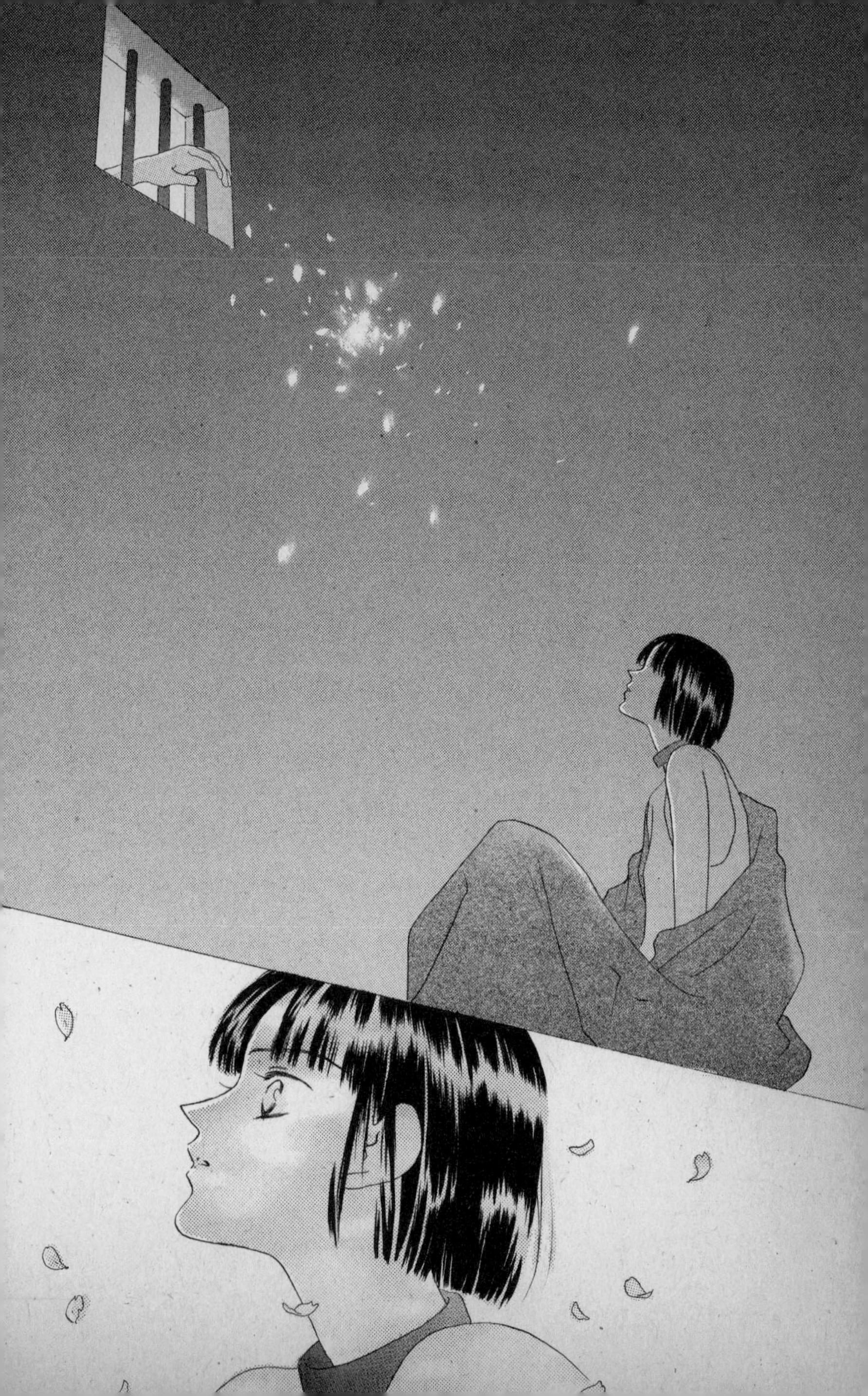

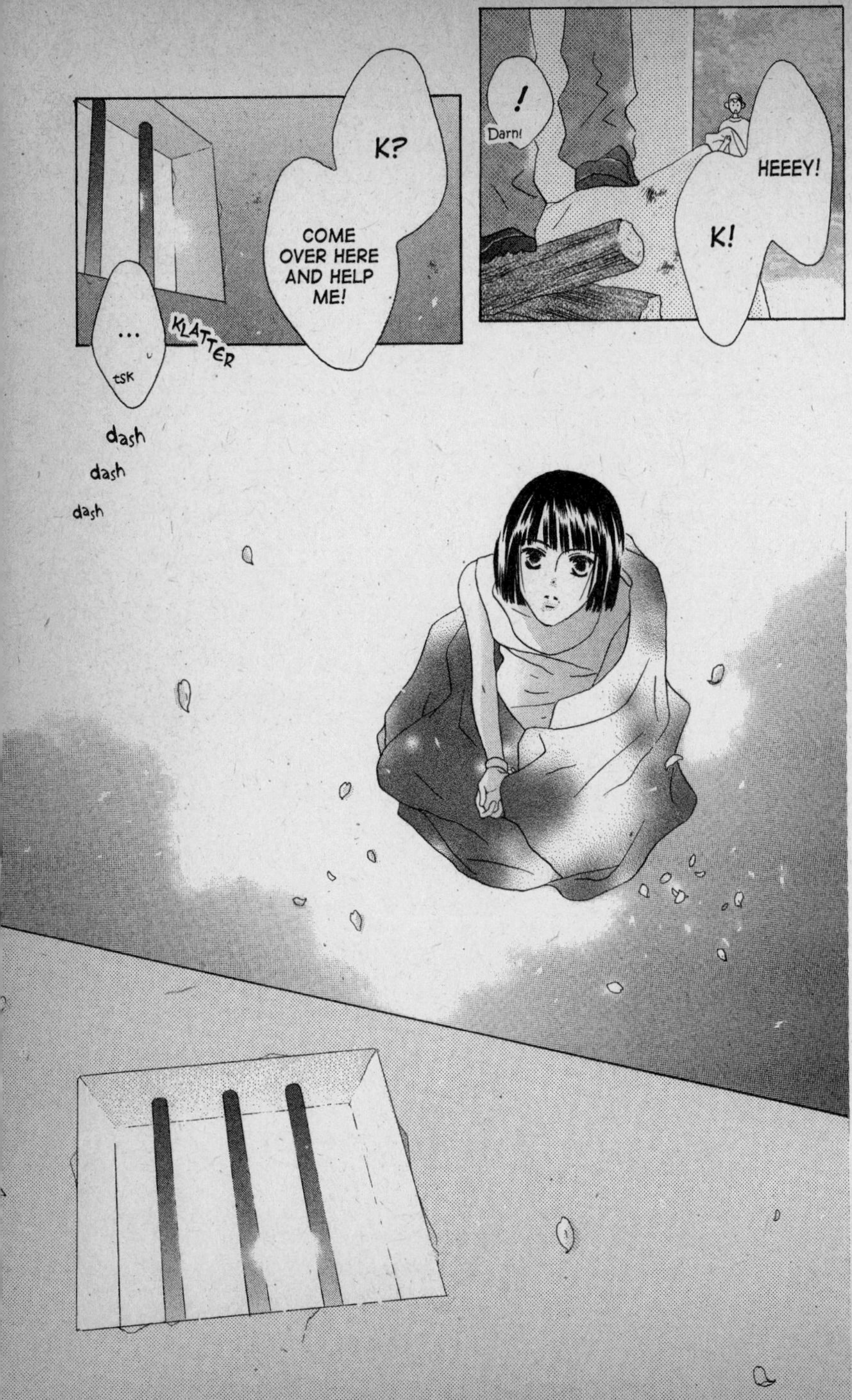
HEEEY!
K!
!
Darn!
K?
COME OVER HERE AND HELP ME!
...
tsk
KLATTER
dash
dash
dash

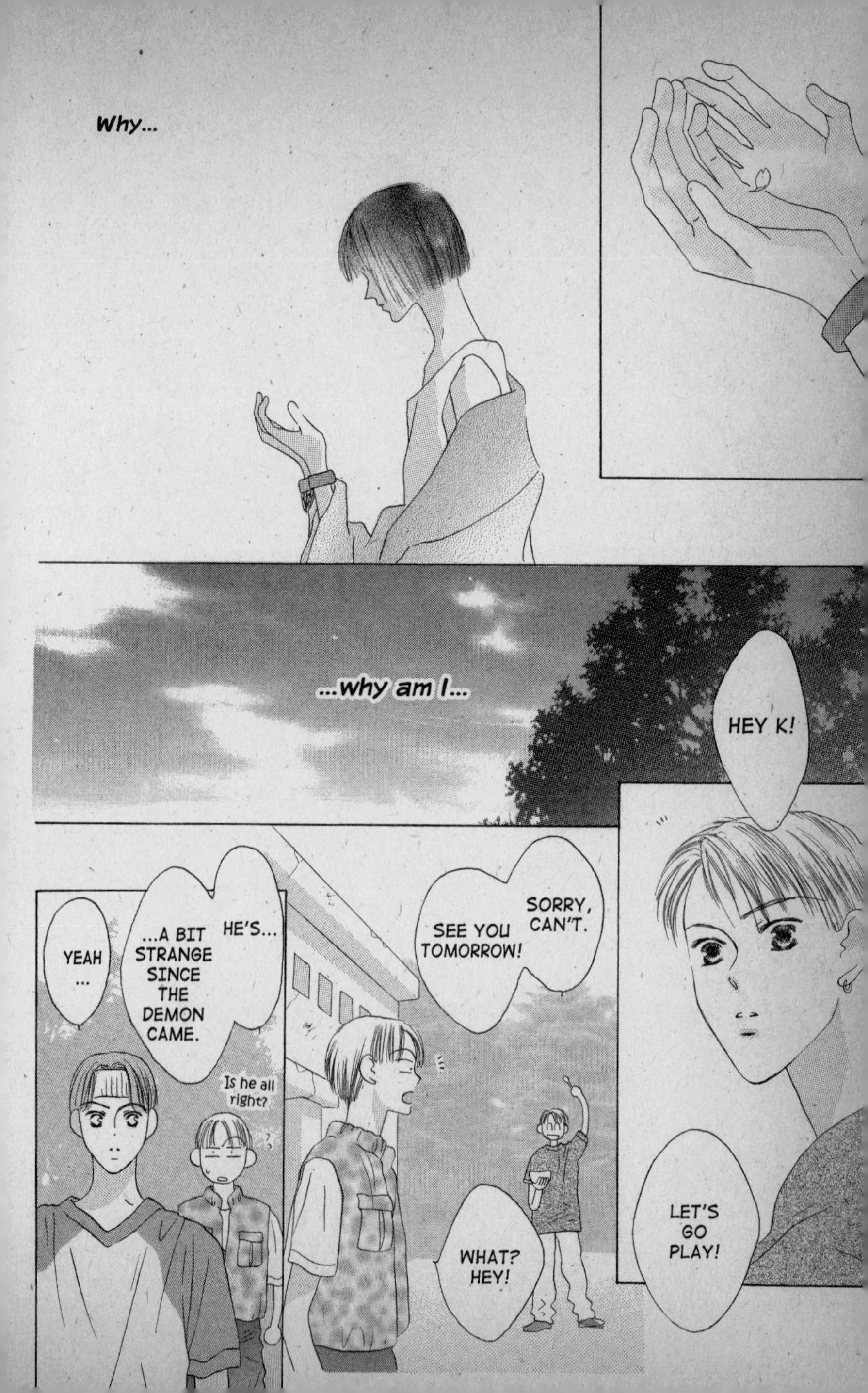
Why...
...why am I...
HEY K!
LET'S GO PLAY!
SORRY, CAN'T.
SEE YOU TOMORROW!
WHAT? HEY!
HE'S...
...A BIT STRANGE SINCE THE DEMON CAME.
Is he all right?
YEAH ...

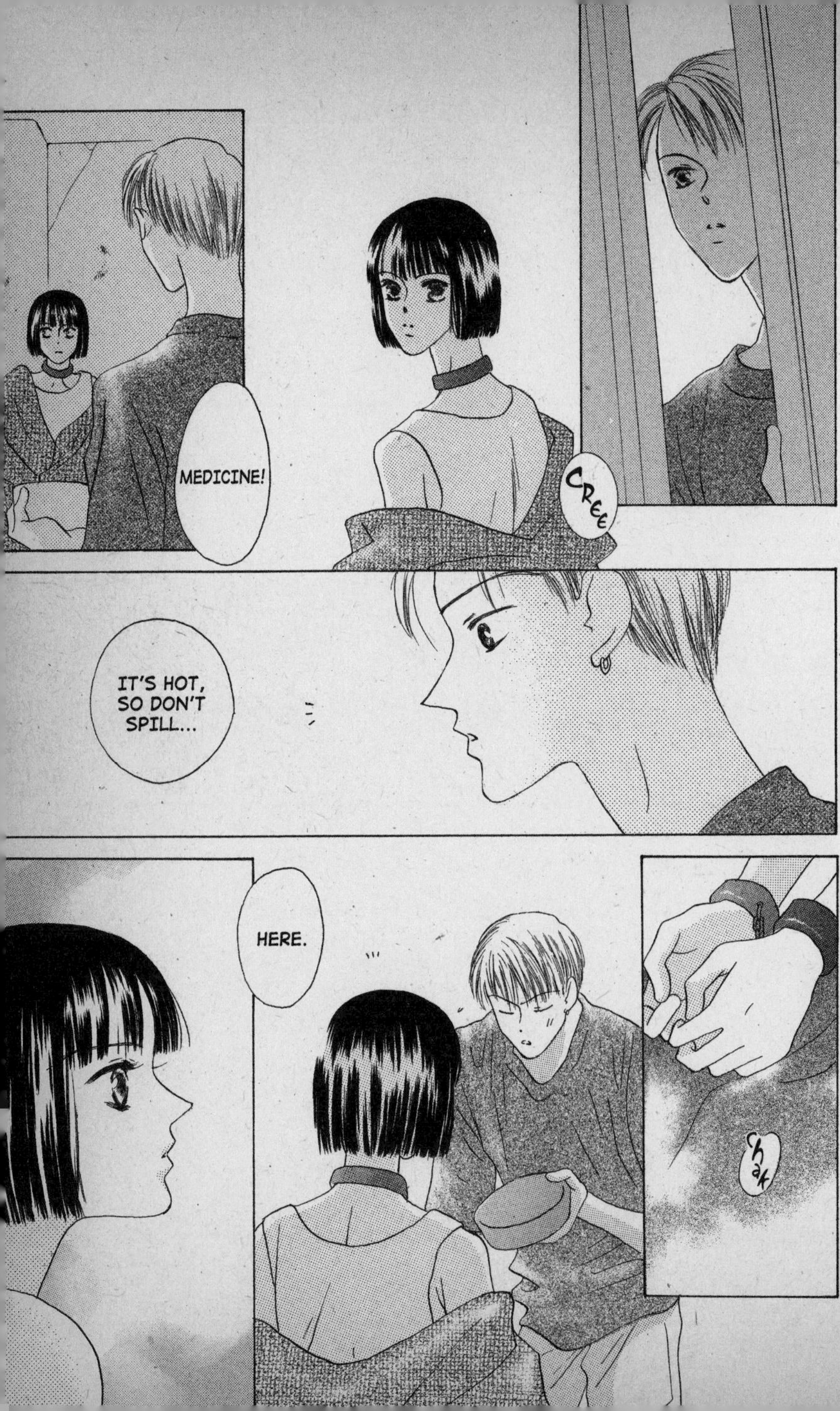
CREE
MEDICINE!
IT'S HOT, SO DON'T SPILL...
chak
HERE.

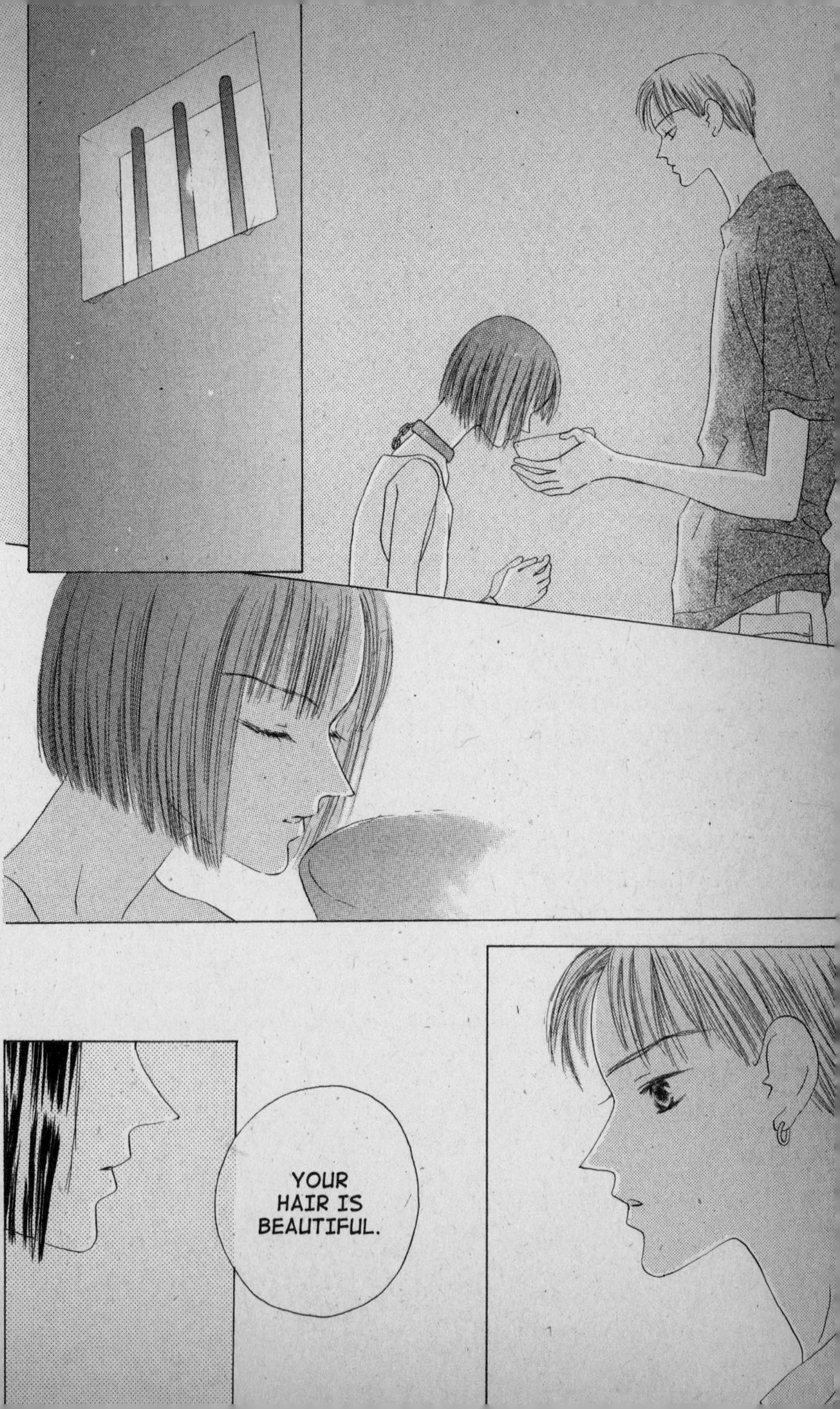
YOUR HAIR IS BEAUTIFUL.

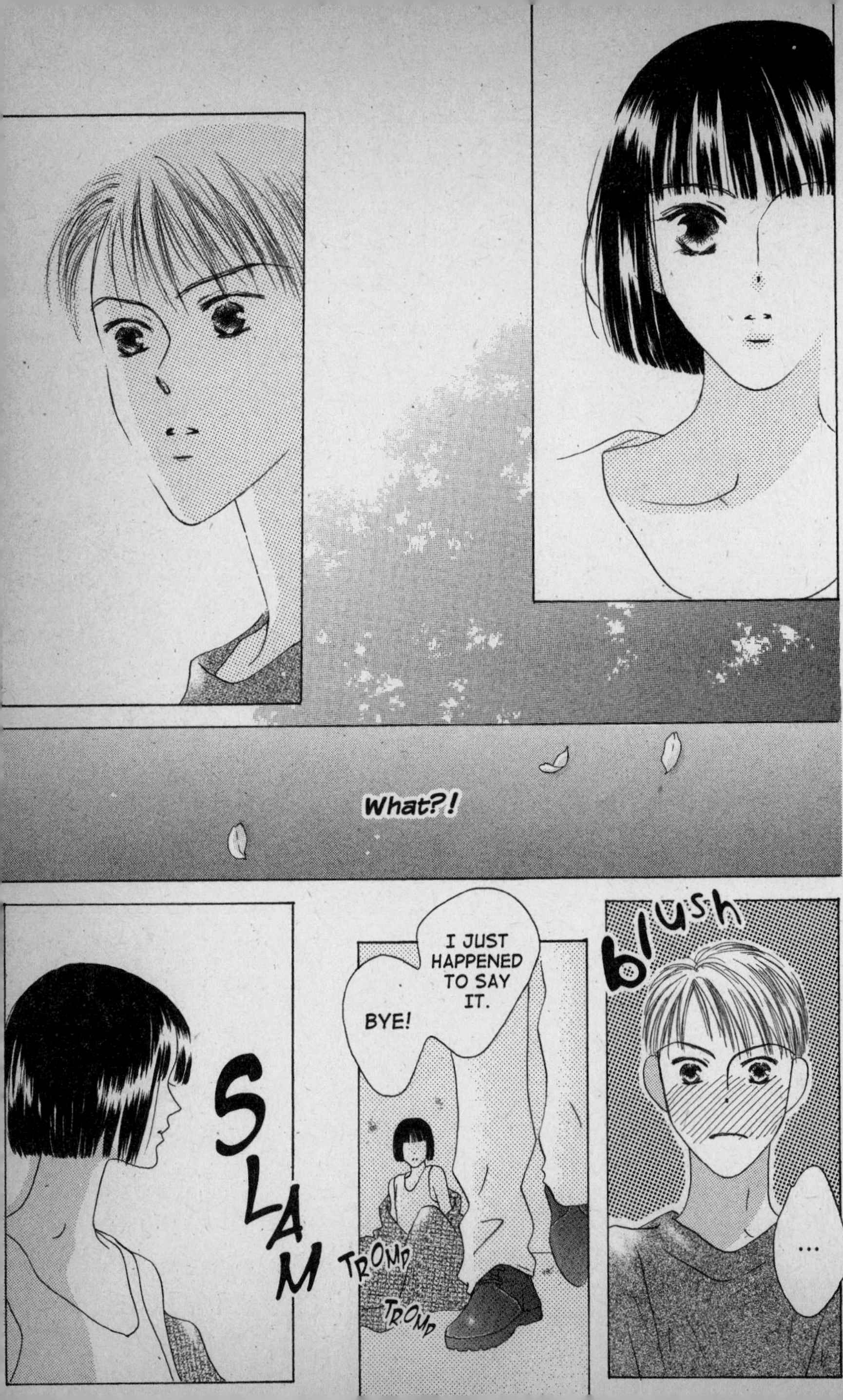
What?!
blush
...
I JUST HAPPENED TO SAY IT.
BYE!
TROMP
TROMP
SLAM

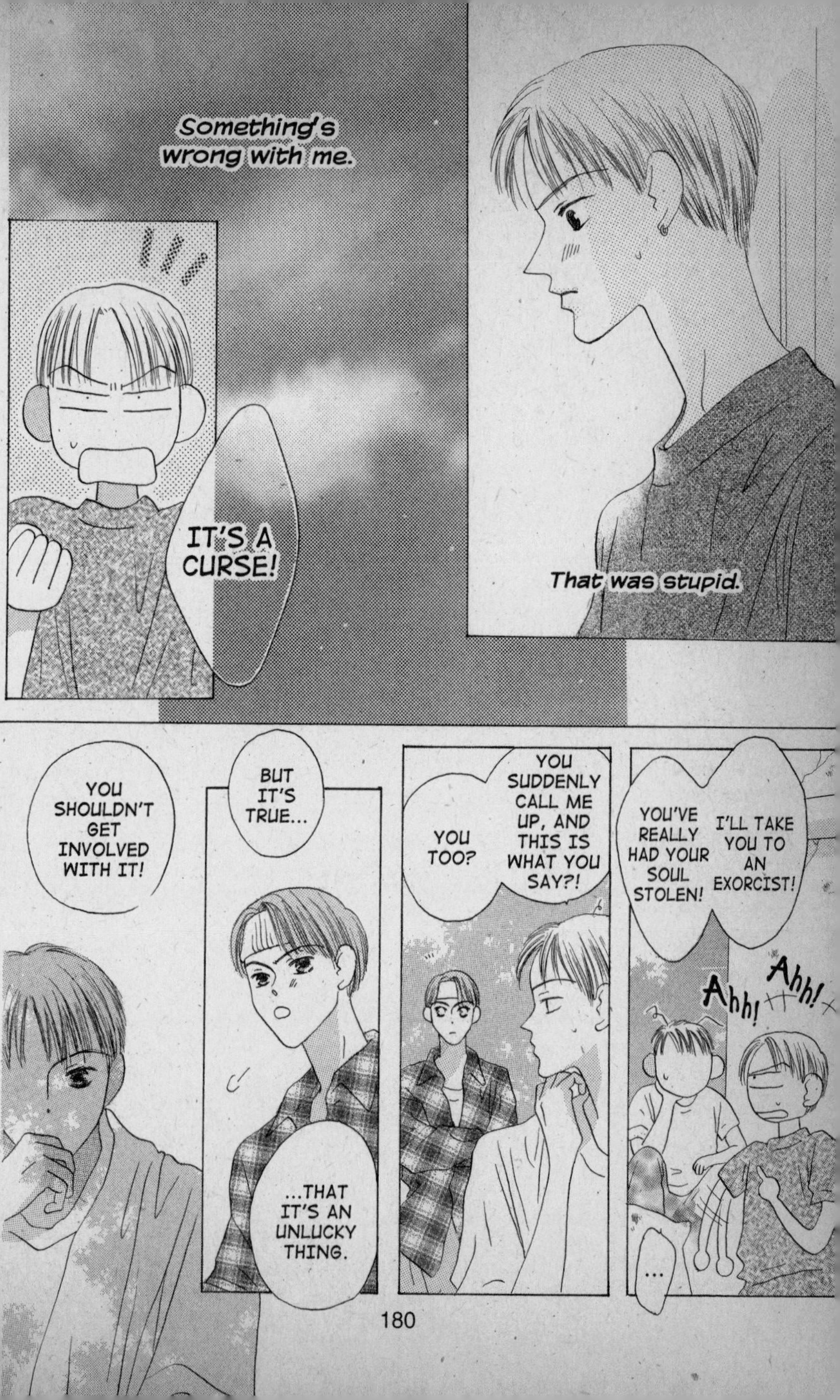
That was stupid.
Something's wrong with me.
IT'S A CURSE!
I'LL TAKE YOU TO AN EXORCIST!
YOU'VE REALLY HAD YOUR SOUL STOLEN!
Ahh! Ahh!
...
YOU SUDDENLY CALL ME UP, AND THIS IS WHAT YOU SAY?!
YOU TOO?
BUT IT'S TRUE...
...THAT IT'S AN UNLUCKY THING.
YOU SHOULDN'T GET INVOLVED WITH IT!

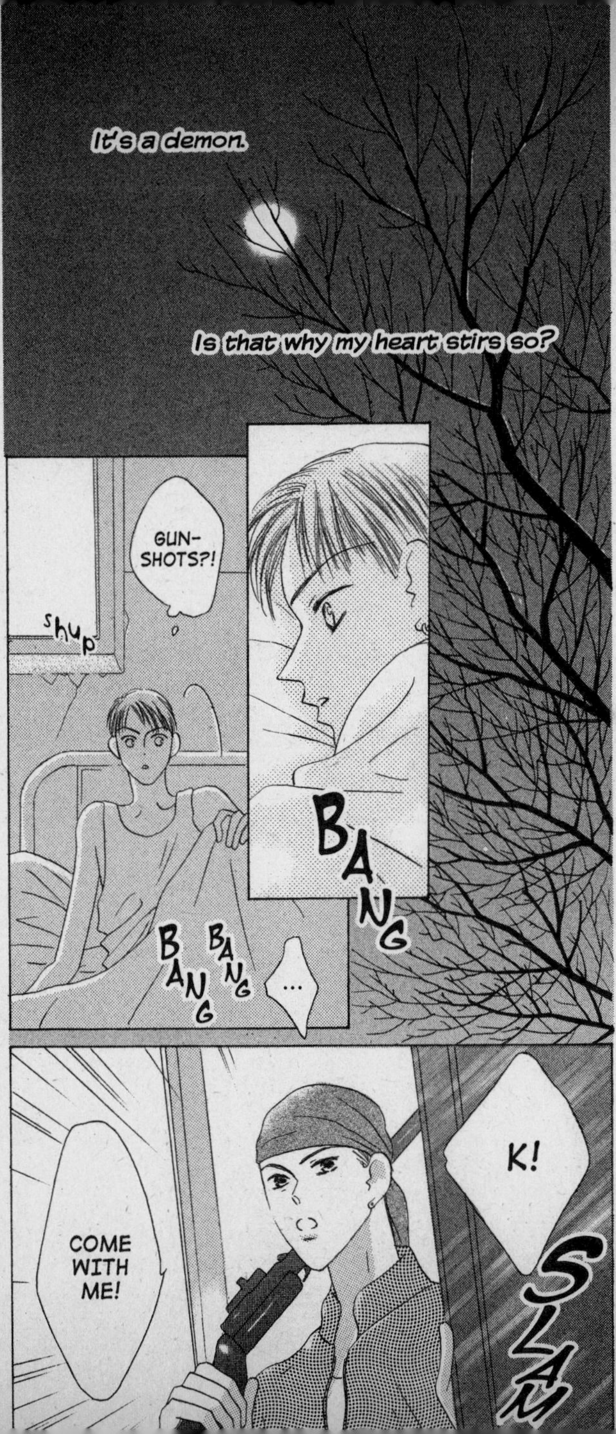

It's a demon.
Is that why my heart stirs so?
BANG
GUN-SHOTS?!
shup
BANG
BANG
...
K!
SLAM
COME WITH ME!

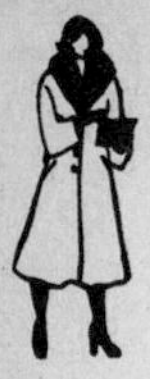

⑥

"The Release" was drawn about eight years (!) ago.
I thought I wasn't the type to have my drawing change over time but... it... it has changed quite a bit...!!
(Ahhh!)
The story has portions that need more explanation, but I left it that way intentionally.

Beauty Is the Beast was initially supposed to be a three-chapter series, so I'm surprised it continued this long without my missing any deadlines. (☺)
I sincerely thank my editor, all my staff, and everyone who read it! Yes.

Thank you so very much.

See you again!

This was
Tomo Matsumoto.

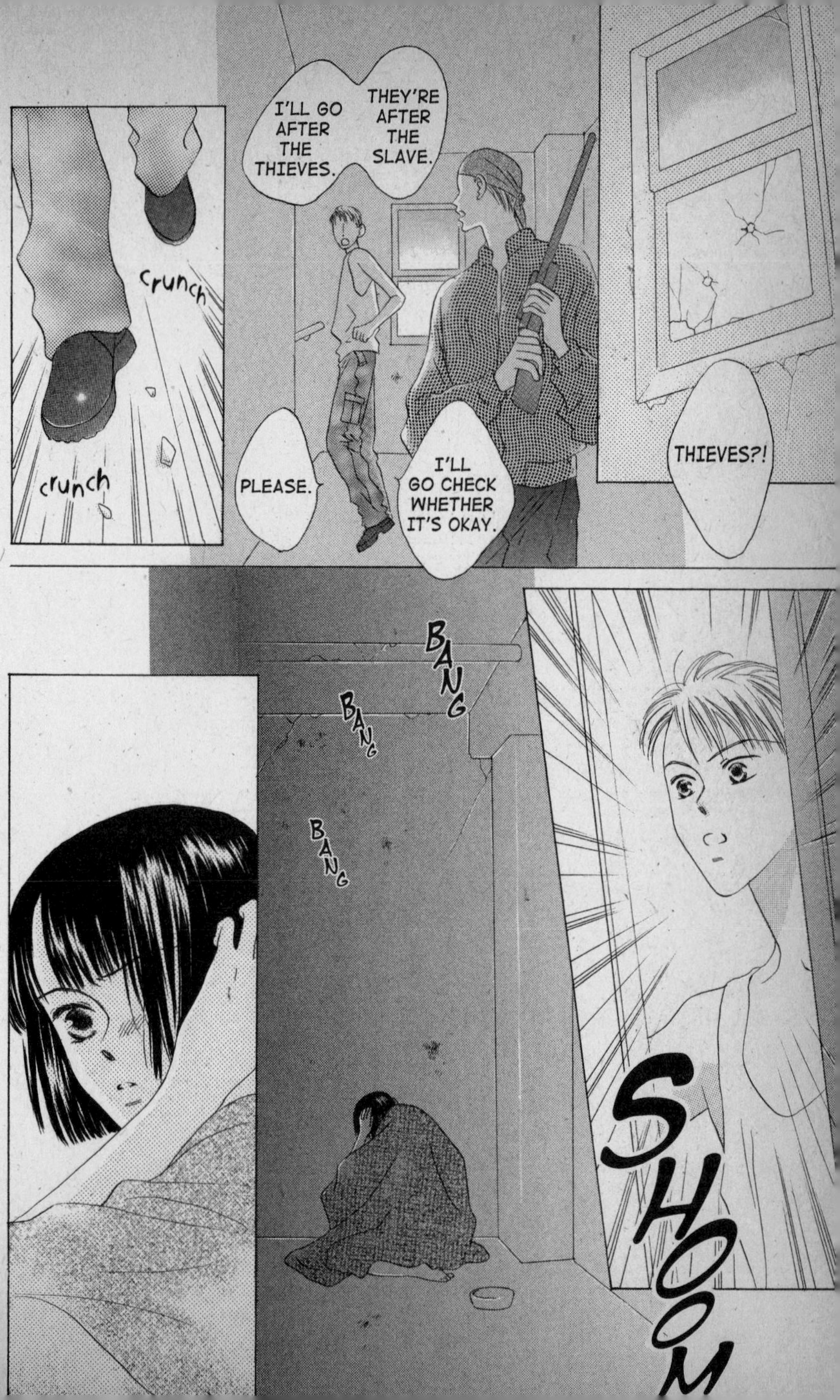
THIEVES?!
THEY'RE AFTER THE SLAVE.
I'LL GO AFTER THE THIEVES.
I'LL GO CHECK WHETHER IT'S OKAY.
PLEASE.
crunch
crunch
SHOOM
BANG
BANG
BANG

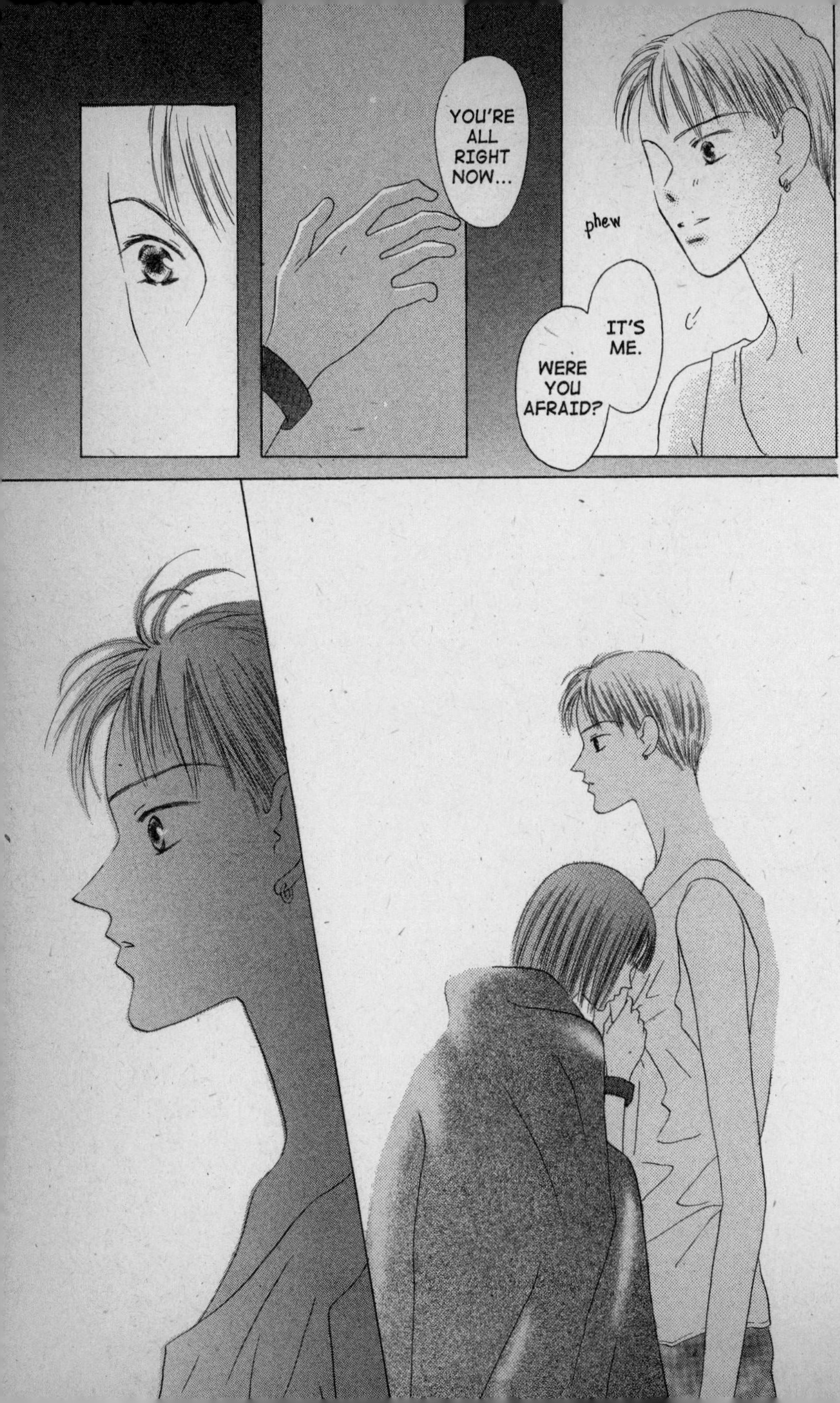
phew
IT'S ME. WERE YOU AFRAID?
YOU'RE ALL RIGHT NOW...

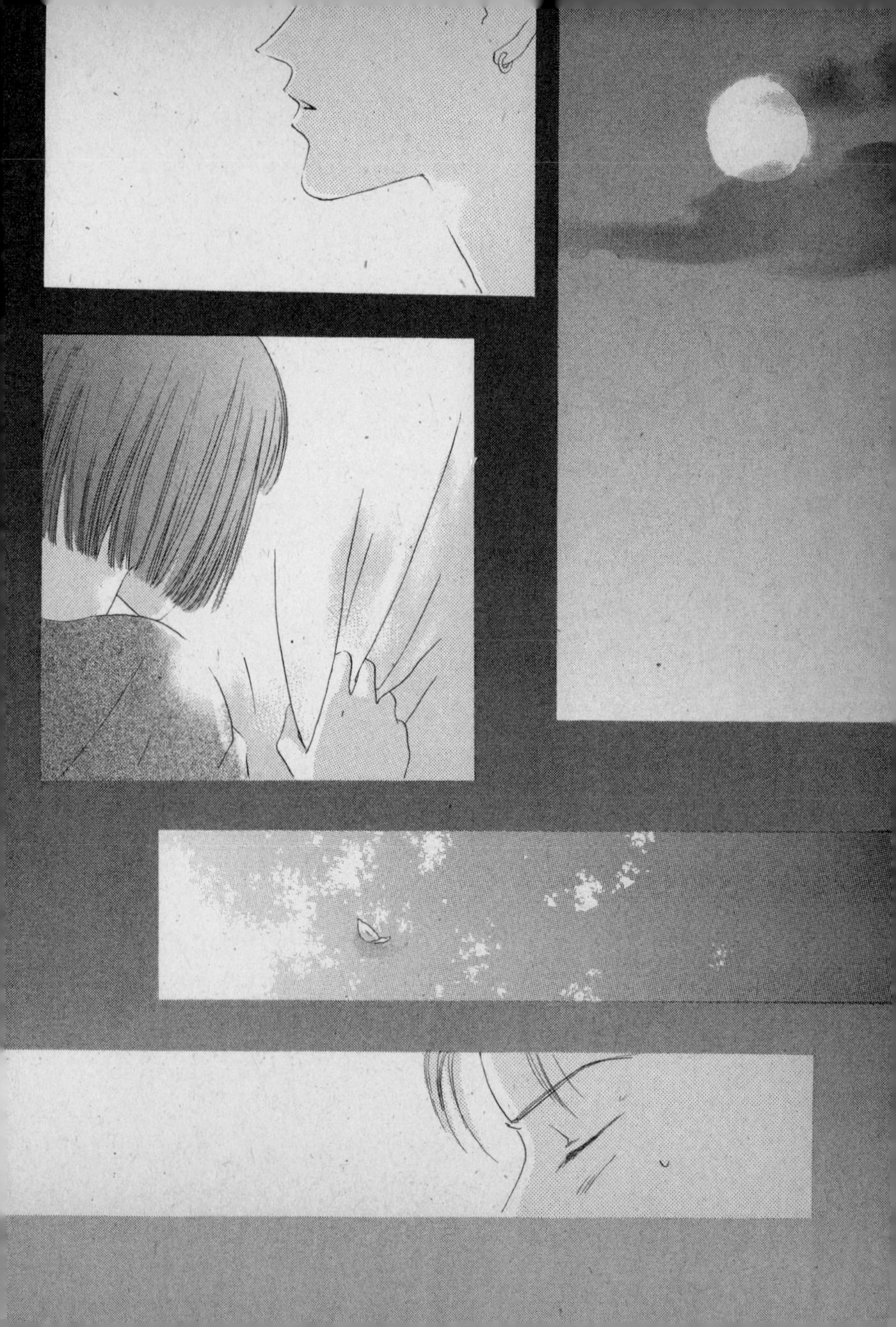

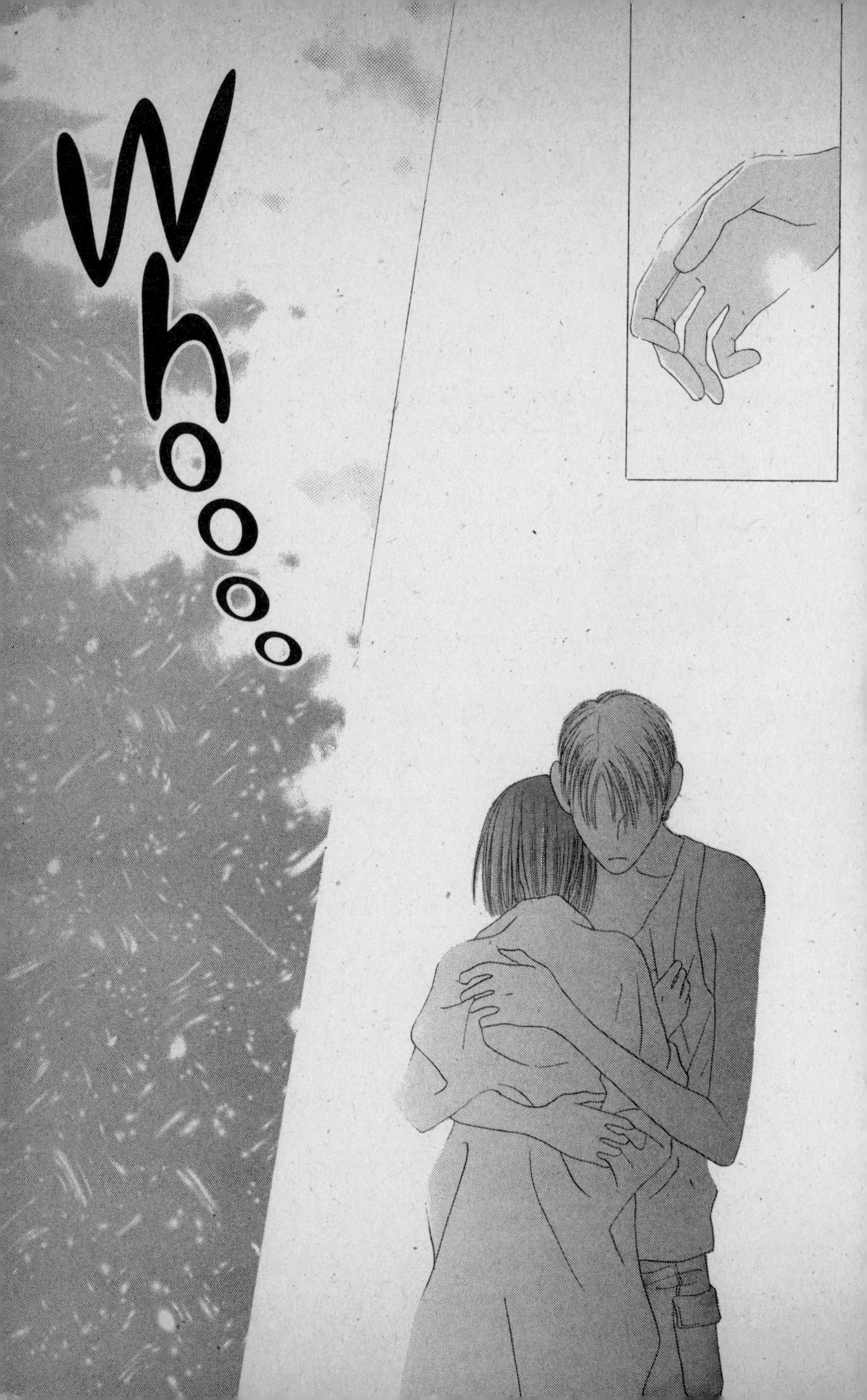
Whoooo

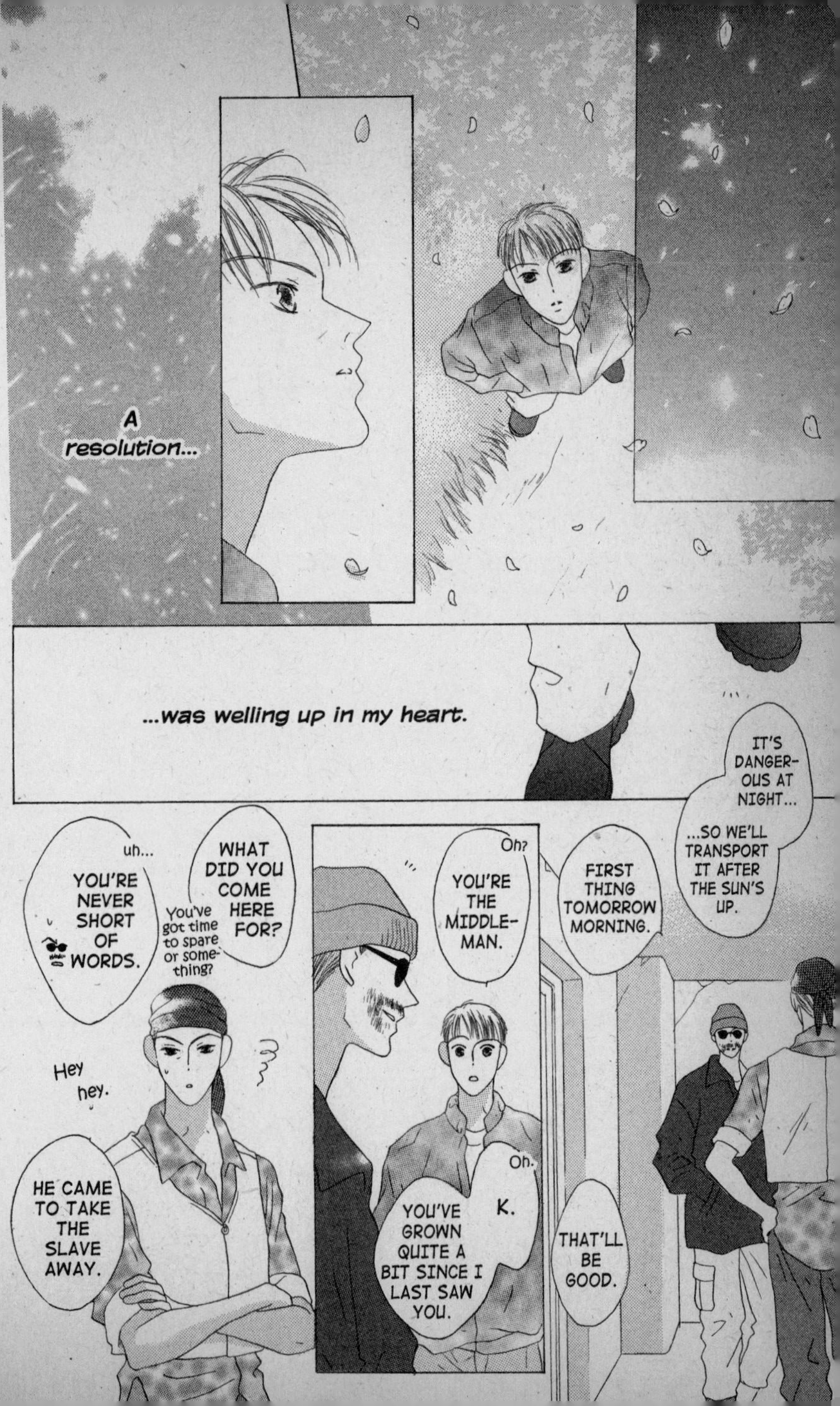
A resolution...
...was welling up in my heart.
IT'S DANGEROUS AT NIGHT...
...SO WE'LL TRANSPORT IT AFTER THE SUN'S UP.
FIRST THING TOMORROW MORNING.
THAT'LL BE GOOD.
Oh?
YOU'RE THE MIDDLE-MAN.
Oh.
K.
YOU'VE GROWN QUITE A BIT SINCE I LAST SAW YOU.
WHAT DID YOU COME HERE FOR?
You've got time to spare or some-thing?
uh...
YOU'RE NEVER SHORT OF WORDS.
Hey hey.
HE CAME TO TAKE THE SLAVE AWAY.

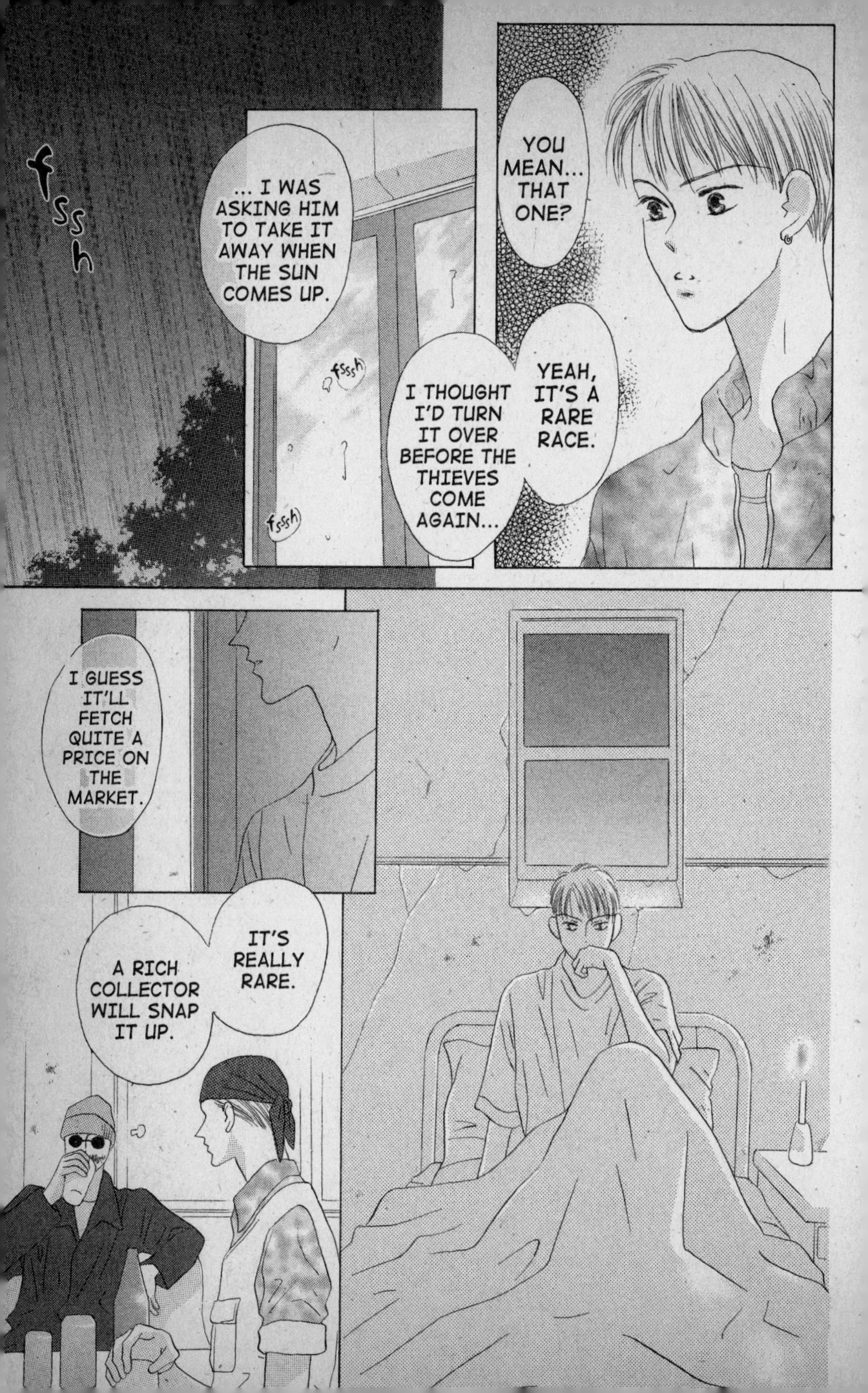
YOU MEAN... THAT ONE?
YEAH, IT'S A RARE RACE.
I THOUGHT I'D TURN IT OVER BEFORE THE THIEVES COME AGAIN...
... I WAS ASKING HIM TO TAKE IT AWAY WHEN THE SUN COMES UP.
fsssh
fsssh
fssh
I GUESS IT'LL FETCH QUITE A PRICE ON THE MARKET.
IT'S REALLY RARE.
A RICH COLLECTOR WILL SNAP IT UP.

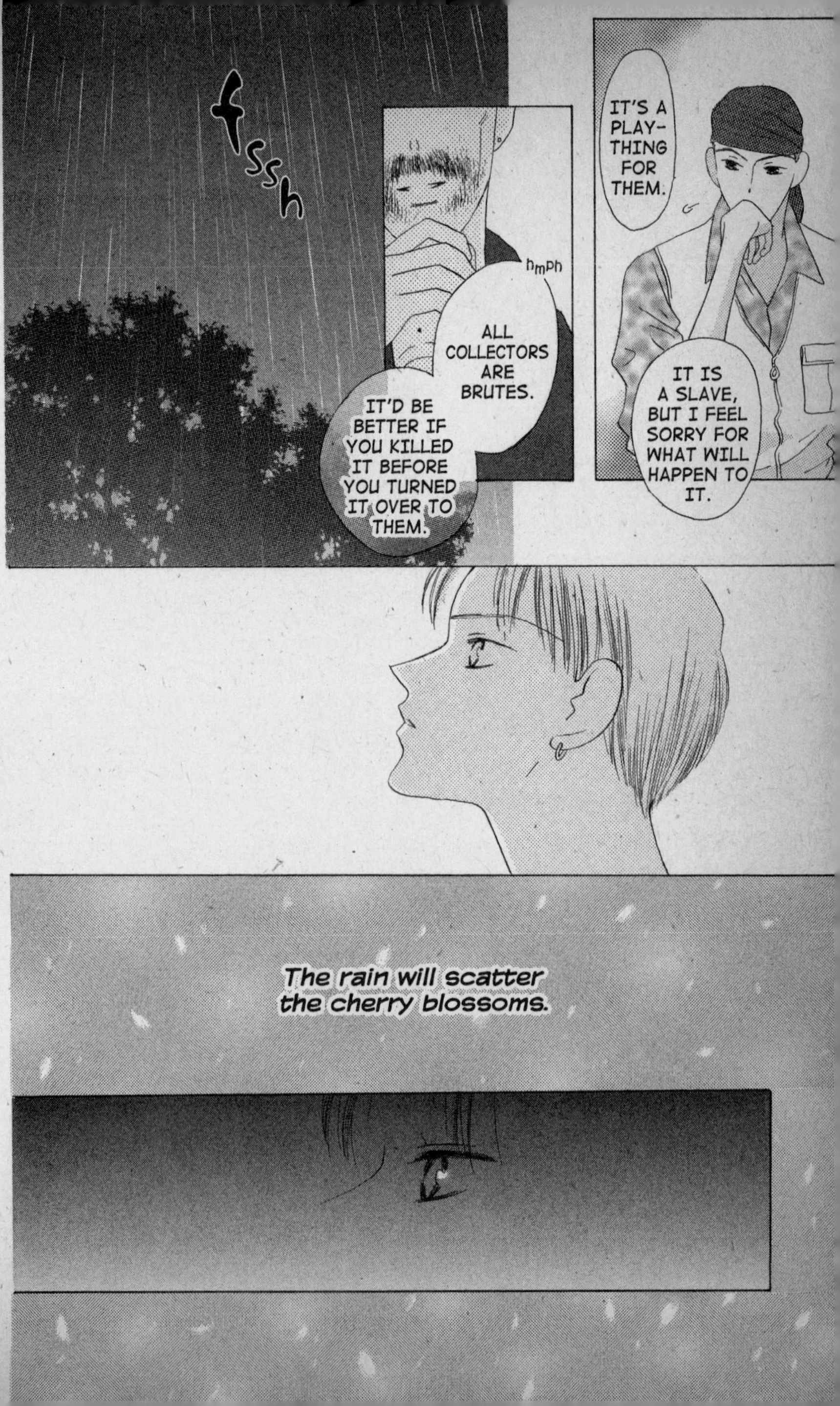
IT'S A PLAYTHING FOR THEM.
IT IS A SLAVE, BUT I FEEL SORRY FOR WHAT WILL HAPPEN TO IT.
hmph
ALL COLLECTORS ARE BRUTES.
IT'D BE BETTER IF YOU KILLED IT BEFORE YOU TURNED IT OVER TO THEM.
fssh
The rain will scatter the cherry blossoms.

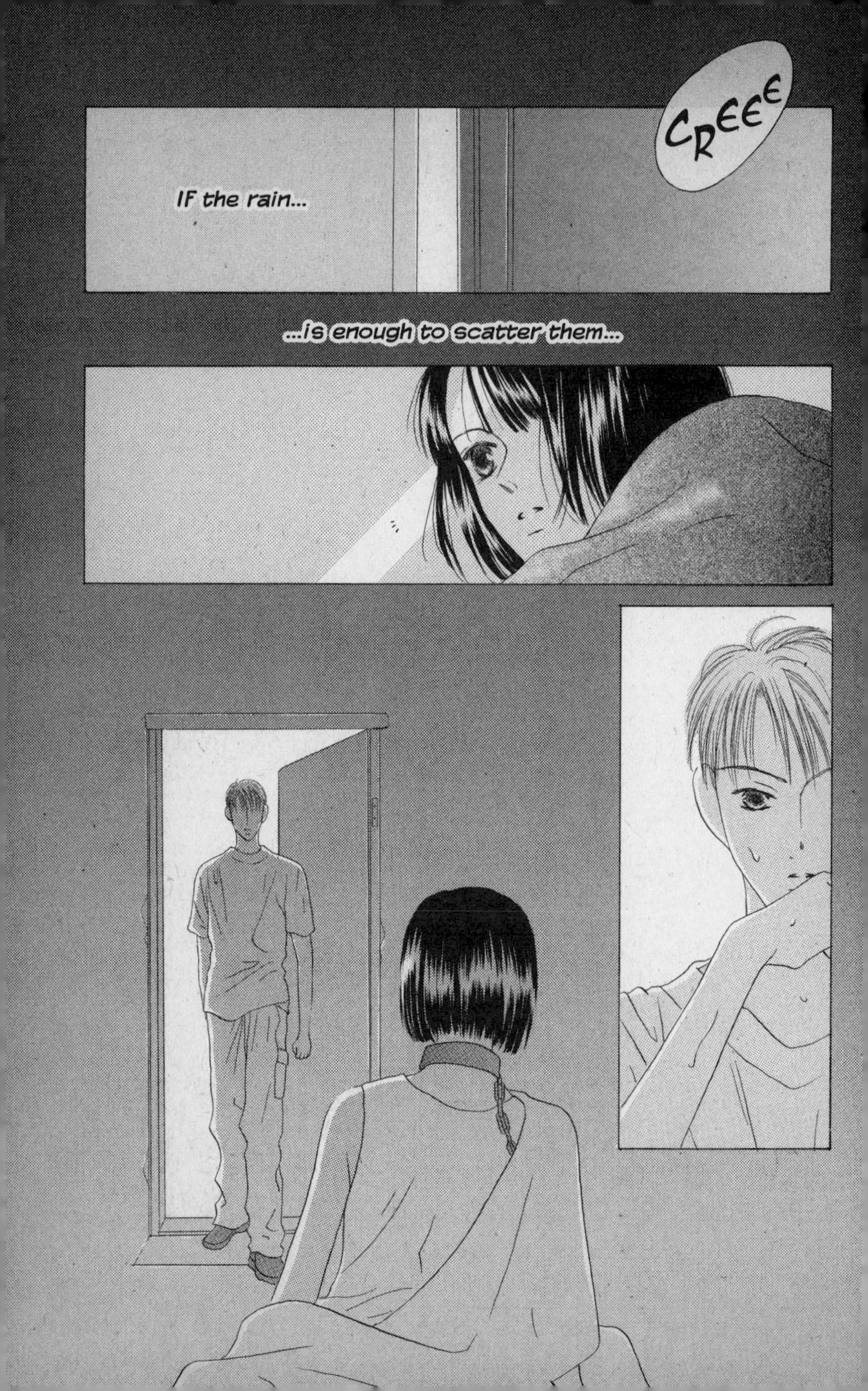
CREEE
IF the rain...
...is enough to scatter them...

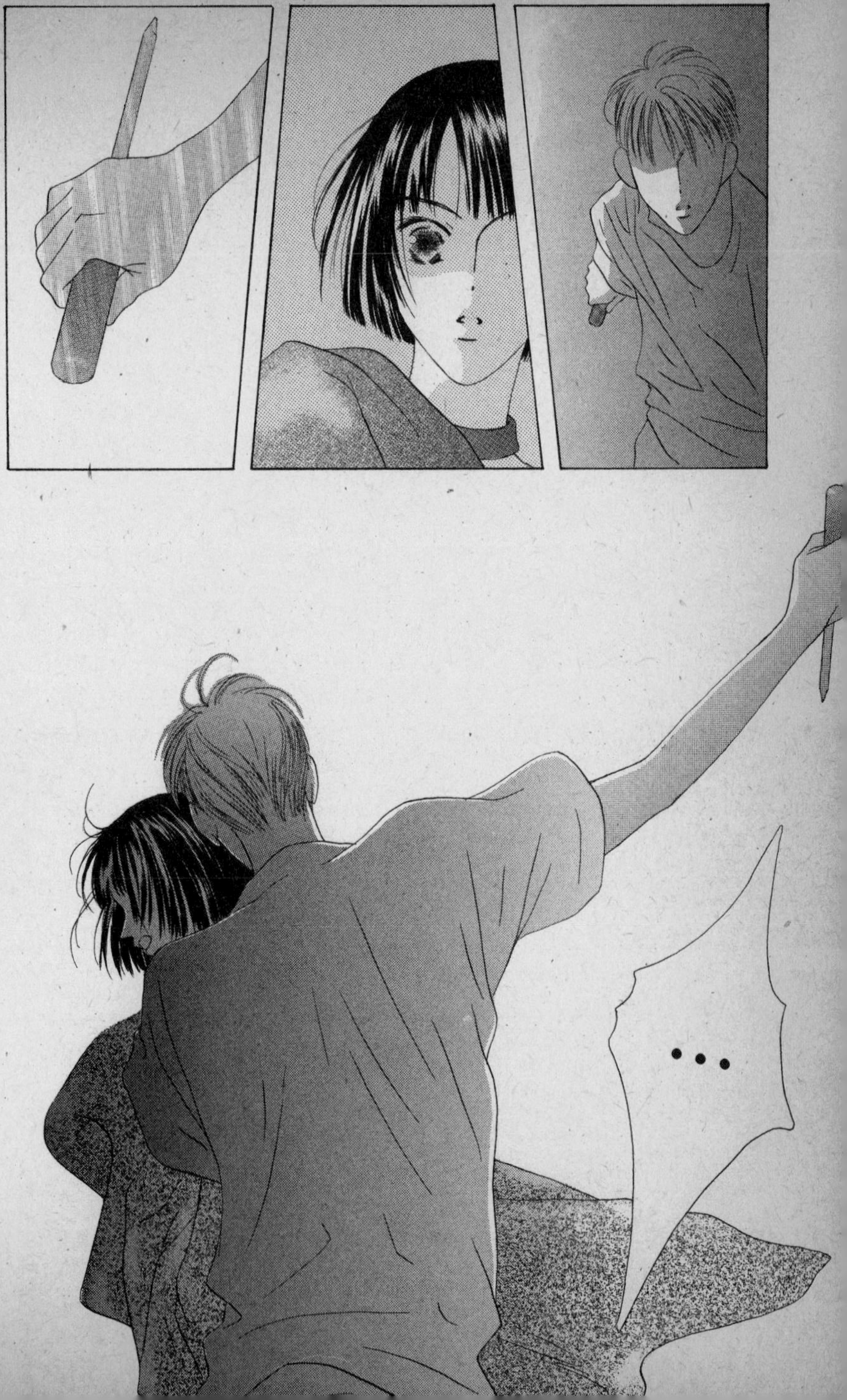
...

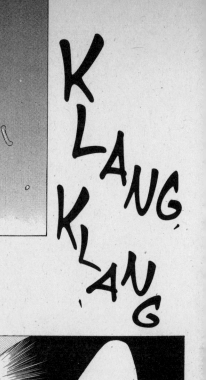

KLANG, KLANG

KLATTER

COME!

huff

huff

huff

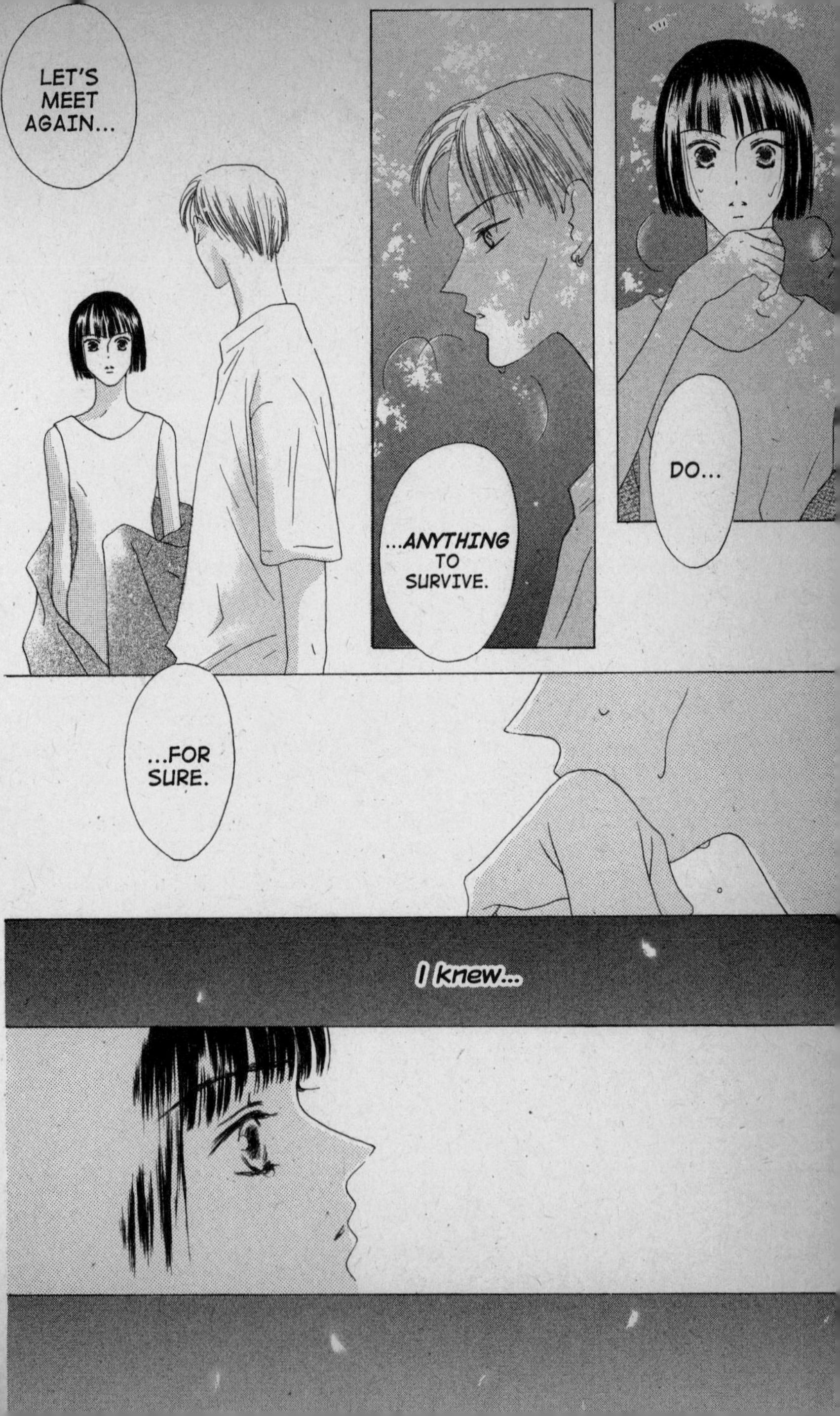
DO...
...ANYTHING TO SURVIVE.
LET'S MEET AGAIN...
...FOR SURE.
I knew...

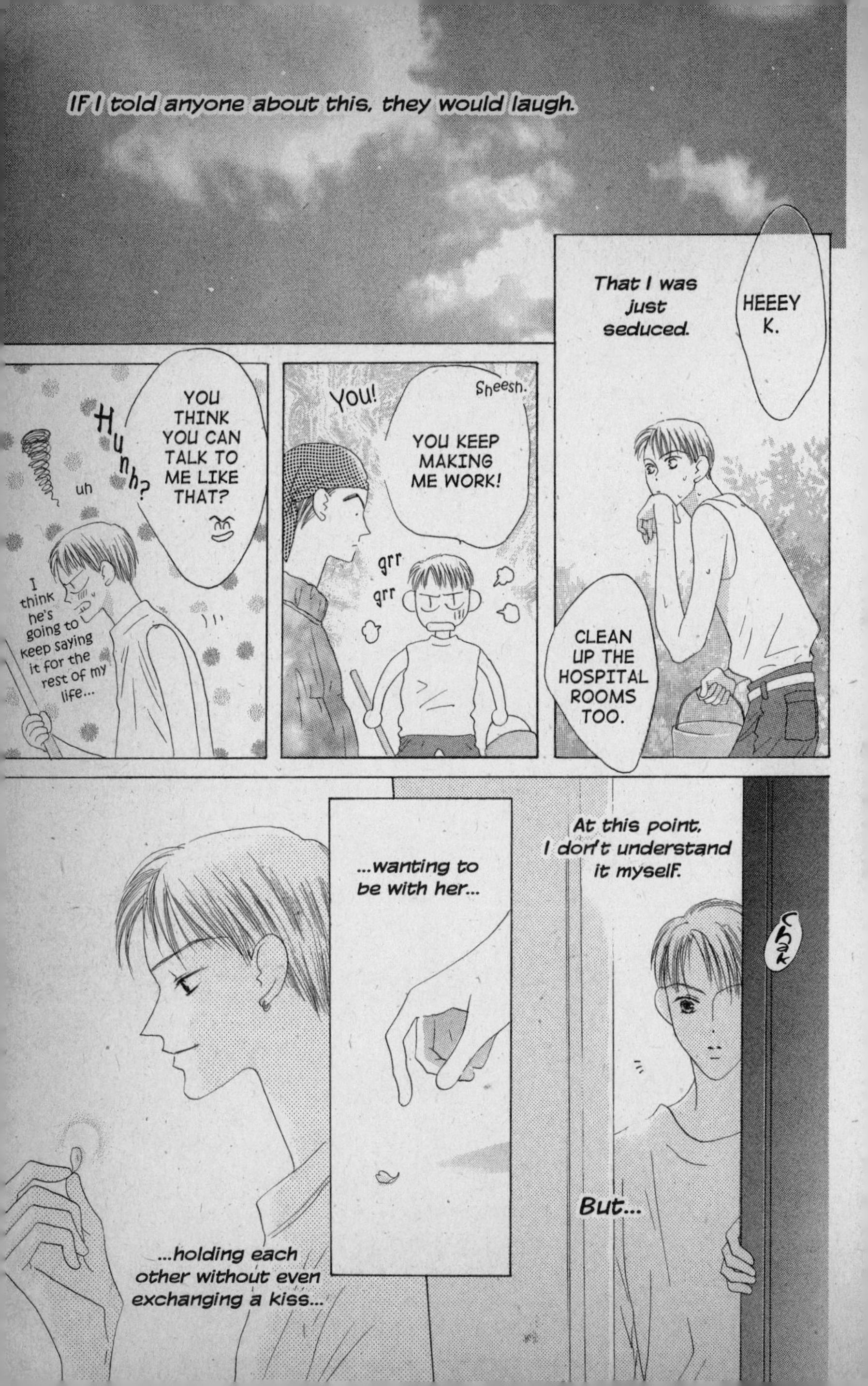
If I told anyone about this, they would laugh.
HEEEY K.
That I was just seduced.
CLEAN UP THE HOSPITAL ROOMS TOO.
Sheesh.
YOU KEEP MAKING ME WORK!
You!
grr
grr
YOU THINK YOU CAN TALK TO ME LIKE THAT?
Hunh?
uh
I think he's going to keep saying it for the rest of my life...
At this point, I don't understand it myself.
Chak
But...
...wanting to be with her...
...holding each other without even exchanging a kiss...

Such a love can exist, too.

The Release

The End

FAMILY PORTRAIT

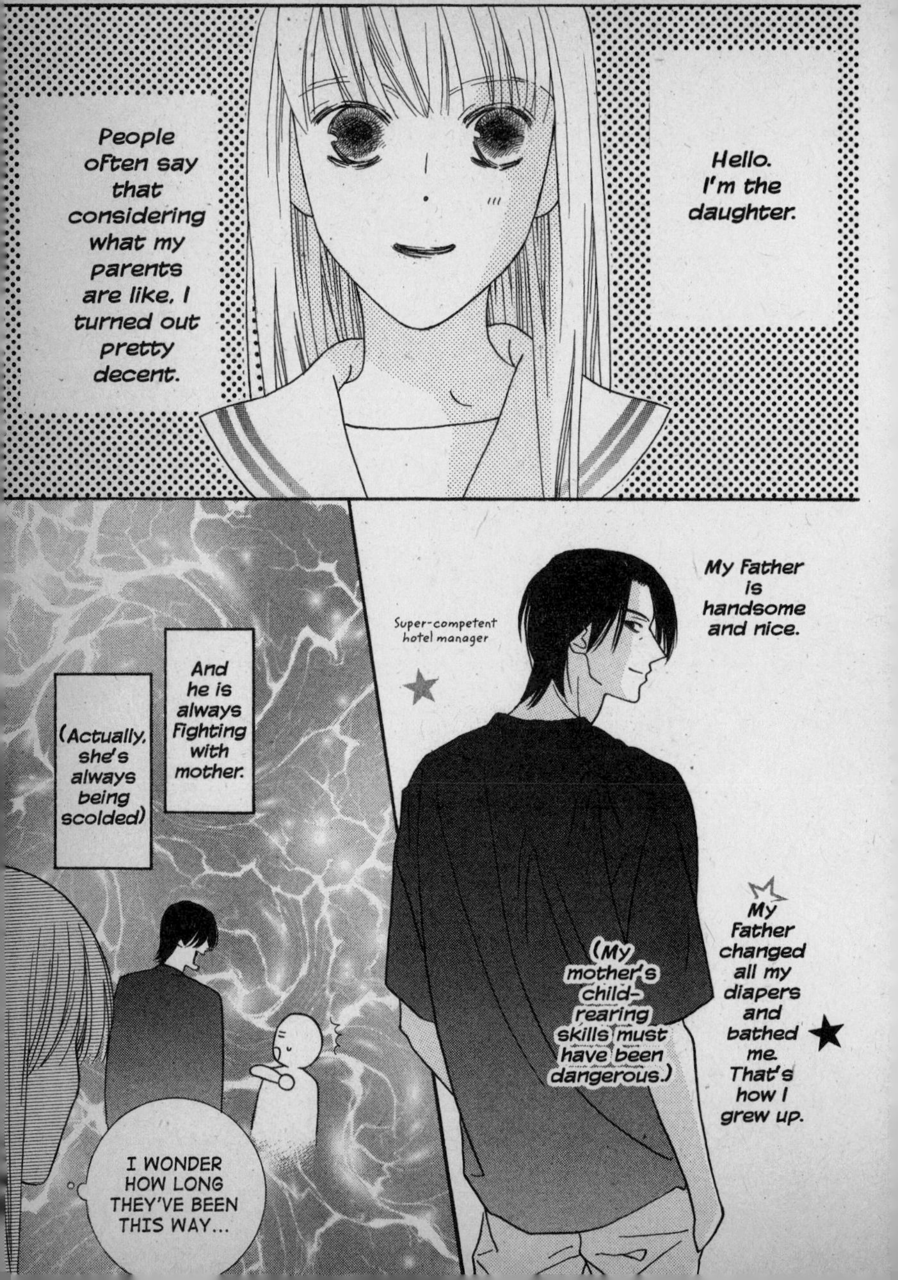
Hello. I'm the daughter.
People often say that considering what my parents are like, I turned out pretty decent.
My Father is handsome and nice.
Super-competent hotel manager
My Father changed all my diapers and bathed me. That's how I grew up.
(My mother's child-rearing skills must have been dangerous.)
And he is always Fighting with mother.
(Actually, she's always being scolded)
I WONDER HOW LONG THEY'VE BEEN THIS WAY...

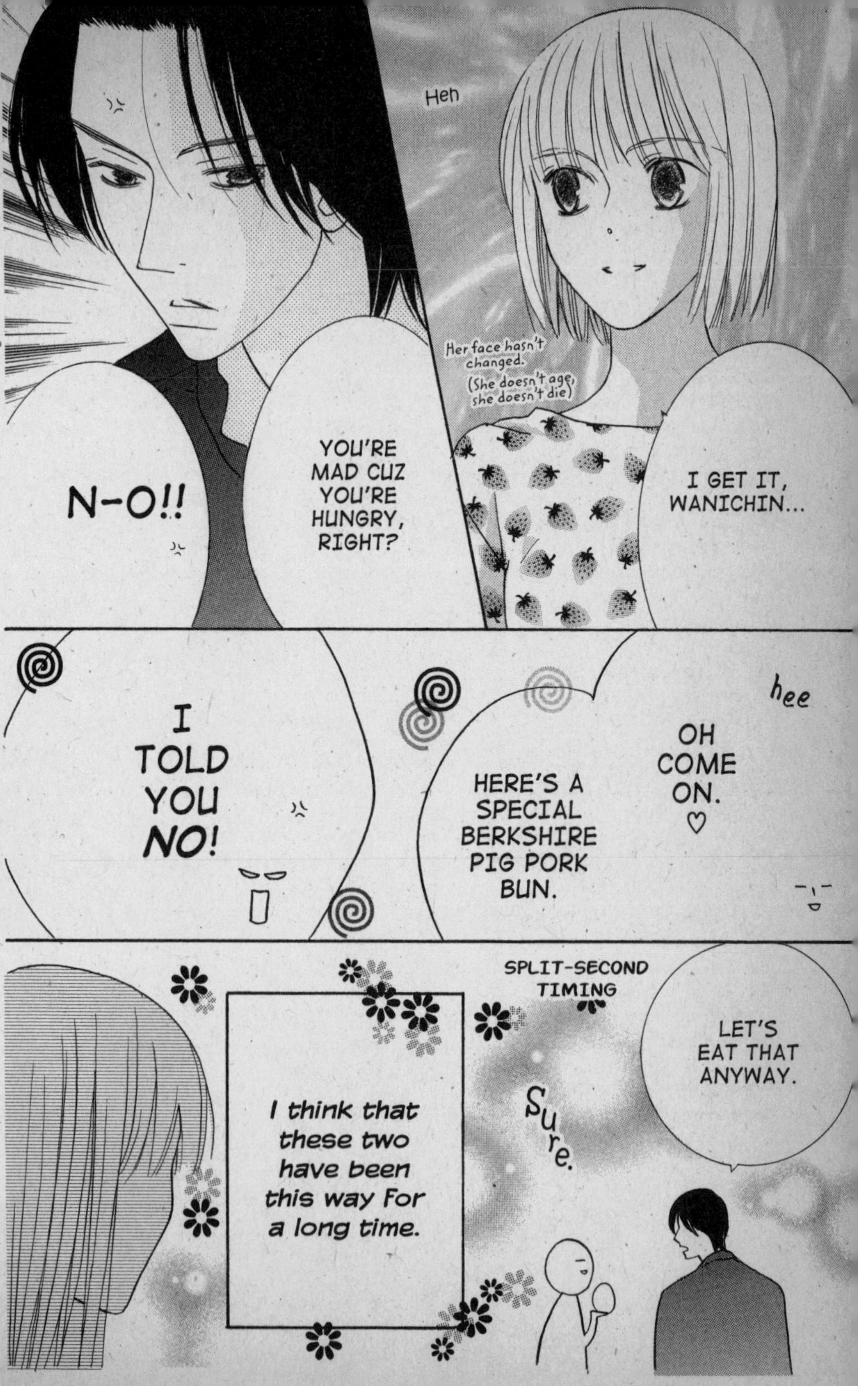
I GET IT, WANICHIN...
Heh
Her face hasn't changed.
(She doesn't age, she doesn't die)
YOU'RE MAD CUZ YOU'RE HUNGRY, RIGHT?
N-O!!
hee
OH COME ON. ♡
HERE'S A SPECIAL BERKSHIRE PIG PORK BUN.
I TOLD YOU NO!
LET'S EAT THAT ANYWAY.
SPLIT-SECOND TIMING
Sure.
I think that these two have been this way for a long time.

Glossary

Some high school experiences are universal. Others need a little more explanation. In these notes you will find interesting information to enhance your *Beauty Is the Beast* reading enjoyment.

Page 3, panel 3: Chiaki Kuri[redacted]
Most likely refers to the actress Chiaki Kuriyama, who appeared in *Kill Bill*.

Page 24, panel 1: Shokado obento
This is an ekiben (*eki* means station), the bento boxes sold at train stations. Ekiben usually feature the local specialty, such as Kobe beef in Kobe.

Page 27, panel 3: Koshihikari
An expensive but tasty brand of rice.

Page 31, panel 2: Agepan
Deep-fried bun, usually filled with sweet red bean paste.

Page 31, panel 2: Hoji-cha
Pan-fried or oven roasted green tea.

Page 41, panel 1: Horsemeat ice cream
Horsemeat is commonly eaten in Kyushu.

Page 43, panel 5: Takana
Chinese mustard, also known as "wrapped-heart mustard." A vegetable often used in soups and stir-fries.

Page 52, panel 4: Megum[redacted]
Most likely the model and singer MEGUMI.

Page 52, panel 5: Aya Sugi[redacted]
Most likely the actress and voice actress Aya Sugimoto.

Page 72, panel 3: The Aroma of Travel, the Play of Time
This is the name of a travel show on television.

Page 84, panel 4: Jun[redacted]chi Ishida
Junichi Ishida is an actor with a reputation as a ladies' man and a son from a previous marriage.

Page 85, panel 2: [redacted]tsuo Umemiya
Tatsuo Umemiya is another actor, known for his culinary skills.

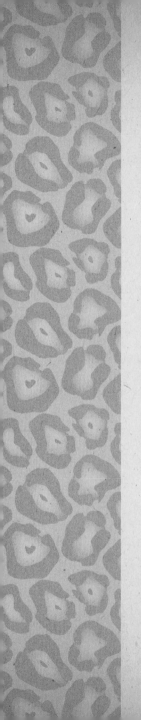

Page 99, panel 1: Purikura
This is a contraction of the Japanese pronunciation of "print club," and refers to the photo booths found in arcades and game centers and the photos they dispense.

Page 100, panel 1: Yakuza method
Yakuza are the Japanese mafia, and Simonuki's sister is blackmailing him in the grand gangster tradition.

Page 103, Author Note: A lewd Suke-san
Suke-san is a character in the period drama *Mito Komon*. The original Japanese phrase is *Sukebe na Suke-san*, a play on words.

Page 114, panel 1: Katsudon
Fried pork cutlet and egg over rice, simple fare.

Page 116, panel 4: Karashi Mentaiko
A common Kyushu souvenir of salted cod roe seasoned with hot peppers.

Page 128, panel 5: Ukokkei
An exclusive breed of chicken with silky white feathers and black skin. This chicken is known in traditional Chinese medicine for its revitalizing properties.

Page 129, panel 4: Chicken Naban
Fried chicken served with sweet vinegar and tartar sauce.

Page 150, panel 1: Gastroenteritis
The acute irritation and inflammation of the digestive tract. Stress is one of the factors that can cause gastroenteritis.

Page 156, Kotomi Takeuchi: 4649
A Yanki way of writing *yoroshiku* which means "regards" or "remember me."
(4 = yon. 6 = ro. 4 = shi. 9 = ku.)

Page 156, Yuka Yasuda: Yasuura-san
The main character of the detective show *Hagure Keiji*.

BEAUTY IS THE BEAST
Vol. 5
The Shojo Beat Manga Edition

STORY & ART BY
TOMO MATSUMOTO

English Translation & Adaptation/Tomo Kimura
Touch-up & Lettering/Inori Fukuda Trant
Graphics & Cover Design/Yukiko Whitley
Editor/Pancha Diaz

Managing Editor/Megan Bates
Editorial Director/Elizabeth Kawasaki
Vice President & Editor in Chief/Yumi Hoashi
Sr. Director of Acquisitions/Rika Inouye
Sr. VP of Marketing/Liza Coppola
Exec. VP of Sales & Marketing/John Easum
Publisher/Hyoe Narita

Printed in Canada

Published by VIZ Media, LLC
P.O. Box 77010
San Francisco, CA 94107

Shojo Beat Manga Edition
10 9 8 7 6 5 4 3 2 1
First printing, November 2006

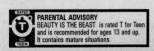
store.viz.com

Tomo Matsumoto was born on January 8th in Osaka and made the switch from nurse to mangaka with her debut story *"Nemuru Hime"* (Sleeping Princess) in *Lunatic LaLa* magazine in 1995. Her other works include *Kiss*, a series about piano lessons and love, *23:00*, a book about street dancing, and *Eikaiwa School Wars* (English School Wars), which is currently serialized in *LaLa Monthly* magazine. Ms. Matsumoto loves dancing and taking English lessons.

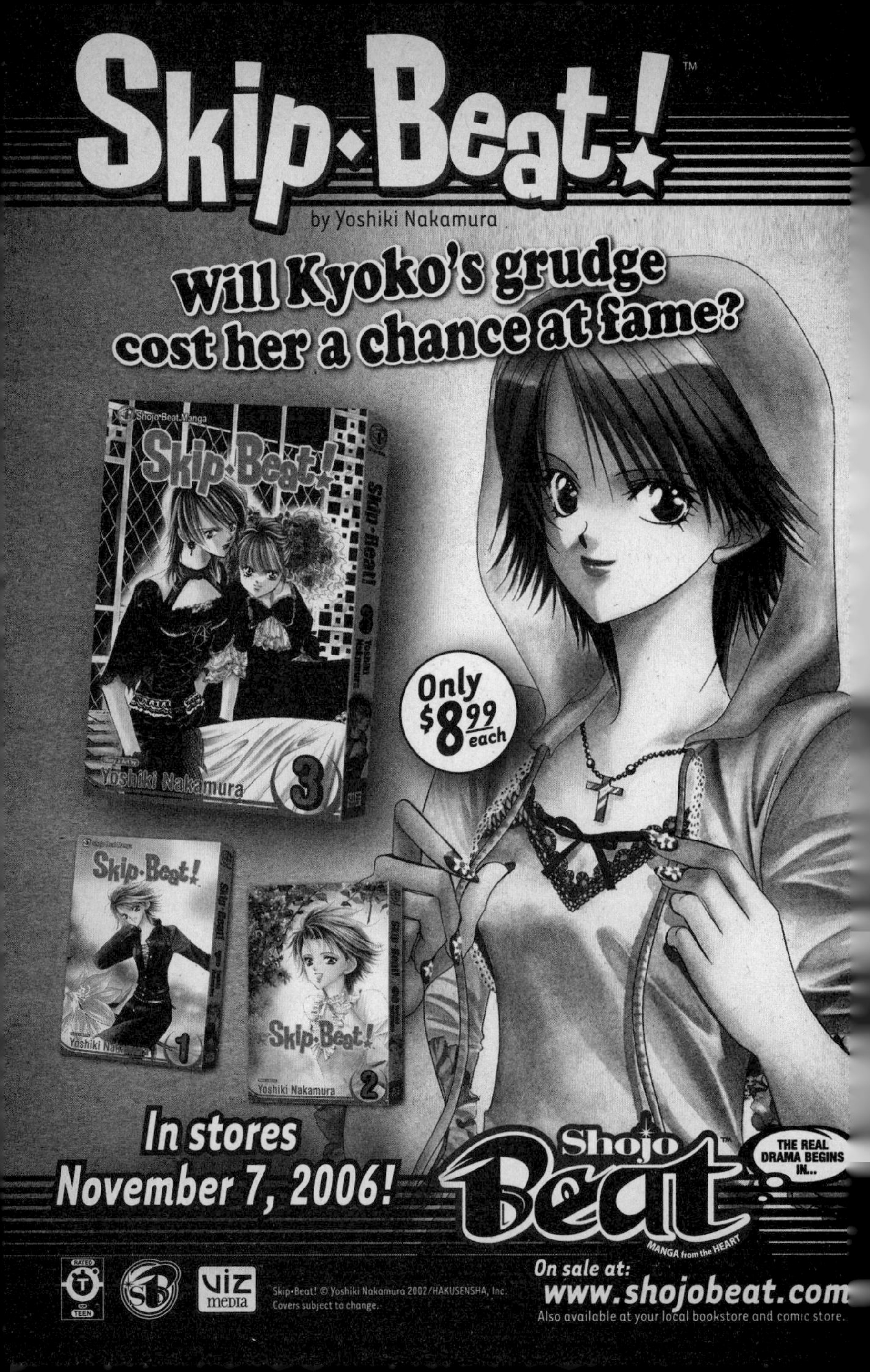

Skip·Beat!™
by Yoshiki Nakamura
Will Kyoko's grudge cost her a chance at fame?
Shojo Beat Manga
Skip·Beat!
Yoshiki Nakamura
3
Only $8.99 each
Skip·Beat!
Yoshiki Nakamura
1
Skip·Beat!
Yoshiki Nakamura
2
In stores November 7, 2006!
THE REAL DRAMA BEGINS IN...
Shojo Beat™
MANGA from the HEART
Skip·Beat! © Yoshiki Nakamura 2002/HAKUSENSHA, Inc.
Covers subject to change.
On sale at:
www.shojobeat.com
Also available at your local bookstore and comic store.

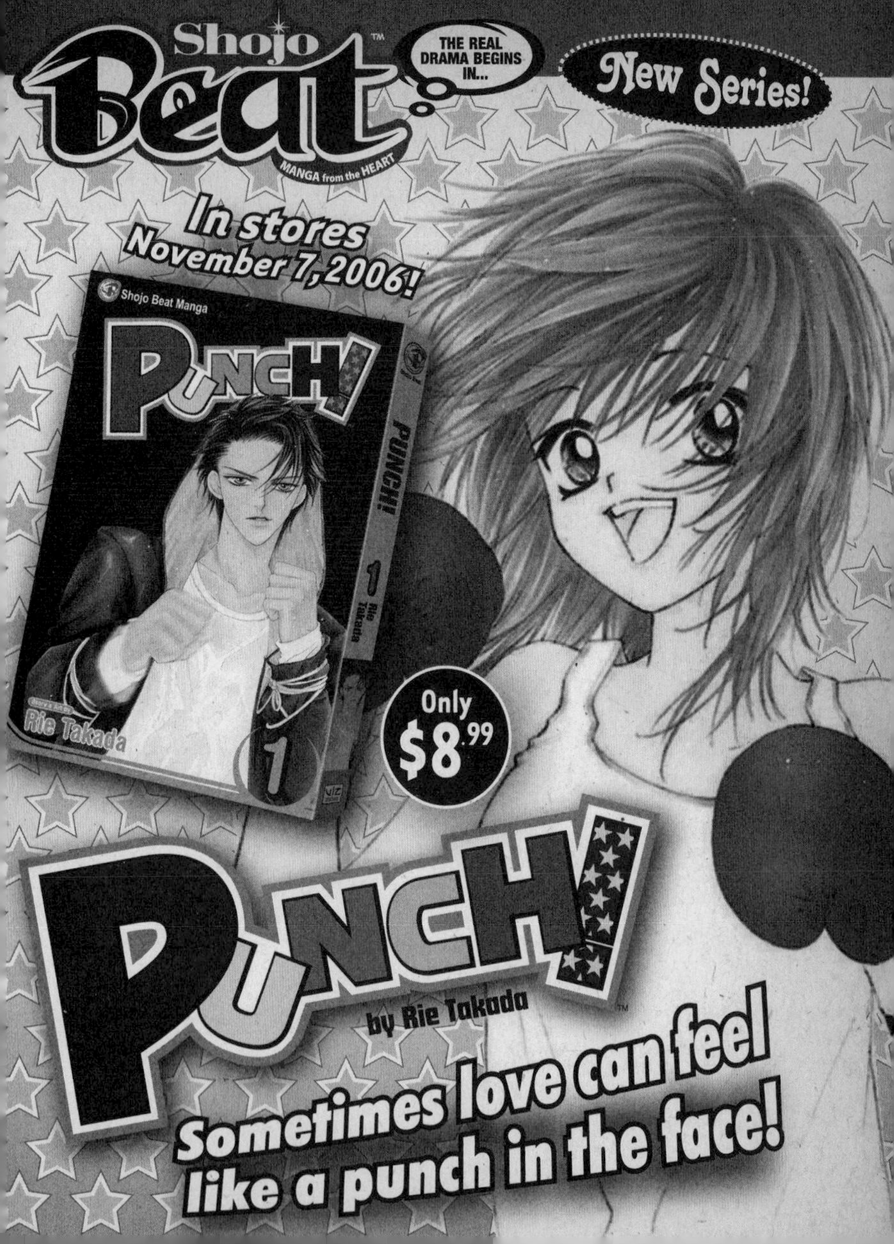

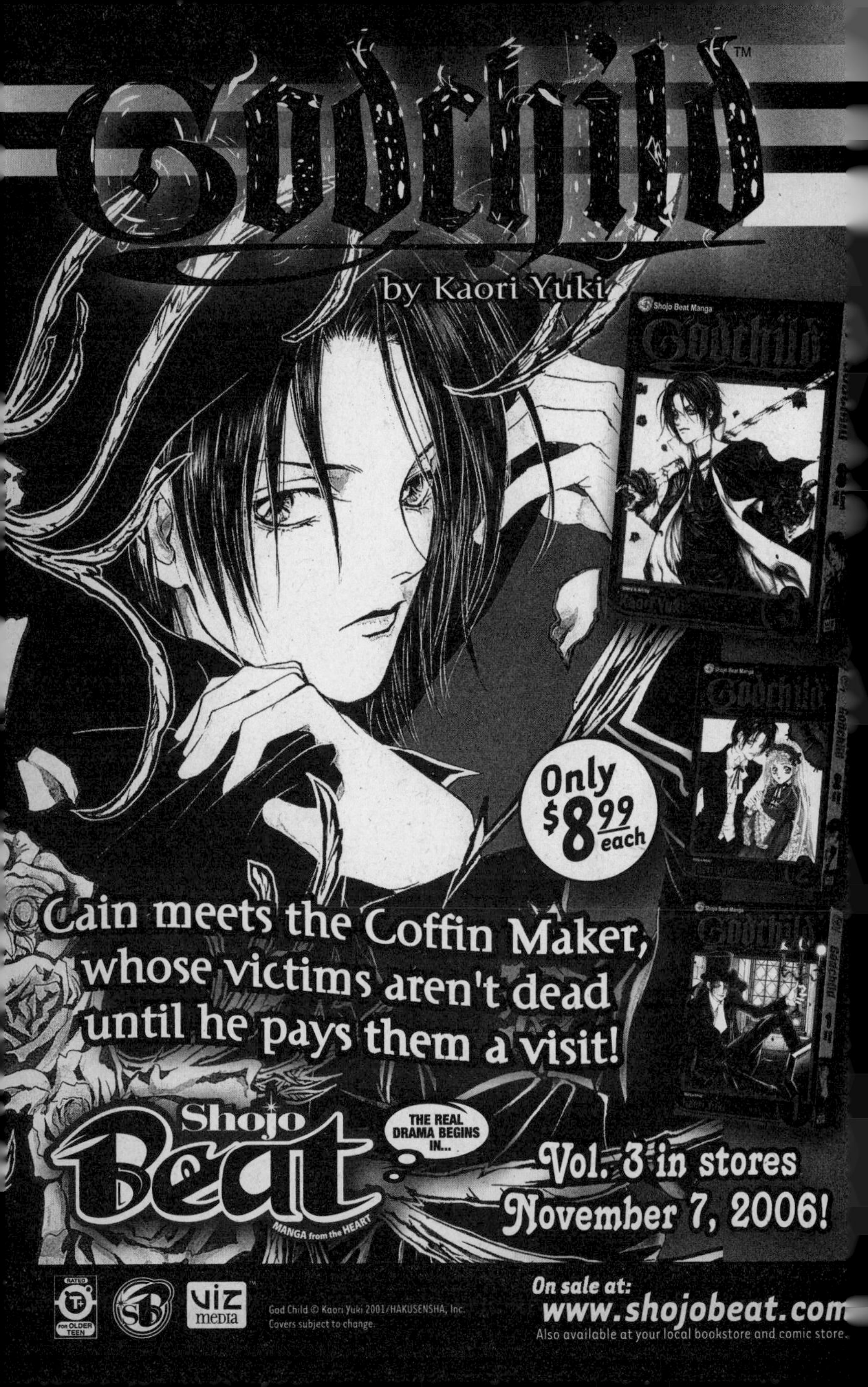

Godchild™
by Kaori Yuki
Only $8.99 each
Cain meets the Coffin Maker, whose victims aren't dead until he pays them a visit!
Shojo Beat
MANGA from the HEART
THE REAL DRAMA BEGINS IN...
Vol. 3 in stores November 7, 2006!
RATED T+ FOR OLDER TEEN
viz media
God Child © Kaori Yuki 2001/HAKUSENSHA, Inc.
Covers subject to change.
On sale at:
www.shojobeat.com
Also available at your local bookstore and comic store.

Don't Miss an Issue!

Shojo Beat
MANGA from the HEART

THE REAL DRAMA BEGINS IN...

Six of the hottest Shojo manga from Japan—
Nana, Baby & Me, Crimson Hero, Vampire Knight, Kaze Hikaru, and Absolute Boyfriend (by superstar creator Yuu Watase!!)*!*

Plus the latest on what's happening in Japanese fashion, music, and art! Save 51% OFF the cover price PLUS enjoy all the benefits of the 🅢 Sub Club with your paid subscription for only $34.99.

Find the Beat online!
Check us out at

www.shojobeat.com!